"Stain" has a certain meaning in English.
Slowly but surely, the character is making his
mark on the story. But anyway, we're getting
the anime I've wanted forever. Amazing!!

KOHEI HORIKOSHI

MY HERO ACADEMIA

6

SHONEN JUMP Manga Edition

STORY & ART KOHEI HORIKOSHI

TRANSLATION & ENGLISH ADAPTATION **Caleb Cook**
TOUCH-UP ART & LETTERING **John Hunt**
DESIGNER **Shawn Carrico**
SHONEN JUMP SERIES EDITOR **John Bae**
GRAPHIC NOVEL EDITOR **Mike Montesa**

BOKU NO HERO ACADEMIA © 2014 by Kohei Horikoshi
All rights reserved.
First published in Japan in 2014 by SHUEISHA Inc., Tokyo.
English translation rights arranged by SHUEISHA Inc.

Printed in the U.S.A.

Published by VIZ Media, LLC
P.O. Box 77010
San Francisco, CA 94107

10 9 8 7 6 5 4 3
First printing, November 2016
Third printing, July 2017

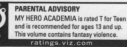
www.viz.com

www.shonenjump.com

MY HERO ACADEMIA

MY HERO ACADEMIA

Vol. 6

Struggling

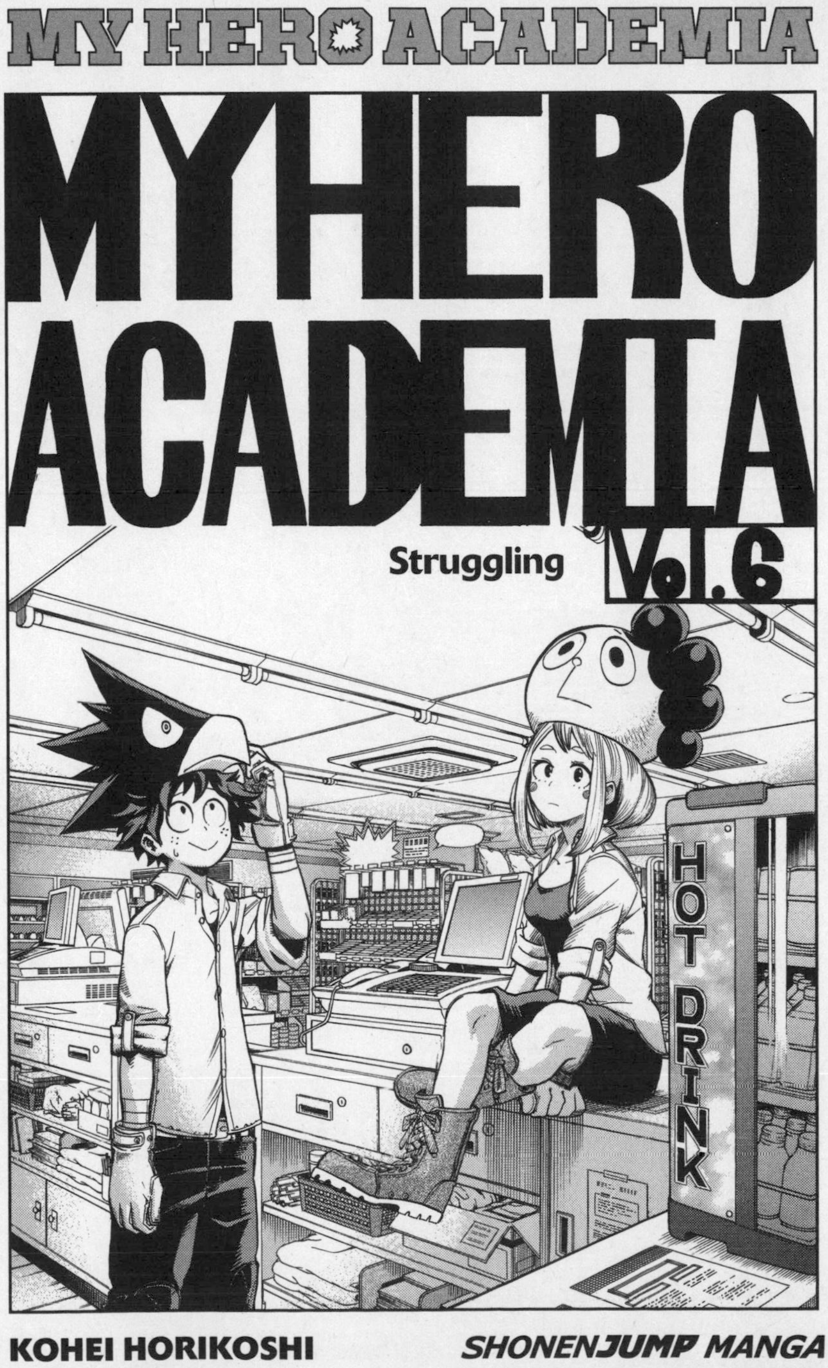
HOT DRINK

KOHEI HORIKOSHI

SHONEN JUMP MANGA

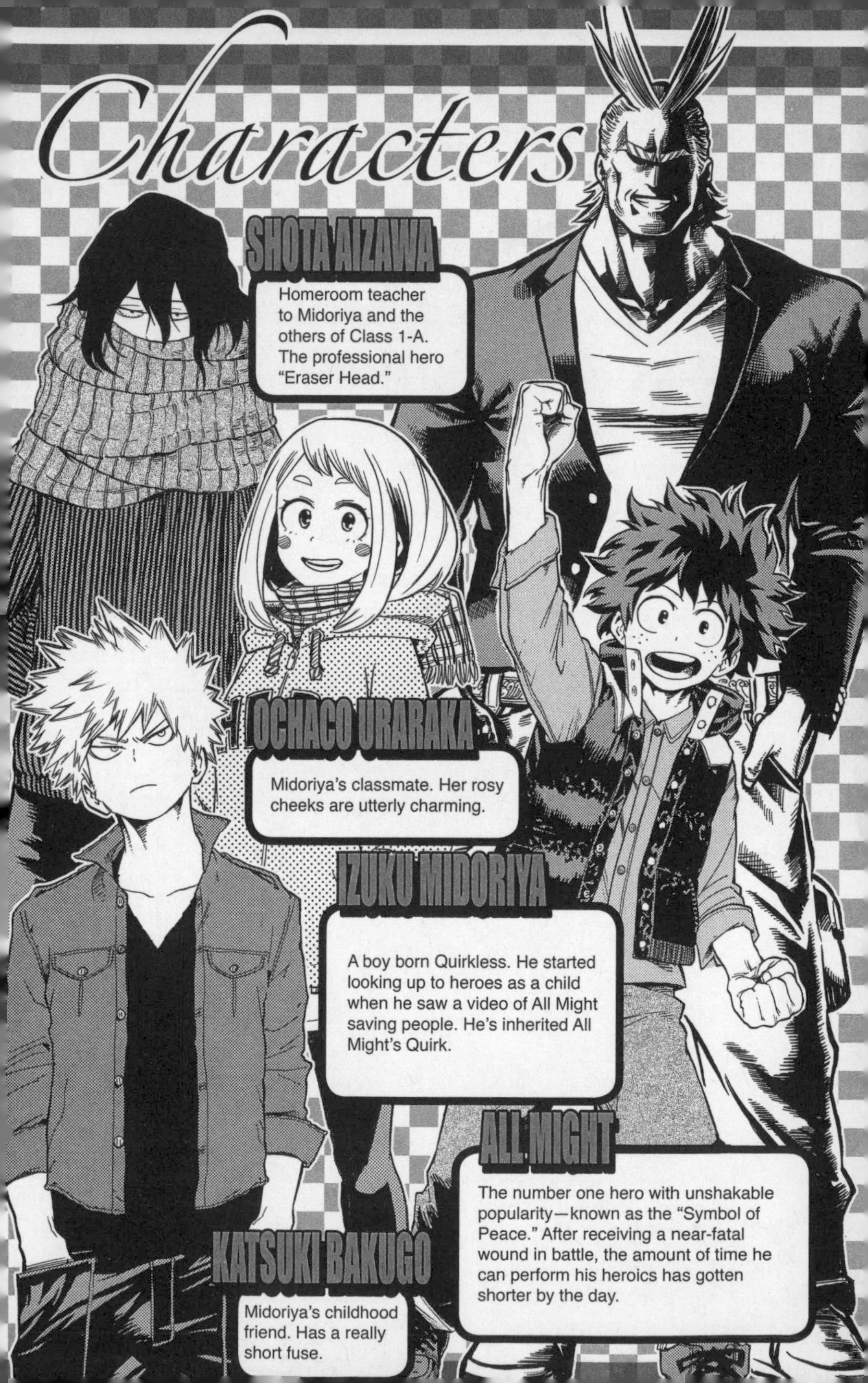
Characters
SHOTA AIZAWA
Homeroom teacher to Midoriya and the others of Class 1-A. The professional hero "Eraser Head."
OCHACO URARAKA
Midoriya's classmate. Her rosy cheeks are utterly charming.
IZUKU MIDORIYA
A boy born Quirkless. He started looking up to heroes as a child when he saw a video of All Might saving people. He's inherited All Might's Quirk.
ALL MIGHT
The number one hero with unshakable popularity—known as the "Symbol of Peace." After receiving a near-fatal wound in battle, the amount of time he can perform his heroics has gotten shorter by the day.
KATSUKI BAKUGO
Midoriya's childhood friend. Has a really short fuse.

STORY

One day, people began manifesting special abilities that came to be known as "Quirks," and before long, society became full of these superpowered humans. But with the advent of these exceptional individuals came an increase in crime, and governments were unable to deal with the situation. At the same time, others emerged to oppose the spread of evil! As if straight from the comic books, these heroes keep the peace and are even officially authorized to fight crime. Our story begins when a certain Quirkless boy and lifelong hero fan meets the world's number one hero, starting him on his path to becoming the greatest hero ever!

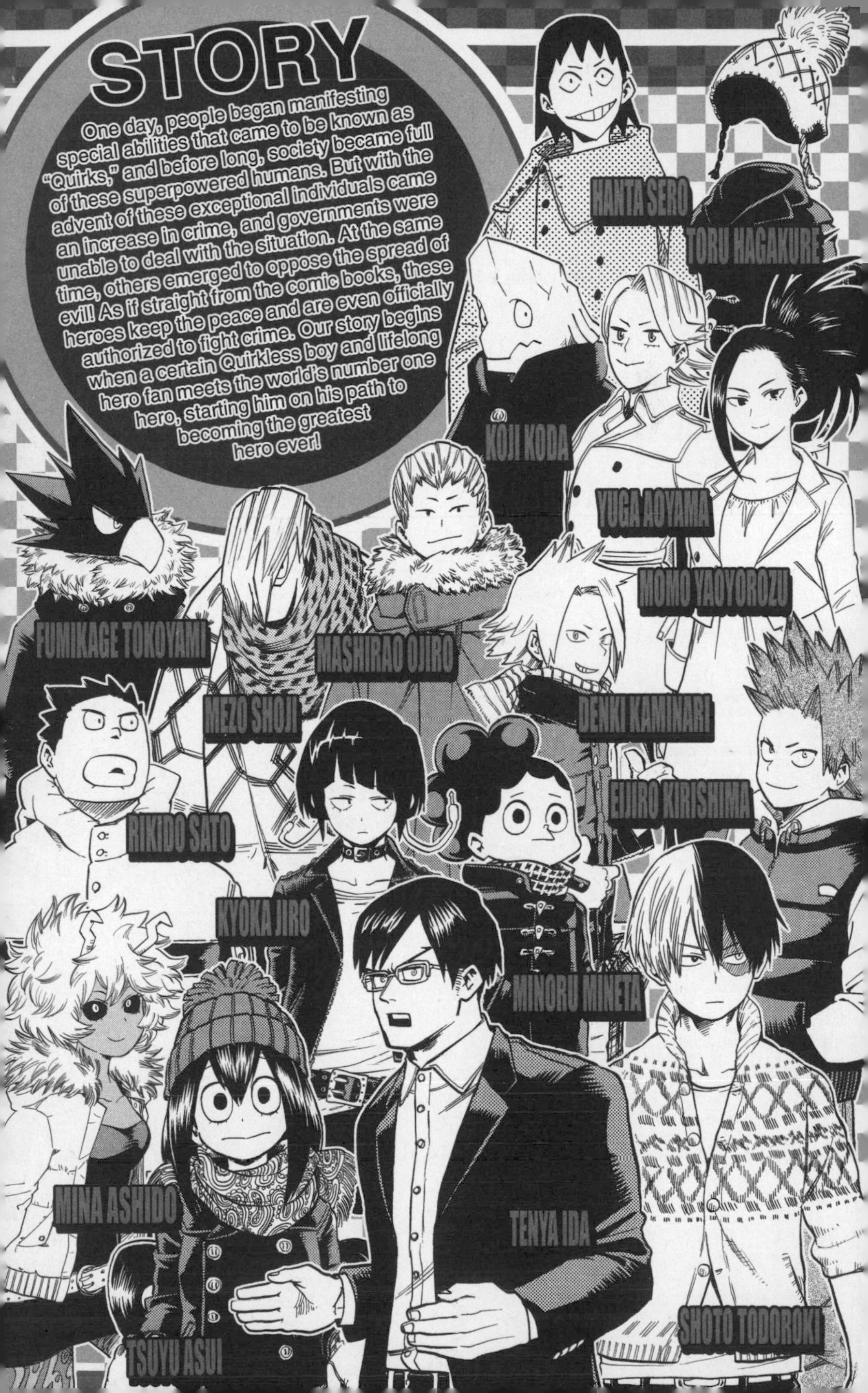
HANTA SERO
TORU HAGAKURE
KOJI KODA
YUGA AOYAMA
MOMO YAOYOROZU
FUMIKAGE TOKOYAMI
MASHIRAO OJIRO
DENKI KAMINARI
MEZO SHOJI
EIJIRO KIRISHIMA
RIKIDO SATO
KYOKA JIRO
MINORU MINETA
MINA ASHIDO
TENYA IDA
SHOTO TODOROKI
TSUYU ASUI

Vol. 6

MY HERO ACADEMIA

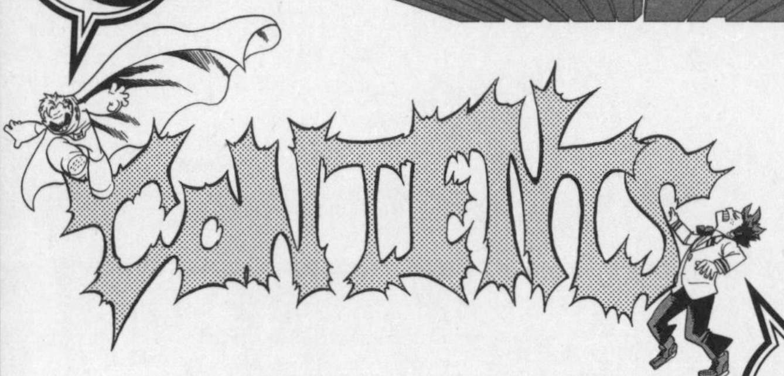

Contents

Struggling

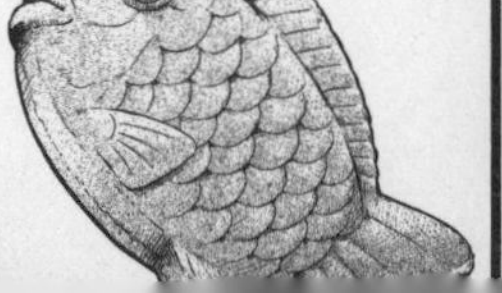

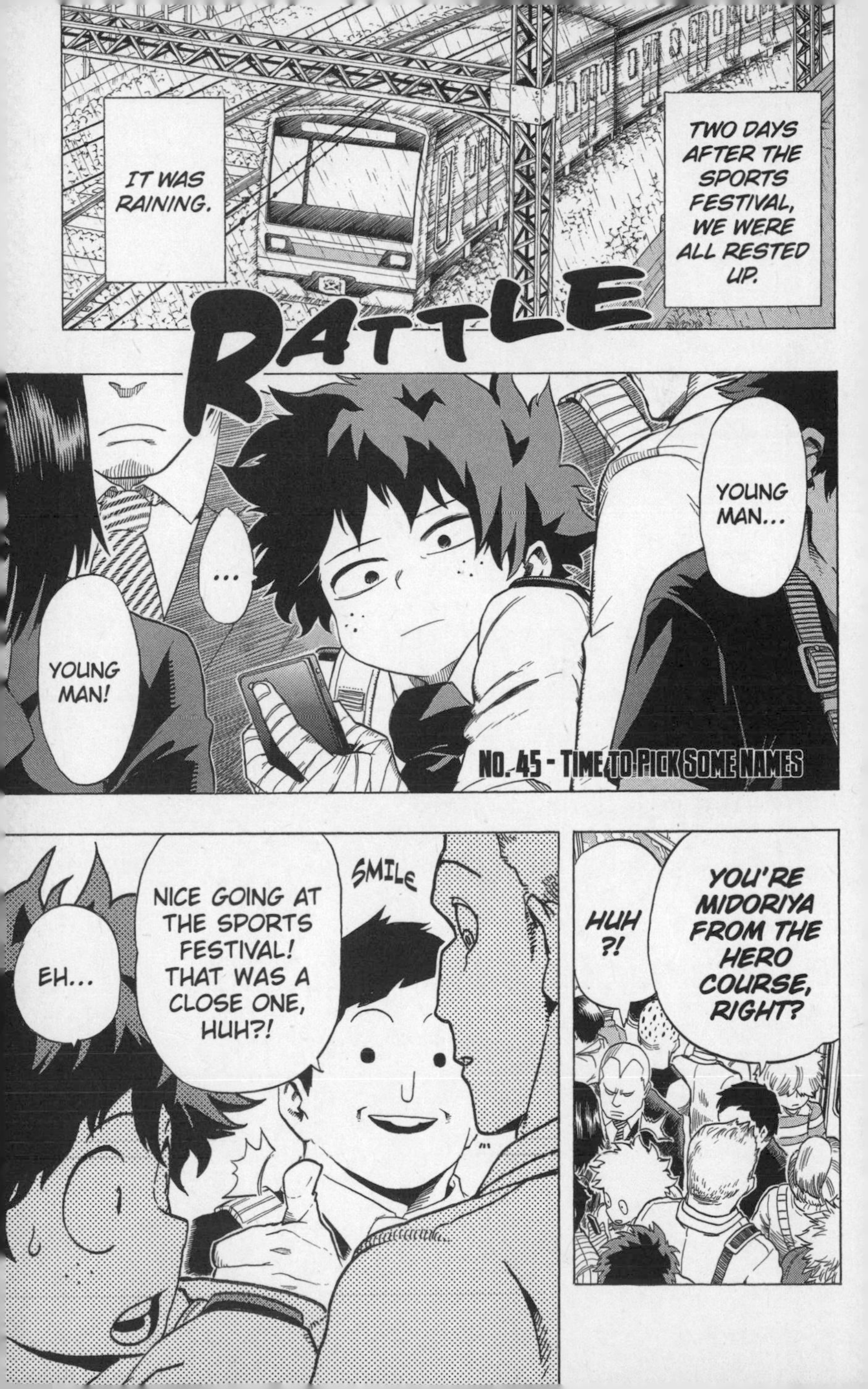
TWO DAYS AFTER THE SPORTS FESTIVAL, WE WERE ALL RESTED UP.
IT WAS RAINING.
RATTLE
YOUNG MAN...
...
YOUNG MAN!
No. 45 - Time to Pick Some Names
YOU'RE MIDORIYA FROM THE HERO COURSE, RIGHT?
HUH?!
SMILE
NICE GOING AT THE SPORTS FESTIVAL! THAT WAS A CLOSE ONE, HUH?!
EH...

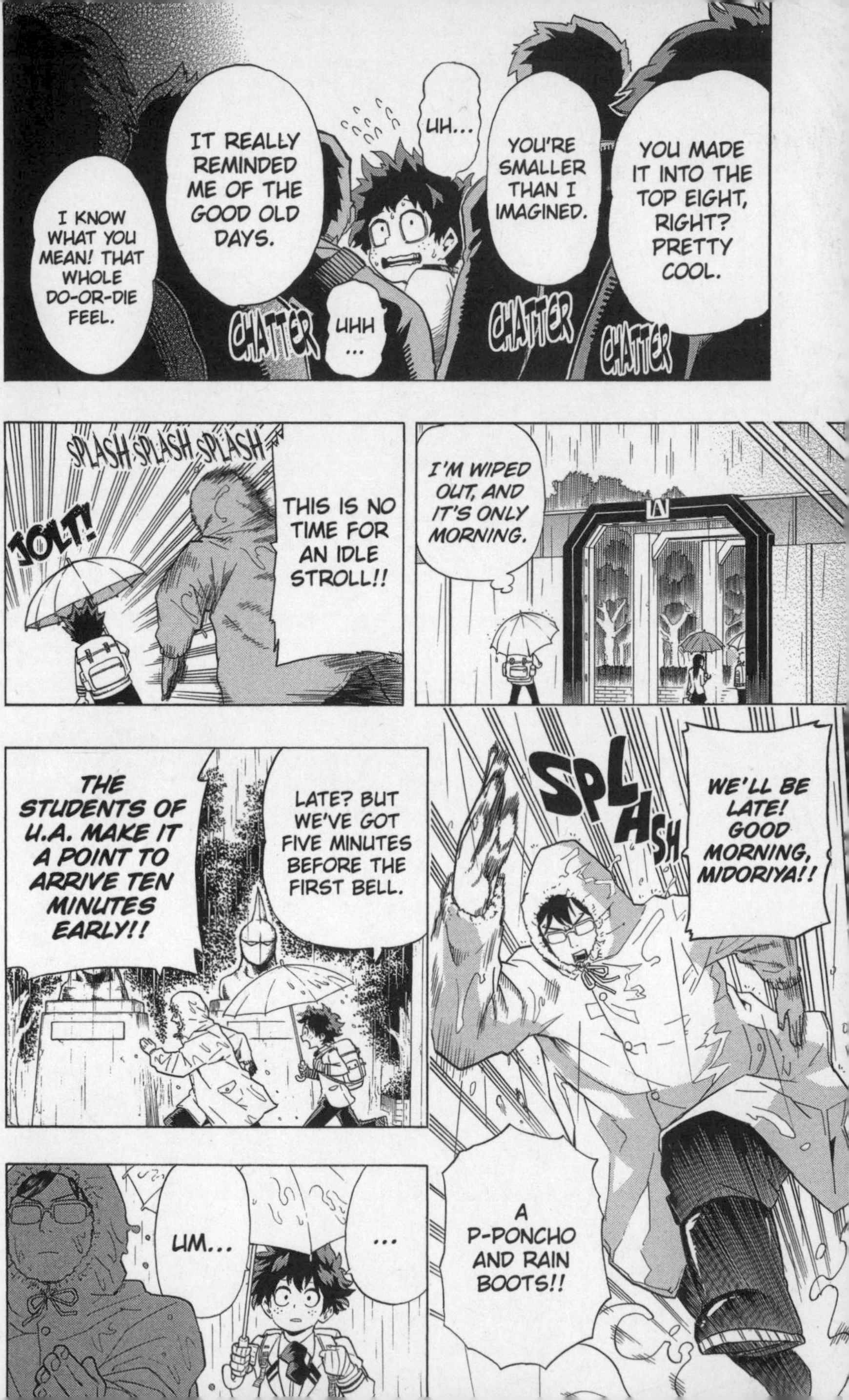
YOU MADE IT INTO THE TOP EIGHT, RIGHT? PRETTY COOL.
CHATTER
YOU'RE SMALLER THAN I IMAGINED.
CHATTER
UH...
IT REALLY REMINDED ME OF THE GOOD OLD DAYS.
UHH ...
I KNOW WHAT YOU MEAN! THAT WHOLE DO-OR-DIE FEEL.
CHATTER
I'M WIPED OUT, AND IT'S ONLY MORNING.
SPLASH SPLASH SPLASH
THIS IS NO TIME FOR AN IDLE STROLL!!
JOLT!!
WE'LL BE LATE! GOOD MORNING, MIDORIYA!!
SPLASH
A P-PONCHO AND RAIN BOOTS!!
LATE? BUT WE'VE GOT FIVE MINUTES BEFORE THE FIRST BELL.
THE STUDENTS OF U.A. MAKE IT A POINT TO ARRIVE TEN MINUTES EARLY!!
...
UM...

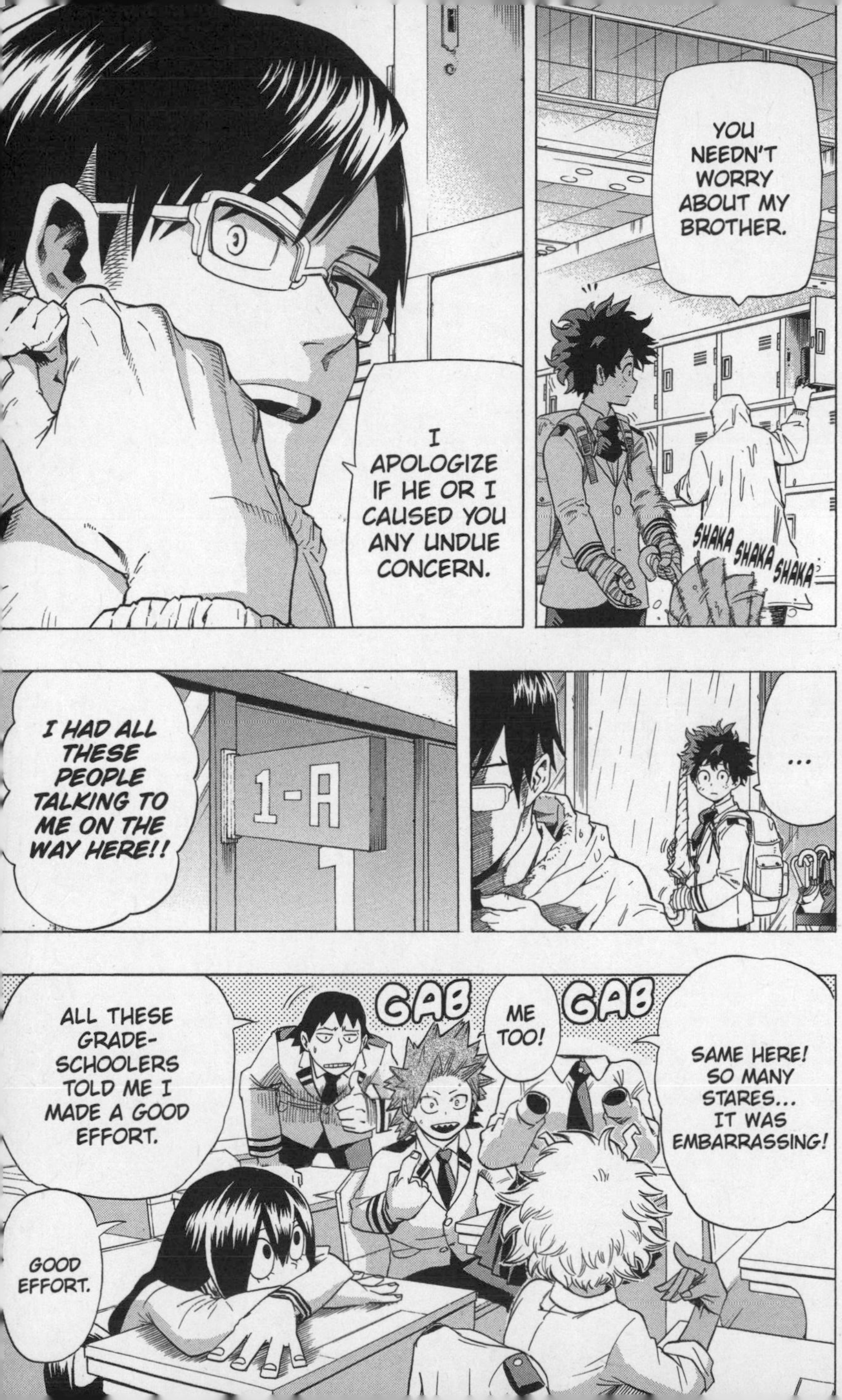
YOU NEEDN'T WORRY ABOUT MY BROTHER.
SHAKA SHAKA SHAKA
I APOLOGIZE IF HE OR I CAUSED YOU ANY UNDUE CONCERN.
...
I HAD ALL THESE PEOPLE TALKING TO ME ON THE WAY HERE!!
1-A
SAME HERE! SO MANY STARES... IT WAS EMBARRASSING!
GAB
ME TOO!
GAB
ALL THESE GRADE-SCHOOLERS TOLD ME I MADE A GOOD EFFORT.
GOOD EFFORT.

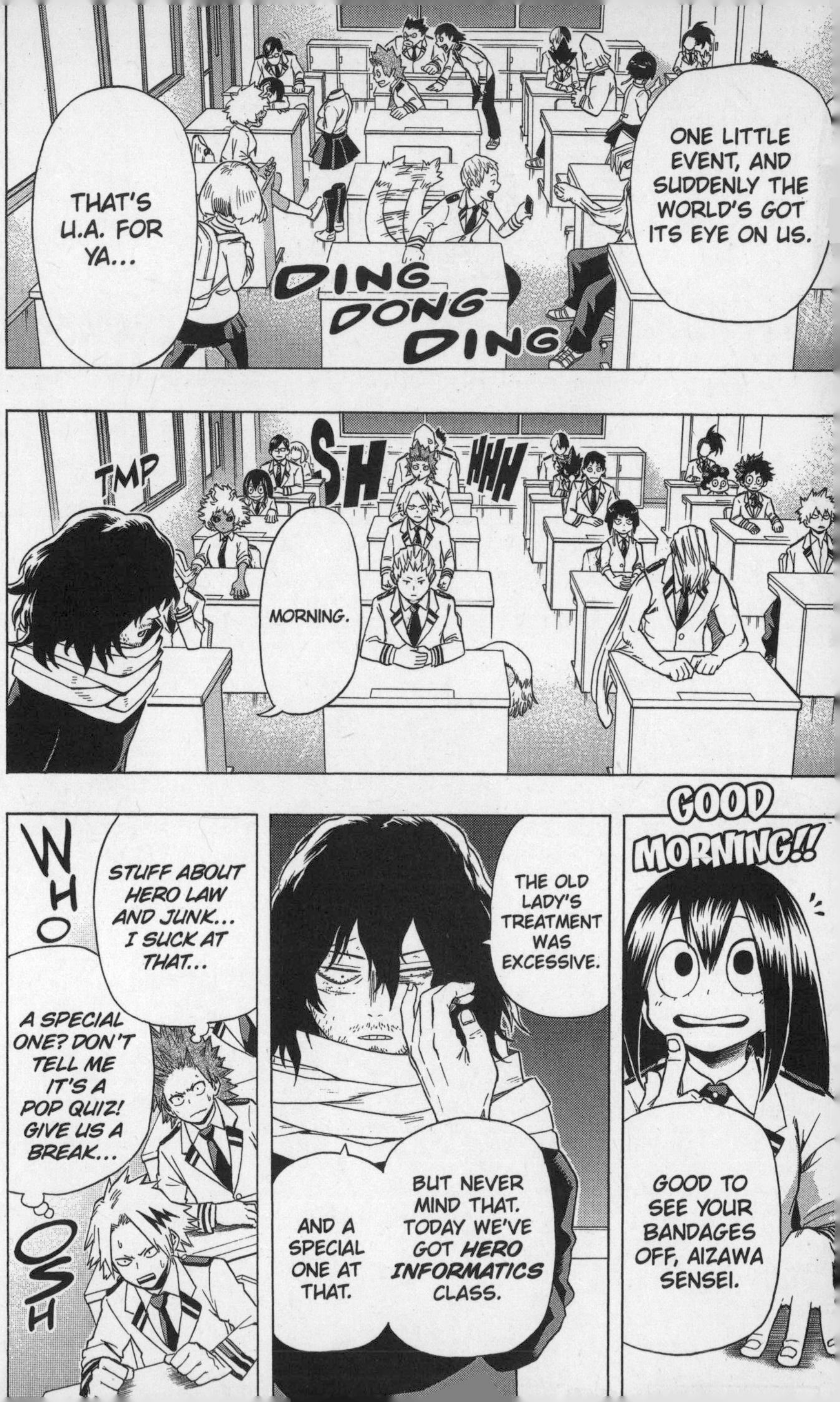
ONE LITTLE EVENT, AND SUDDENLY THE WORLD'S GOT ITS EYE ON US.
THAT'S U.A. FOR YA...
DING DONG DING
SHHHH
TMP
MORNING.
GOOD MORNING!!
GOOD TO SEE YOUR BANDAGES OFF, AIZAWA SENSEI.
THE OLD LADY'S TREATMENT WAS EXCESSIVE.
BUT NEVER MIND THAT. TODAY WE'VE GOT *HERO INFORMATICS* CLASS.
AND A SPECIAL ONE AT THAT.
STUFF ABOUT HERO LAW AND JUNK... I SUCK AT THAT...
WHO
A SPECIAL ONE? DON'T TELL ME IT'S A POP QUIZ! GIVE US A BREAK...
OSH

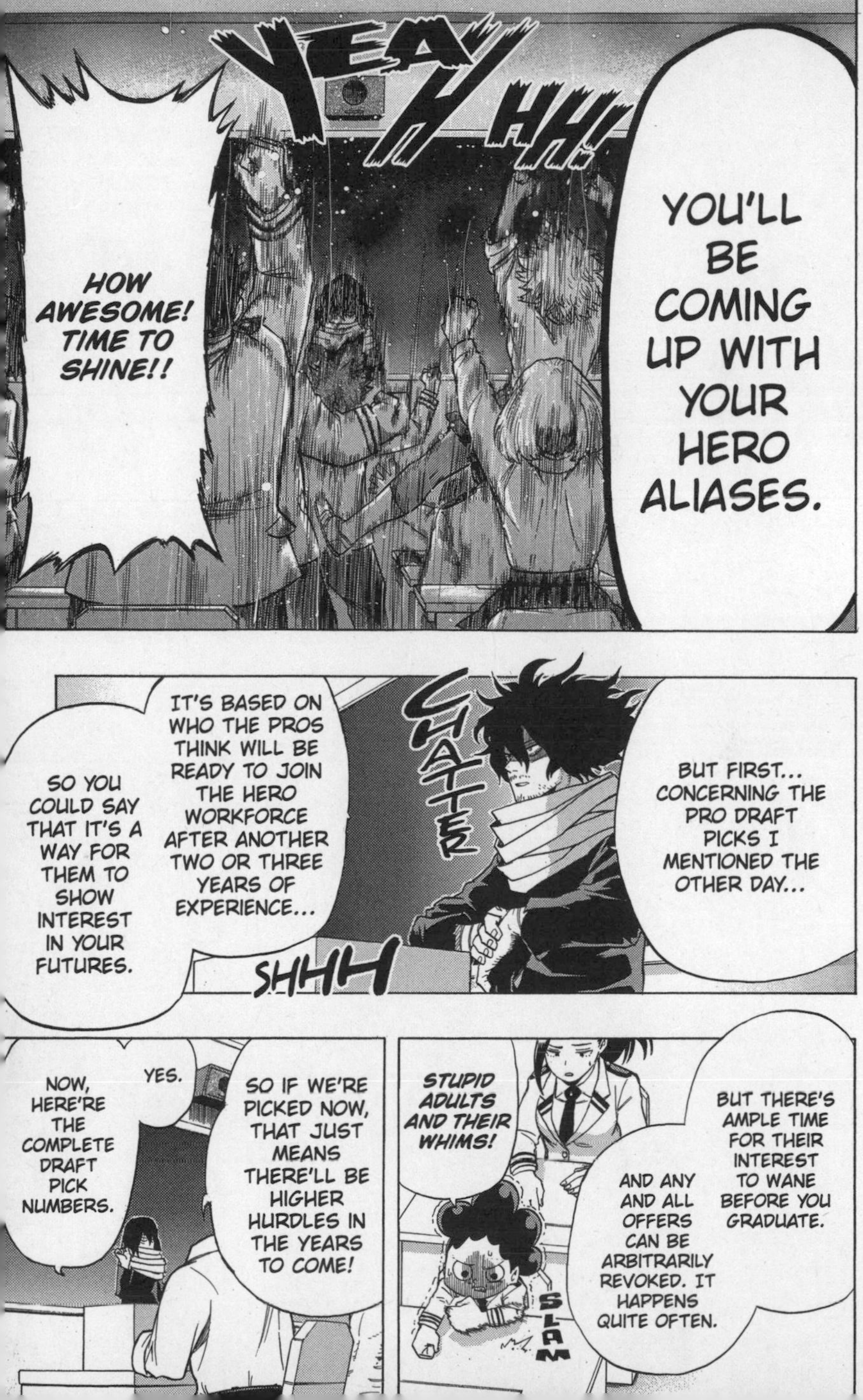
YOU'LL BE COMING UP WITH YOUR HERO ALIASES.
YEAHHH!
HOW AWESOME! TIME TO SHINE!!
BUT FIRST... CONCERNING THE PRO DRAFT PICKS I MENTIONED THE OTHER DAY...
CHATTER
SHHH
IT'S BASED ON WHO THE PROS THINK WILL BE READY TO JOIN THE HERO WORKFORCE AFTER ANOTHER TWO OR THREE YEARS OF EXPERIENCE...
SO YOU COULD SAY THAT IT'S A WAY FOR THEM TO SHOW INTEREST IN YOUR FUTURES.
BUT THERE'S AMPLE TIME FOR THEIR INTEREST TO WANE BEFORE YOU GRADUATE.
AND ANY AND ALL OFFERS CAN BE ARBITRARILY REVOKED. IT HAPPENS QUITE OFTEN.
STUPID ADULTS AND THEIR WHIMS!
SLAM
SO IF WE'RE PICKED NOW, THAT JUST MEANS THERE'LL BE HIGHER HURDLES IN THE YEARS TO COME!
YES.
NOW, HERE'RE THE COMPLETE DRAFT PICK NUMBERS.

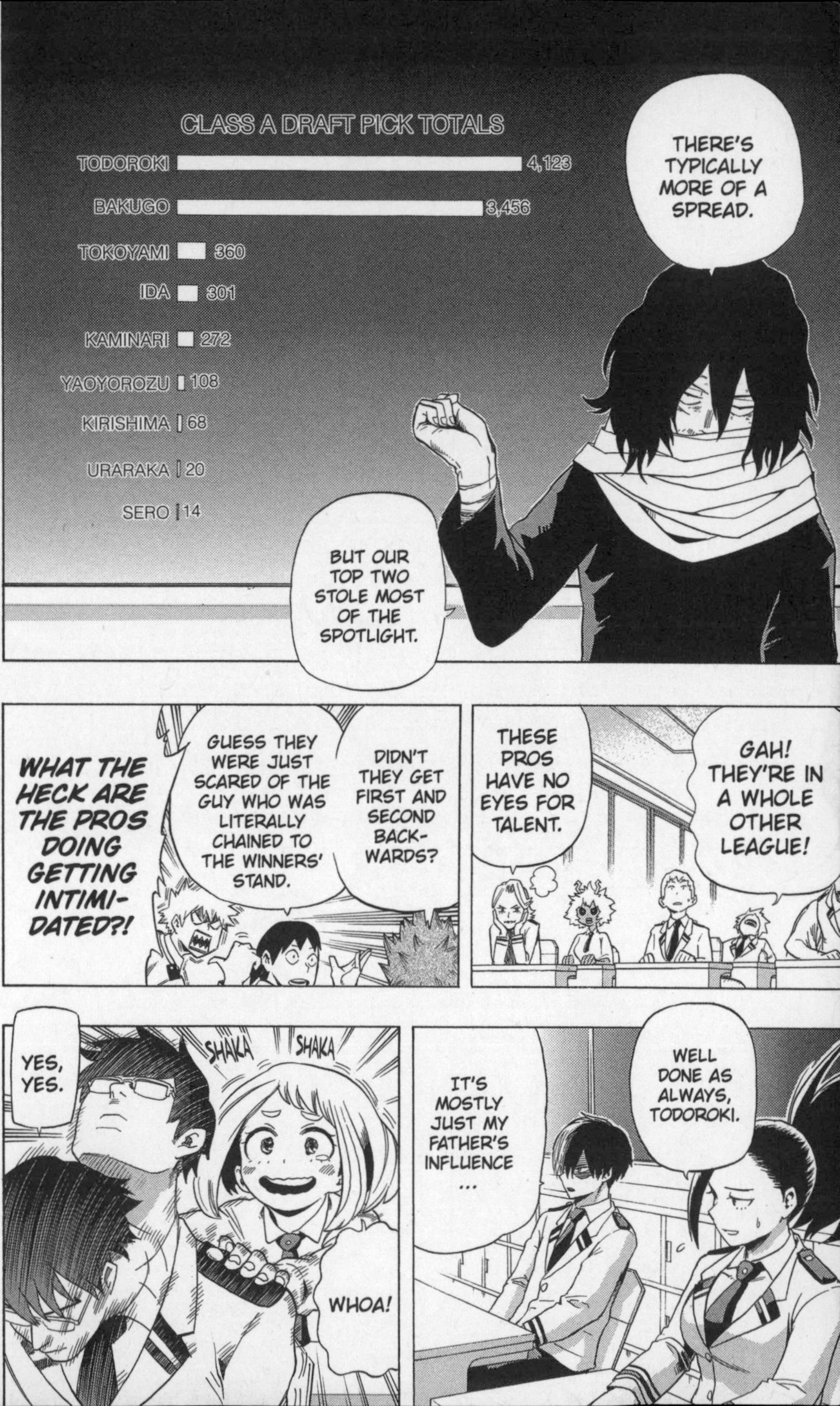

THERE'S TYPICALLY MORE OF A SPREAD.
CLASS A DRAFT PICK TOTALS
TODOROKI 4,123
BAKUGO 3,456
TOKOYAMI 360
IDA 301
KAMINARI 272
YAOYOROZU 108
KIRISHIMA 68
URARAKA 20
SERO 14
BUT OUR TOP TWO STOLE MOST OF THE SPOTLIGHT.
GAH! THEY'RE IN A WHOLE OTHER LEAGUE!
THESE PROS HAVE NO EYES FOR TALENT.
DIDN'T THEY GET FIRST AND SECOND BACK-WARDS?
GUESS THEY WERE JUST SCARED OF THE GUY WHO WAS LITERALLY CHAINED TO THE WINNERS' STAND.
WHAT THE HECK ARE THE PROS DOING GETTING INTIMI-DATED?!
WELL DONE AS ALWAYS, TODOROKI.
IT'S MOSTLY JUST MY FATHER'S INFLUENCE ...
SHAKA
SHAKA
YES, YES.
WHOA!

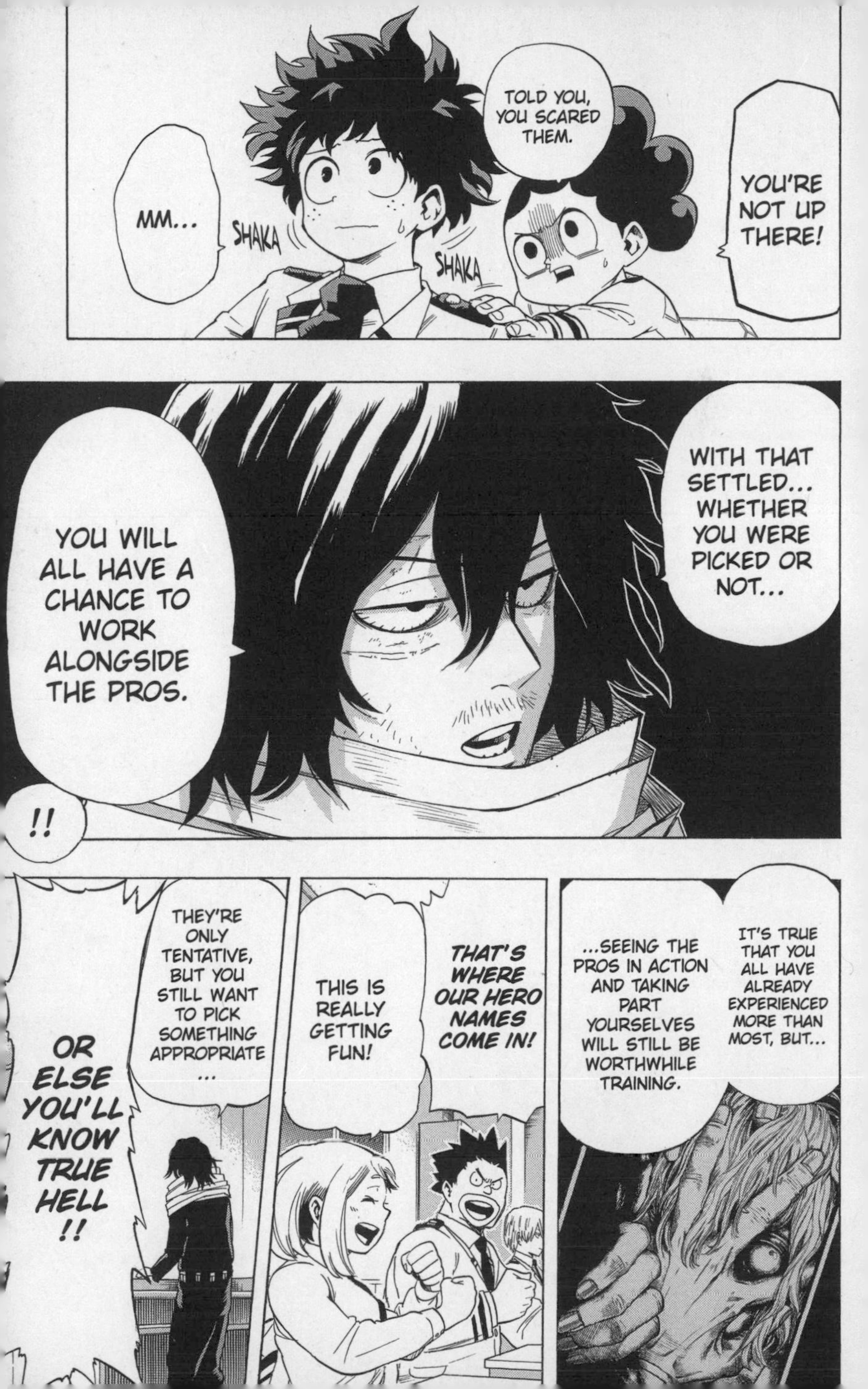
YOU'RE NOT UP THERE!
TOLD YOU, YOU SCARED THEM.
SHAKA
SHAKA
MM...
WITH THAT SETTLED... WHETHER YOU WERE PICKED OR NOT...
YOU WILL ALL HAVE A CHANCE TO WORK ALONGSIDE THE PROS.
!!
IT'S TRUE THAT YOU ALL HAVE ALREADY EXPERIENCED MORE THAN MOST, BUT...
...SEEING THE PROS IN ACTION AND TAKING PART YOURSELVES WILL STILL BE WORTHWHILE TRAINING.
THAT'S WHERE OUR HERO NAMES COME IN!
THIS IS REALLY GETTING FUN!
THEY'RE ONLY TENTATIVE, BUT YOU STILL WANT TO PICK SOMETHING APPROPRIATE...
OR ELSE YOU'LL KNOW TRUE HELL!!

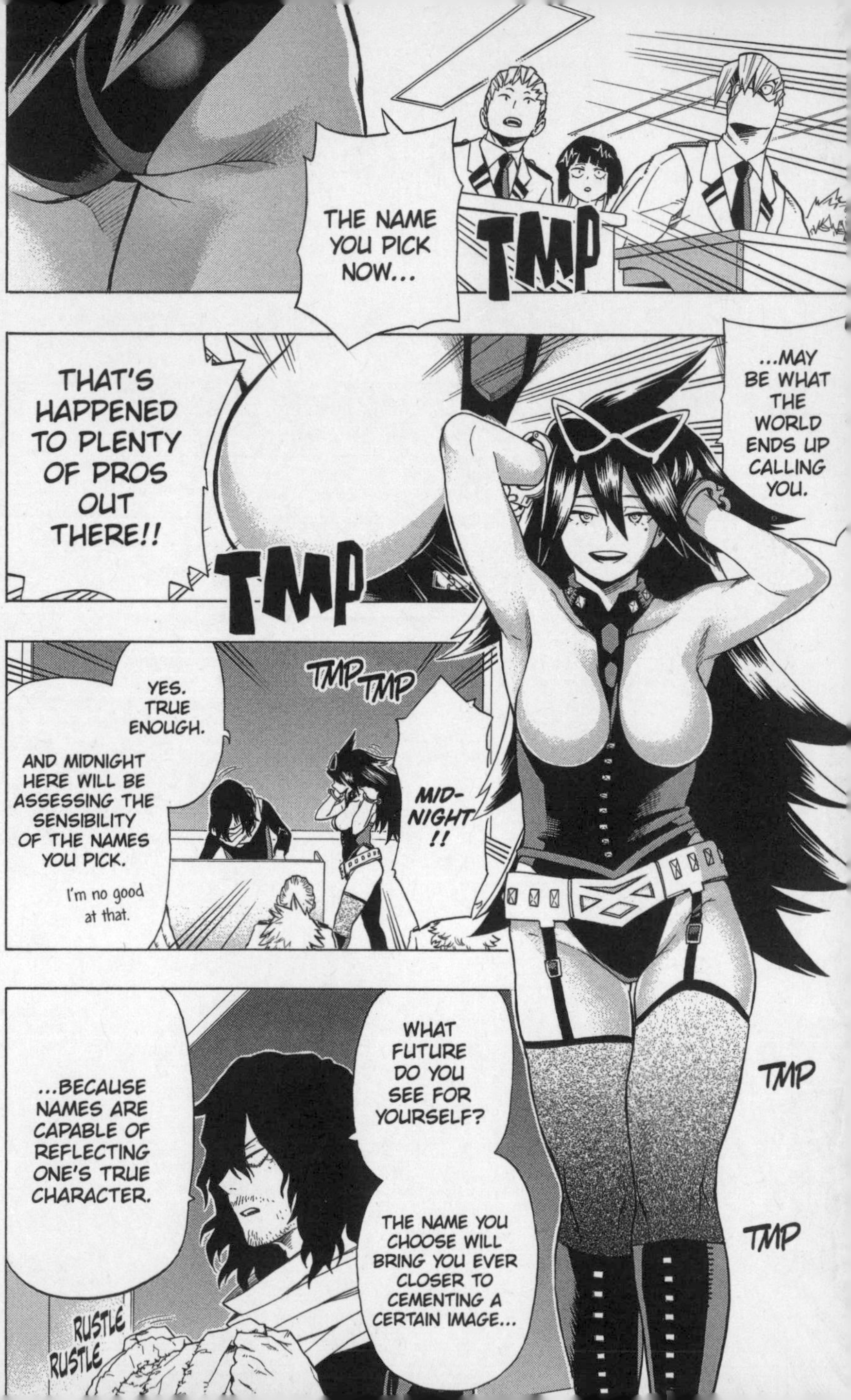
THE NAME YOU PICK NOW...
TMP
...MAY BE WHAT THE WORLD ENDS UP CALLING YOU.
TMP
TMP
THAT'S HAPPENED TO PLENTY OF PROS OUT THERE!!
TMP
TMP TMP
MID-NIGHT!!
YES. TRUE ENOUGH.
AND MIDNIGHT HERE WILL BE ASSESSING THE SENSIBILITY OF THE NAMES YOU PICK.
I'm no good at that.
WHAT FUTURE DO YOU SEE FOR YOURSELF?
THE NAME YOU CHOOSE WILL BRING YOU EVER CLOSER TO CEMENTING A CERTAIN IMAGE...
...BECAUSE NAMES ARE CAPABLE OF REFLECTING ONE'S TRUE CHARACTER.
RUSTLE RUSTLE

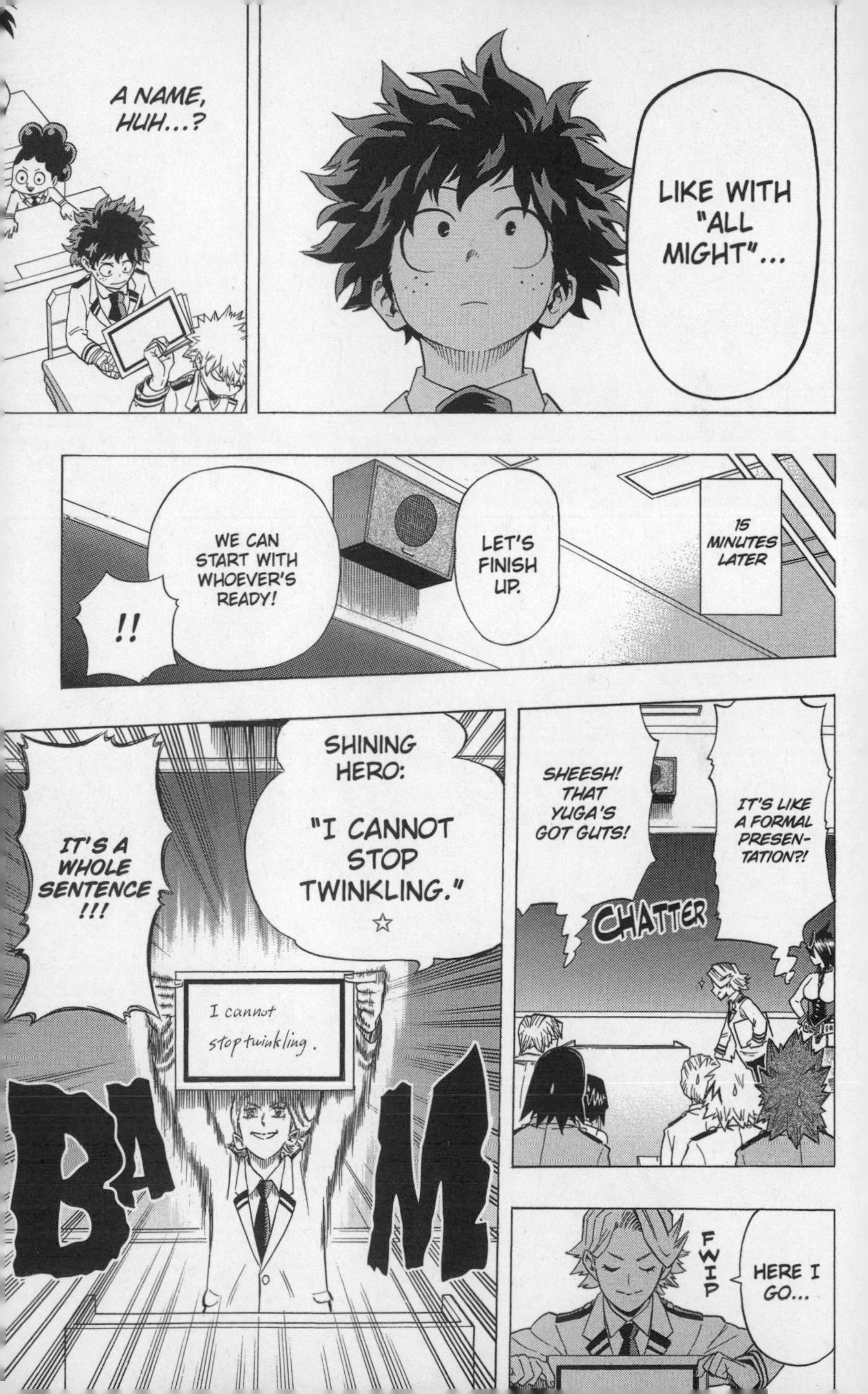
LIKE WITH "ALL MIGHT"...
A NAME, HUH...?
15 MINUTES LATER
LET'S FINISH UP.
WE CAN START WITH WHOEVER'S READY!
!!
IT'S LIKE A FORMAL PRESEN- TATION?!
SHEESH! THAT YUGA'S GOT GUTS!
CHATTER
HERE I GO...
FWIP
SHINING HERO:
"I CANNOT STOP TWINKLING." ☆
IT'S A WHOLE SENTENCE !!!
I cannot stop twinkling.
BAM

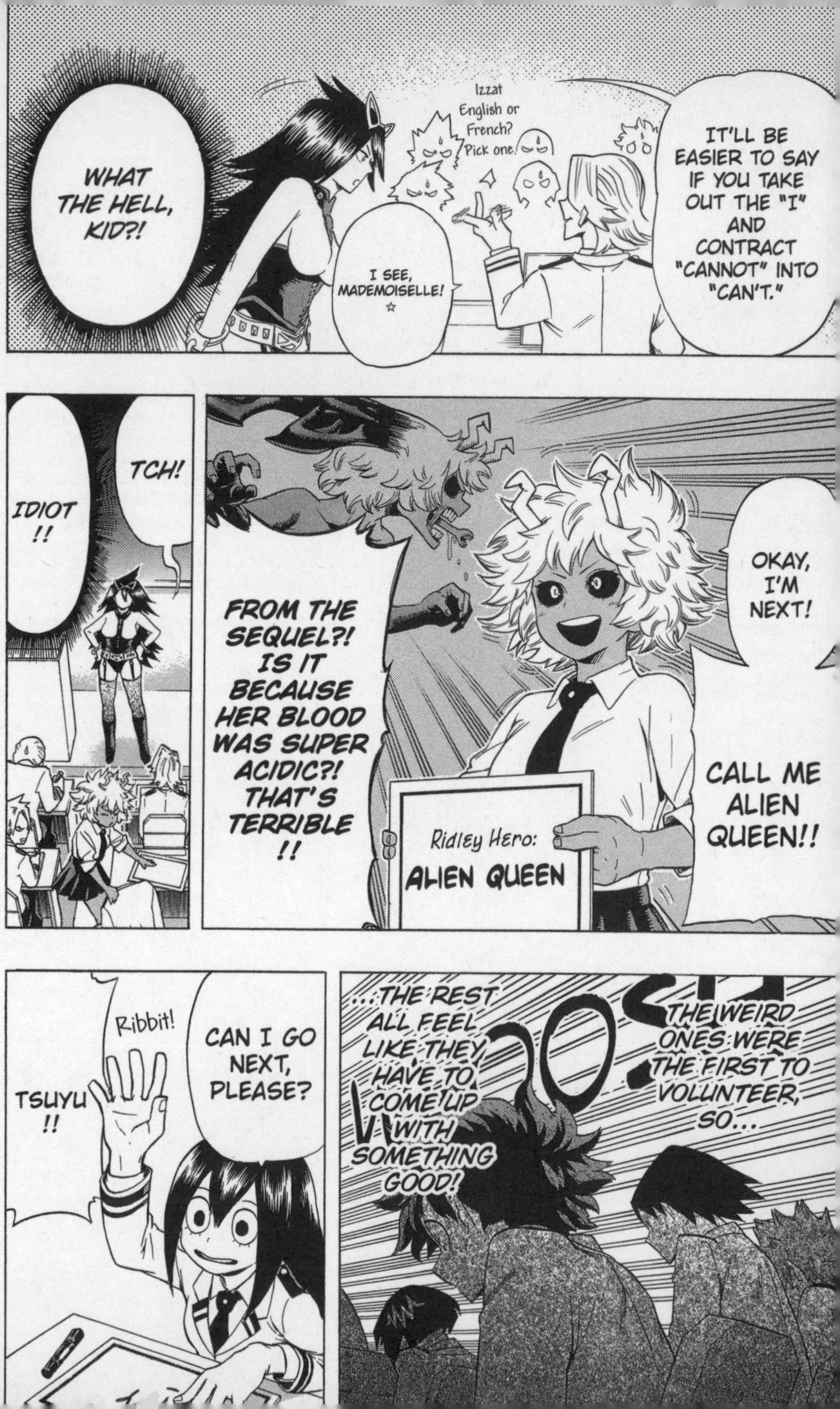
IT'LL BE EASIER TO SAY IF YOU TAKE OUT THE "I" AND CONTRACT "CANNOT" INTO "CAN'T."
Izzat English or French? Pick one.
I SEE, MADEMOISELLE! ☆
WHAT THE HELL, KID?!
OKAY, I'M NEXT!
CALL ME ALIEN QUEEN!!
Ridley Hero: ALIEN QUEEN
FROM THE SEQUEL?! IS IT BECAUSE HER BLOOD WAS SUPER ACIDIC?! THAT'S TERRIBLE!!
TCH!
IDIOT!!
THE WEIRD ONES WERE THE FIRST TO VOLUNTEER, SO...
...THE REST ALL FEEL LIKE THEY HAVE TO COME UP WITH SOMETHING GOOD!
CAN I GO NEXT, PLEASE?
Ribbit!
TSUYU!!

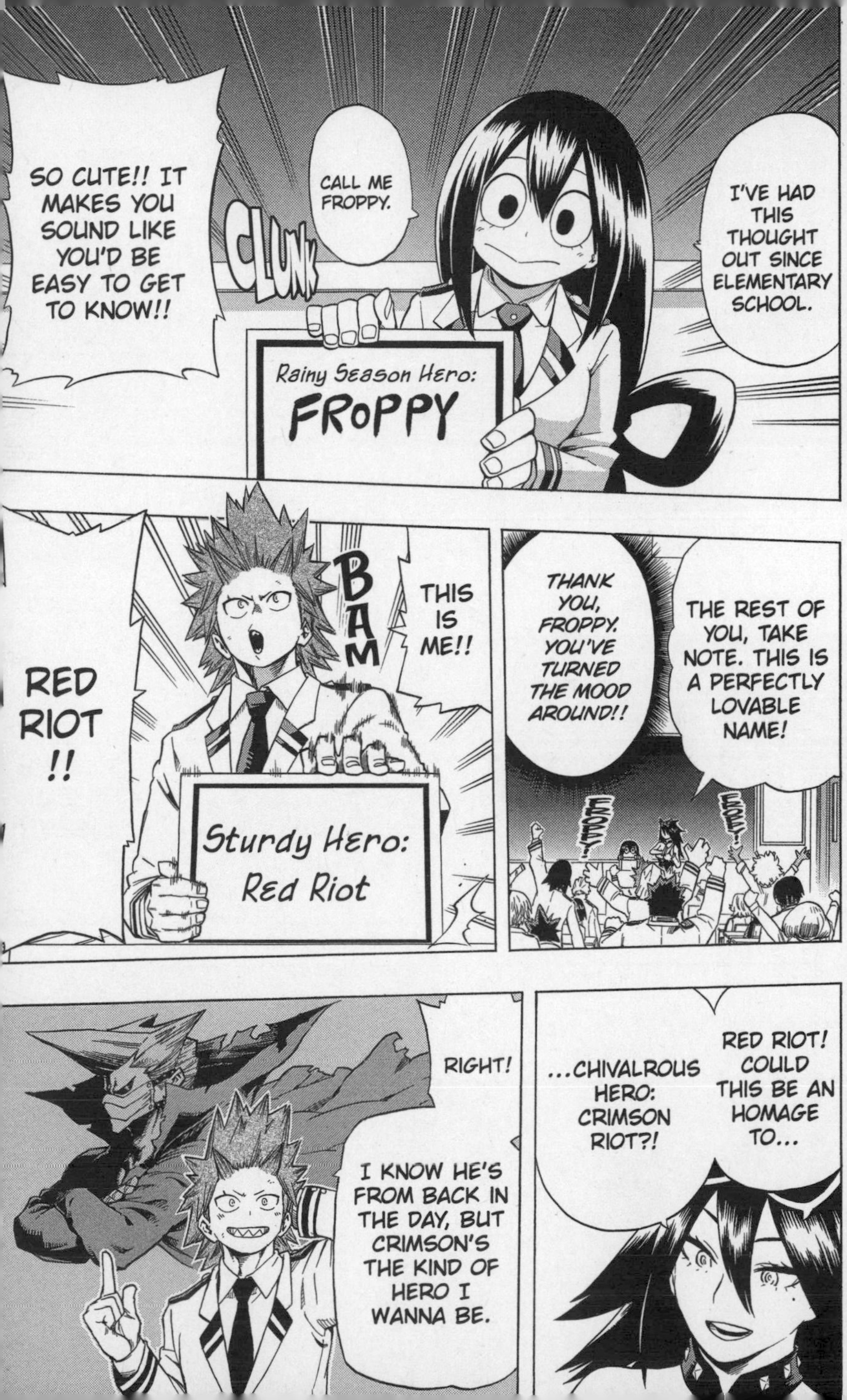

I'VE HAD THIS THOUGHT OUT SINCE ELEMENTARY SCHOOL.
CALL ME FROPPY.
CLUNK
Rainy Season Hero: FROPPY
SO CUTE!! IT MAKES YOU SOUND LIKE YOU'D BE EASY TO GET TO KNOW!!
THE REST OF YOU, TAKE NOTE. THIS IS A PERFECTLY LOVABLE NAME!
THANK YOU, FROPPY. YOU'VE TURNED THE MOOD AROUND!!
THIS IS ME!!
BAM
RED RIOT!!
Sturdy Hero: Red Riot
RED RIOT! COULD THIS BE AN HOMAGE TO...
...CHIVALROUS HERO: CRIMSON RIOT?!
RIGHT!
I KNOW HE'S FROM BACK IN THE DAY, BUT CRIMSON'S THE KIND OF HERO I WANNA BE.

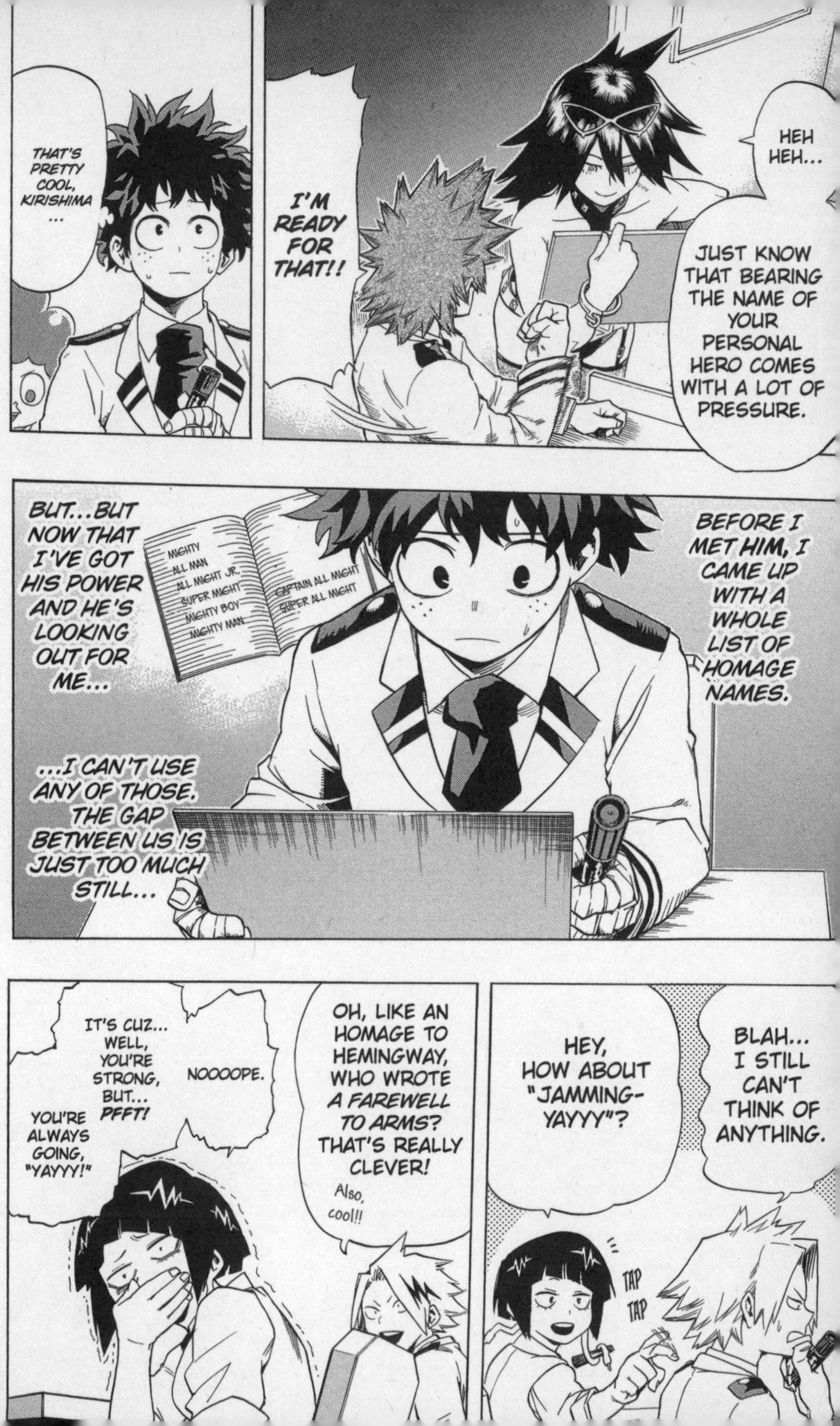
HEH HEH...
JUST KNOW THAT BEARING THE NAME OF YOUR PERSONAL HERO COMES WITH A LOT OF PRESSURE.
I'M READY FOR THAT!!
THAT'S PRETTY COOL, KIRISHIMA ...
BEFORE I MET HIM, I CAME UP WITH A WHOLE LIST OF HOMAGE NAMES.
BUT...BUT NOW THAT I'VE GOT HIS POWER AND HE'S LOOKING OUT FOR ME...
MIGHTY
ALL MAN
ALL MIGHT JR.
SUPER MIGHT
MIGHTY BOY
MIGHTY MAN
CAPTAIN ALL MIGHT
SUPER ALL MIGHT
...I CAN'T USE ANY OF THOSE. THE GAP BETWEEN US IS JUST TOO MUCH STILL...
BLAH... I STILL CAN'T THINK OF ANYTHING.
HEY, HOW ABOUT "JAMMING-YAYYY"?
TAP TAP
OH, LIKE AN HOMAGE TO HEMINGWAY, WHO WROTE A FAREWELL TO ARMS? THAT'S REALLY CLEVER!
Also, cool!!
NOOOOPE.
IT'S CUZ... WELL, YOU'RE STRONG, BUT... PFFT!
YOU'RE ALWAYS GOING, "YAYYY!"

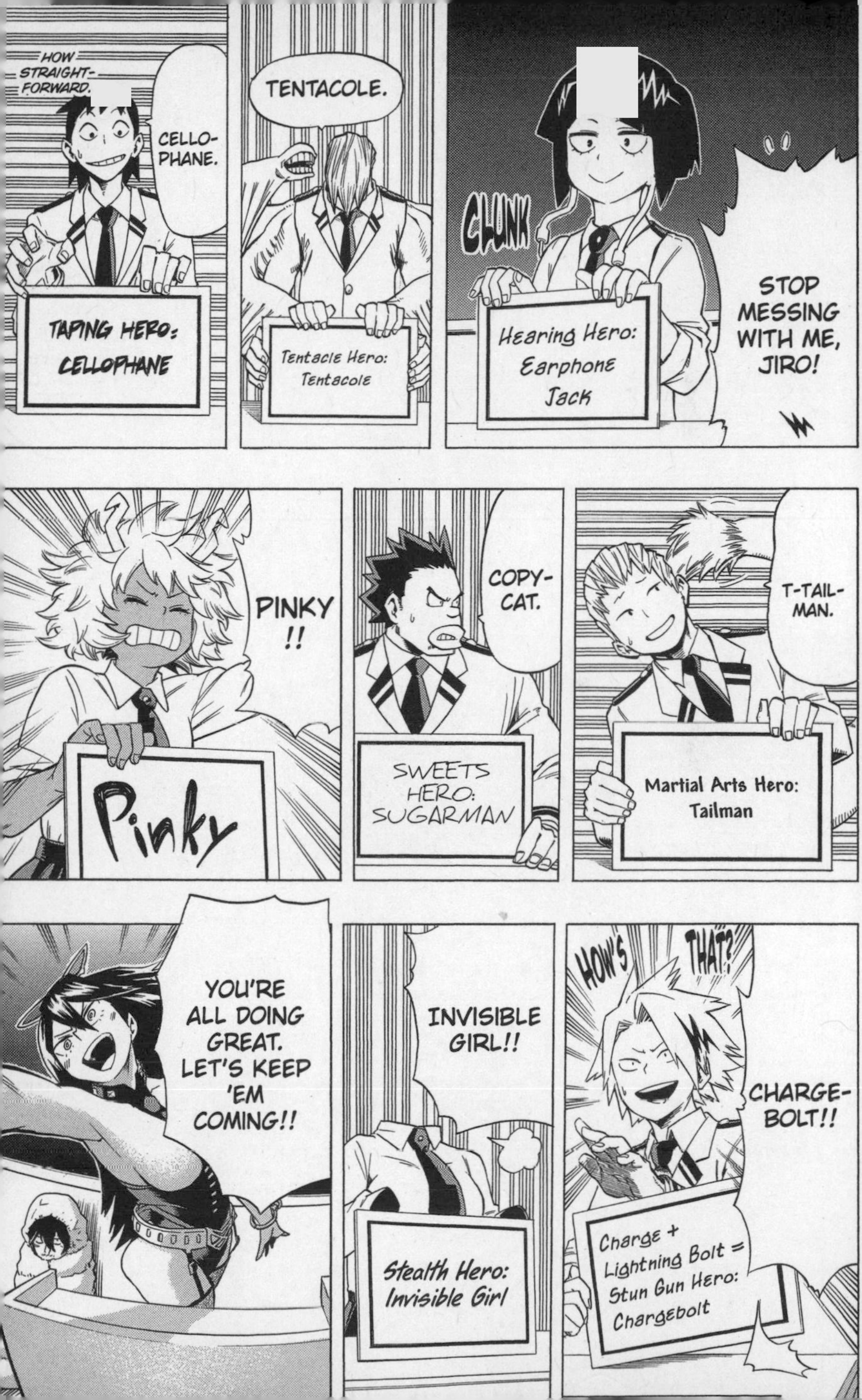
CLUNK
Hearing Hero: Earphone Jack
STOP MESSING WITH ME, JIRO!
TENTACOLE.
Tentacle Hero: Tentacole
CELLO-PHANE.
HOW STRAIGHT-FORWARD.
TAPING HERO: CELLOPHANE
T-TAIL-MAN.
Martial Arts Hero: Tailman
COPY-CAT.
SWEETS HERO: SUGARMAN
PINKY!!
Pinky
HOW'S THAT?
CHARGE-BOLT!!
Charge + Lightning Bolt = Stun Gun Hero: Chargebolt
INVISIBLE GIRL!!
Stealth Hero: Invisible Girl
YOU'RE ALL DOING GREAT. LET'S KEEP 'EM COMING!!

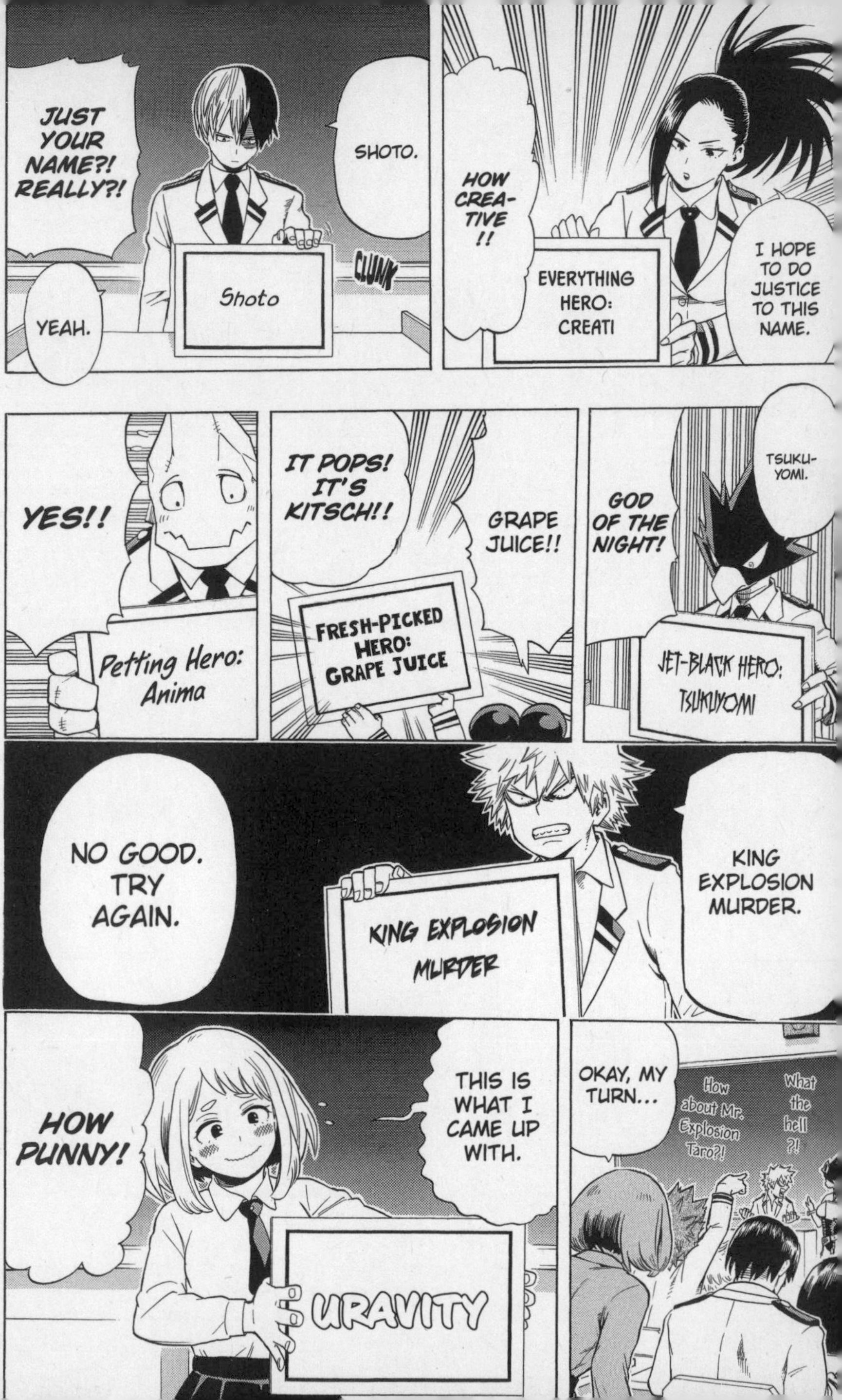
I HOPE TO DO JUSTICE TO THIS NAME.
EVERYTHING HERO: CREATI
HOW CREA-TIVE !!
SHOTO.
CLUNK
Shoto
JUST YOUR NAME?! REALLY?!
YEAH.
TSUKU-YOMI.
JET-BLACK HERO: TSUKUYOMI
GOD OF THE NIGHT!
GRAPE JUICE!!
IT POPS! IT'S KITSCH!!
FRESH-PICKED HERO: GRAPE JUICE
YES!!
Petting Hero: Anima
KING EXPLOSION MURDER.
KING EXPLOSION MURDER
NO GOOD. TRY AGAIN.
What the hell ?!
How about Mr. Explosion Taro?!
OKAY, MY TURN...
THIS IS WHAT I CAME UP WITH.
URAVITY
HOW PUNNY!

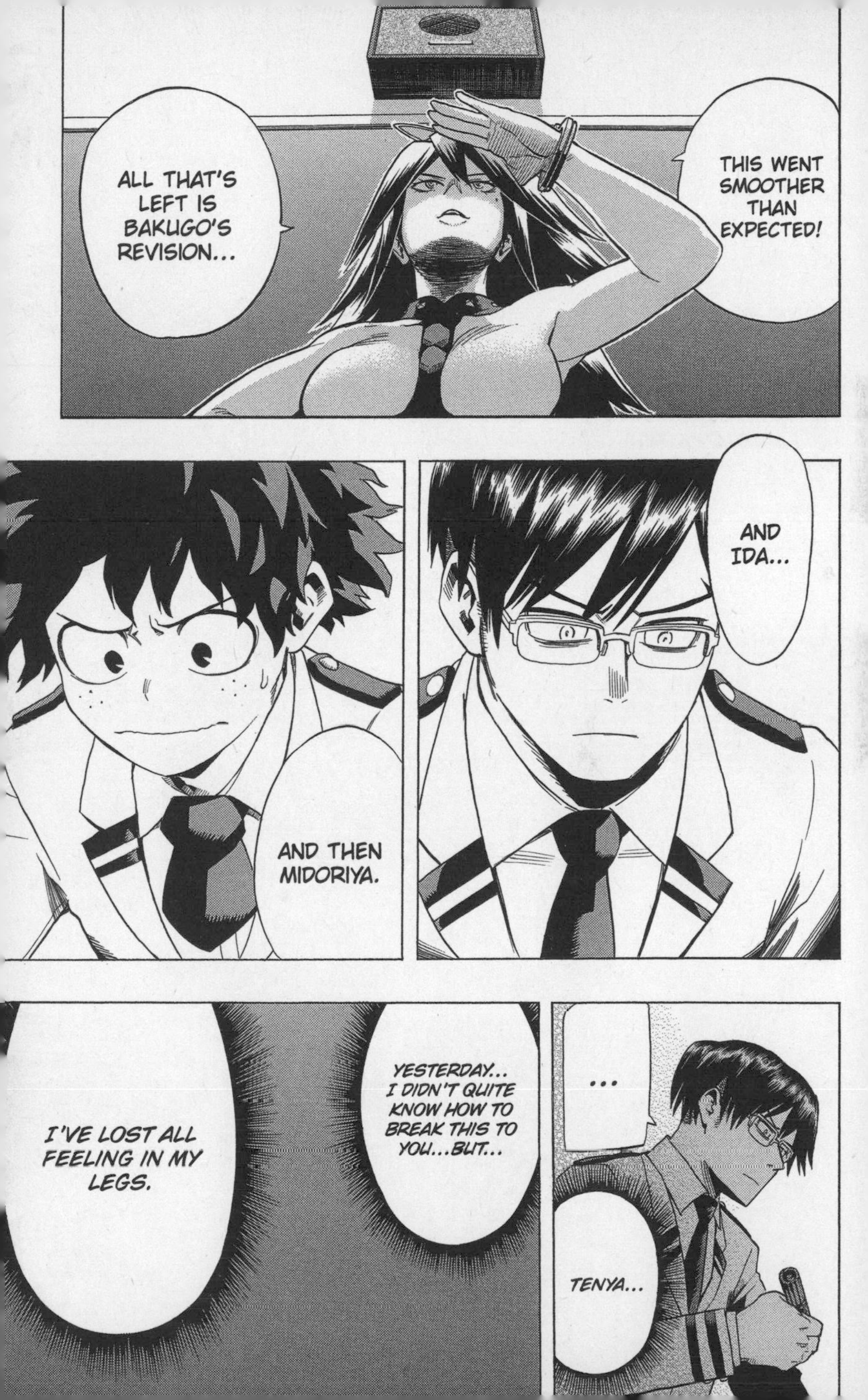
THIS WENT SMOOTHER THAN EXPECTED!
ALL THAT'S LEFT IS BAKUGO'S REVISION...
AND IDA...
AND THEN MIDORIYA.
...
TENYA...
YESTERDAY... I DIDN'T QUITE KNOW HOW TO BREAK THIS TO YOU...BUT...
I'VE LOST ALL FEELING IN MY LEGS.

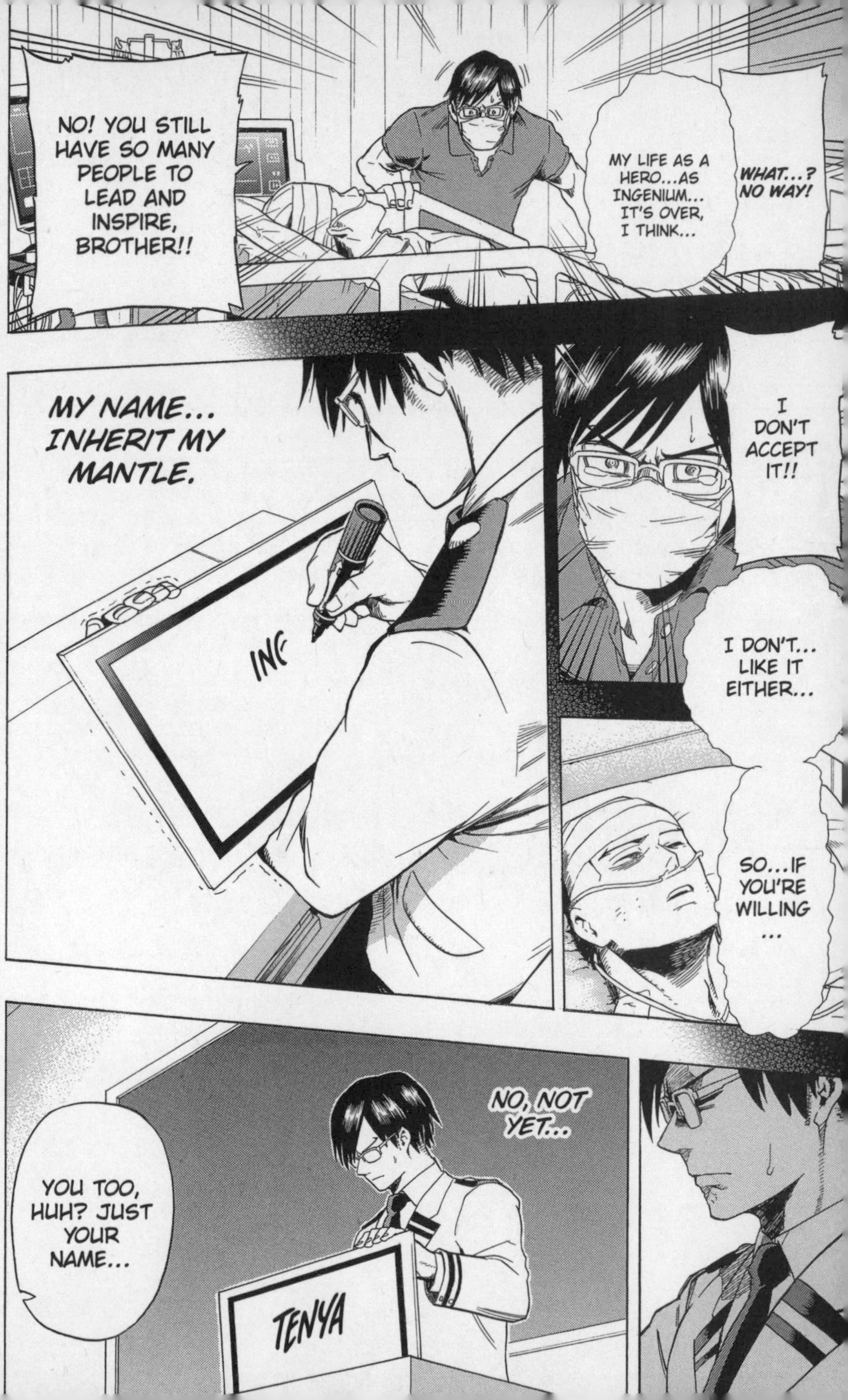
MY LIFE AS A HERO...AS INGENIUM... IT'S OVER, I THINK...
WHAT...? NO WAY!
NO! YOU STILL HAVE SO MANY PEOPLE TO LEAD AND INSPIRE, BROTHER!!
I DON'T ACCEPT IT!!
I DON'T... LIKE IT EITHER...
SO...IF YOU'RE WILLING...
MY NAME... INHERIT MY MANTLE.
INC
NO, NOT YET...
YOU TOO, HUH? JUST YOUR NAME...
TENYA

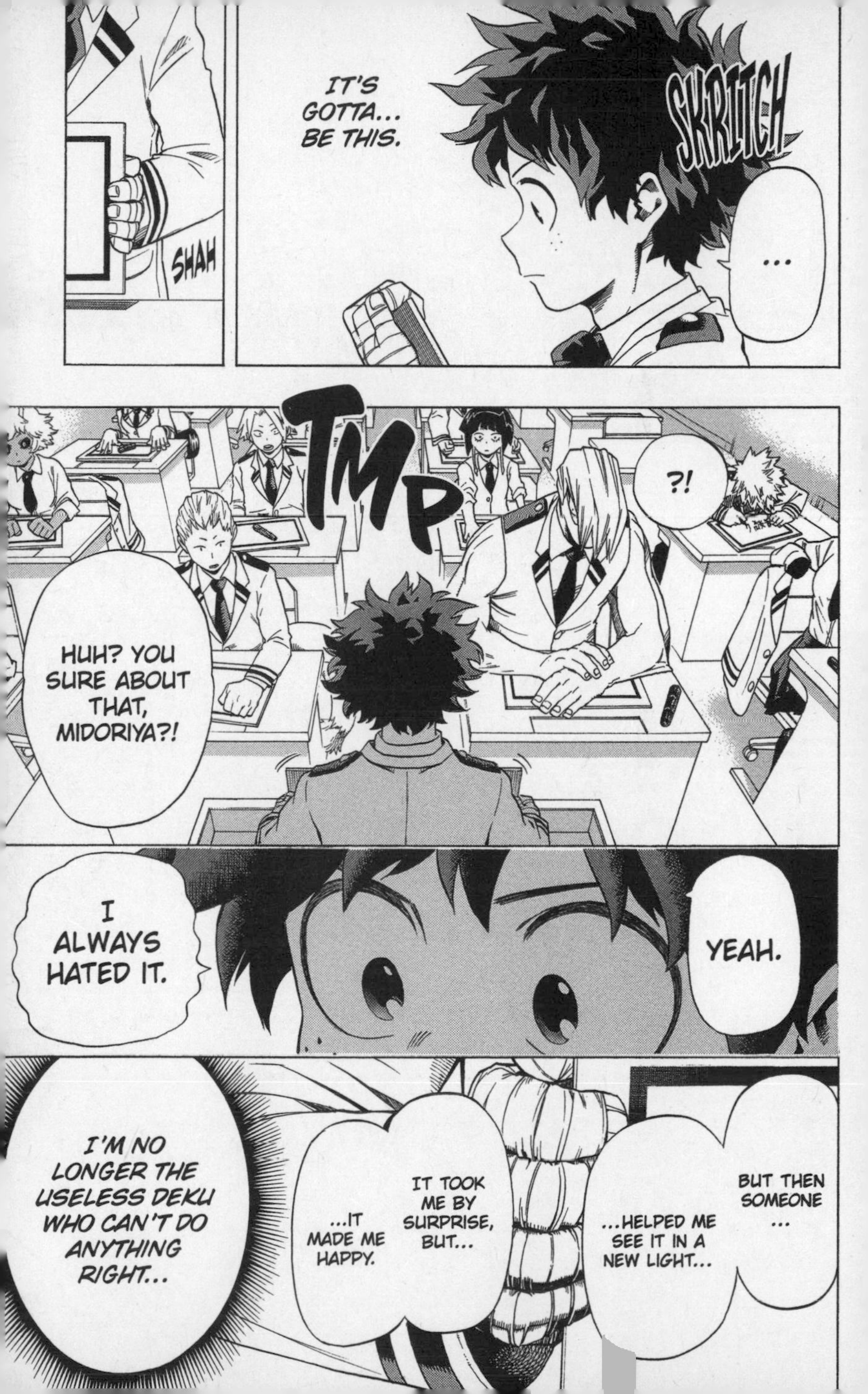
SKRITCH
...
IT'S GOTTA... BE THIS.
SHAH
?!
TMP
HUH? YOU SURE ABOUT THAT, MIDORIYA?!
YEAH.
I ALWAYS HATED IT.
BUT THEN SOMEONE...
...HELPED ME SEE IT IN A NEW LIGHT...
IT TOOK ME BY SURPRISE, BUT...
...IT MADE ME HAPPY.
I'M NO LONGER THE USELESS DEKU WHO CAN'T DO ANYTHING RIGHT...

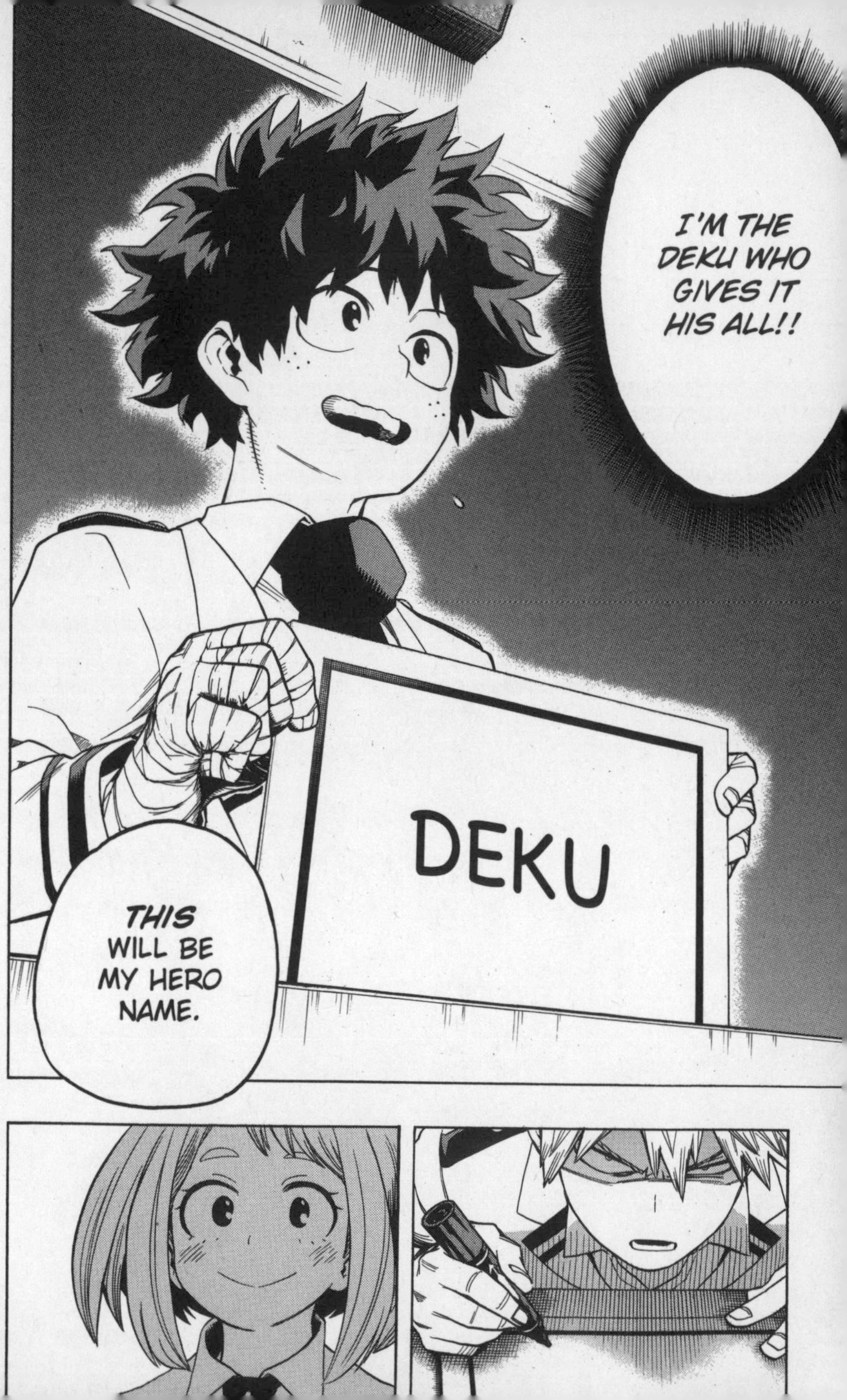
I'M THE DEKU WHO GIVES IT HIS ALL!!
DEKU
THIS WILL BE MY HERO NAME.

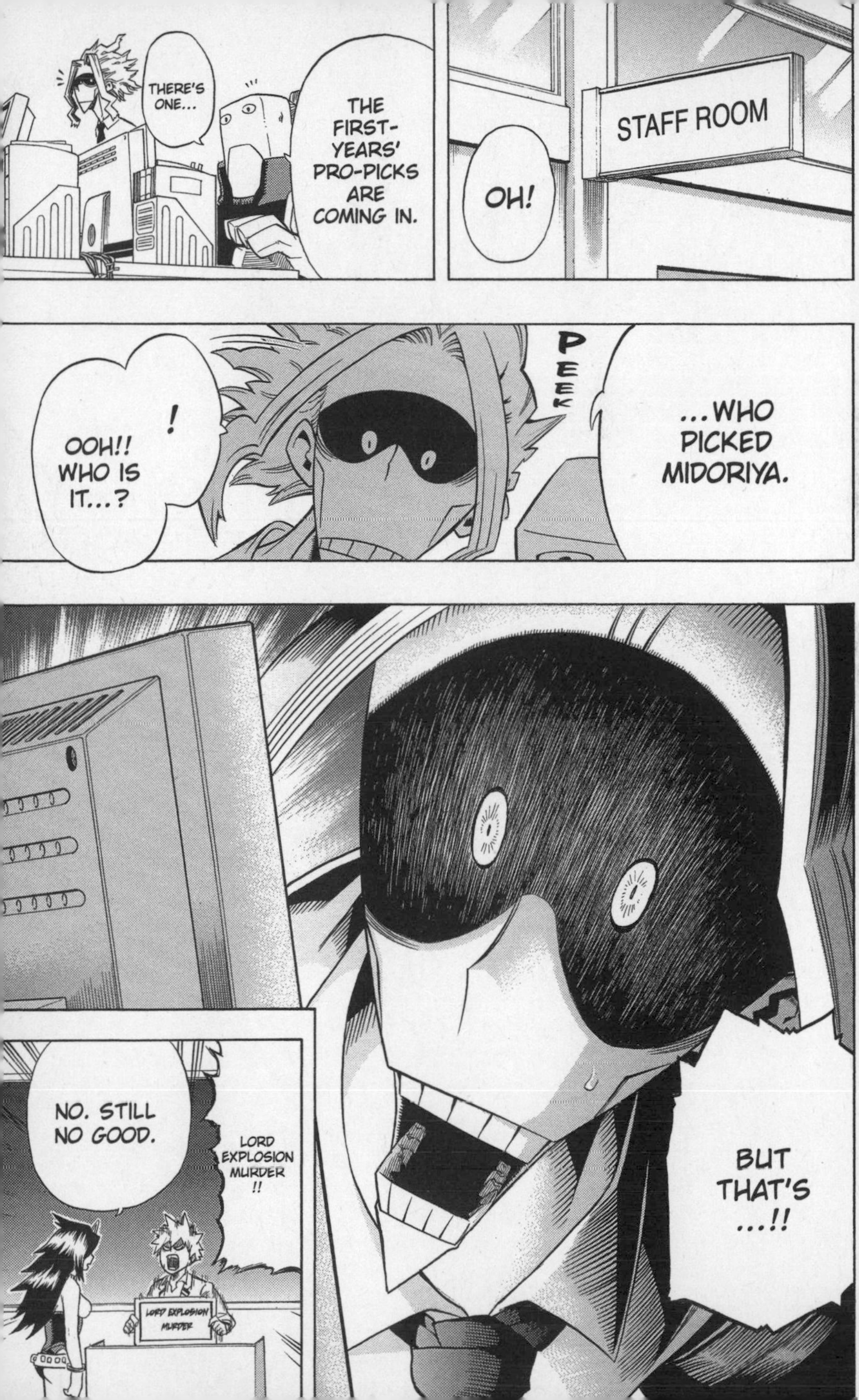
STAFF ROOM
OH!
THE FIRST-YEARS' PRO-PICKS ARE COMING IN.
THERE'S ONE...
...WHO PICKED MIDORIYA.
PEEK
!
OOH!! WHO IS IT...?
BUT THAT'S ...!!
NO. STILL NO GOOD.
LORD EXPLOSION MURDER !!
LORD EXPLOSION MURDER

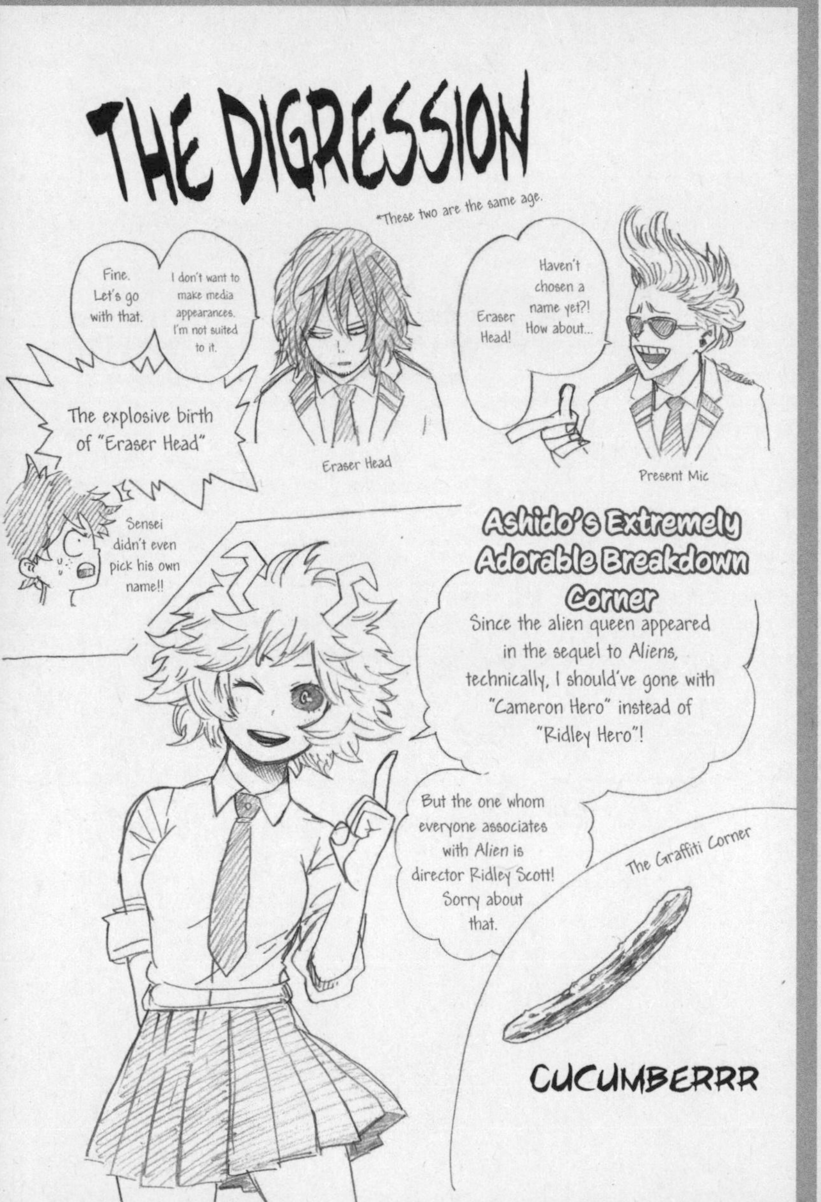
THE DIGRESSION
*These two are the same age.
Haven't chosen a name yet?! How about...
Eraser Head!
Present Mic
I don't want to make media appearances. I'm not suited to it.
Fine. Let's go with that.
Eraser Head
The explosive birth of "Eraser Head"
Sensei didn't even pick his own name!!
Ashido's Extremely Adorable Breakdown Corner
Since the alien queen appeared in the sequel to Aliens, technically, I should've gone with "Cameron Hero" instead of "Ridley Hero"!
But the one whom everyone associates with Alien is director Ridley Scott! Sorry about that.
The Graffiti Corner
CUCUMBERRR

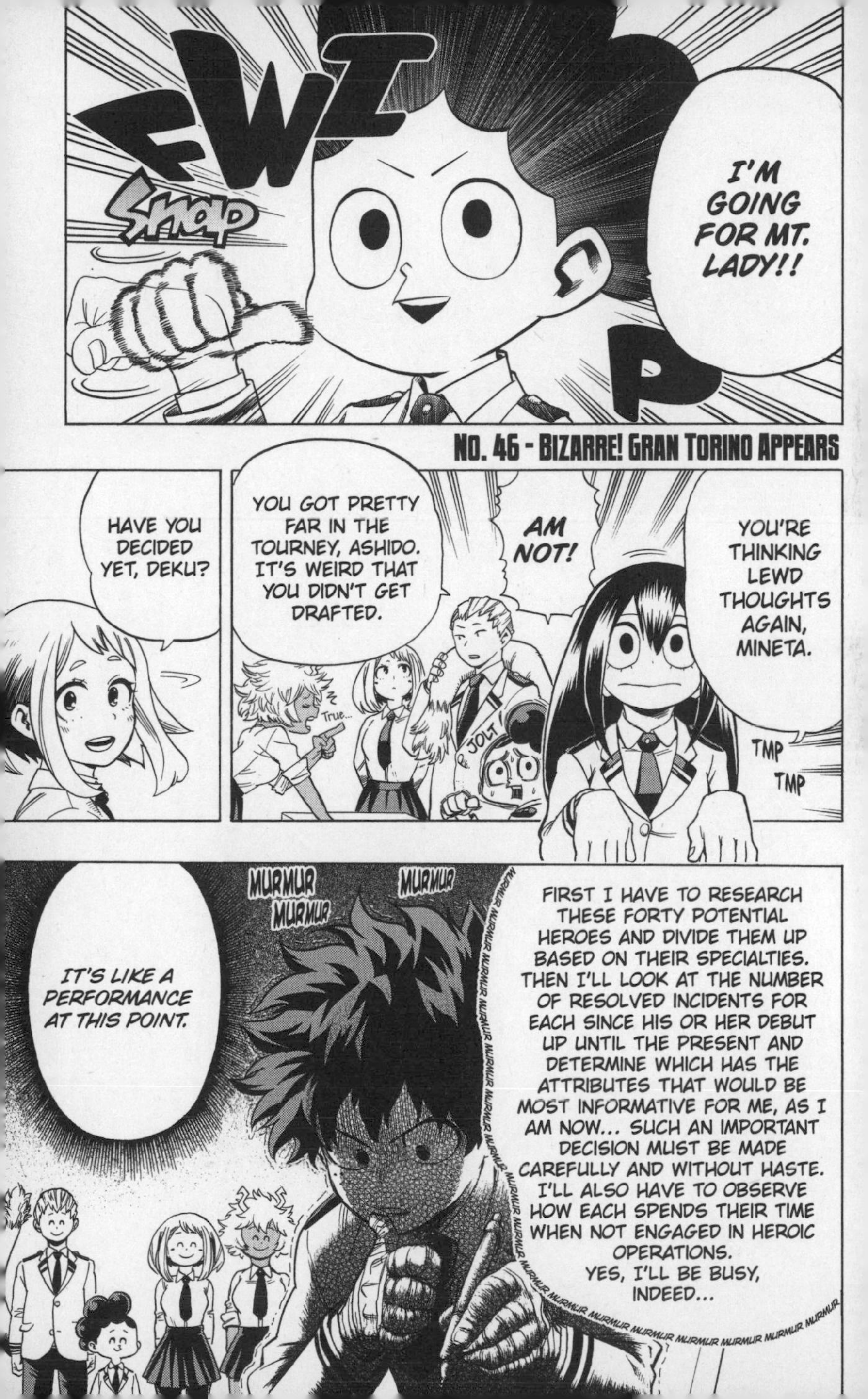
I'M GOING FOR MT. LADY!!
FWIP
SNAP
NO. 46 - BIZARRE! GRAN TORINO APPEARS
YOU'RE THINKING LEWD THOUGHTS AGAIN, MINETA.
TMP TMP
AM NOT!
JOLT
YOU GOT PRETTY FAR IN THE TOURNEY, ASHIDO. IT'S WEIRD THAT YOU DIDN'T GET DRAFTED.
True...
HAVE YOU DECIDED YET, DEKU?
FIRST I HAVE TO RESEARCH THESE FORTY POTENTIAL HEROES AND DIVIDE THEM UP BASED ON THEIR SPECIALTIES. THEN I'LL LOOK AT THE NUMBER OF RESOLVED INCIDENTS FOR EACH SINCE HIS OR HER DEBUT UP UNTIL THE PRESENT AND DETERMINE WHICH HAS THE ATTRIBUTES THAT WOULD BE MOST INFORMATIVE FOR ME, AS I AM NOW... SUCH AN IMPORTANT DECISION MUST BE MADE CAREFULLY AND WITHOUT HASTE. I'LL ALSO HAVE TO OBSERVE HOW EACH SPENDS THEIR TIME WHEN NOT ENGAGED IN HEROIC OPERATIONS. YES, I'LL BE BUSY, INDEED...
MURMUR MURMUR
MURMUR
IT'S LIKE A PERFORMANCE AT THIS POINT.

No. 46
BIZARRE!
GRAN TORINO APPEARS

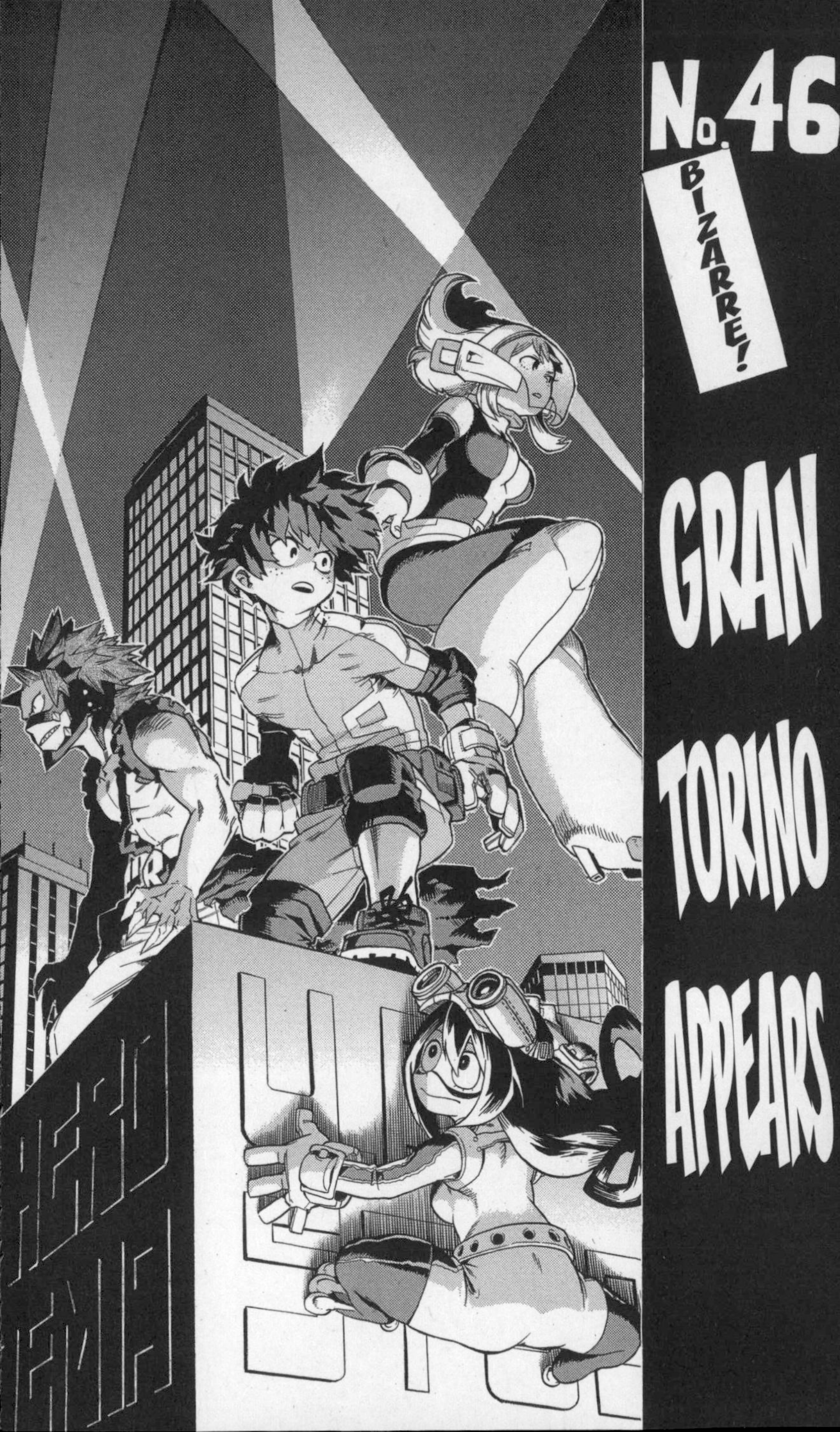

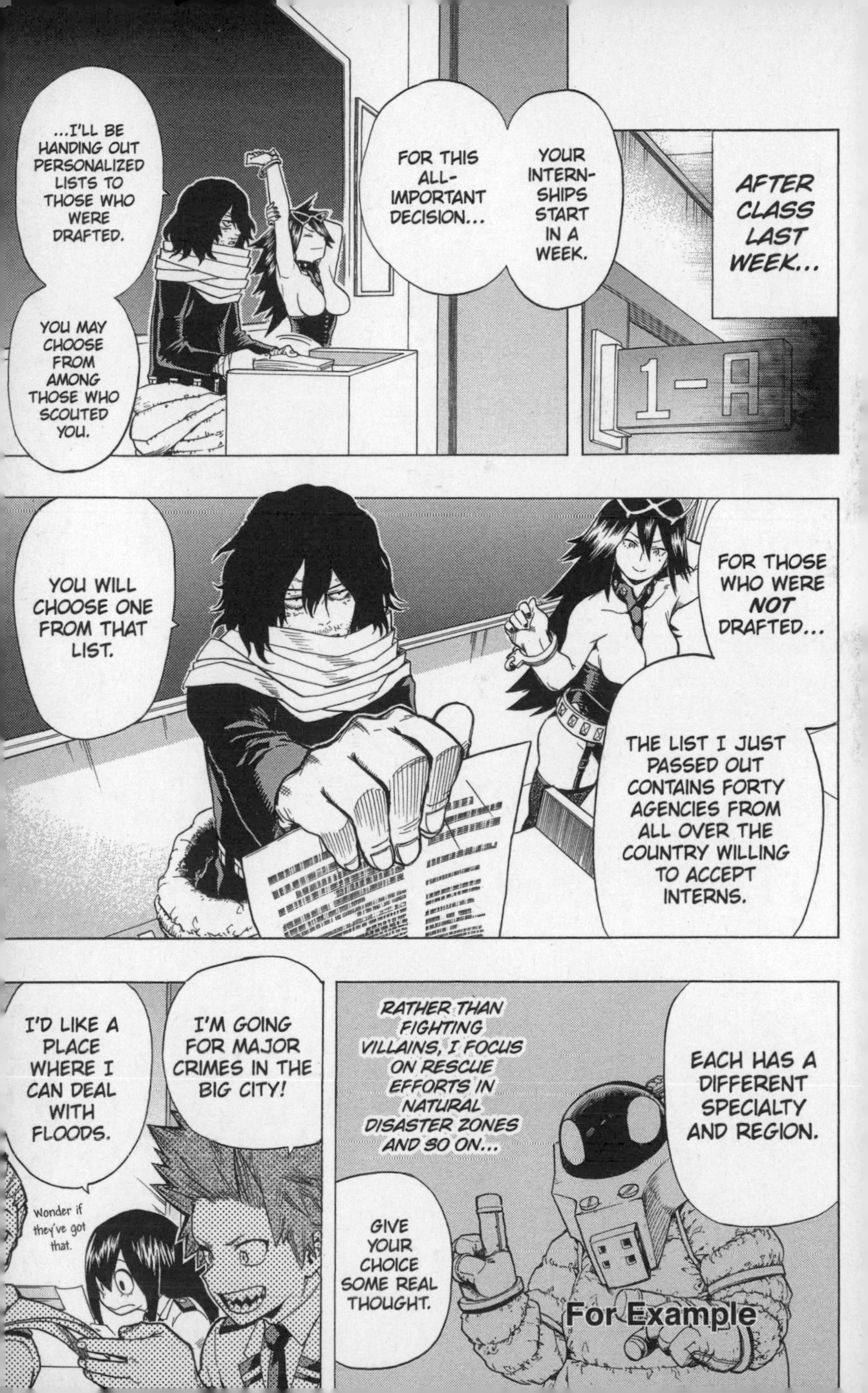
AFTER CLASS LAST WEEK...
YOUR INTERNSHIPS START IN A WEEK.
FOR THIS ALL-IMPORTANT DECISION...
...I'LL BE HANDING OUT PERSONALIZED LISTS TO THOSE WHO WERE DRAFTED.
YOU MAY CHOOSE FROM AMONG THOSE WHO SCOUTED YOU.
FOR THOSE WHO WERE *NOT* DRAFTED...
THE LIST I JUST PASSED OUT CONTAINS FORTY AGENCIES FROM ALL OVER THE COUNTRY WILLING TO ACCEPT INTERNS.
YOU WILL CHOOSE ONE FROM THAT LIST.
EACH HAS A DIFFERENT SPECIALTY AND REGION.
RATHER THAN FIGHTING VILLAINS, I FOCUS ON RESCUE EFFORTS IN NATURAL DISASTER ZONES AND SO ON...
GIVE YOUR CHOICE SOME REAL THOUGHT.
For Example
I'M GOING FOR MAJOR CRIMES IN THE BIG CITY!
I'D LIKE A PLACE WHERE I CAN DEAL WITH FLOODS.
Wonder if they've got that.

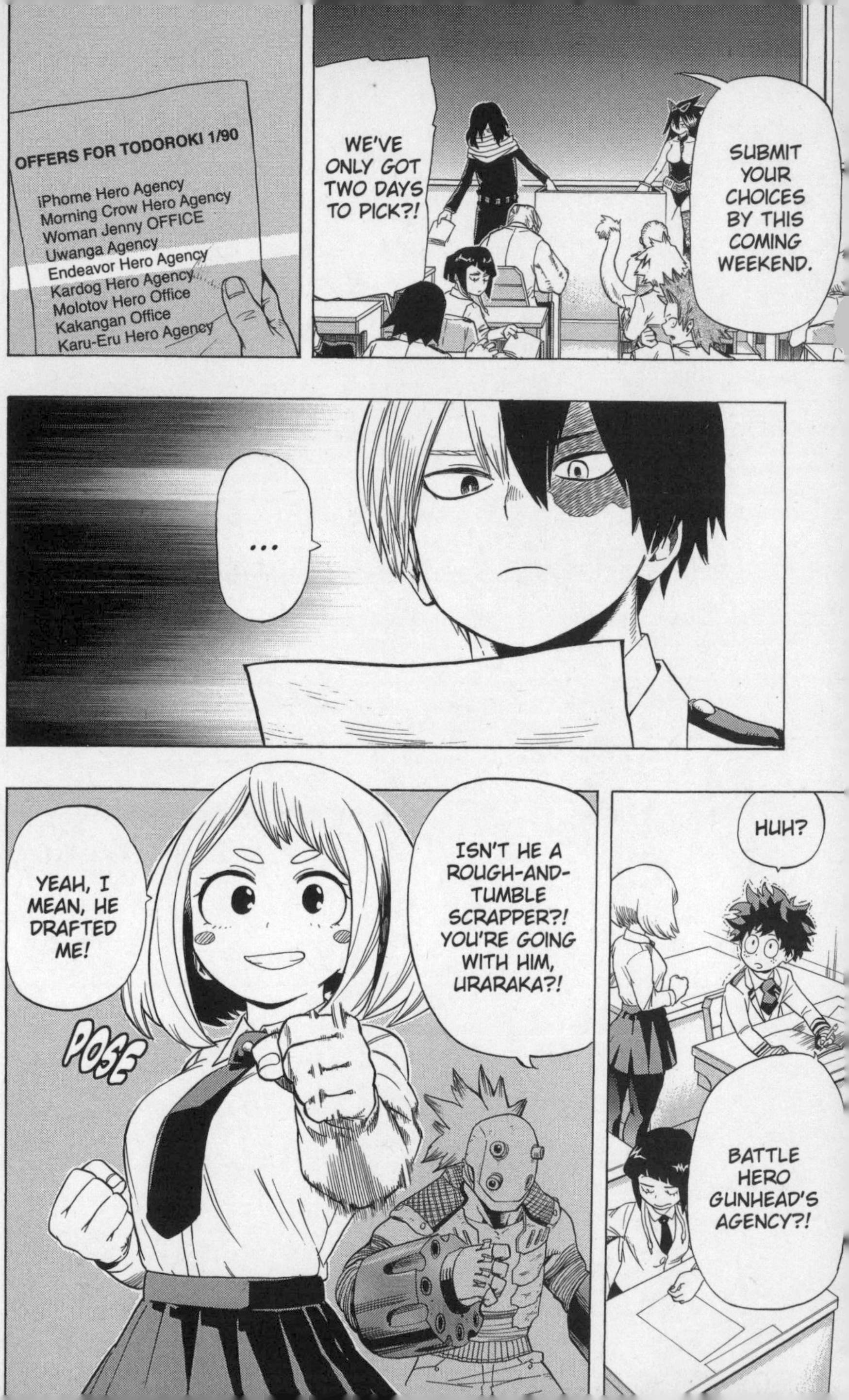
SUBMIT YOUR CHOICES BY THIS COMING WEEKEND.
WE'VE ONLY GOT TWO DAYS TO PICK?!
OFFERS FOR TODOROKI 1/90
iPhome Hero Agency
Morning Crow Hero Agency
Woman Jenny OFFICE
Uwanga Agency
Endeavor Hero Agency
Kardog Hero Agency
Molotov Hero Office
Kakangan Office
Karu-Eru Hero Agency
...
HUH?
BATTLE HERO GUNHEAD'S AGENCY?!
ISN'T HE A ROUGH-AND-TUMBLE SCRAPPER?! YOU'RE GOING WITH HIM, URARAKA?!
YEAH, I MEAN, HE DRAFTED ME!
POSE

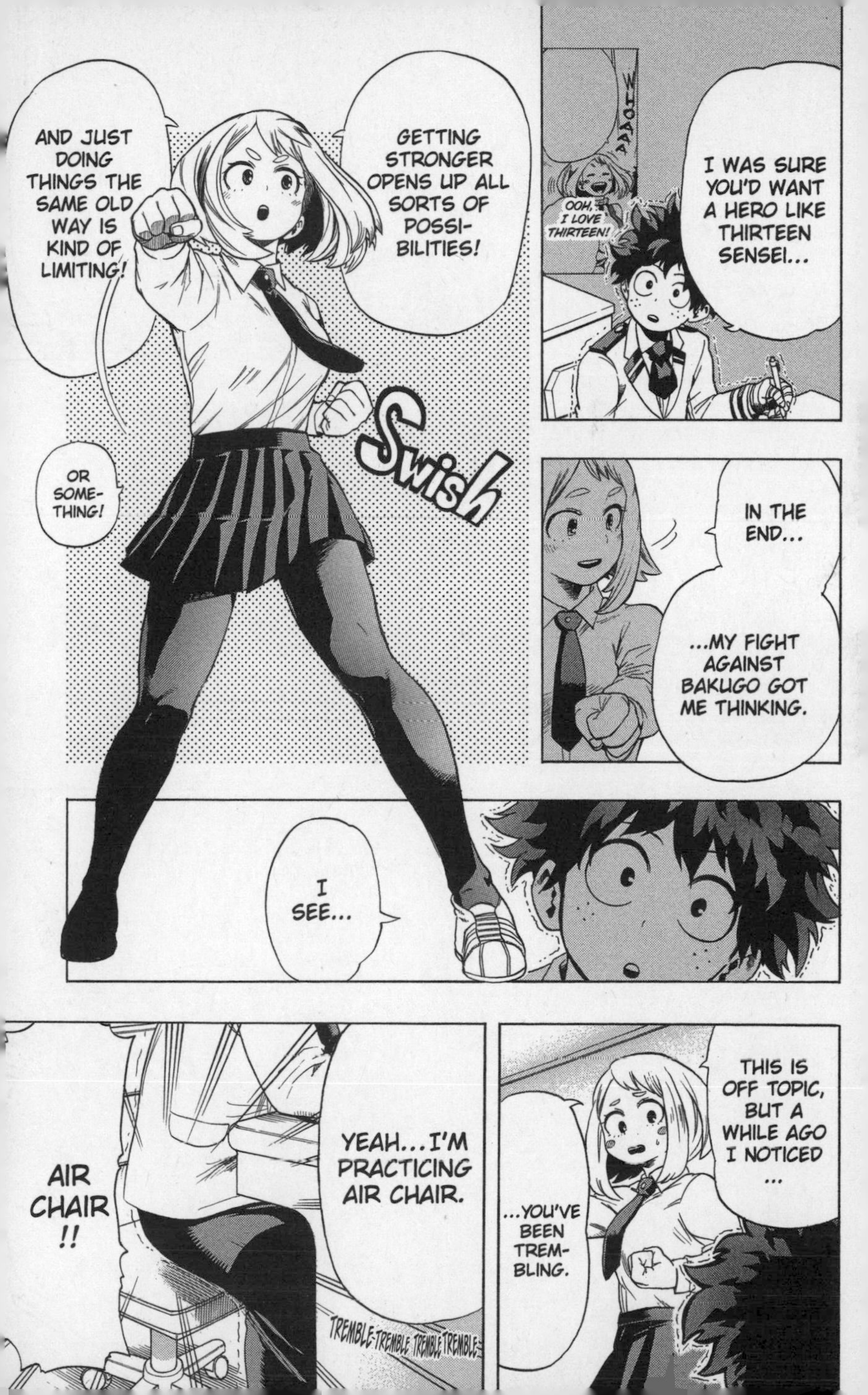
I WAS SURE YOU'D WANT A HERO LIKE THIRTEEN SENSEI...
WHOAAA
OOH, I LOVE THIRTEEN!
IN THE END...
...MY FIGHT AGAINST BAKUGO GOT ME THINKING.
GETTING STRONGER OPENS UP ALL SORTS OF POSSI-BILITIES!
AND JUST DOING THINGS THE SAME OLD WAY IS KIND OF LIMITING!
Swish
OR SOME-THING!
I SEE...
THIS IS OFF TOPIC, BUT A WHILE AGO I NOTICED ...
...YOU'VE BEEN TREM-BLING.
YEAH...I'M PRACTICING AIR CHAIR.
AIR CHAIR !!
TREMBLE-TREMBLE TREMBLE-TREMBLE

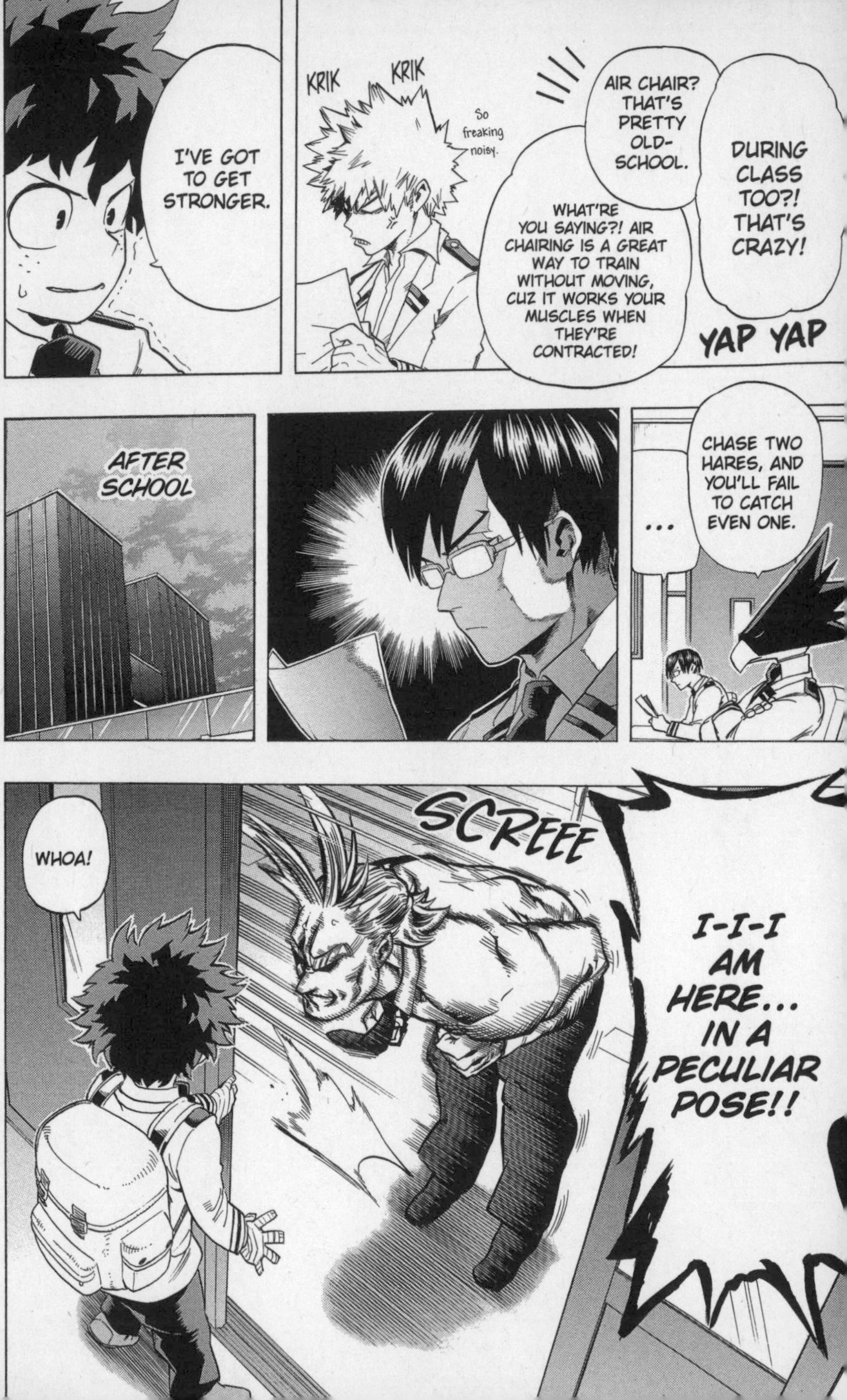
DURING CLASS TOO?! THAT'S CRAZY!
AIR CHAIR? THAT'S PRETTY OLD-SCHOOL.
WHAT'RE YOU SAYING?! AIR CHAIRING IS A GREAT WAY TO TRAIN WITHOUT MOVING, CUZ IT WORKS YOUR MUSCLES WHEN THEY'RE CONTRACTED!
YAP YAP
KRIK KRIK
So freaking noisy.
I'VE GOT TO GET STRONGER.
CHASE TWO HARES, AND YOU'LL FAIL TO CATCH EVEN ONE.
...
AFTER SCHOOL
I-I-I AM HERE... IN A PECULIAR POSE!!
SCREEEE
WHOA!

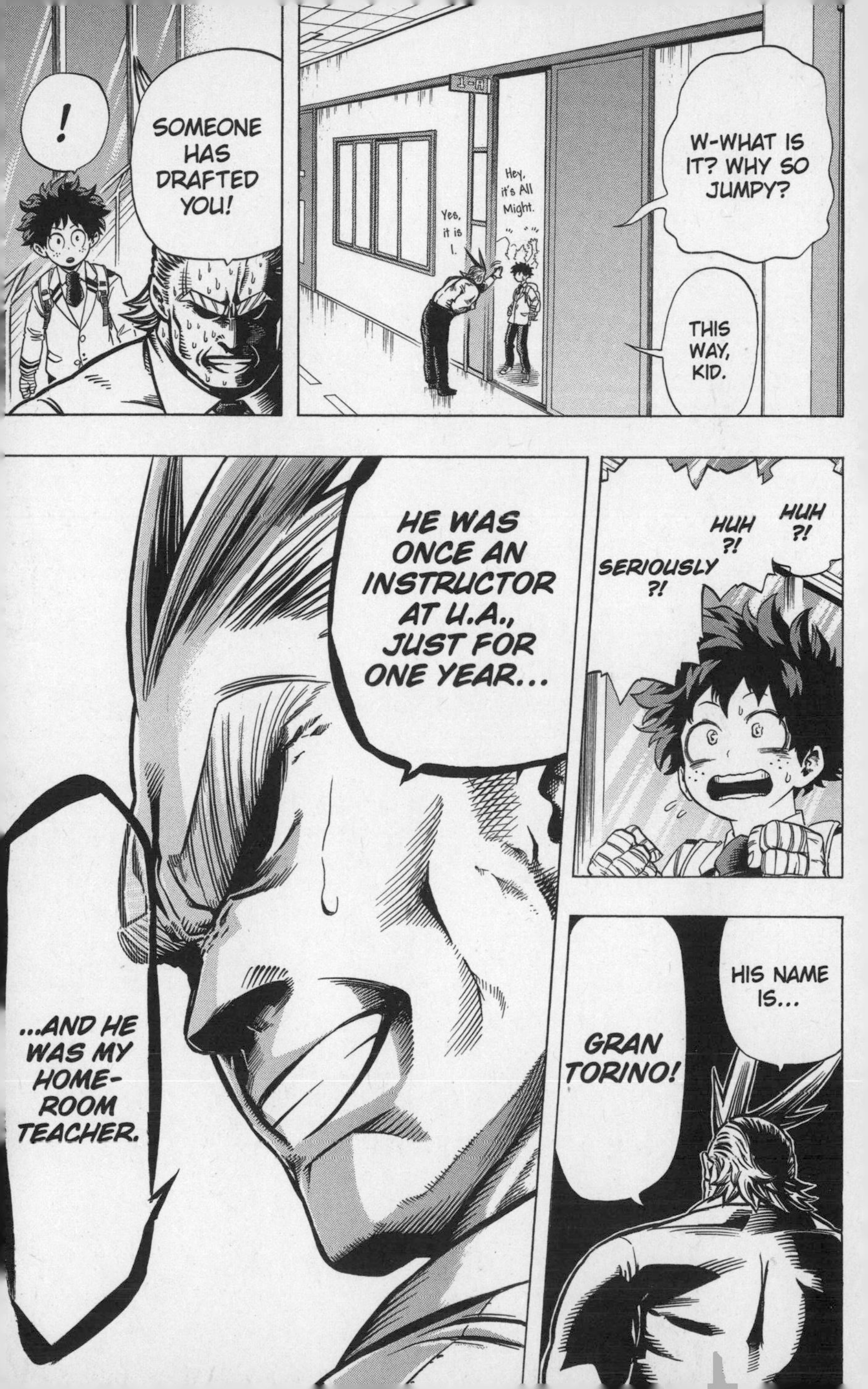
W-WHAT IS IT? WHY SO JUMPY?
Hey, it's All Might.
Yes, it is I.
THIS WAY, KID.
SOMEONE HAS DRAFTED YOU!
!
HUH ?!
HUH ?!
SERIOUSLY ?!
HIS NAME IS...
GRAN TORINO!
HE WAS ONCE AN INSTRUCTOR AT U.A., JUST FOR ONE YEAR...
...AND HE WAS MY HOME-ROOM TEACHER.

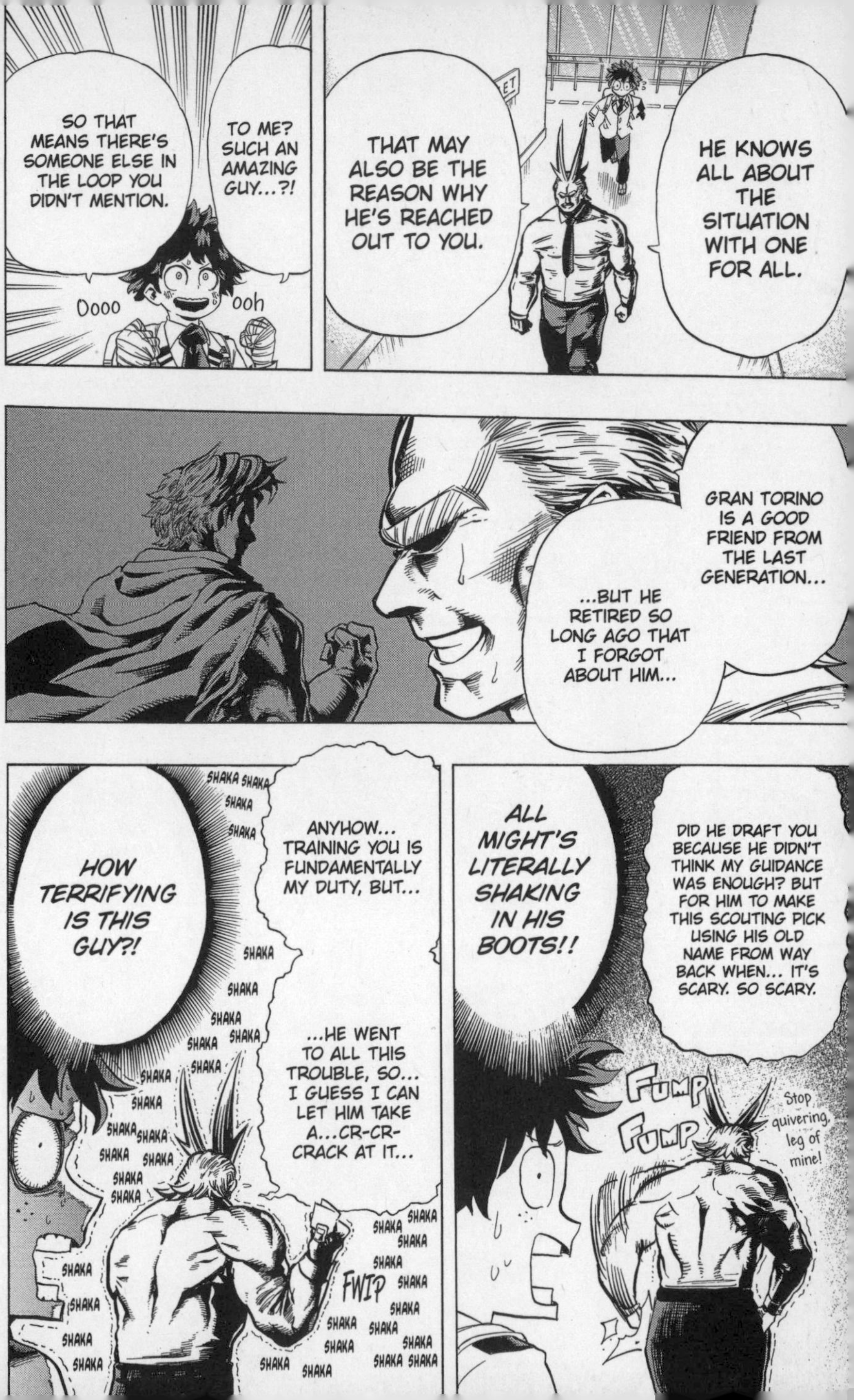
HE KNOWS ALL ABOUT THE SITUATION WITH ONE FOR ALL.
THAT MAY ALSO BE THE REASON WHY HE'S REACHED OUT TO YOU.
TO ME? SUCH AN AMAZING GUY...?!
SO THAT MEANS THERE'S SOMEONE ELSE IN THE LOOP YOU DIDN'T MENTION.
Oooo
ooh
GRAN TORINO IS A GOOD FRIEND FROM THE LAST GENERATION...
...BUT HE RETIRED SO LONG AGO THAT I FORGOT ABOUT HIM...
DID HE DRAFT YOU BECAUSE HE DIDN'T THINK MY GUIDANCE WAS ENOUGH? BUT FOR HIM TO MAKE THIS SCOUTING PICK USING HIS OLD NAME FROM WAY BACK WHEN... IT'S SCARY. SO SCARY.
ALL MIGHT'S LITERALLY SHAKING IN HIS BOOTS!!
FUMP
FUMP
Stop quivering, leg of mine!
ANYHOW... TRAINING YOU IS FUNDAMENTALLY MY DUTY, BUT...
...HE WENT TO ALL THIS TROUBLE, SO... I GUESS I CAN LET HIM TAKE A...CR-CR-CRACK AT IT...
HOW TERRIFYING IS THIS GUY?!
SHAKA SHAKA SHAKA SHAKA
FWIP

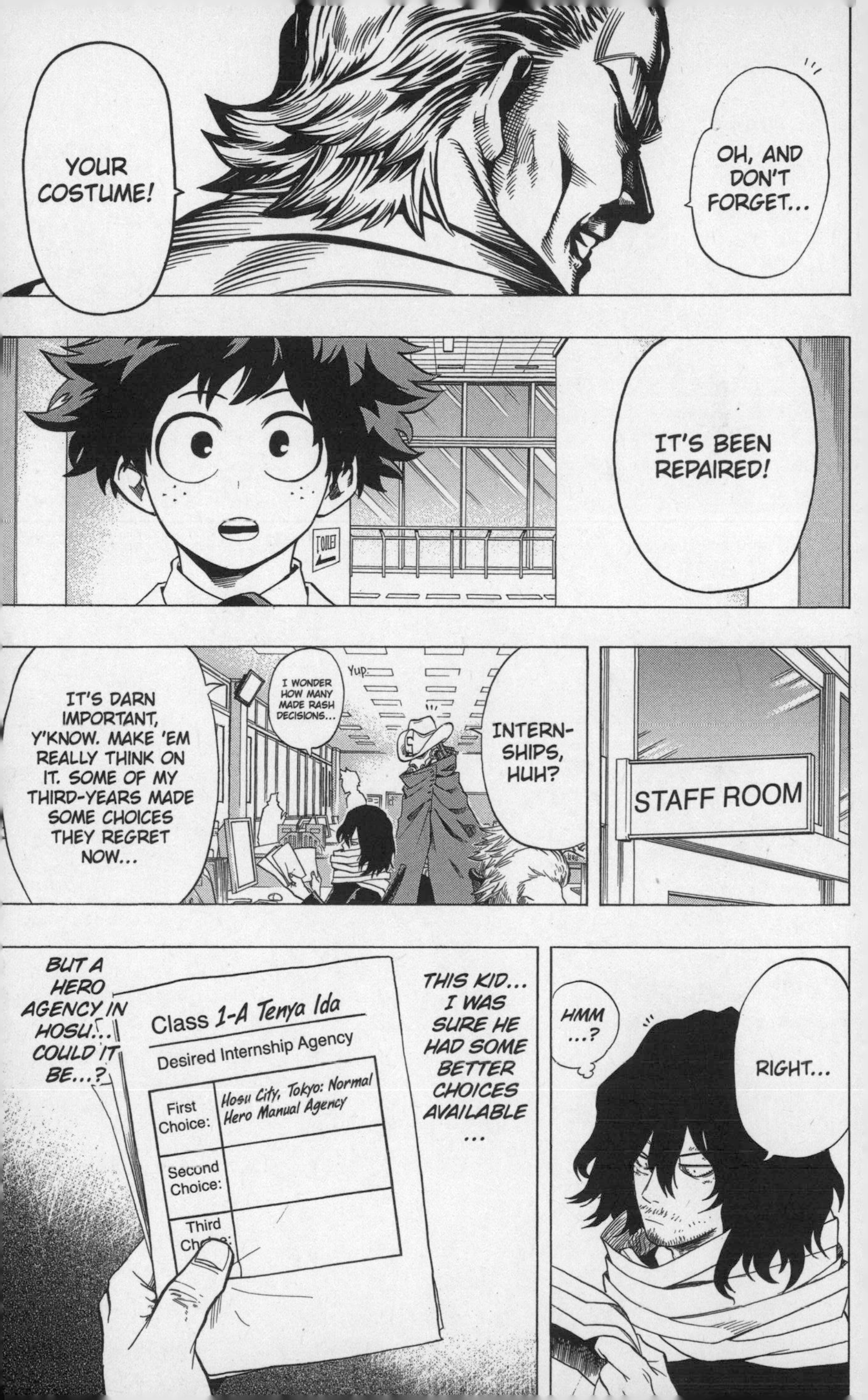
OH, AND DON'T FORGET...
YOUR COSTUME!
IT'S BEEN REPAIRED!
STAFF ROOM
INTERN-SHIPS, HUH?
Yup.
I WONDER HOW MANY MADE RASH DECISIONS...
IT'S DARN IMPORTANT, Y'KNOW. MAKE 'EM REALLY THINK ON IT. SOME OF MY THIRD-YEARS MADE SOME CHOICES THEY REGRET NOW...
RIGHT...
HMM ...?
THIS KID... I WAS SURE HE HAD SOME BETTER CHOICES AVAILABLE ...
Class 1-A Tenya Ida
Desired Internship Agency
First Choice:
Hosu City, Tokyo: Normal Hero Manual Agency
Second Choice:
Third
BUT A HERO AGENCY IN HOSU... COULD IT BE...?

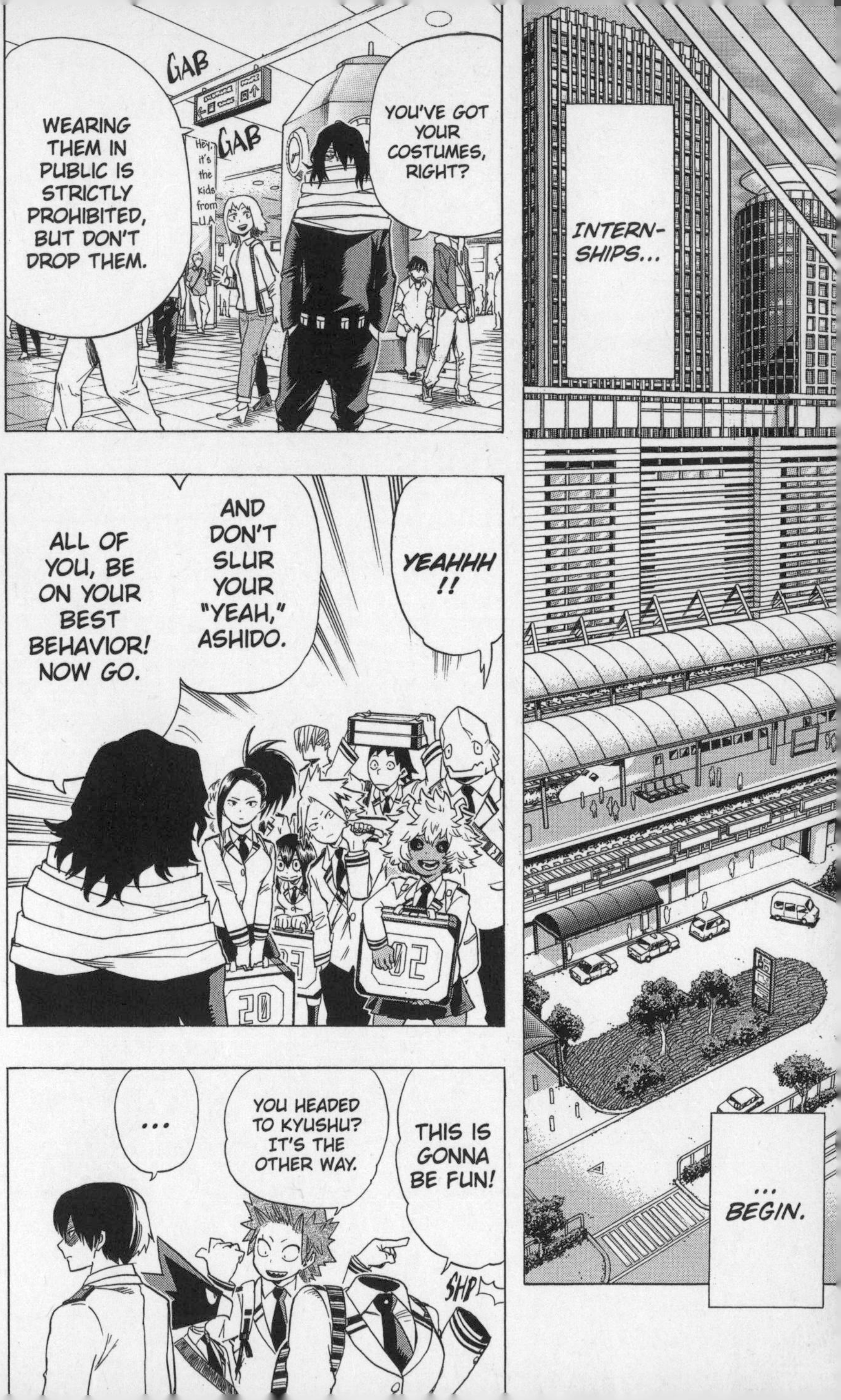
INTERN-SHIPS...
...BEGIN.
YOU'VE GOT YOUR COSTUMES, RIGHT?
GAB
GAB
Hey, it's the kids from U.A.
WEARING THEM IN PUBLIC IS STRICTLY PROHIBITED, BUT DON'T DROP THEM.
YEAHHH !!
AND DON'T SLUR YOUR "YEAH," ASHIDO.
ALL OF YOU, BE ON YOUR BEST BEHAVIOR! NOW GO.
THIS IS GONNA BE FUN!
SHP
YOU HEADED TO KYUSHU? IT'S THE OTHER WAY.
...

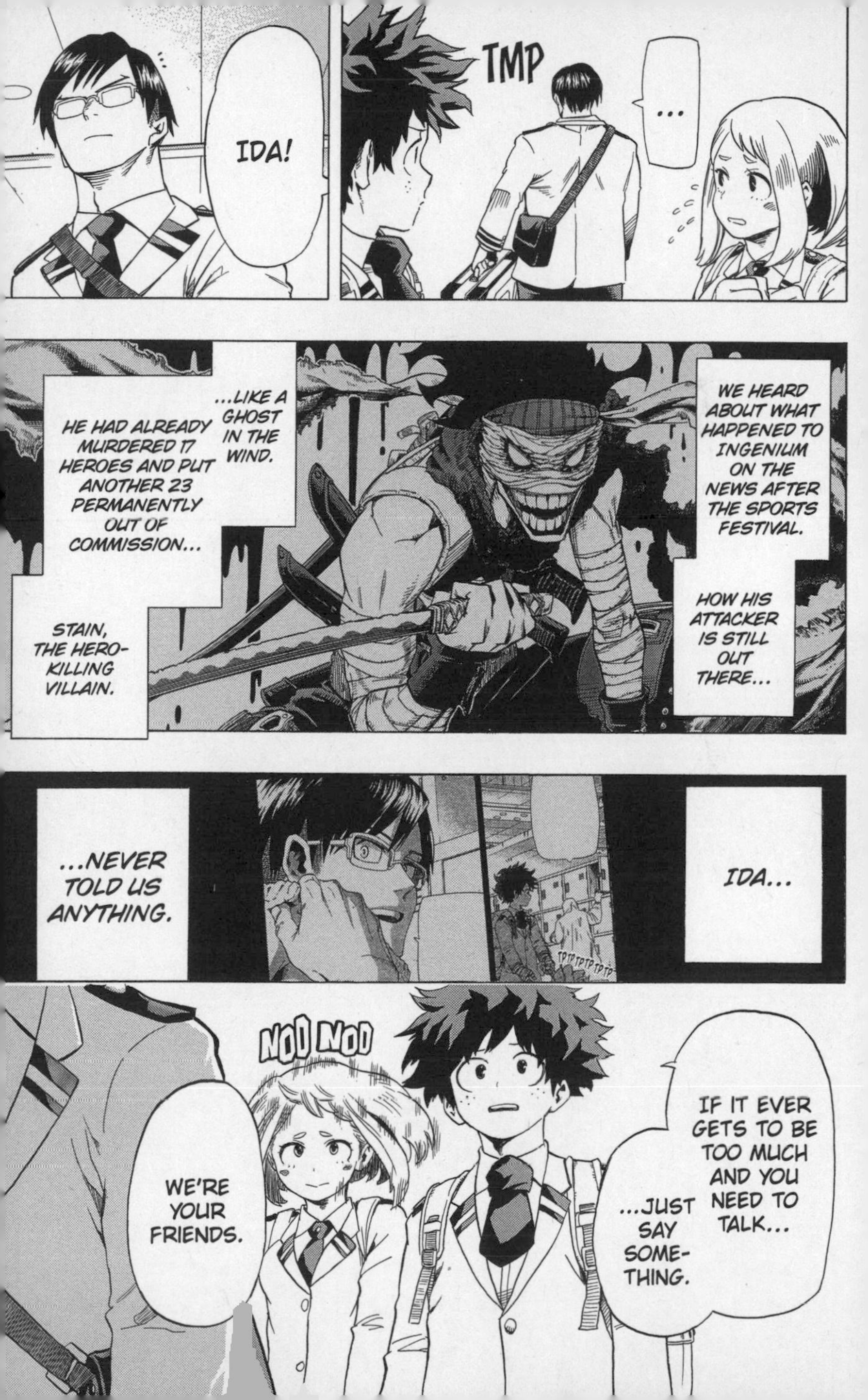
TMP
...
IDA!
WE HEARD ABOUT WHAT HAPPENED TO INGENIUM ON THE NEWS AFTER THE SPORTS FESTIVAL.
HOW HIS ATTACKER IS STILL OUT THERE...
...LIKE A GHOST IN THE WIND.
HE HAD ALREADY MURDERED 17 HEROES AND PUT ANOTHER 23 PERMANENTLY OUT OF COMMISSION...
STAIN, THE HERO-KILLING VILLAIN.
IDA...
...NEVER TOLD US ANYTHING.
IF IT EVER GETS TO BE TOO MUCH AND YOU NEED TO TALK...
...JUST SAY SOME-THING.
NOD NOD
WE'RE YOUR FRIENDS.

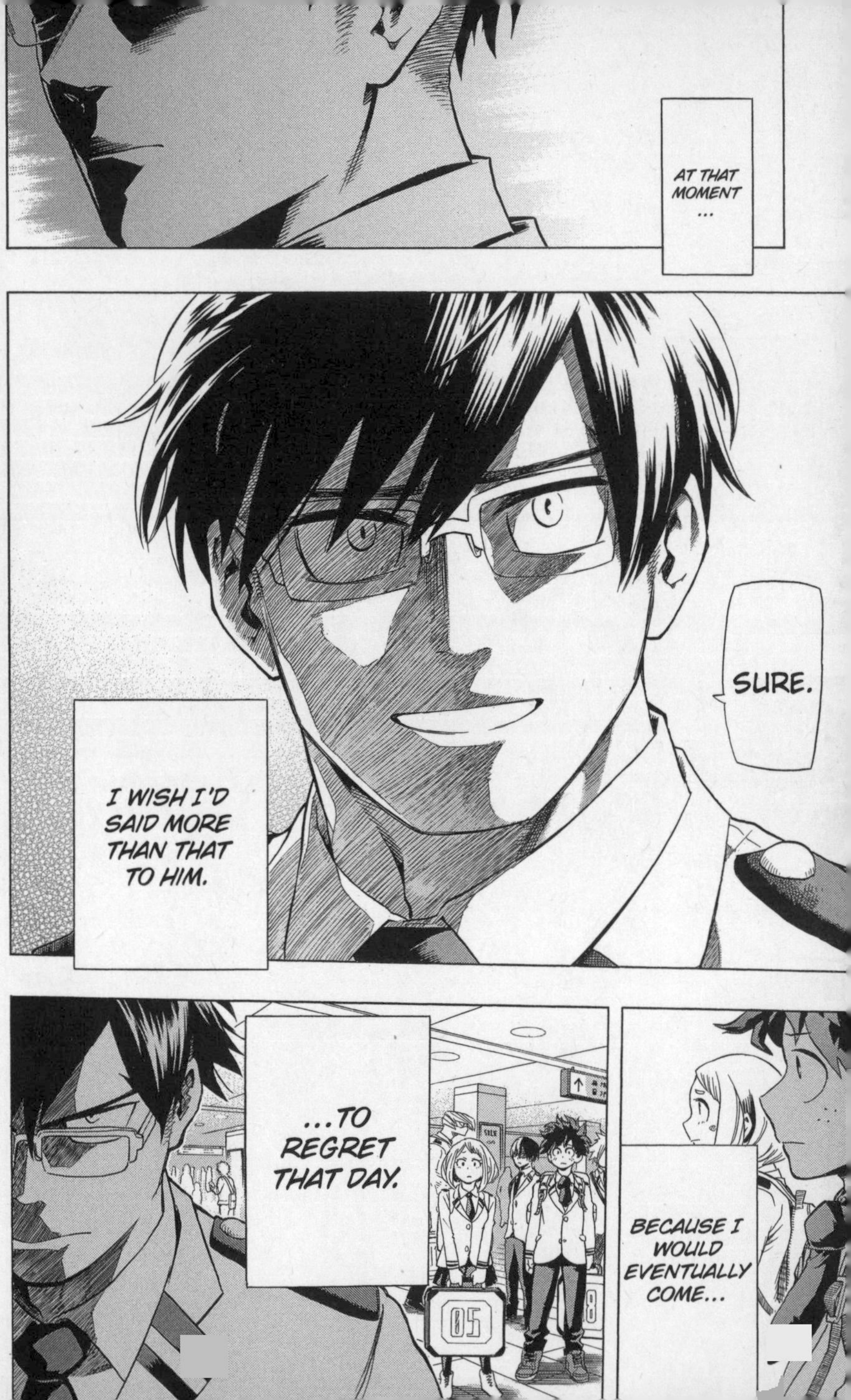
AT THAT MOMENT ...
SURE.
I WISH I'D SAID MORE THAN THAT TO HIM.
BECAUSE I WOULD EVENTUALLY COME...
...TO REGRET THAT DAY.
05

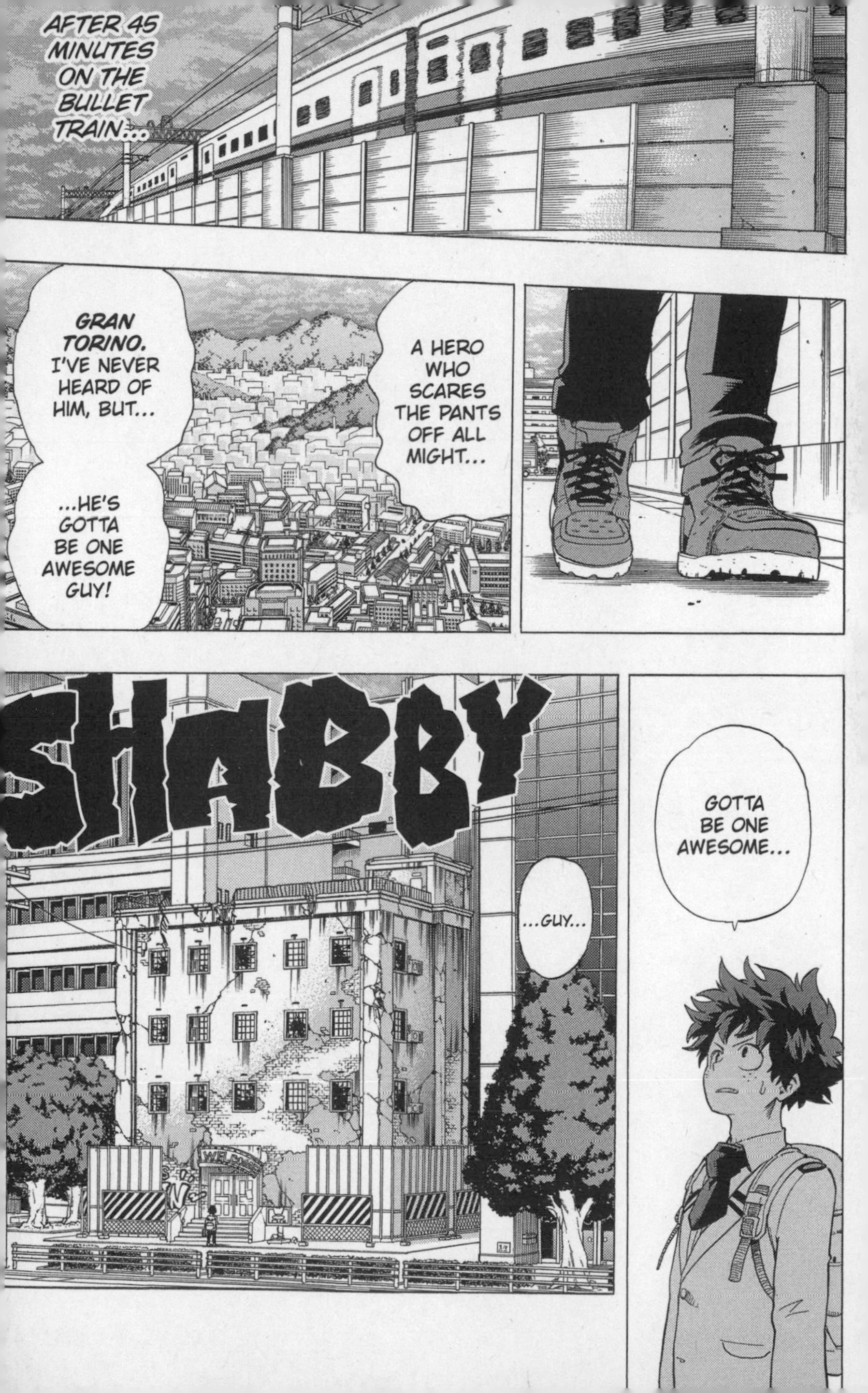
AFTER 45 MINUTES ON THE BULLET TRAIN...
A HERO WHO SCARES THE PANTS OFF ALL MIGHT...
GRAN TORINO. I'VE NEVER HEARD OF HIM, BUT...
...HE'S GOTTA BE ONE AWESOME GUY!
GOTTA BE ONE AWESOME...
SHABBY
...GUY...
WELCOME

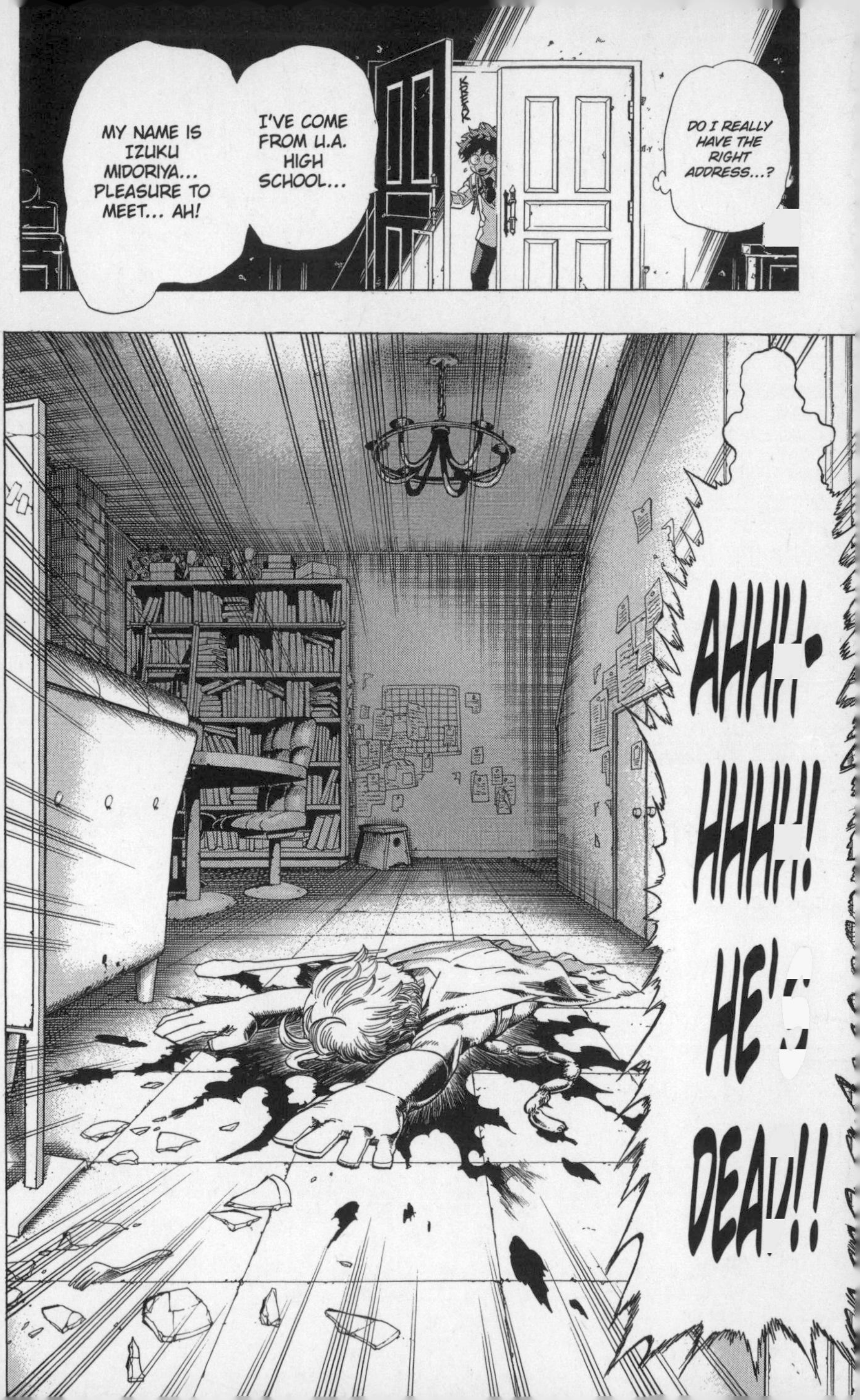
DO I REALLY HAVE THE RIGHT ADDRESS...?
I'VE COME FROM U.A. HIGH SCHOOL...
MY NAME IS IZUKU MIDORIYA... PLEASURE TO MEET... AH!
AHHH-HHHH!! HE'S DEAD!!

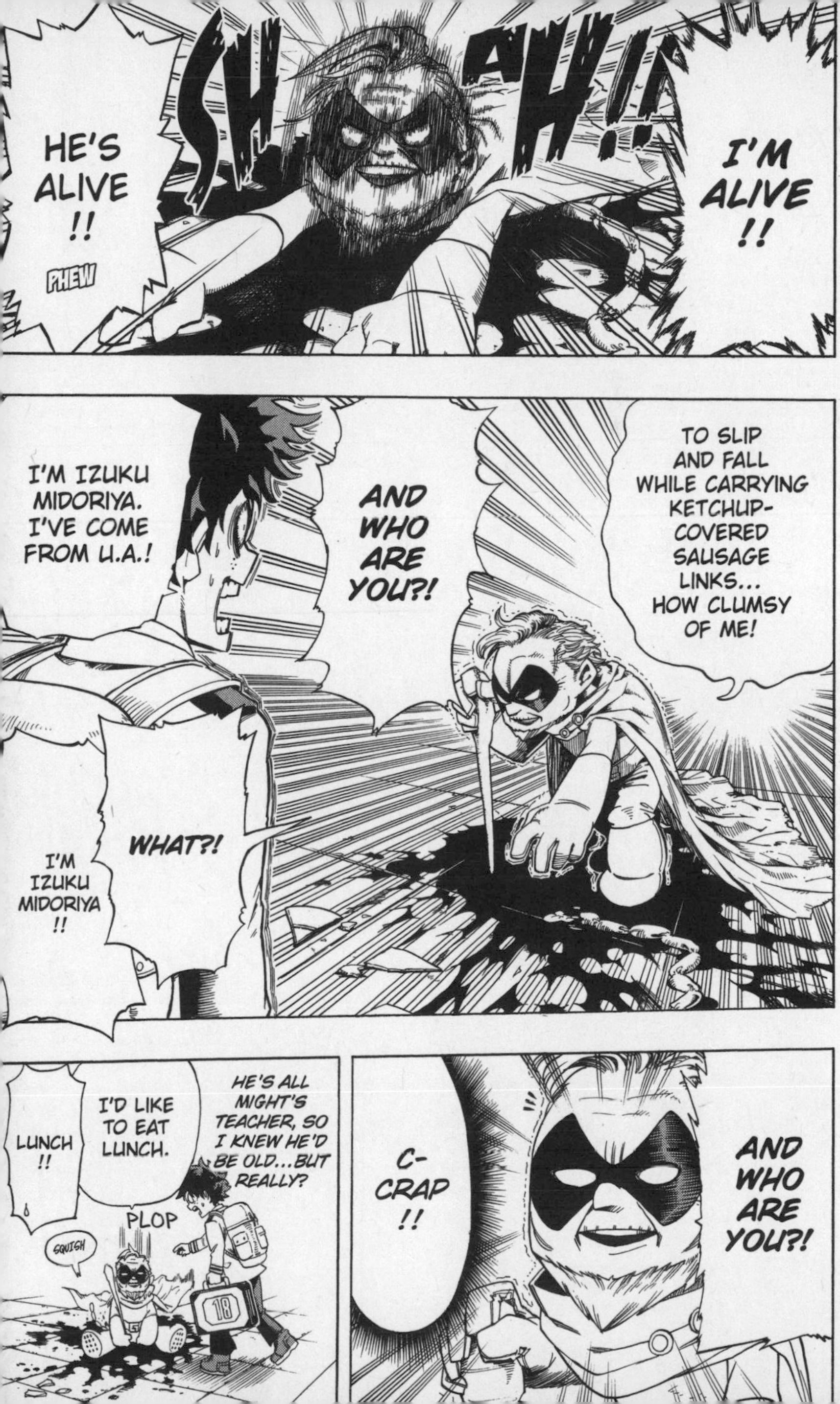
SHPAH!!
I'M ALIVE !!
HE'S ALIVE !!
PHEW
TO SLIP AND FALL WHILE CARRYING KETCHUP-COVERED SAUSAGE LINKS... HOW CLUMSY OF ME!
AND WHO ARE YOU?!
I'M IZUKU MIDORIYA. I'VE COME FROM U.A.!
WHAT?!
I'M IZUKU MIDORIYA !!
AND WHO ARE YOU?!
C-CRAP !!
HE'S ALL MIGHT'S TEACHER, SO I KNEW HE'D BE OLD...BUT REALLY?
I'D LIKE TO EAT LUNCH.
LUNCH !!
PLOP
SQUISH

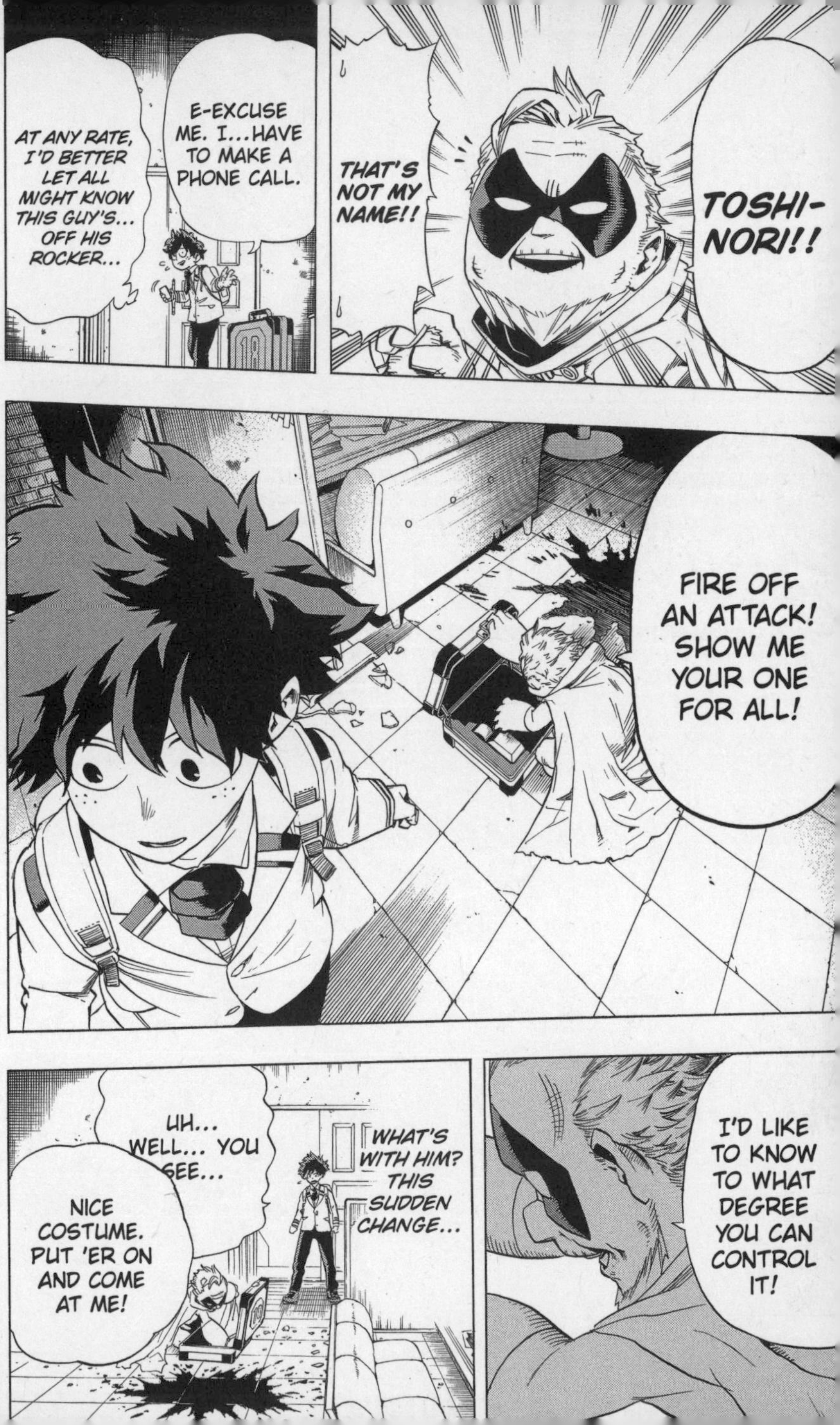
TOSHI-NORI!!
THAT'S NOT MY NAME!!
E-EXCUSE ME. I...HAVE TO MAKE A PHONE CALL.
AT ANY RATE, I'D BETTER LET ALL MIGHT KNOW THIS GUY'S... OFF HIS ROCKER...
FIRE OFF AN ATTACK! SHOW ME YOUR ONE FOR ALL!
I'D LIKE TO KNOW TO WHAT DEGREE YOU CAN CONTROL IT!
WHAT'S WITH HIM? THIS SUDDEN CHANGE...
UH... WELL... YOU SEE...
NICE COSTUME. PUT 'ER ON AND COME AT ME!

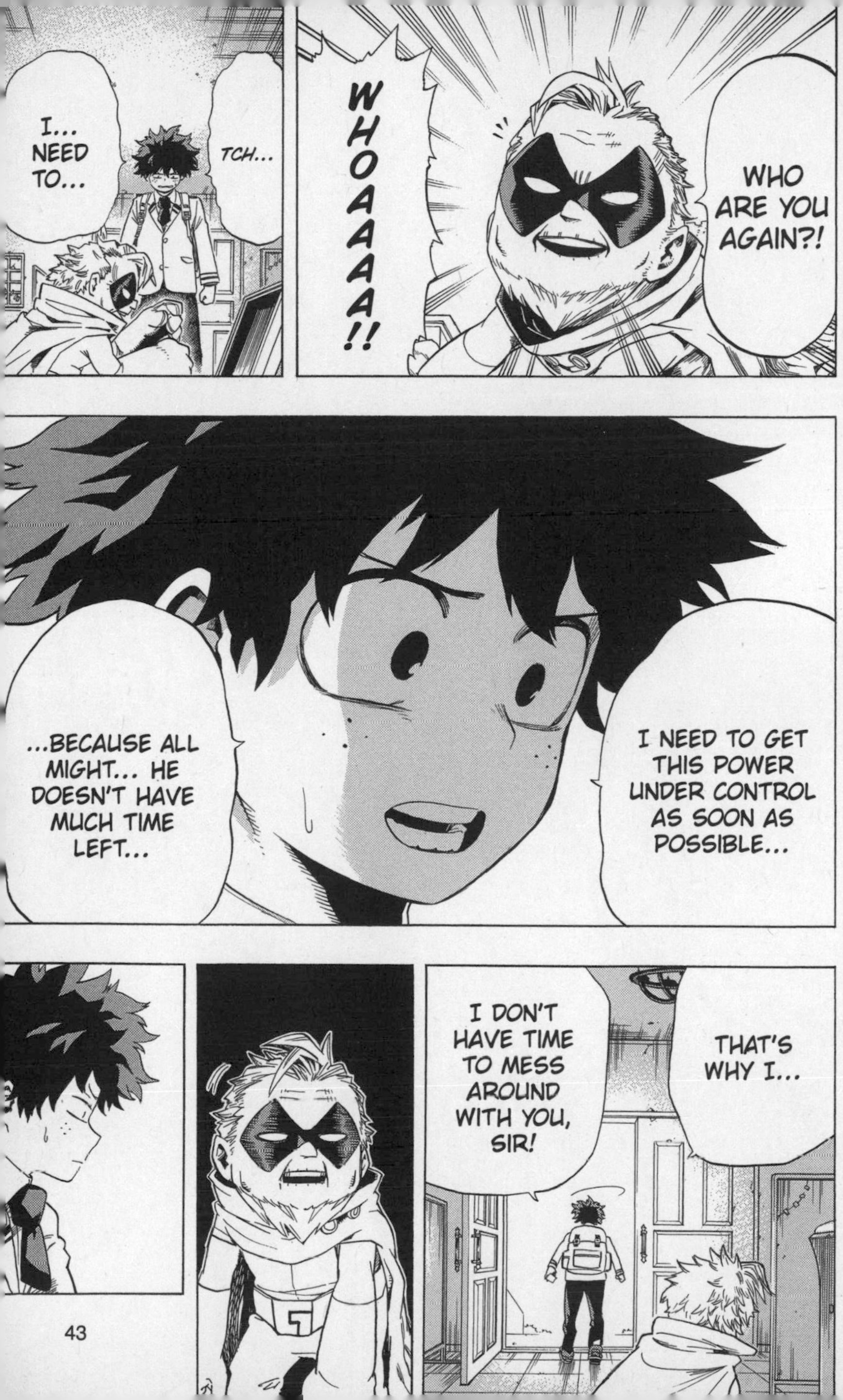
WHO ARE YOU AGAIN?!
WHOAAAAA!!
TCH...
I... NEED TO...
I NEED TO GET THIS POWER UNDER CONTROL AS SOON AS POSSIBLE...
...BECAUSE ALL MIGHT... HE DOESN'T HAVE MUCH TIME LEFT...
THAT'S WHY I...
I DON'T HAVE TIME TO MESS AROUND WITH YOU, SIR!

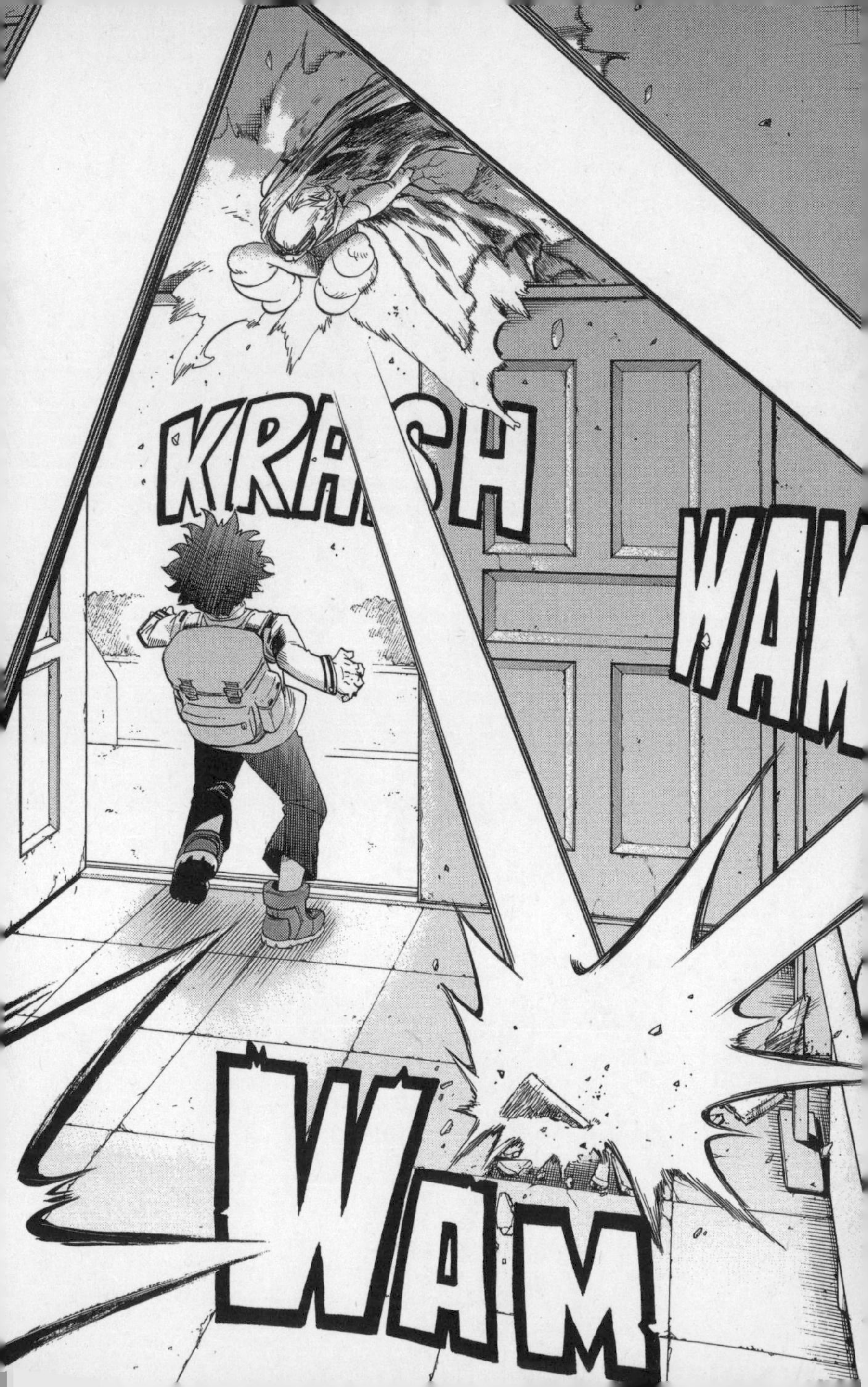
KRASH
WAM
WAM

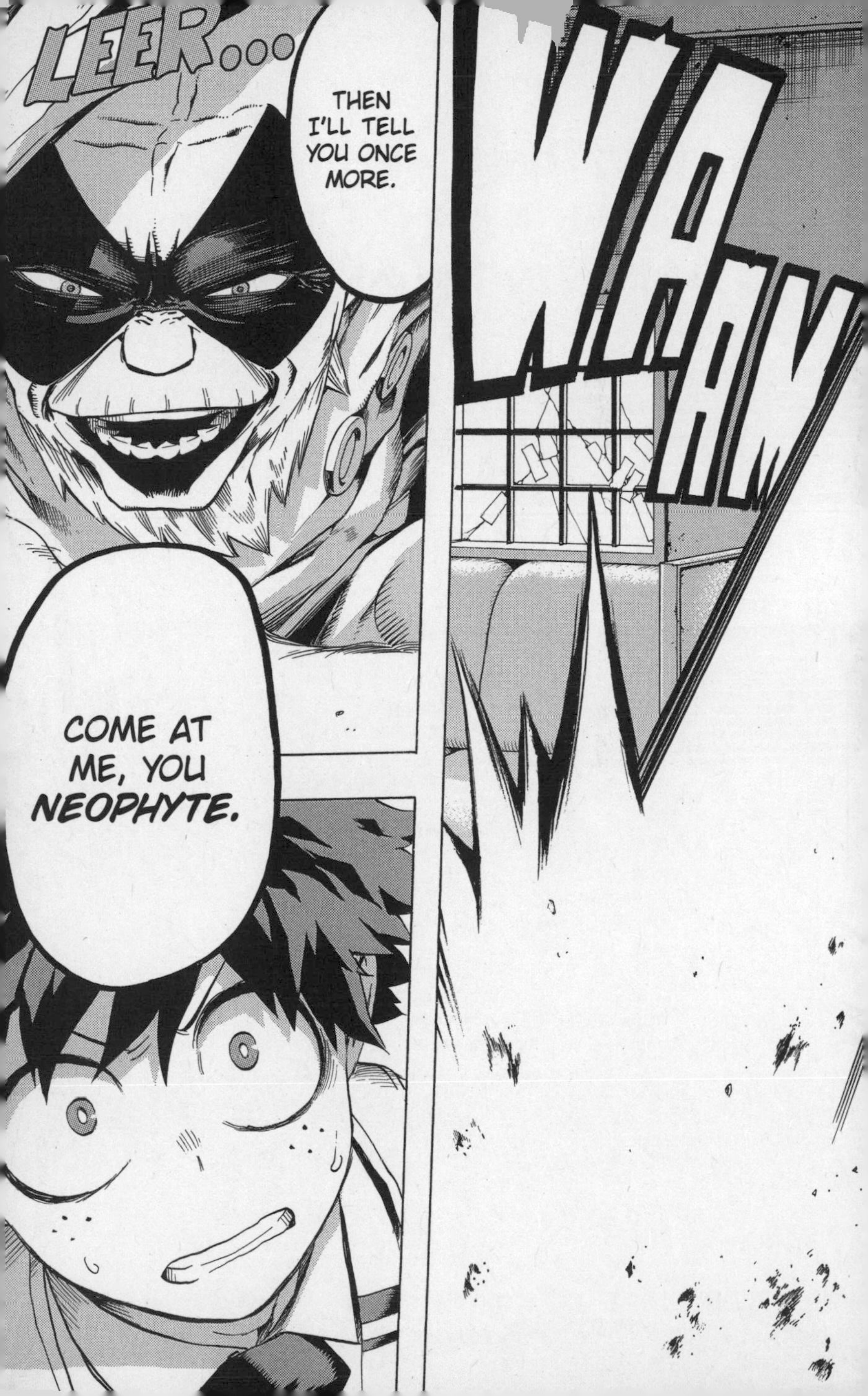
WHAM
LEER...
THEN I'LL TELL YOU ONCE MORE.
COME AT ME, YOU NEOPHYTE.

THE "COSTUME EXPLANATIONS TO FILL IN THE ANNOYING BLANK PAGES" CORNER

OCHACO URARAKA'S COSTUME

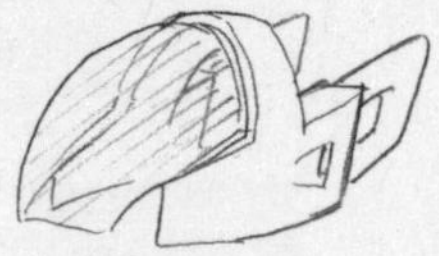

Urarakamet
Reduces stress on the ears' semicircular canals.

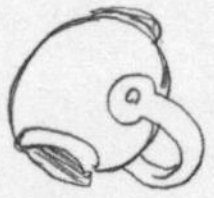

Urarakawrist
Contains blood pressure cuff-like devices to increase and decrease pressure. Bumps at the wrist help to suppress nausea via pressure point stimulation.

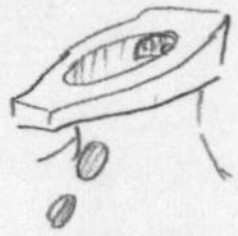

Urarakaneck
The pressure point bumps here help reduce the severity of headaches and the like.

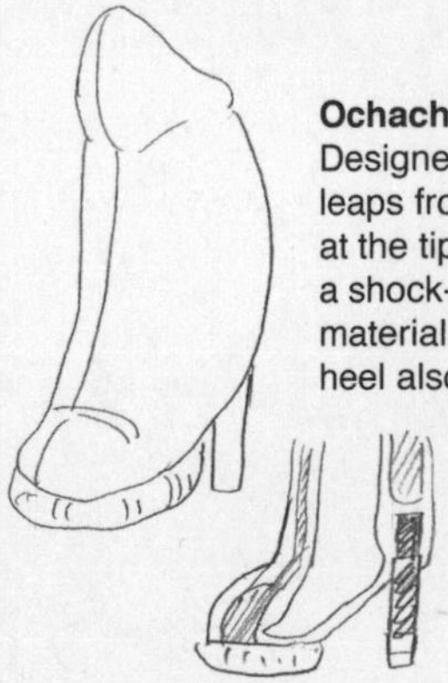

Ochachakaleg
Designed to aid in landing after leaps from high places. The sole at the tips of the toes is made of a shock-absorbent, cushiony material. The stiff spring in the heel also softens landings.

ALL IN ALL: MOSTLY THERE TO COUNTERACT NAUSEA

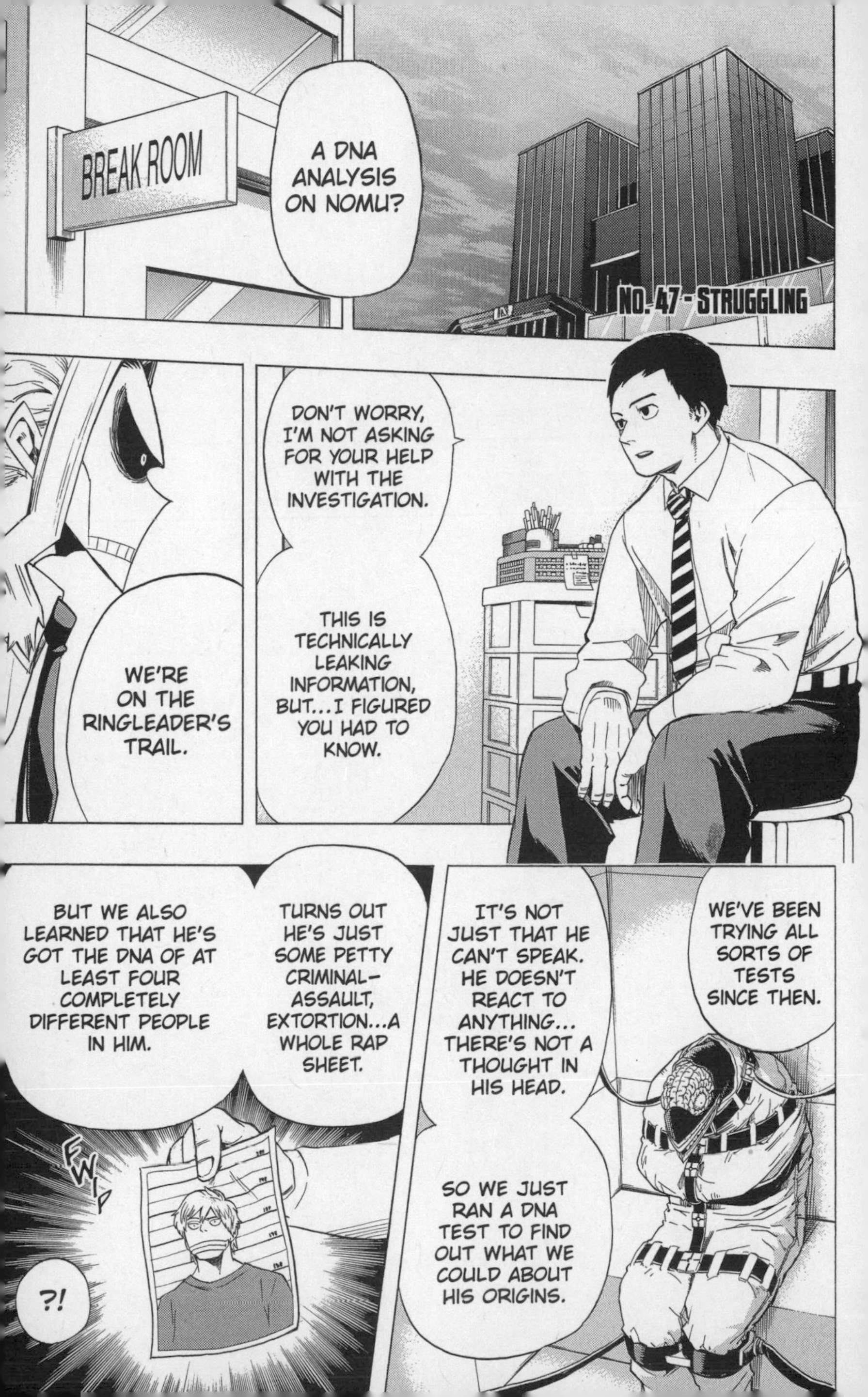
No. 47 - Struggling
A DNA ANALYSIS ON NOMU?
BREAK ROOM
DON'T WORRY, I'M NOT ASKING FOR YOUR HELP WITH THE INVESTIGATION.
THIS IS TECHNICALLY LEAKING INFORMATION, BUT...I FIGURED YOU HAD TO KNOW.
WE'RE ON THE RINGLEADER'S TRAIL.
WE'VE BEEN TRYING ALL SORTS OF TESTS SINCE THEN.
IT'S NOT JUST THAT HE CAN'T SPEAK. HE DOESN'T REACT TO ANYTHING... THERE'S NOT A THOUGHT IN HIS HEAD.
SO WE JUST RAN A DNA TEST TO FIND OUT WHAT WE COULD ABOUT HIS ORIGINS.
TURNS OUT HE'S JUST SOME PETTY CRIMINAL-ASSAULT, EXTORTION...A WHOLE RAP SHEET.
BUT WE ALSO LEARNED THAT HE'S GOT THE DNA OF AT LEAST FOUR COMPLETELY DIFFERENT PEOPLE IN HIM.
FWIP
?!

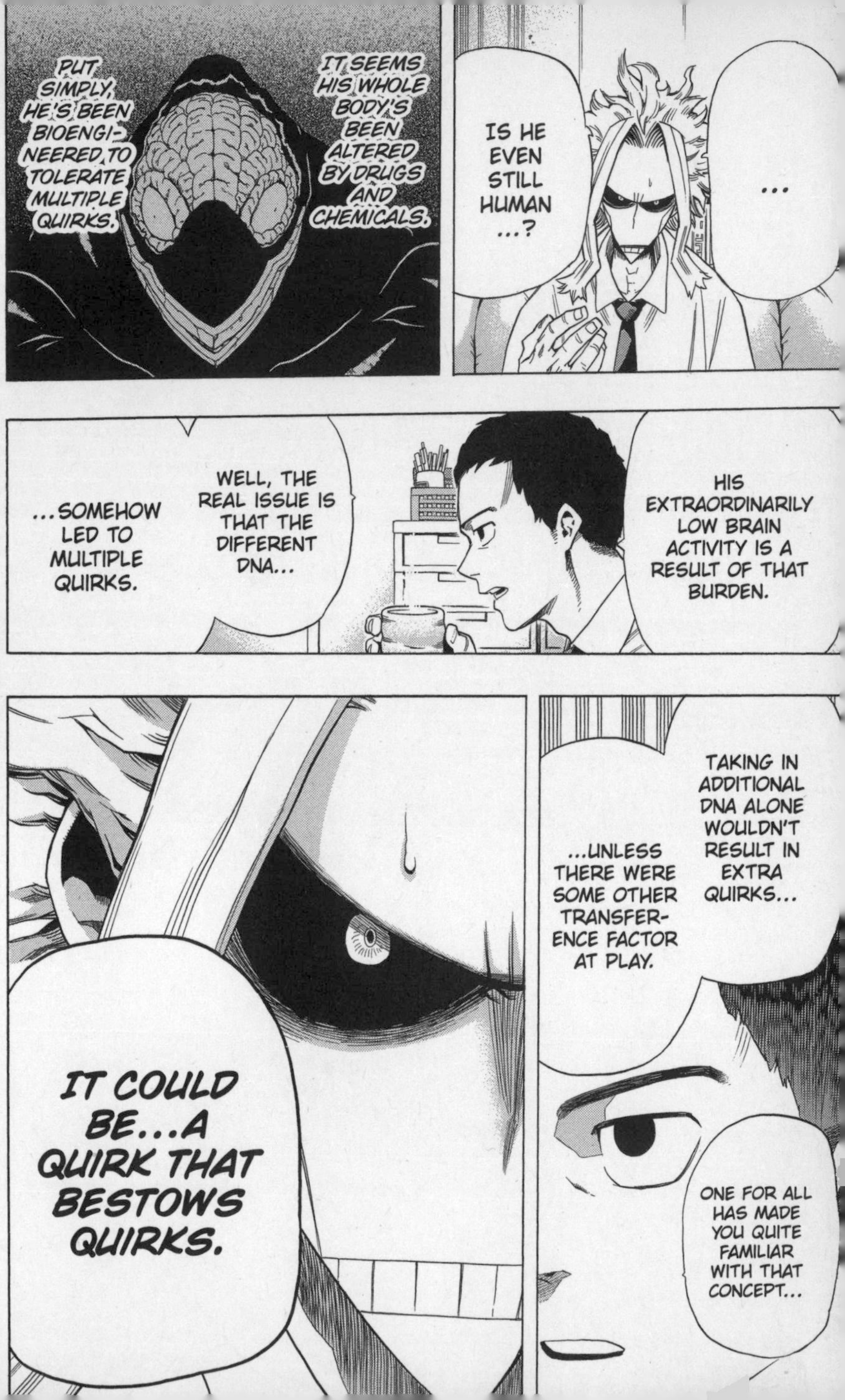
...
IS HE EVEN STILL HUMAN ...?
IT SEEMS HIS WHOLE BODY'S BEEN ALTERED BY DRUGS AND CHEMICALS.
PUT SIMPLY, HE'S BEEN BIOENGINEERED TO TOLERATE MULTIPLE QUIRKS.
HIS EXTRAORDINARILY LOW BRAIN ACTIVITY IS A RESULT OF THAT BURDEN.
WELL, THE REAL ISSUE IS THAT THE DIFFERENT DNA...
...SOMEHOW LED TO MULTIPLE QUIRKS.
TAKING IN ADDITIONAL DNA ALONE WOULDN'T RESULT IN EXTRA QUIRKS...
...UNLESS THERE WERE SOME OTHER TRANSFERENCE FACTOR AT PLAY.
ONE FOR ALL HAS MADE YOU QUITE FAMILIAR WITH THAT CONCEPT...
IT COULD BE...A QUIRK THAT BESTOWS QUIRKS.

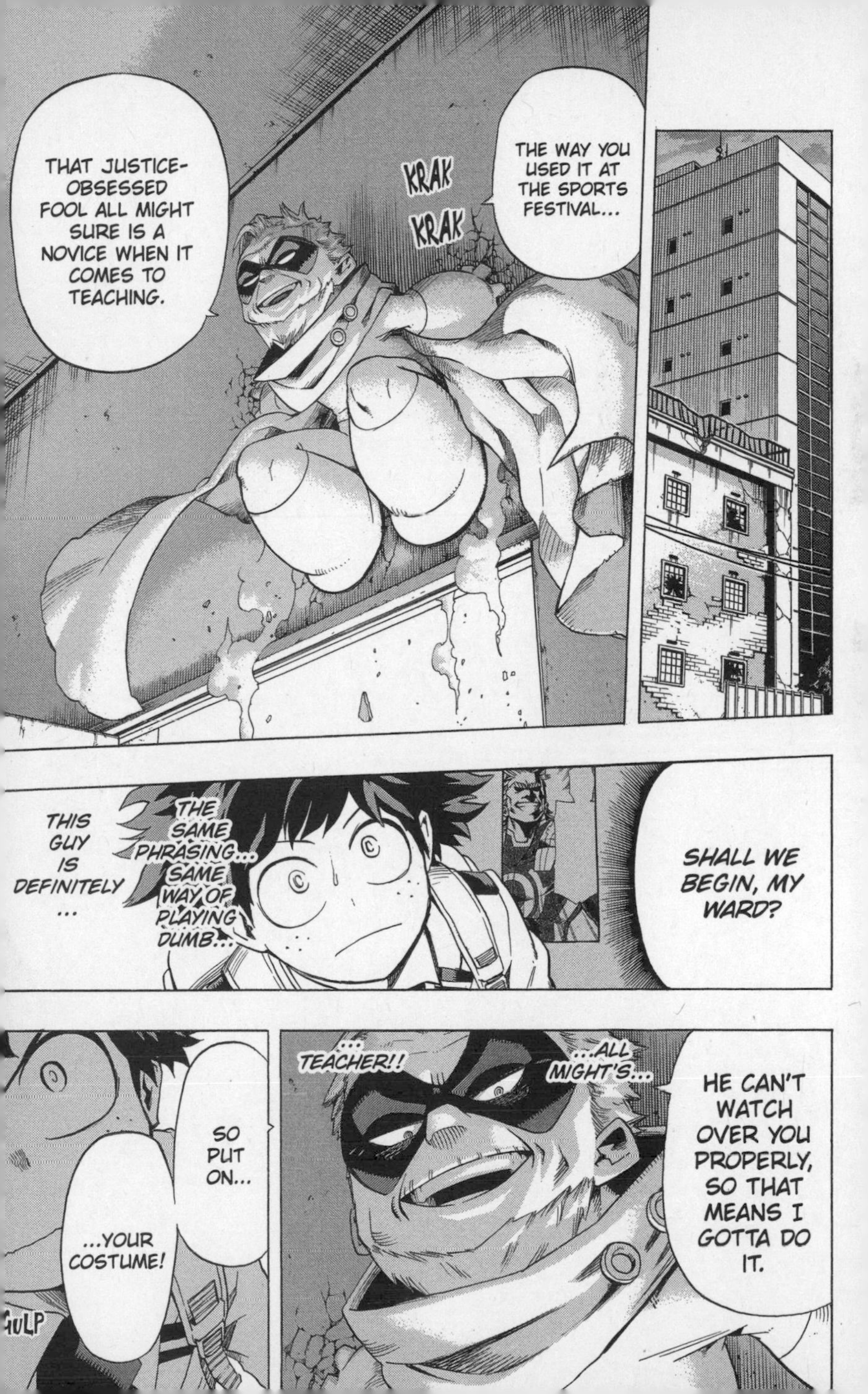

THE WAY YOU USED IT AT THE SPORTS FESTIVAL...
KRAK
KRAK
THAT JUSTICE-OBSESSED FOOL ALL MIGHT SURE IS A NOVICE WHEN IT COMES TO TEACHING.
SHALL WE BEGIN, MY WARD?
THE SAME PHRASING... SAME WAY OF PLAYING DUMB...
THIS GUY IS DEFINITELY...
HE CAN'T WATCH OVER YOU PROPERLY, SO THAT MEANS I GOTTA DO IT.
...ALL MIGHT'S...
...TEACHER!!
SO PUT ON...
...YOUR COSTUME!
GULP

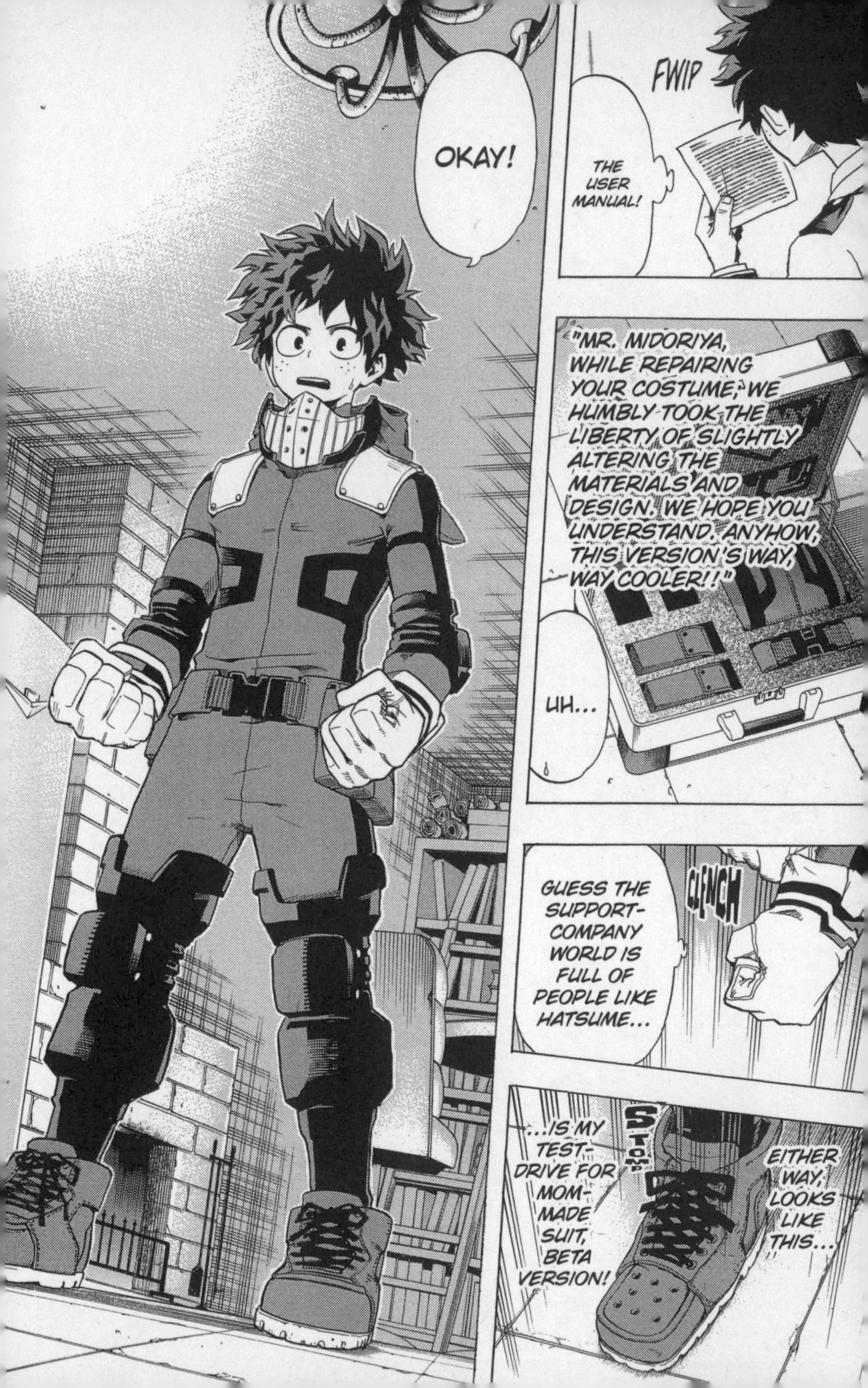
FWIP
THE USER MANUAL!
"MR. MIDORIYA, WHILE REPAIRING YOUR COSTUME, WE HUMBLY TOOK THE LIBERTY OF SLIGHTLY ALTERING THE MATERIALS AND DESIGN. WE HOPE YOU UNDERSTAND. ANYHOW, THIS VERSION'S WAY, WAY COOLER!!"
UH...
CLENCH
GUESS THE SUPPORT-COMPANY WORLD IS FULL OF PEOPLE LIKE HATSUME...
EITHER WAY, LOOKS LIKE THIS...
STOMP
...IS MY TEST-DRIVE FOR MOM-MADE SUIT, BETA VERSION!
OKAY!

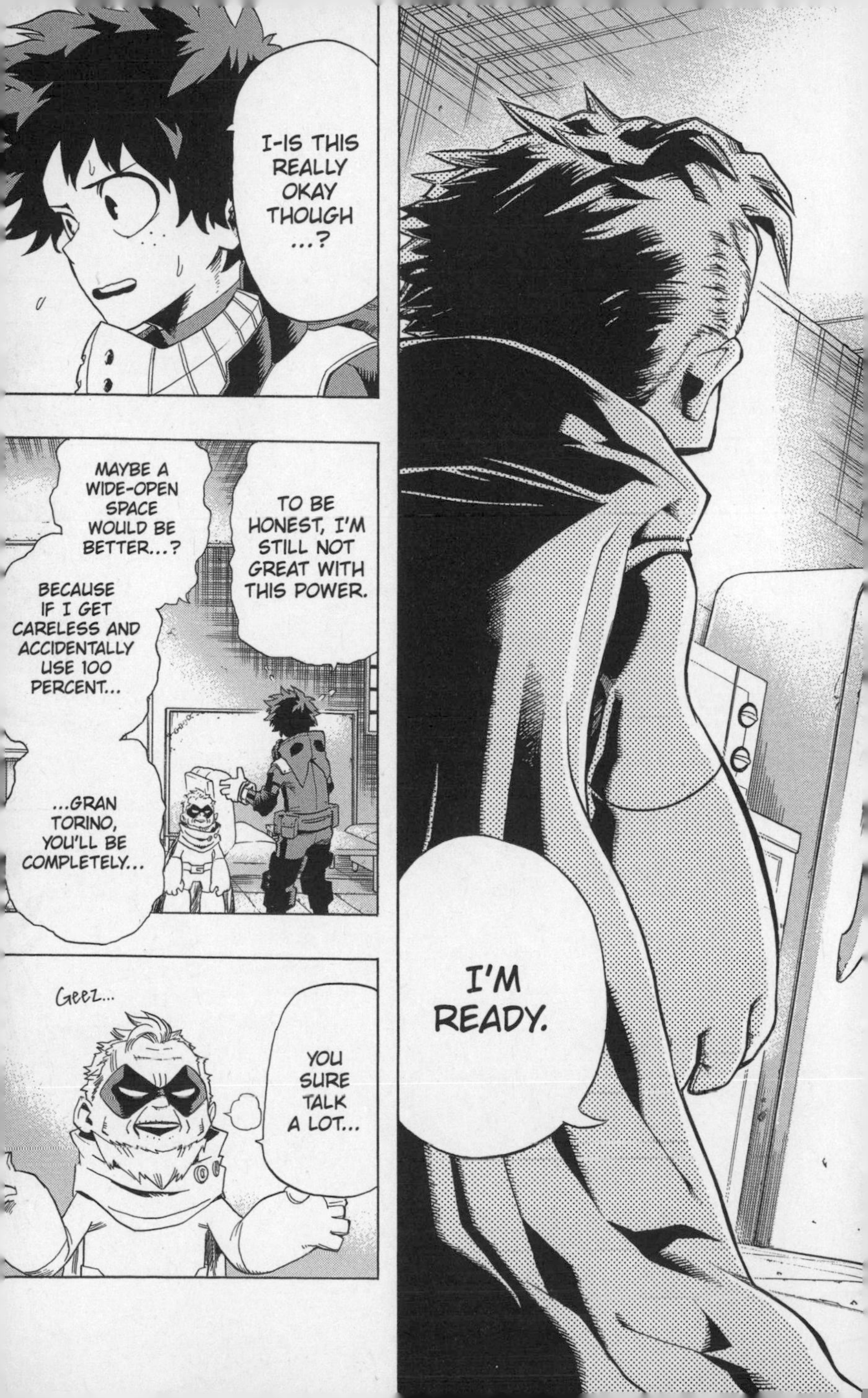
I'M READY.
I-IS THIS REALLY OKAY THOUGH ...?
TO BE HONEST, I'M STILL NOT GREAT WITH THIS POWER.
MAYBE A WIDE-OPEN SPACE WOULD BE BETTER...?
BECAUSE IF I GET CARELESS AND ACCIDENTALLY USE 100 PERCENT...
...GRAN TORINO, YOU'LL BE COMPLETELY...
YOU SURE TALK A LOT...
Geez...

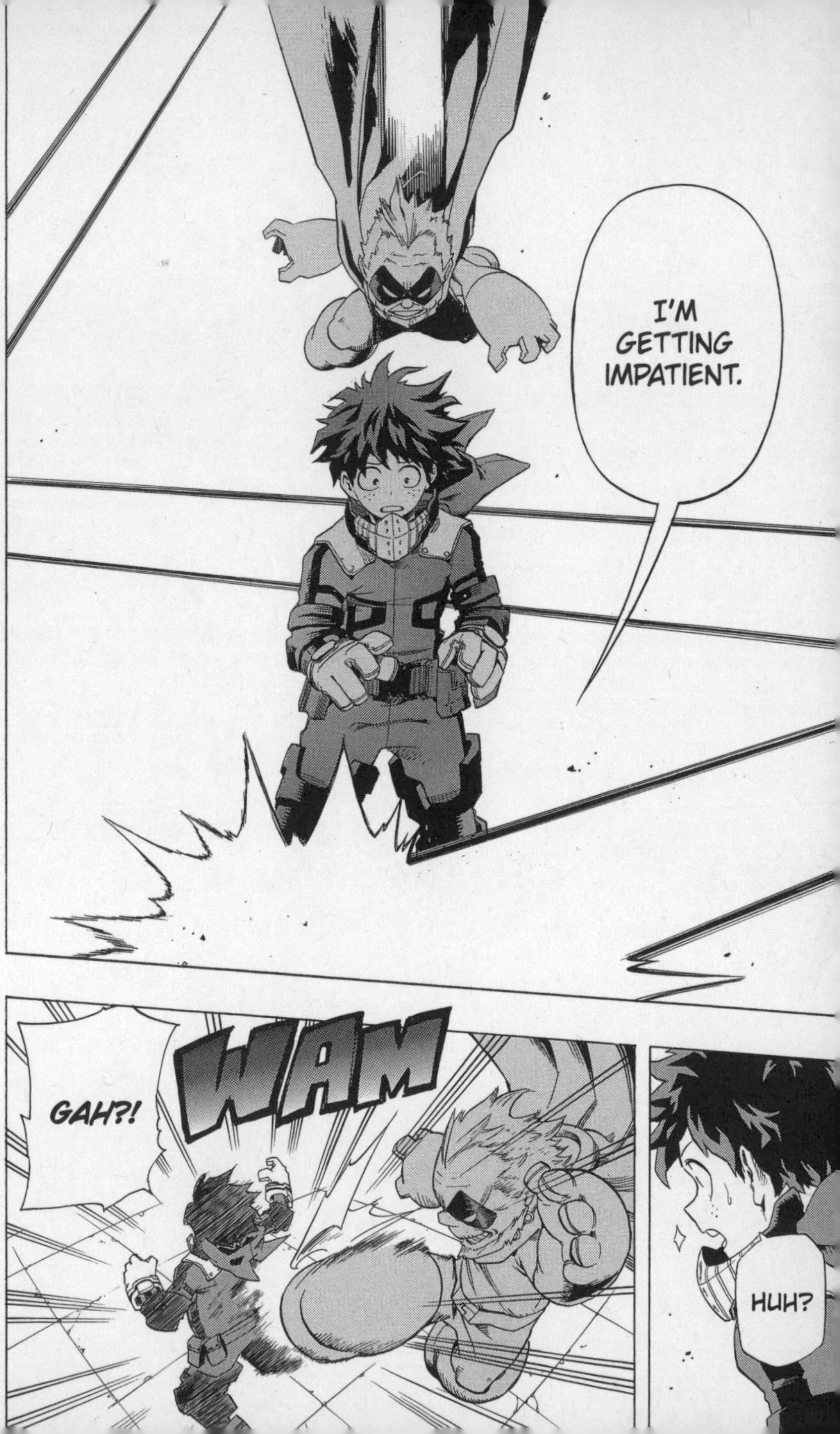
I'M GETTING IMPATIENT.
HUH?
WAM
GAH?!

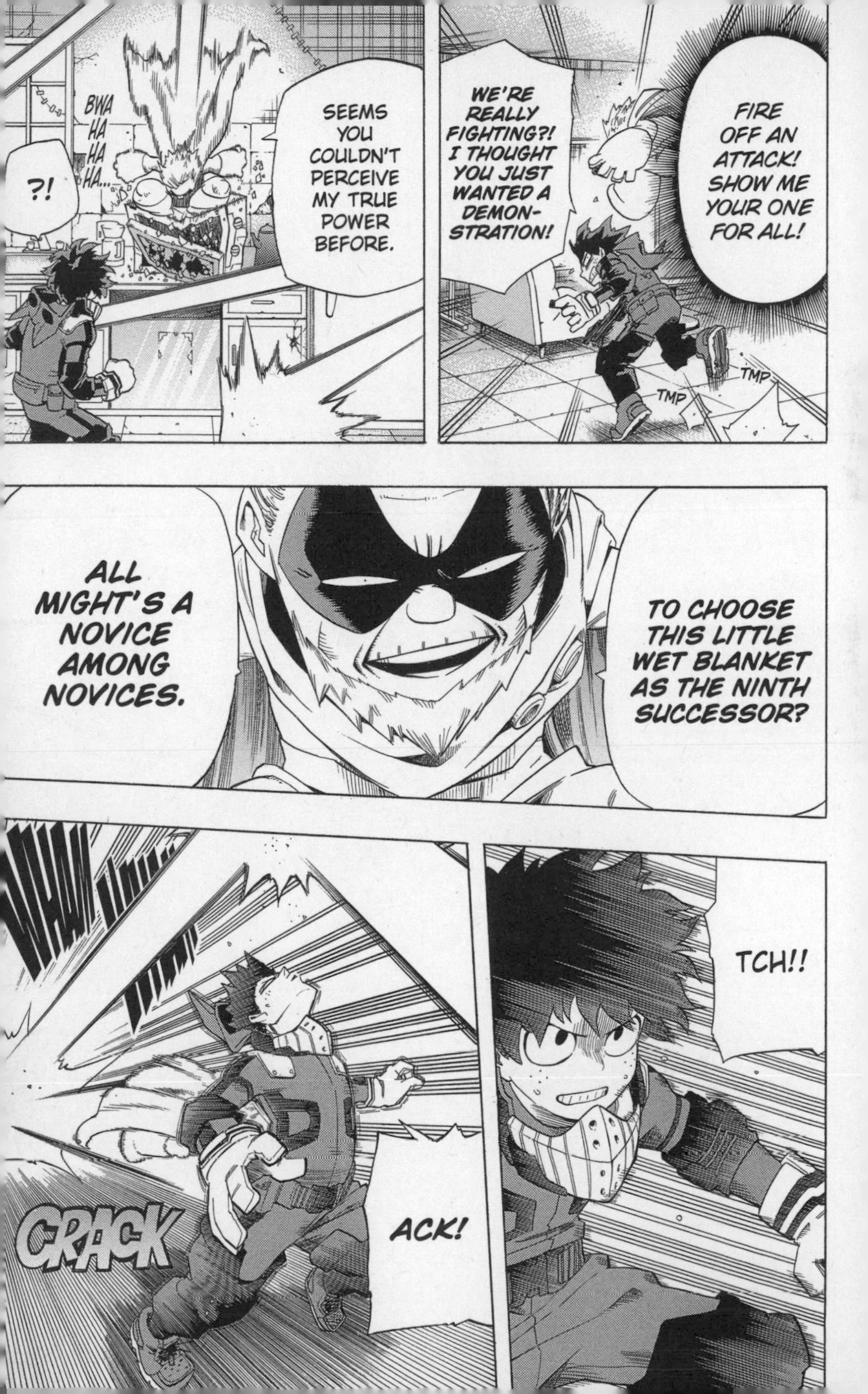
FIRE OFF AN ATTACK! SHOW ME YOUR ONE FOR ALL!
WE'RE REALLY FIGHTING?! I THOUGHT YOU JUST WANTED A DEMONSTRATION!
TMP
TMP
SEEMS YOU COULDN'T PERCEIVE MY TRUE POWER BEFORE.
BWA HA HA HA...
?!
TO CHOOSE THIS LITTLE WET BLANKET AS THE NINTH SUCCESSOR?
ALL MIGHT'S A NOVICE AMONG NOVICES.
TCH!!
WHAM
ACK!
CRACK

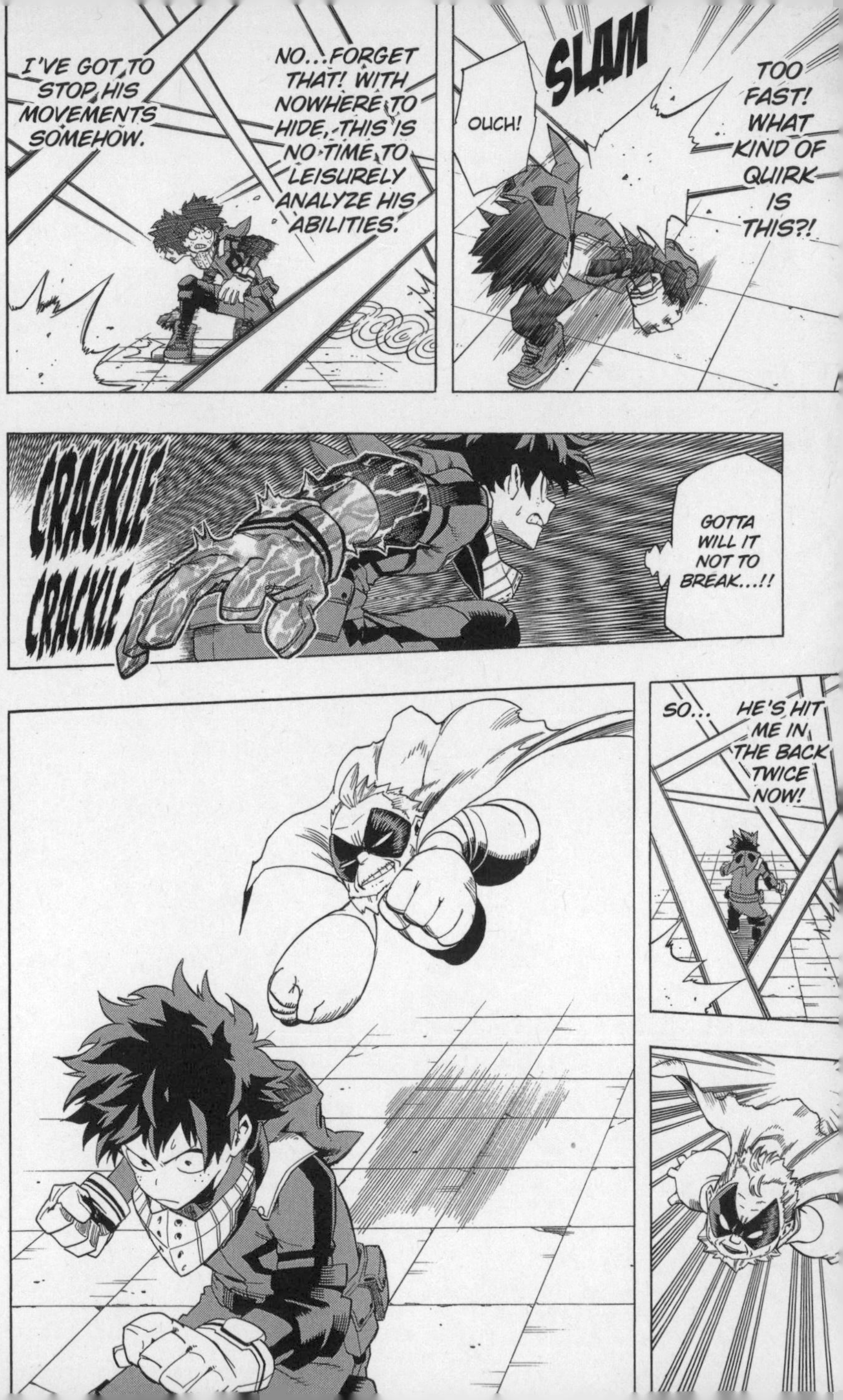
SLAM
TOO FAST! WHAT KIND OF QUIRK IS THIS?!
OUCH!
NO...FORGET THAT! WITH NOWHERE TO HIDE, THIS IS NO TIME TO LEISURELY ANALYZE HIS ABILITIES.
I'VE GOT TO STOP HIS MOVEMENTS SOMEHOW.
GOTTA WILL IT NOT TO BREAK...!!
CRACKLE CRACKLE
HE'S HIT ME IN THE BACK TWICE NOW!
SO...

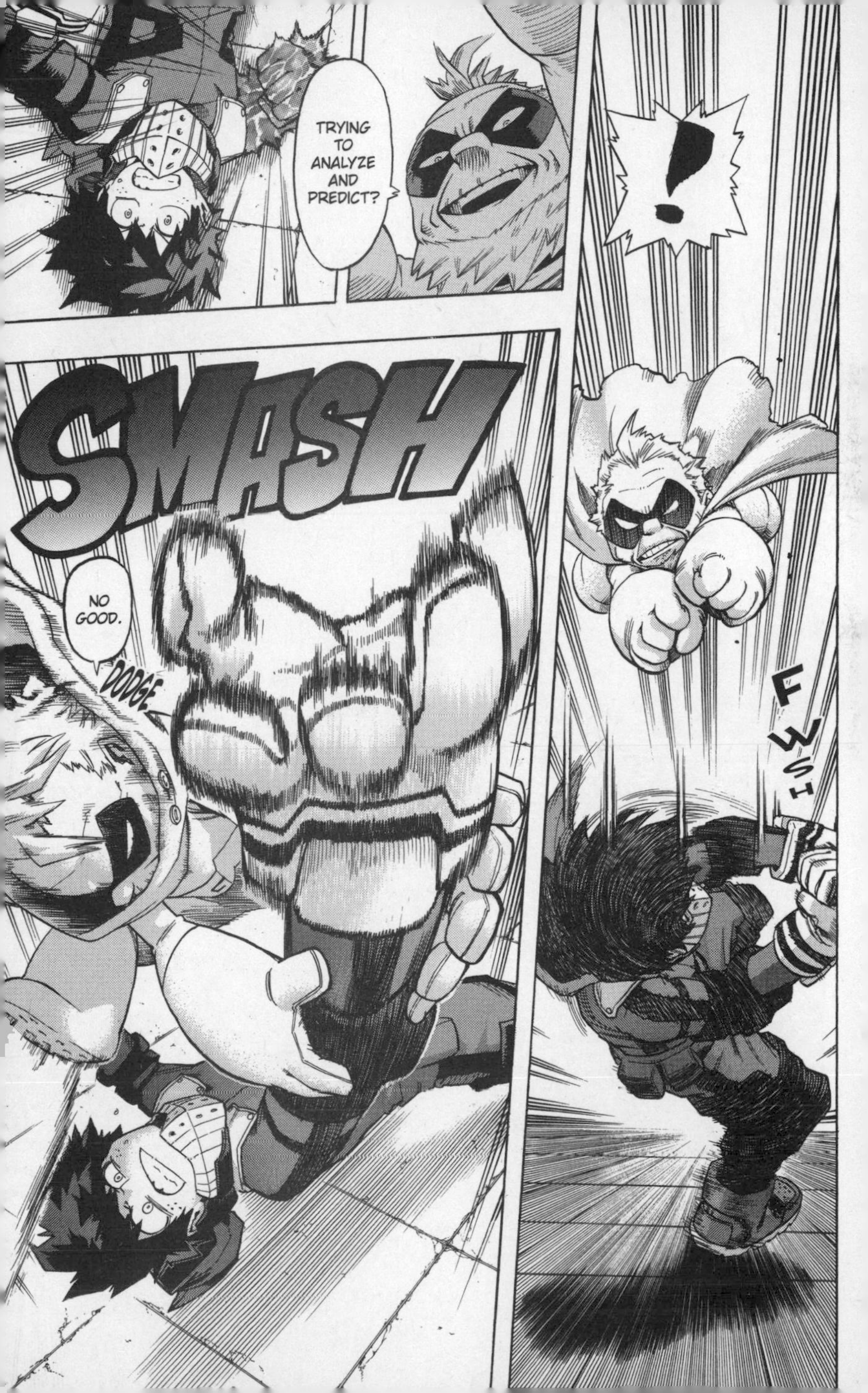
!
FWSH
TRYING TO ANALYZE AND PREDICT?
SMASH
NO GOOD.
DODGE

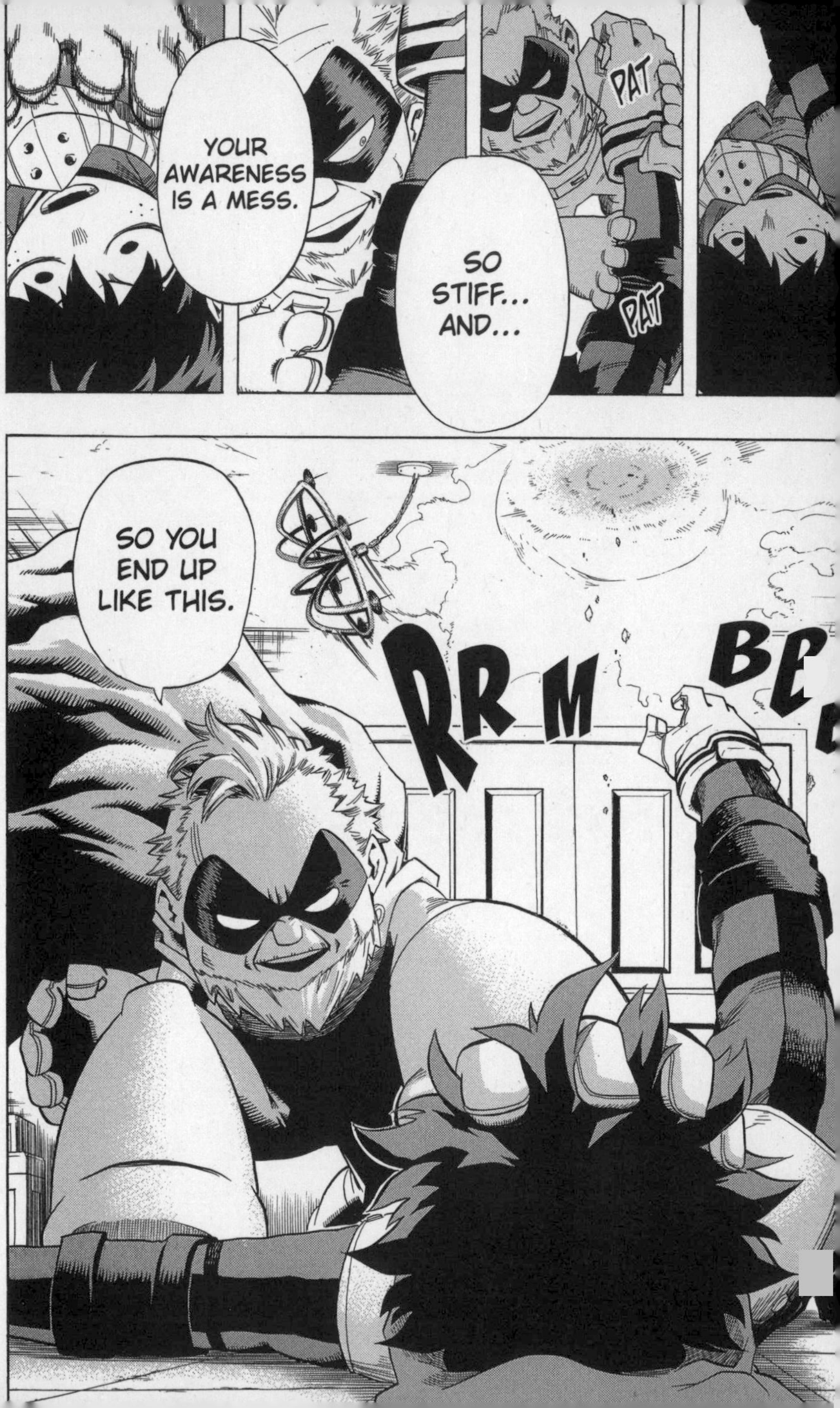
PAT
PAT
YOUR AWARENESS IS A MESS.
SO STIFF... AND...
SO YOU END UP LIKE THIS.
RRM

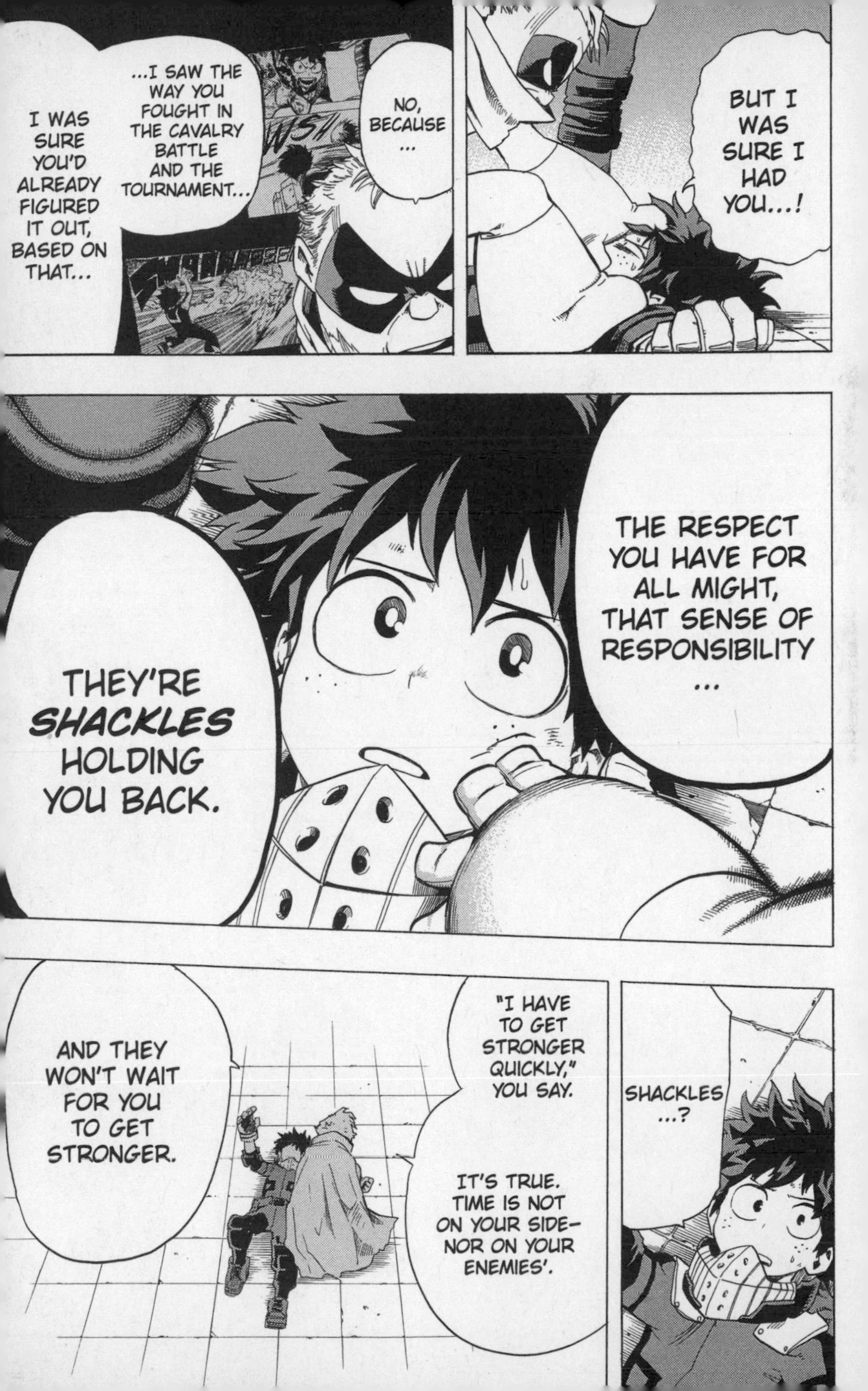
BUT I WAS SURE I HAD YOU...!
NO, BECAUSE ...
...I SAW THE WAY YOU FOUGHT IN THE CAVALRY BATTLE AND THE TOURNAMENT...
I WAS SURE YOU'D ALREADY FIGURED IT OUT, BASED ON THAT...
THE RESPECT YOU HAVE FOR ALL MIGHT, THAT SENSE OF RESPONSIBILITY ...
THEY'RE *SHACKLES* HOLDING YOU BACK.
SHACKLES ...?
"I HAVE TO GET STRONGER QUICKLY," YOU SAY.
IT'S TRUE. TIME IS NOT ON YOUR SIDE-NOR ON YOUR ENEMIES'.
AND THEY WON'T WAIT FOR YOU TO GET STRONGER.

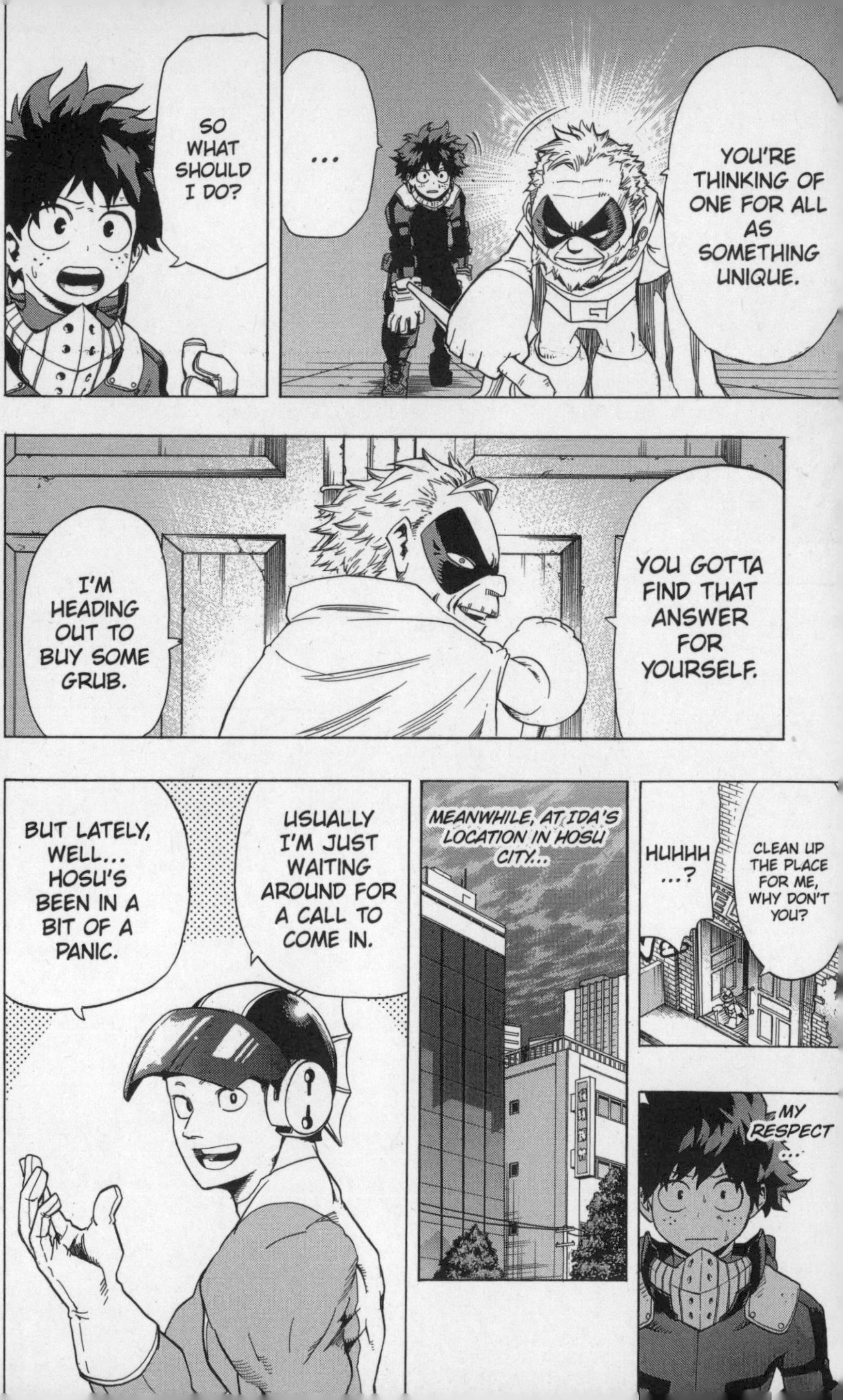
YOU'RE THINKING OF ONE FOR ALL AS SOMETHING UNIQUE.
...
SO WHAT SHOULD I DO?
YOU GOTTA FIND THAT ANSWER FOR YOURSELF.
I'M HEADING OUT TO BUY SOME GRUB.
CLEAN UP THE PLACE FOR ME, WHY DON'T YOU?
HUHHH ...?
MY RESPECT ...
MEANWHILE, AT IDA'S LOCATION IN HOSU CITY...
USUALLY I'M JUST WAITING AROUND FOR A CALL TO COME IN.
BUT LATELY, WELL... HOSU'S BEEN IN A BIT OF A PANIC.

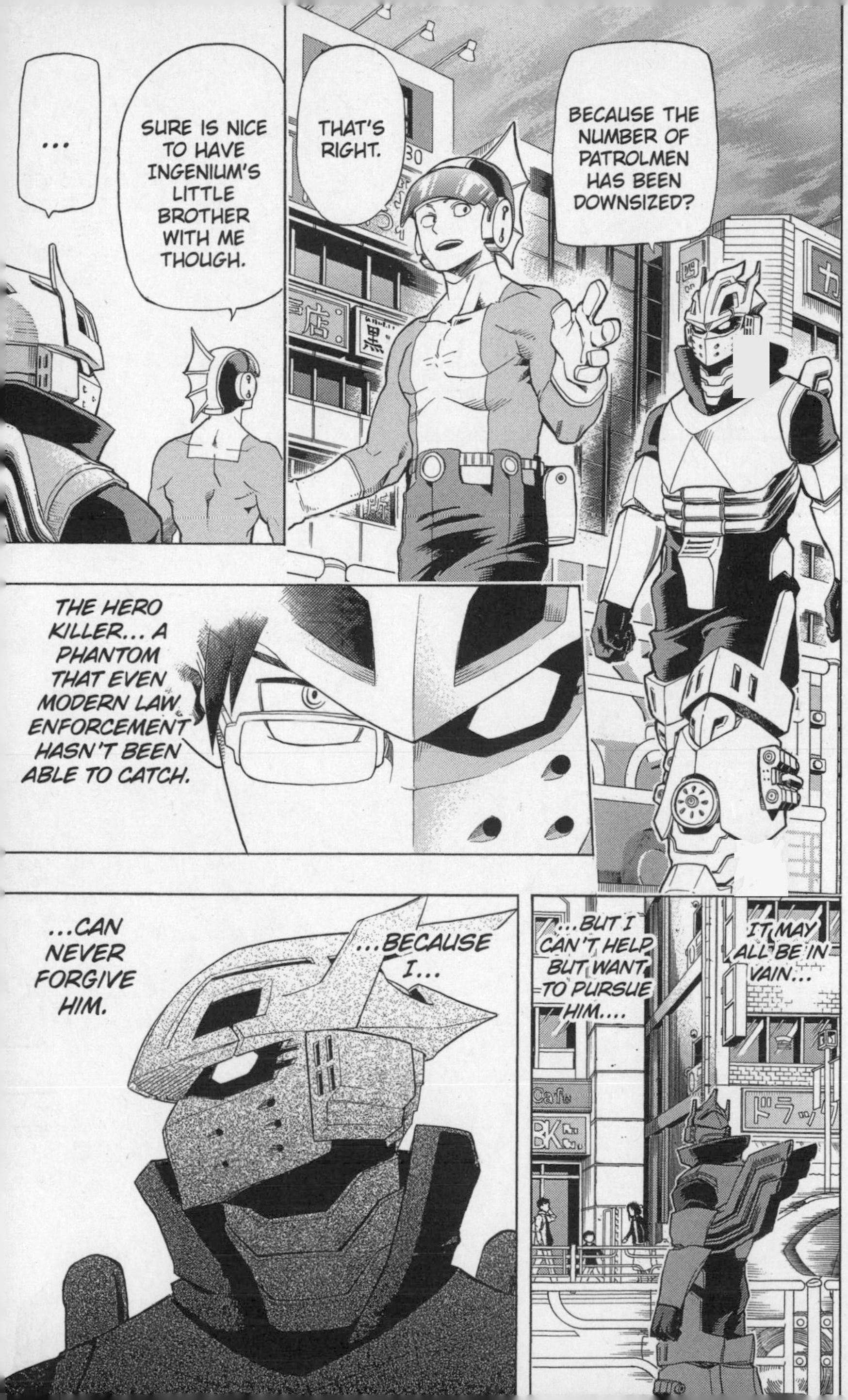
BECAUSE THE NUMBER OF PATROLMEN HAS BEEN DOWNSIZED?
THAT'S RIGHT.
SURE IS NICE TO HAVE INGENIUM'S LITTLE BROTHER WITH ME THOUGH.
...
THE HERO KILLER... A PHANTOM THAT EVEN MODERN LAW ENFORCEMENT HASN'T BEEN ABLE TO CATCH.
IT MAY ALL BE IN VAIN...
...BUT I CAN'T HELP BUT WANT TO PURSUE HIM....
...BECAUSE I...
...CAN NEVER FORGIVE HIM.

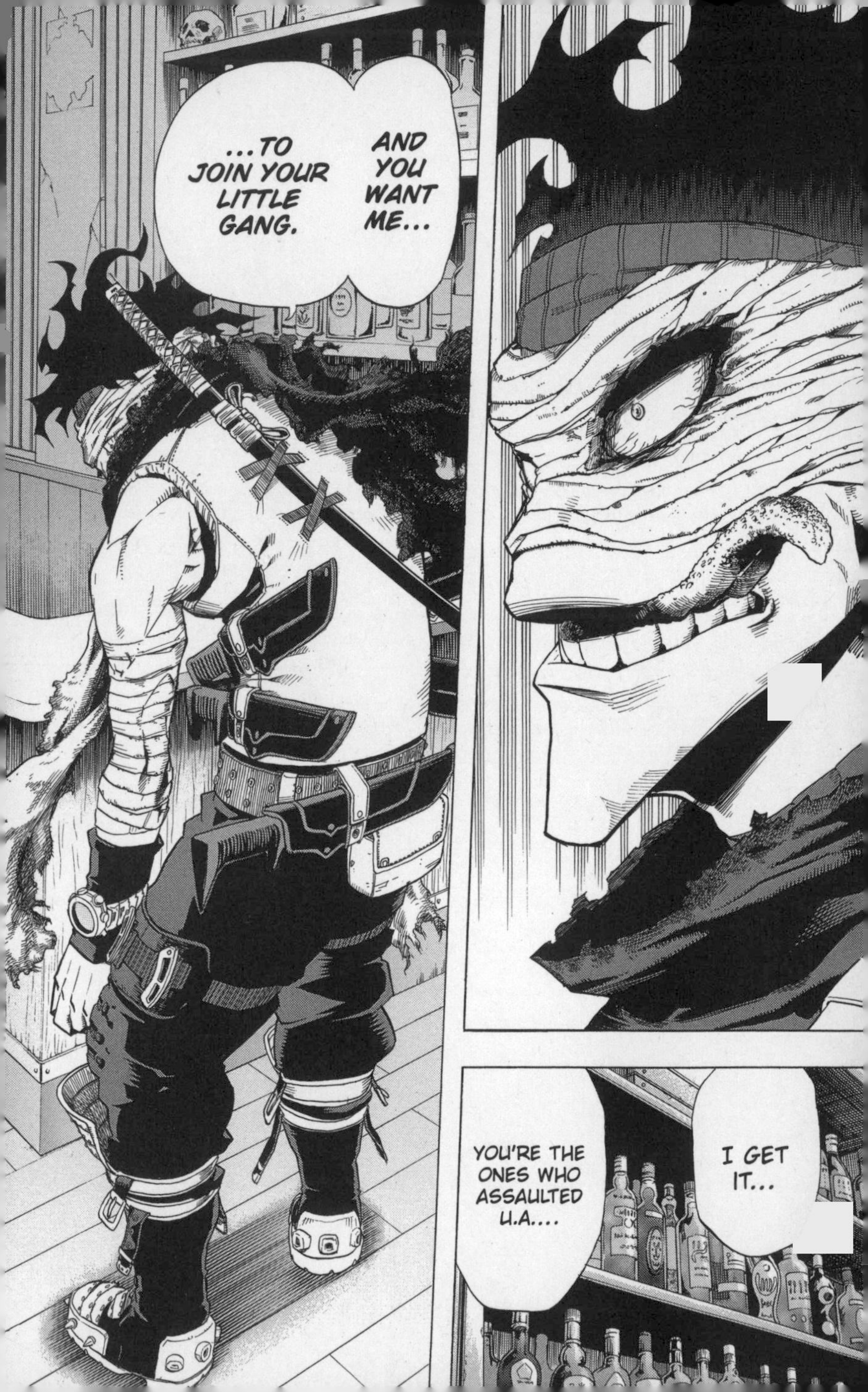
I GET IT...
YOU'RE THE ONES WHO ASSAULTED U.A....
AND YOU WANT ME...
...TO JOIN YOUR LITTLE GANG.

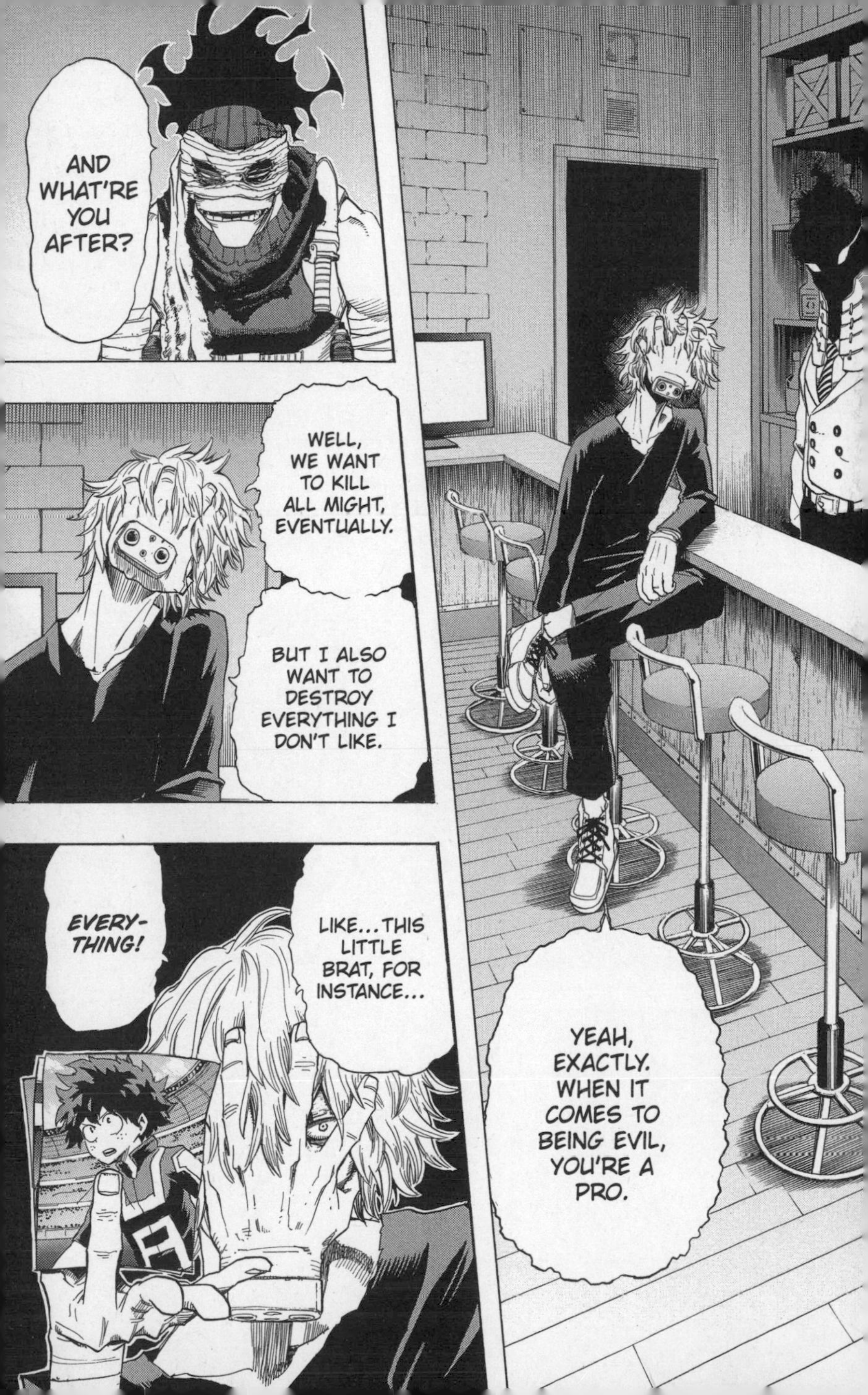
YEAH, EXACTLY. WHEN IT COMES TO BEING EVIL, YOU'RE A PRO.
AND WHAT'RE YOU AFTER?
WELL, WE WANT TO KILL ALL MIGHT, EVENTUALLY.
BUT I ALSO WANT TO DESTROY EVERYTHING I DON'T LIKE.
LIKE... THIS LITTLE BRAT, FOR INSTANCE...
EVERY-THING!

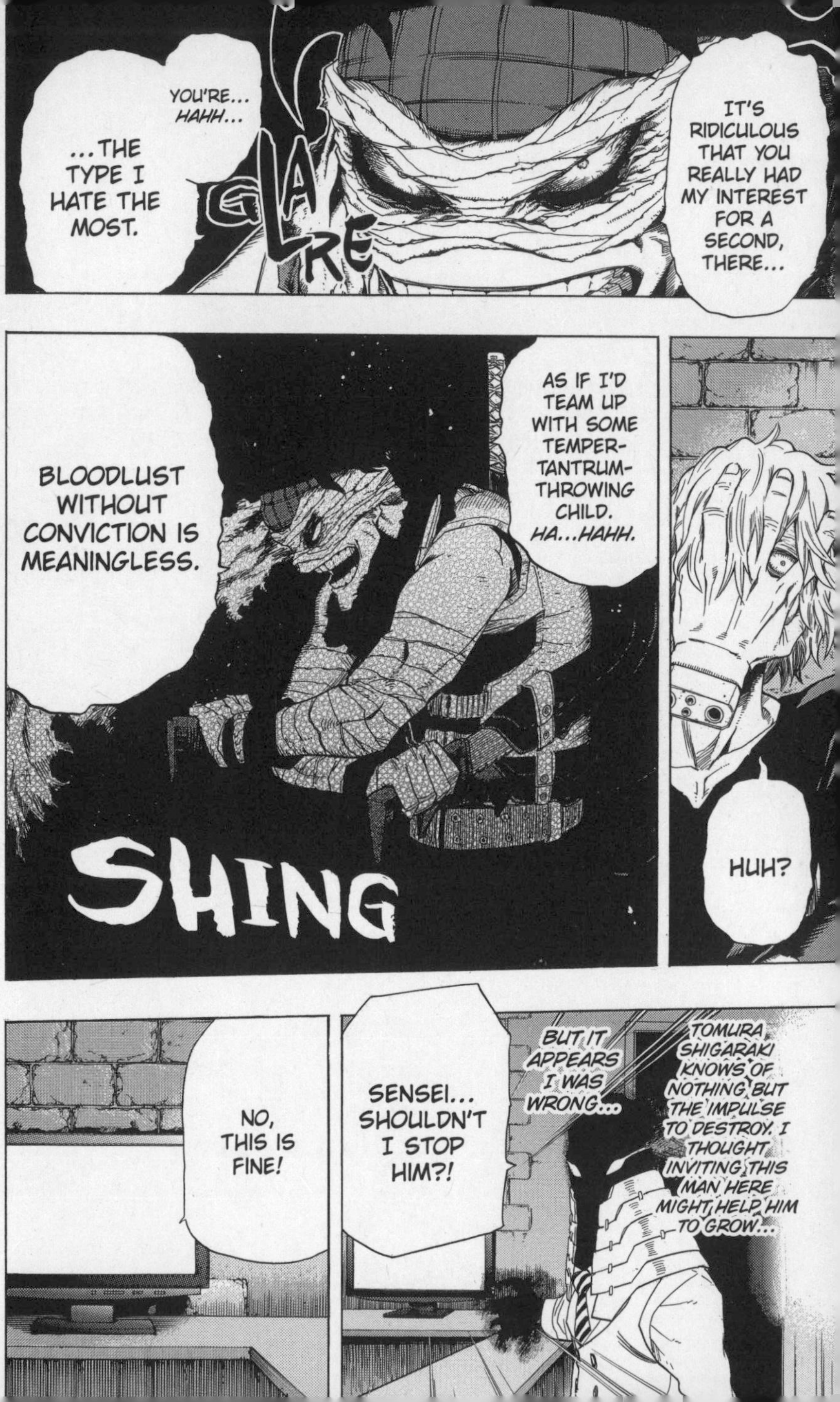
IT'S RIDICULOUS THAT YOU REALLY HAD MY INTEREST FOR A SECOND, THERE...
YOU'RE... HAHH...
...THE TYPE I HATE THE MOST.
GLARE
HUH?
AS IF I'D TEAM UP WITH SOME TEMPER-TANTRUM-THROWING CHILD. HA...HAHH.
BLOODLUST WITHOUT CONVICTION IS MEANINGLESS.
SHING
TOMURA SHIGARAKI KNOWS OF NOTHING BUT THE IMPULSE TO DESTROY. I THOUGHT INVITING THIS MAN HERE MIGHT HELP HIM TO GROW...
BUT IT APPEARS I WAS WRONG...
SENSEI... SHOULDN'T I STOP HIM?!
NO, THIS IS FINE!

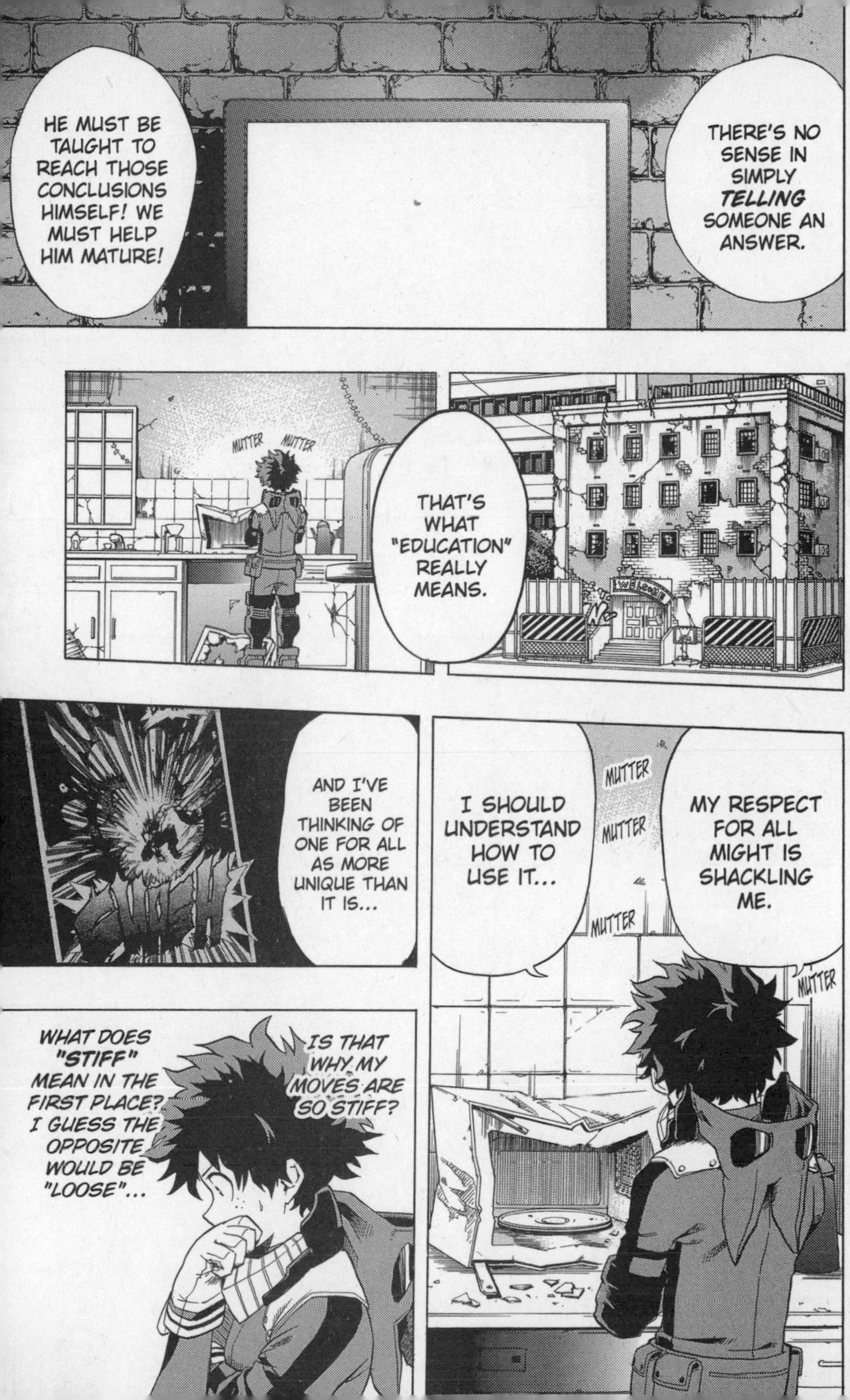

THERE'S NO SENSE IN SIMPLY ***TELLING*** SOMEONE AN ANSWER.
HE MUST BE TAUGHT TO REACH THOSE CONCLUSIONS HIMSELF! WE MUST HELP HIM MATURE!
THAT'S WHAT "EDUCATION" REALLY MEANS.
MUTTER
MUTTER
MY RESPECT FOR ALL MIGHT IS SHACKLING ME.
MUTTER
I SHOULD UNDERSTAND HOW TO USE IT...
MUTTER
MUTTER
MUTTER
AND I'VE BEEN THINKING OF ONE FOR ALL AS MORE UNIQUE THAN IT IS...
IS THAT WHY MY MOVES ARE SO STIFF?
*WHAT DOES **"STIFF"** MEAN IN THE FIRST PLACE? I GUESS THE OPPOSITE WOULD BE "LOOSE"...*

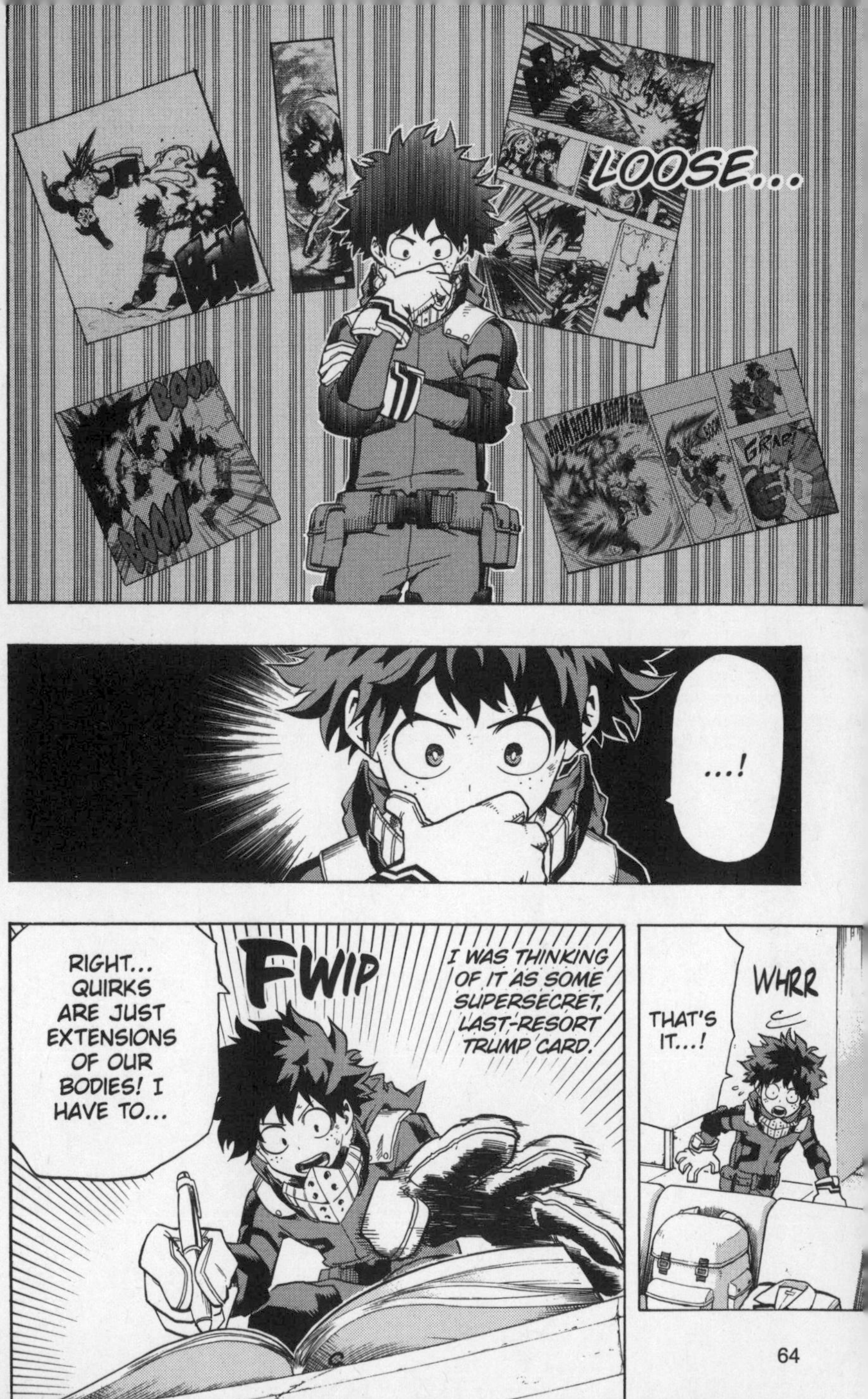
LOOSE...
...!
WHRR
THAT'S IT...!
I WAS THINKING OF IT AS SOME SUPERSECRET, LAST-RESORT TRUMP CARD.
FWIP
RIGHT... QUIRKS ARE JUST EXTENSIONS OF OUR BODIES! I HAVE TO...

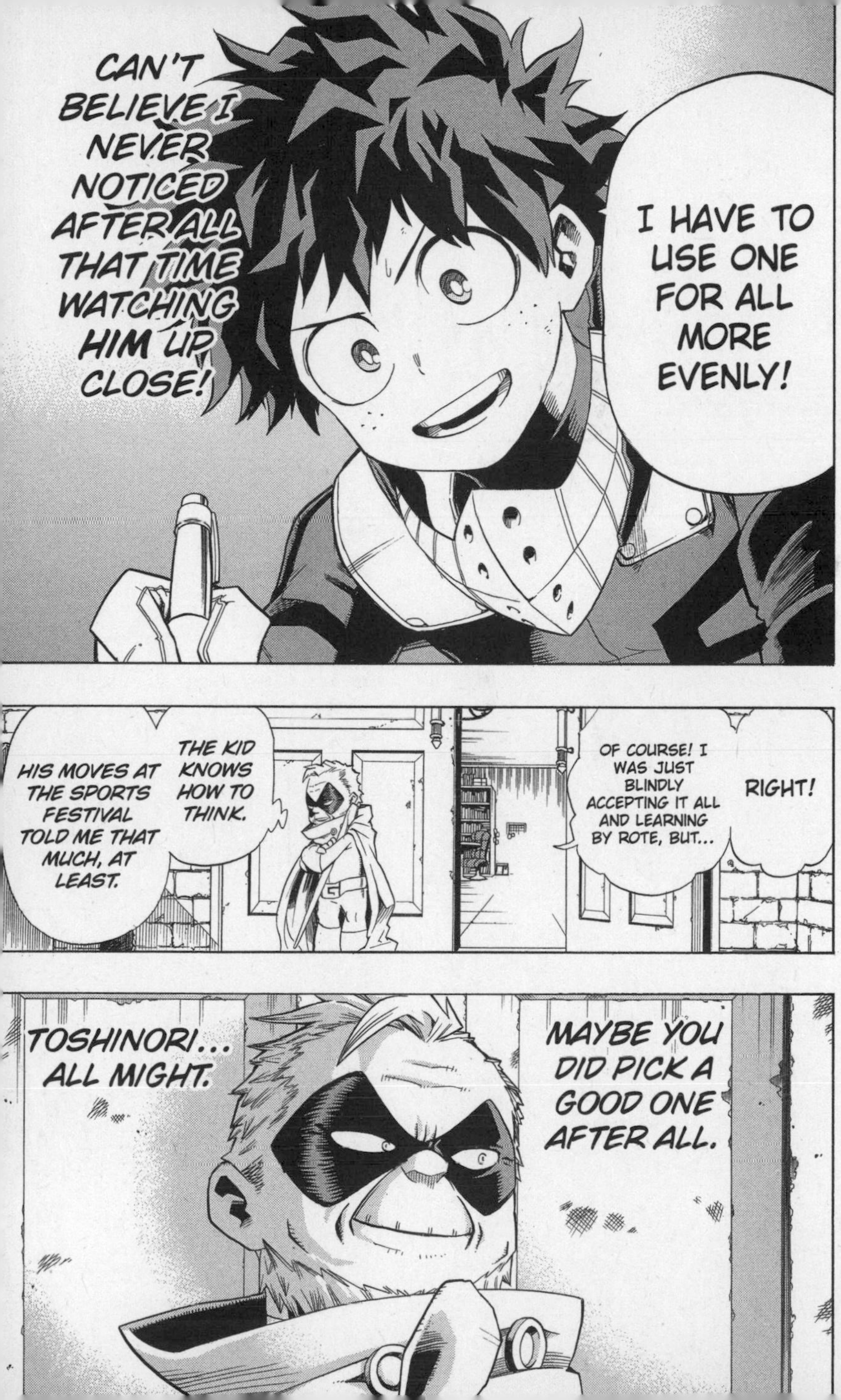
I HAVE TO USE ONE FOR ALL MORE EVENLY!
CAN'T BELIEVE I NEVER NOTICED AFTER ALL THAT TIME WATCHING HIM UP CLOSE!
RIGHT!
OF COURSE! I WAS JUST BLINDLY ACCEPTING IT ALL AND LEARNING BY ROTE, BUT...
THE KID KNOWS HOW TO THINK.
HIS MOVES AT THE SPORTS FESTIVAL TOLD ME THAT MUCH, AT LEAST.
MAYBE YOU DID PICK A GOOD ONE AFTER ALL.
TOSHINORI... ALL MIGHT.

HERO

GRAN TORINO (?)

STREET CLOTHES

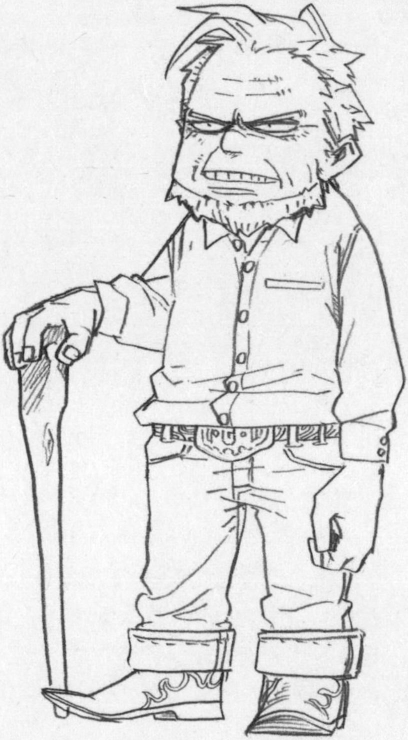

Birthday: 1/28
Height: 120 cm
Favorite Things: Taiyaki, being inactive

BEHIND THE SCENES

Some people will instantly recognize the Dagobah sensibility about him. For the "teacher's teacher," I had to go with this sort of gag-oriented guy.

I absolutely love the fusion of an old man with a simple/cliché superhero costume and the aforementioned Dagobah feel.

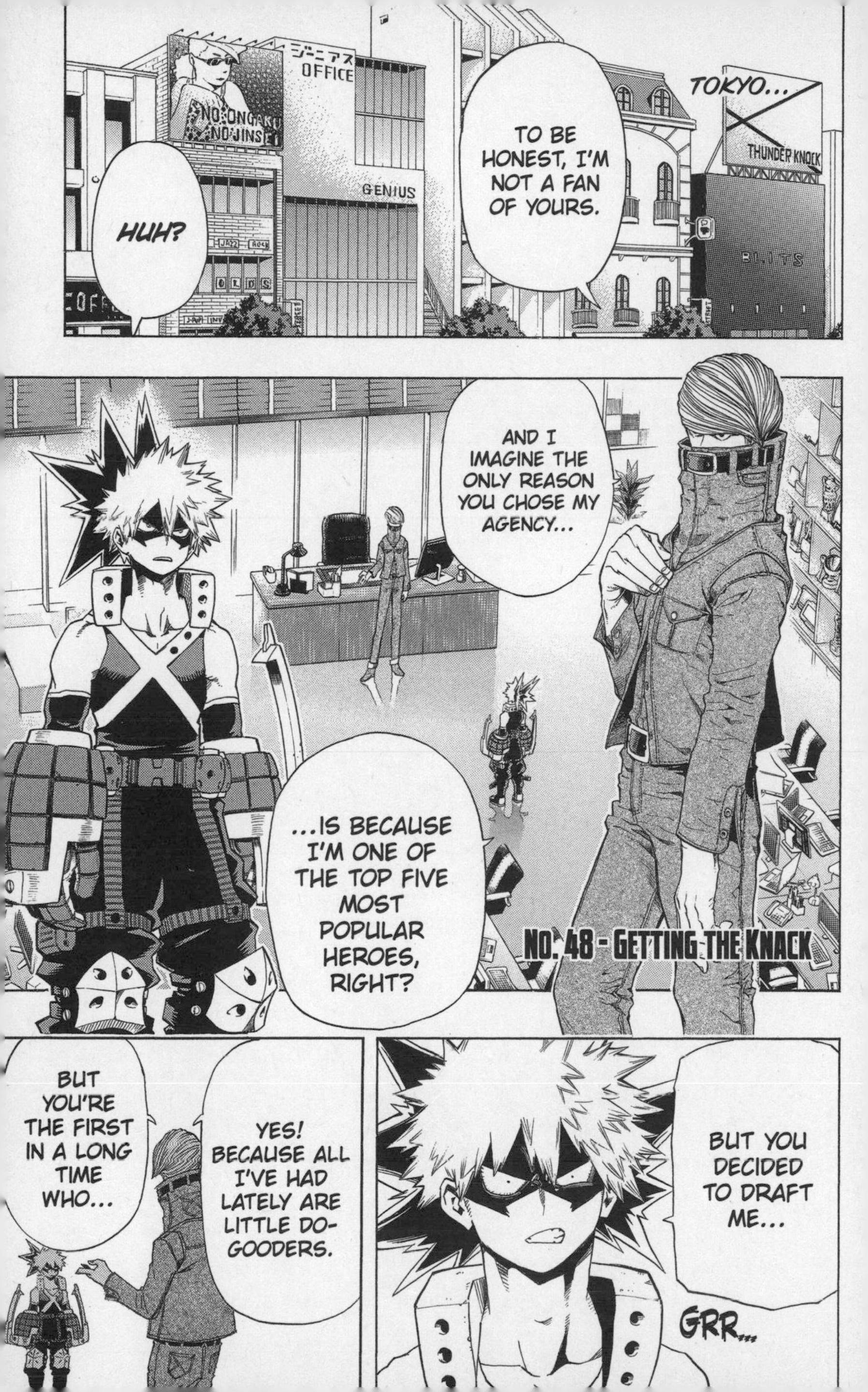
TOKYO...
THUNDER KNOCK
TO BE HONEST, I'M NOT A FAN OF YOURS.
GENIUS
OFFICE
HUH?
AND I IMAGINE THE ONLY REASON YOU CHOSE MY AGENCY...
...IS BECAUSE I'M ONE OF THE TOP FIVE MOST POPULAR HEROES, RIGHT?
No. 48 - Getting the Knack
BUT YOU DECIDED TO DRAFT ME...
GRR...
YES! BECAUSE ALL I'VE HAD LATELY ARE LITTLE DO-GOODERS.
BUT YOU'RE THE FIRST IN A LONG TIME WHO...

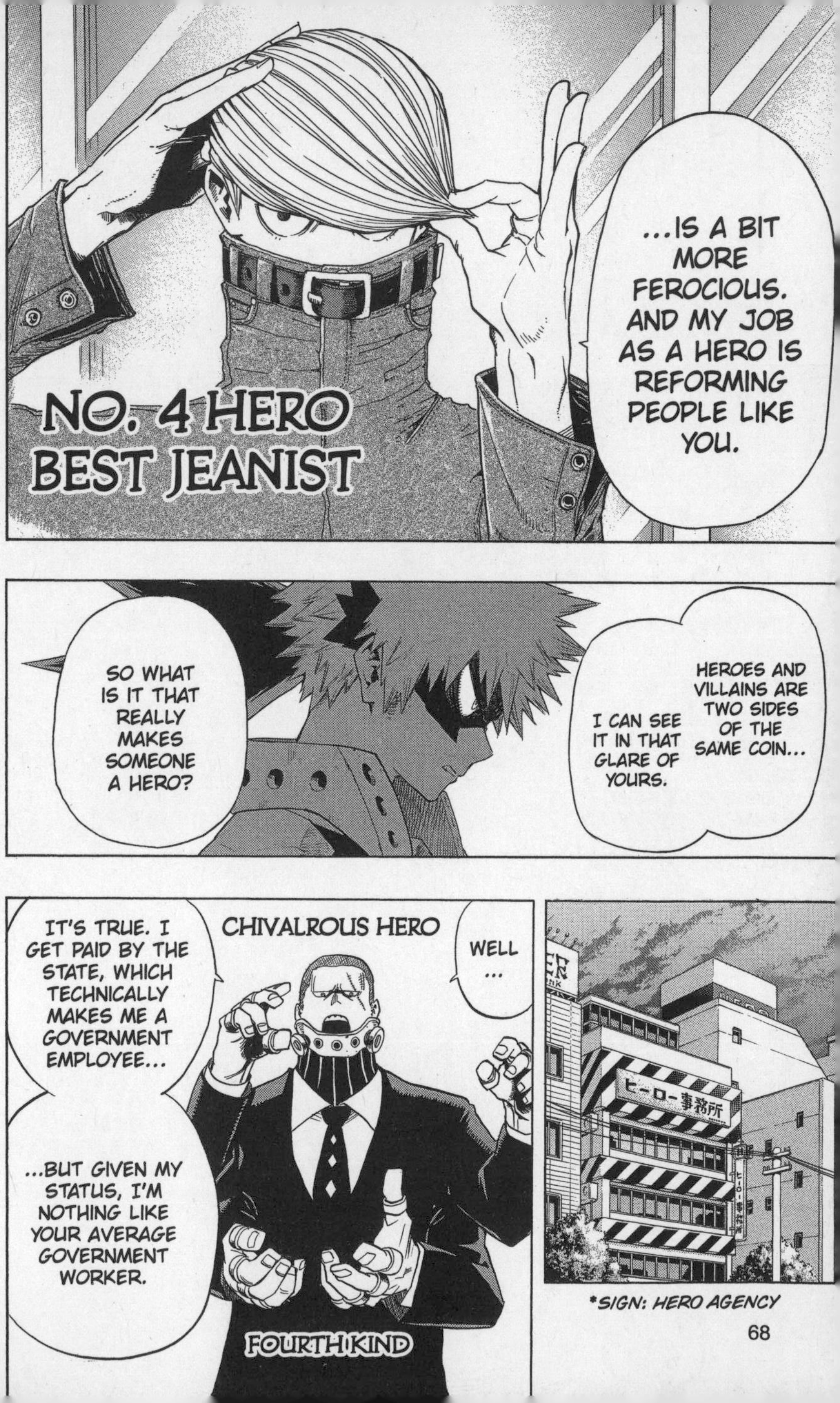
...IS A BIT MORE FEROCIOUS. AND MY JOB AS A HERO IS REFORMING PEOPLE LIKE YOU.
NO. 4 HERO BEST JEANIST
HEROES AND VILLAINS ARE TWO SIDES OF THE SAME COIN...
I CAN SEE IT IN THAT GLARE OF YOURS.
SO WHAT IS IT THAT REALLY MAKES SOMEONE A HERO?
ヒーロー事務所
*SIGN: HERO AGENCY
WELL ...
CHIVALROUS HERO
IT'S TRUE. I GET PAID BY THE STATE, WHICH TECHNICALLY MAKES ME A GOVERNMENT EMPLOYEE...
...BUT GIVEN MY STATUS, I'M NOTHING LIKE YOUR AVERAGE GOVERNMENT WORKER.
FOURTH KIND

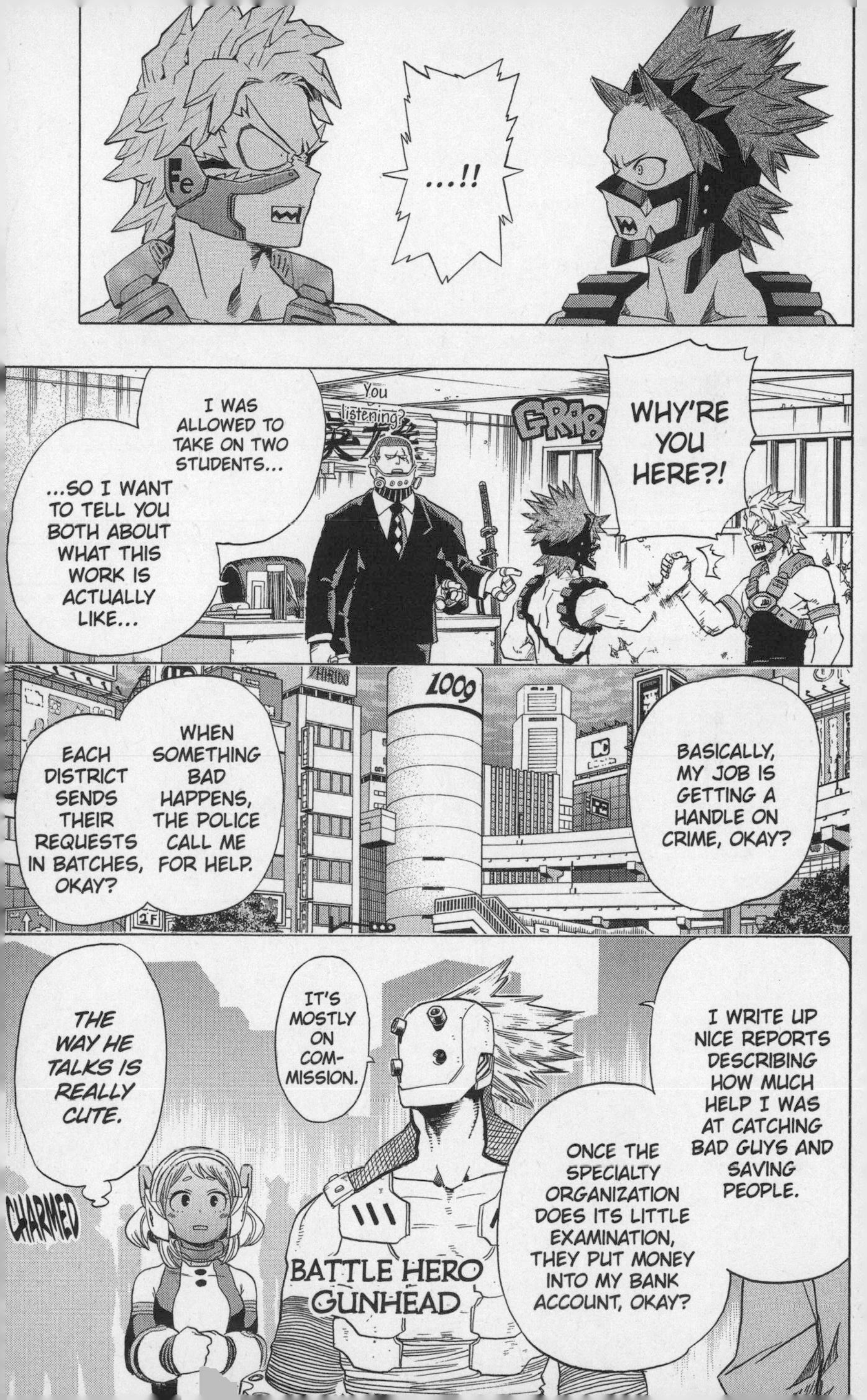
...!!
WHY'RE YOU HERE?!
GRAB
You listening?
I WAS ALLOWED TO TAKE ON TWO STUDENTS...
...SO I WANT TO TELL YOU BOTH ABOUT WHAT THIS WORK IS ACTUALLY LIKE...
BASICALLY, MY JOB IS GETTING A HANDLE ON CRIME, OKAY?
WHEN SOMETHING BAD HAPPENS, THE POLICE CALL ME FOR HELP.
EACH DISTRICT SENDS THEIR REQUESTS IN BATCHES, OKAY?
I WRITE UP NICE REPORTS DESCRIBING HOW MUCH HELP I WAS AT CATCHING BAD GUYS AND SAVING PEOPLE.
ONCE THE SPECIALTY ORGANIZATION DOES ITS LITTLE EXAMINATION, THEY PUT MONEY INTO MY BANK ACCOUNT, OKAY?
IT'S MOSTLY ON COM-MISSION.
BATTLE HERO GUNHEAD
THE WAY HE TALKS IS REALLY CUTE.
CHARMED

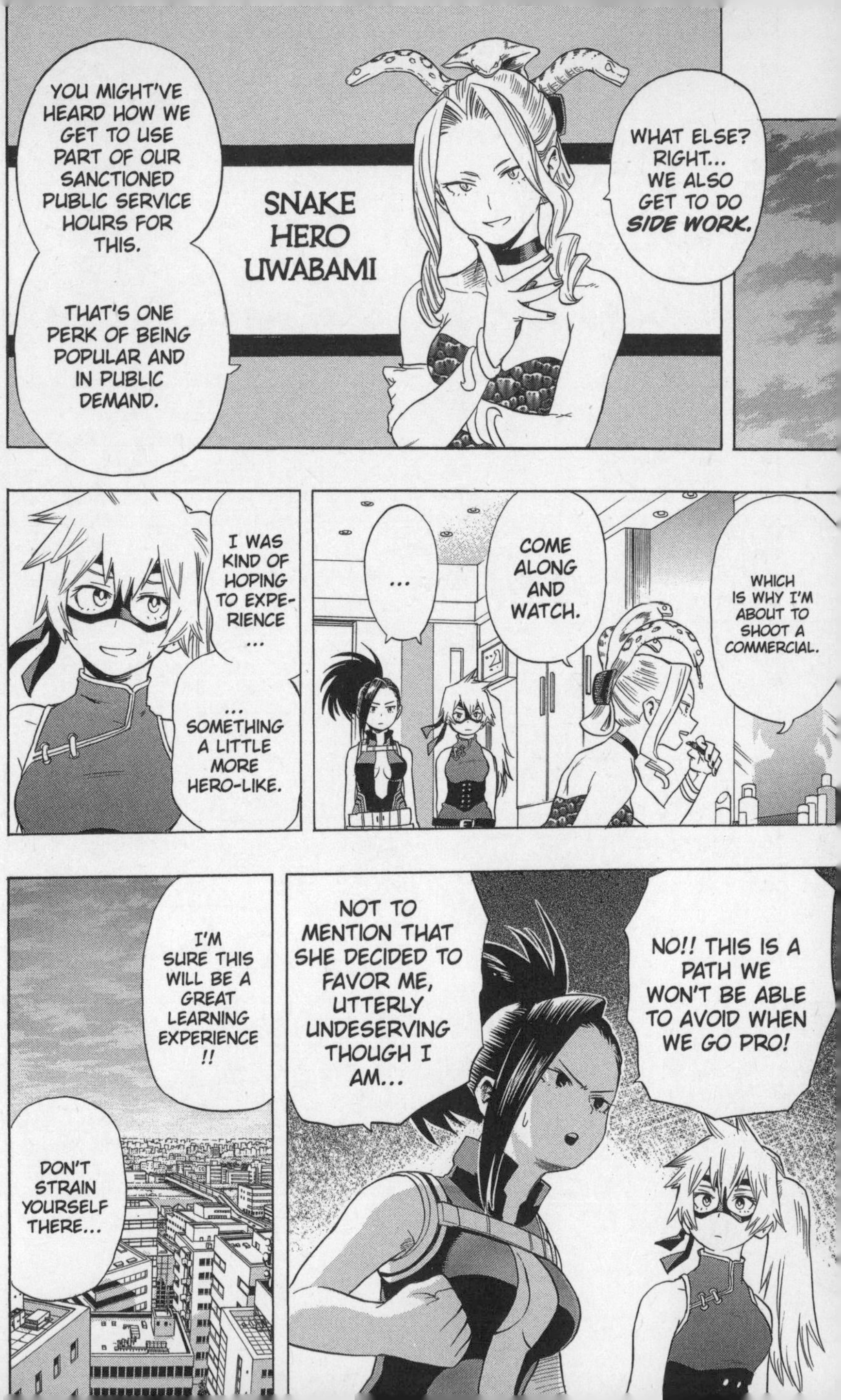
WHAT ELSE? RIGHT... WE ALSO GET TO DO *SIDE WORK.*
SNAKE HERO UWABAMI
YOU MIGHT'VE HEARD HOW WE GET TO USE PART OF OUR SANCTIONED PUBLIC SERVICE HOURS FOR THIS.
THAT'S ONE PERK OF BEING POPULAR AND IN PUBLIC DEMAND.
WHICH IS WHY I'M ABOUT TO SHOOT A COMMERCIAL.
COME ALONG AND WATCH.
...
I WAS KIND OF HOPING TO EXPE-RIENCE...
...SOMETHING A LITTLE MORE HERO-LIKE.
NO!! THIS IS A PATH WE WON'T BE ABLE TO AVOID WHEN WE GO PRO!
NOT TO MENTION THAT SHE DECIDED TO FAVOR ME, UTTERLY UNDESERVING THOUGH I AM...
I'M SURE THIS WILL BE A GREAT LEARNING EXPERIENCE!!
DON'T STRAIN YOURSELF THERE...

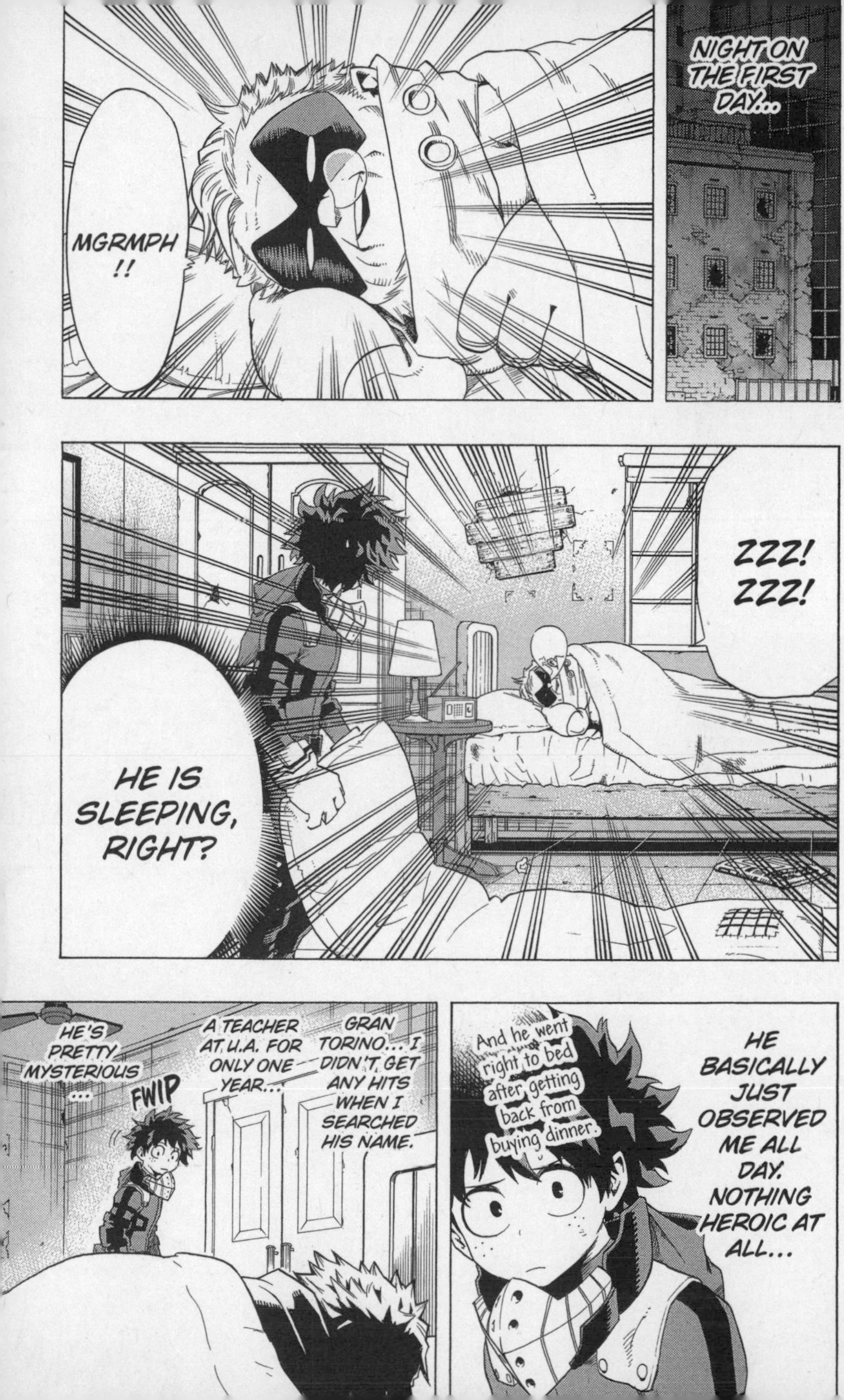
NIGHT ON THE FIRST DAY...
MGRMPH !!
ZZZ! ZZZ!
HE IS SLEEPING, RIGHT?
HE BASICALLY JUST OBSERVED ME ALL DAY. NOTHING HEROIC AT ALL...
And he went right to bed after getting back from buying dinner.
GRAN TORINO... I DIDN'T GET ANY HITS WHEN I SEARCHED HIS NAME.
A TEACHER AT U.A. FOR ONLY ONE YEAR...
HE'S PRETTY MYSTERIOUS...
FWIP

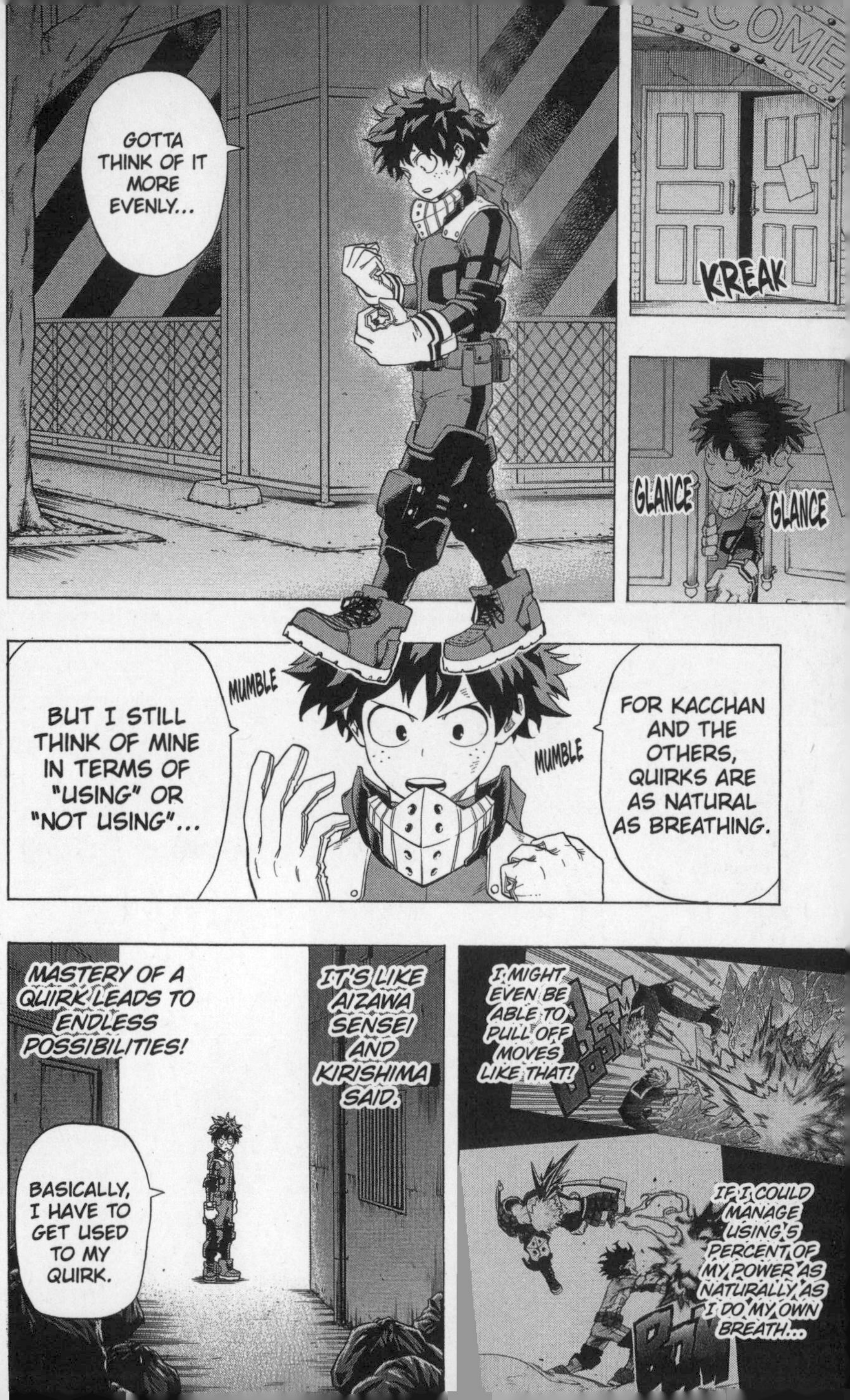
KREAK
GLANCE
GLANCE
GOTTA THINK OF IT MORE EVENLY...
FOR KACCHAN AND THE OTHERS, QUIRKS ARE AS NATURAL AS BREATHING.
MUMBLE
MUMBLE
BUT I STILL THINK OF MINE IN TERMS OF "USING" OR "NOT USING"...
I MIGHT EVEN BE ABLE TO PULL OFF MOVES LIKE THAT!
IF I COULD MANAGE USING 5 PERCENT OF MY POWER AS NATURALLY AS I DO MY OWN BREATH...
IT'S LIKE AIZAWA SENSEI AND KIRISHIMA SAID.
MASTERY OF A QUIRK LEADS TO ENDLESS POSSIBILITIES!
BASICALLY, I HAVE TO GET USED TO MY QUIRK.

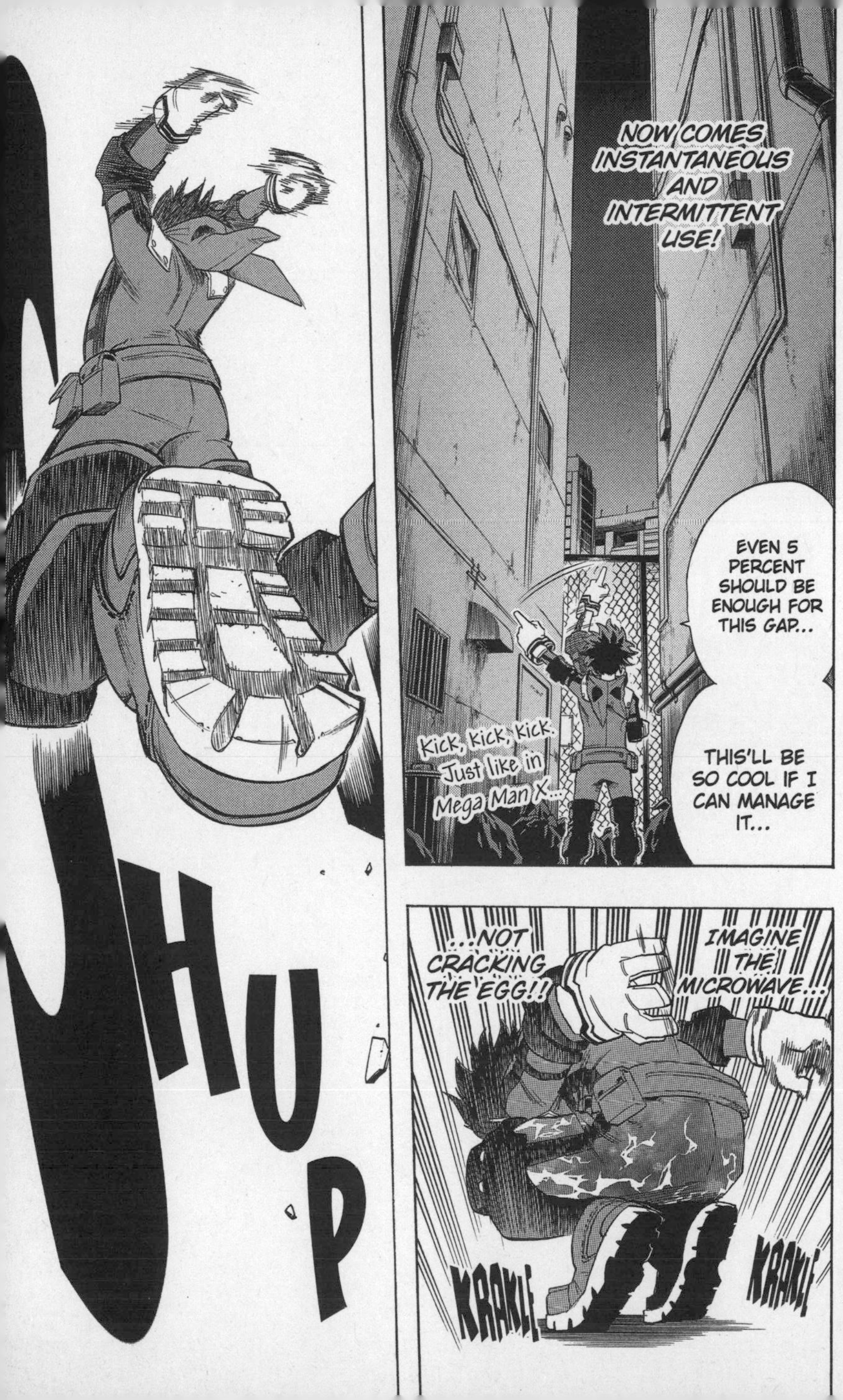
NOW COMES INSTANTANEOUS AND INTERMITTENT USE!
EVEN 5 PERCENT SHOULD BE ENOUGH FOR THIS GAP...
THIS'LL BE SO COOL IF I CAN MANAGE IT...
Kick, kick, kick. Just like in Mega Man X...
IMAGINE THE MICROWAVE...
...NOT CRACKING THE EGG!!
KRAKLE
KRAKLE
SHUP

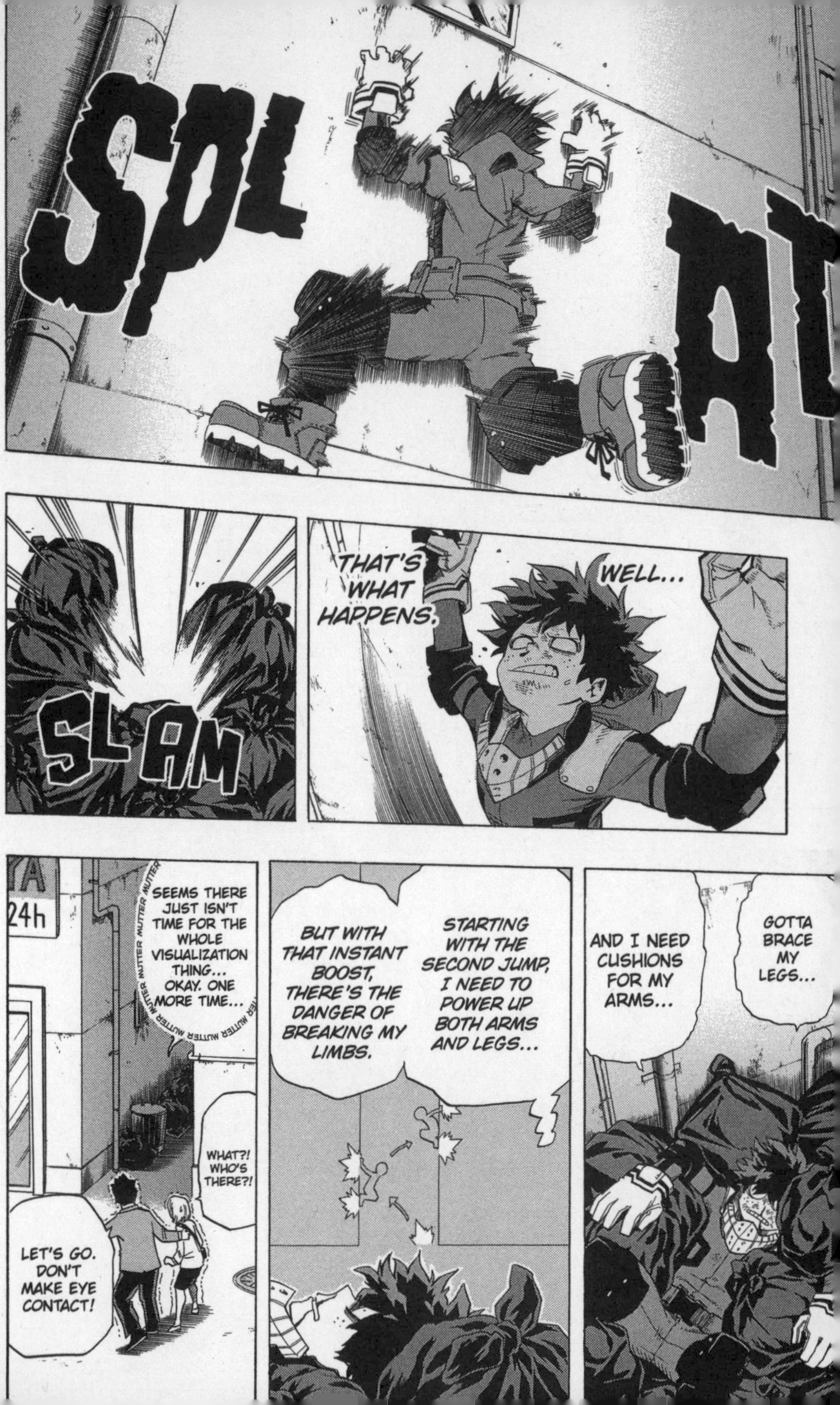
SPLAT
WELL...
THAT'S WHAT HAPPENS.
SLAM
GOTTA BRACE MY LEGS...
AND I NEED CUSHIONS FOR MY ARMS...
STARTING WITH THE SECOND JUMP, I NEED TO POWER UP BOTH ARMS AND LEGS...
BUT WITH THAT INSTANT BOOST, THERE'S THE DANGER OF BREAKING MY LIMBS.
SEEMS THERE JUST ISN'T TIME FOR THE WHOLE VISUALIZATION THING... OKAY. ONE MORE TIME...
MUTTER MUTTER MUTTER MUTTER MUTTER
24h
WHAT?! WHO'S THERE?!
LET'S GO. DON'T MAKE EYE CONTACT!

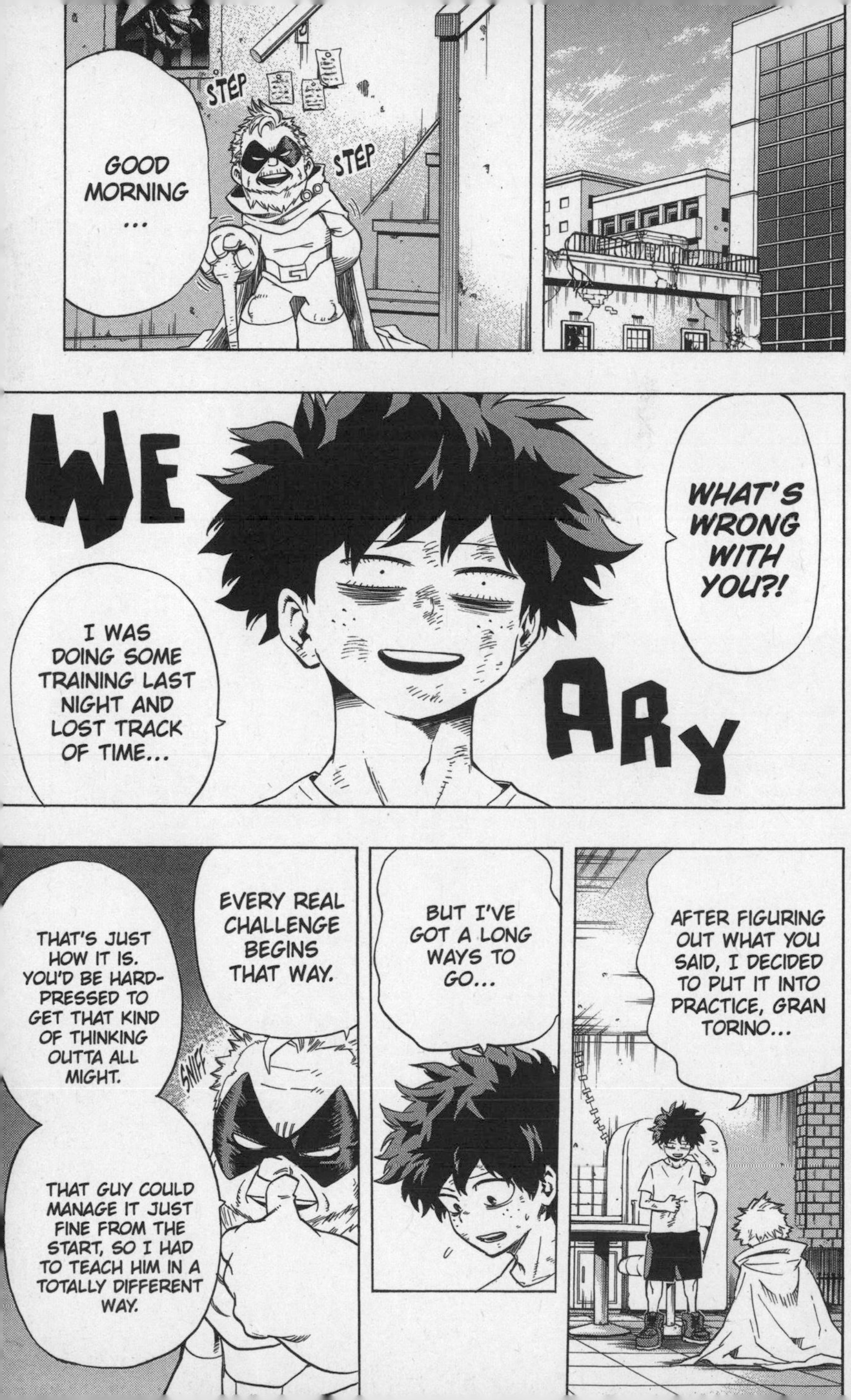
STEP
STEP
GOOD MORNING ...
WHAT'S WRONG WITH YOU?!
WEARY
I WAS DOING SOME TRAINING LAST NIGHT AND LOST TRACK OF TIME...
AFTER FIGURING OUT WHAT YOU SAID, I DECIDED TO PUT IT INTO PRACTICE, GRAN TORINO...
BUT I'VE GOT A LONG WAYS TO GO...
EVERY REAL CHALLENGE BEGINS THAT WAY.
THAT'S JUST HOW IT IS. YOU'D BE HARD-PRESSED TO GET THAT KIND OF THINKING OUTTA ALL MIGHT.
SNIFF
THAT GUY COULD MANAGE IT JUST FINE FROM THE START, SO I HAD TO TEACH HIM IN A TOTALLY DIFFERENT WAY.

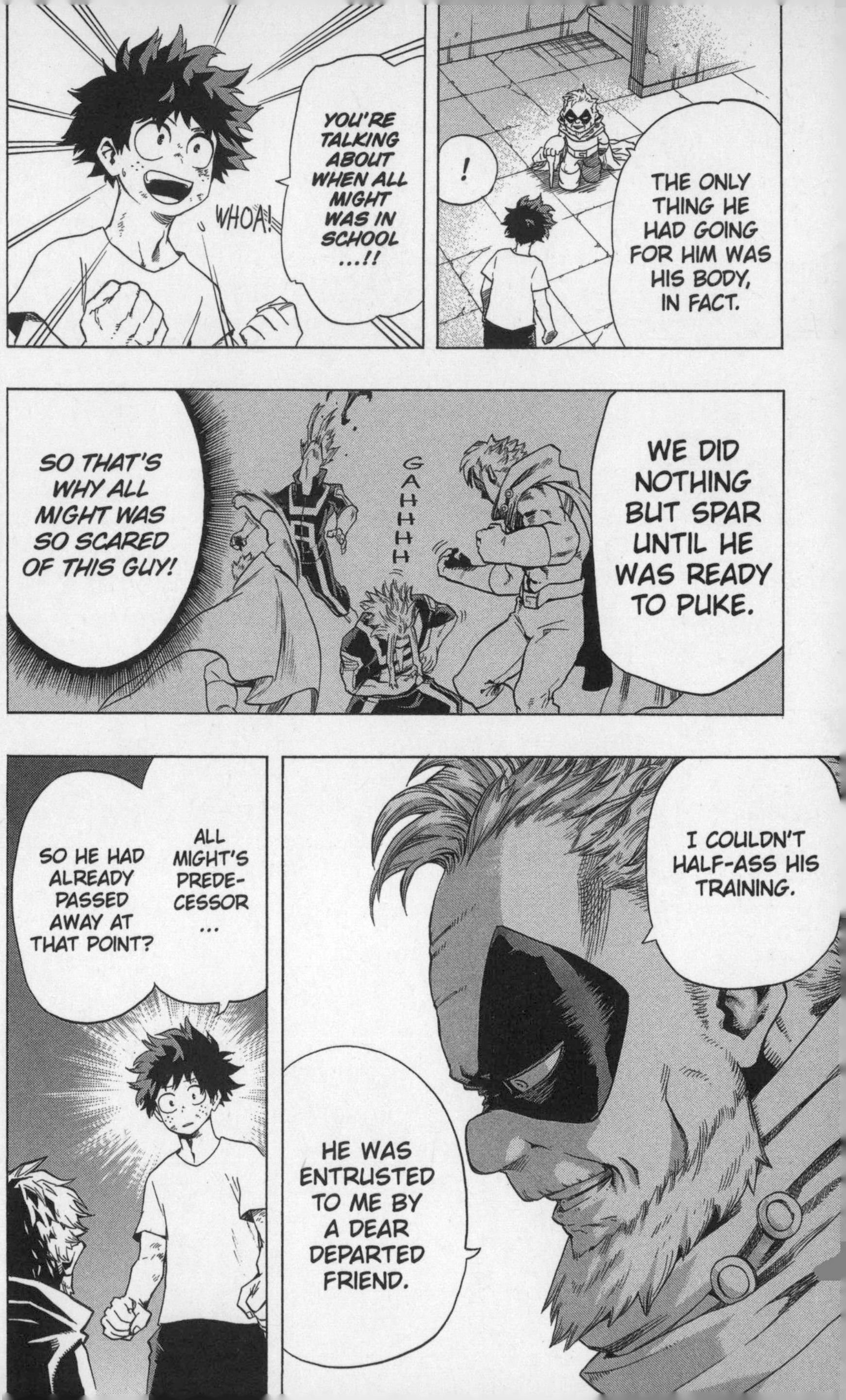
THE ONLY THING HE HAD GOING FOR HIM WAS HIS BODY, IN FACT.
!
YOU'RE TALKING ABOUT WHEN ALL MIGHT WAS IN SCHOOL ...!!
WHOA!
WE DID NOTHING BUT SPAR UNTIL HE WAS READY TO PUKE.
GAHHHHH
SO THAT'S WHY ALL MIGHT WAS SO SCARED OF THIS GUY!
I COULDN'T HALF-ASS HIS TRAINING.
HE WAS ENTRUSTED TO ME BY A DEAR DEPARTED FRIEND.
ALL MIGHT'S PREDE-CESSOR ...
SO HE HAD ALREADY PASSED AWAY AT THAT POINT?

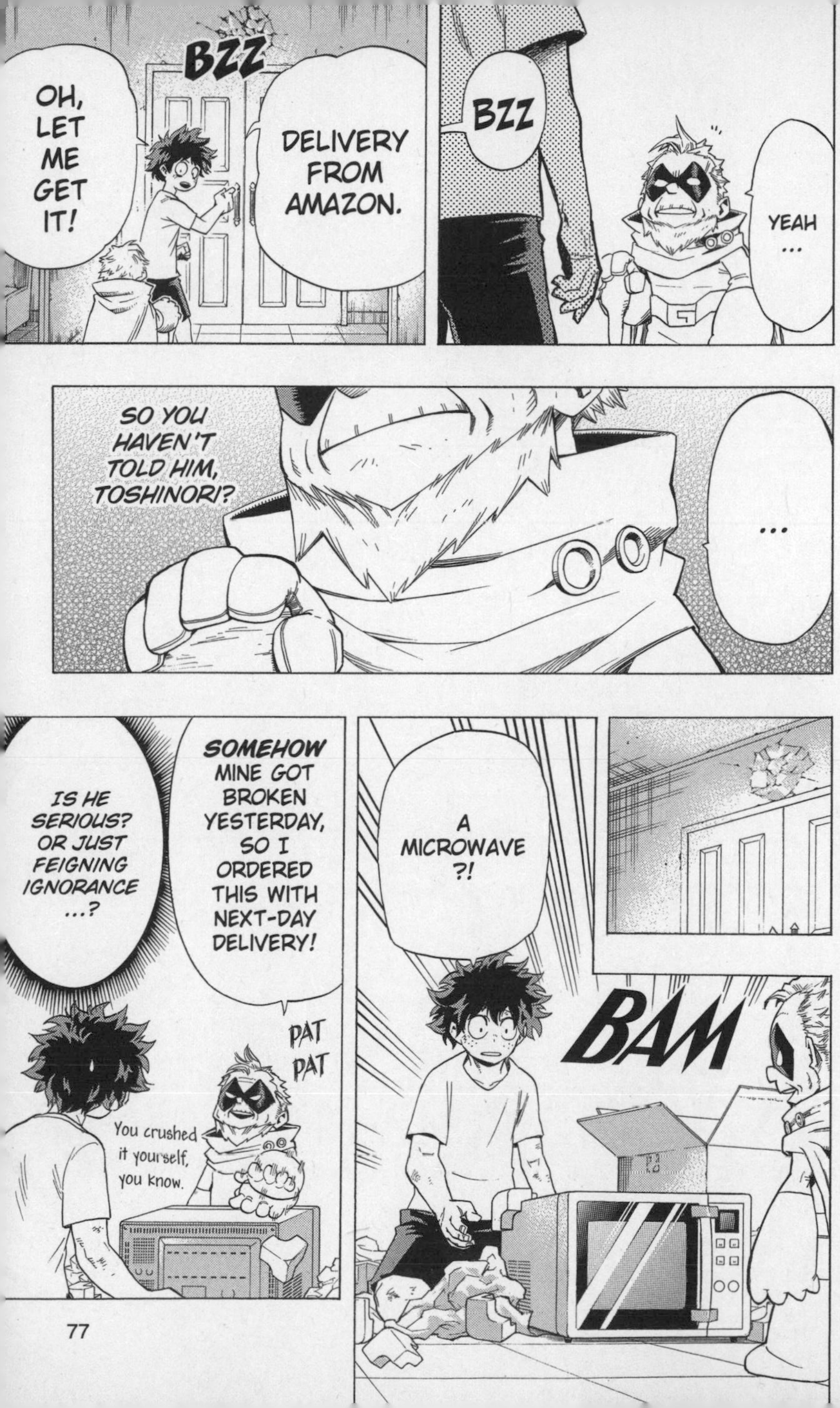
BZZ
YEAH ...
DELIVERY FROM AMAZON.
BZZ
OH, LET ME GET IT!
...
SO YOU HAVEN'T TOLD HIM, TOSHINORI?
A MICROWAVE ?!
BAM
SOMEHOW MINE GOT BROKEN YESTERDAY, SO I ORDERED THIS WITH NEXT-DAY DELIVERY!
IS HE SERIOUS? OR JUST FEIGNING IGNORANCE ...?
PAT PAT
You crushed it yourself, you know.

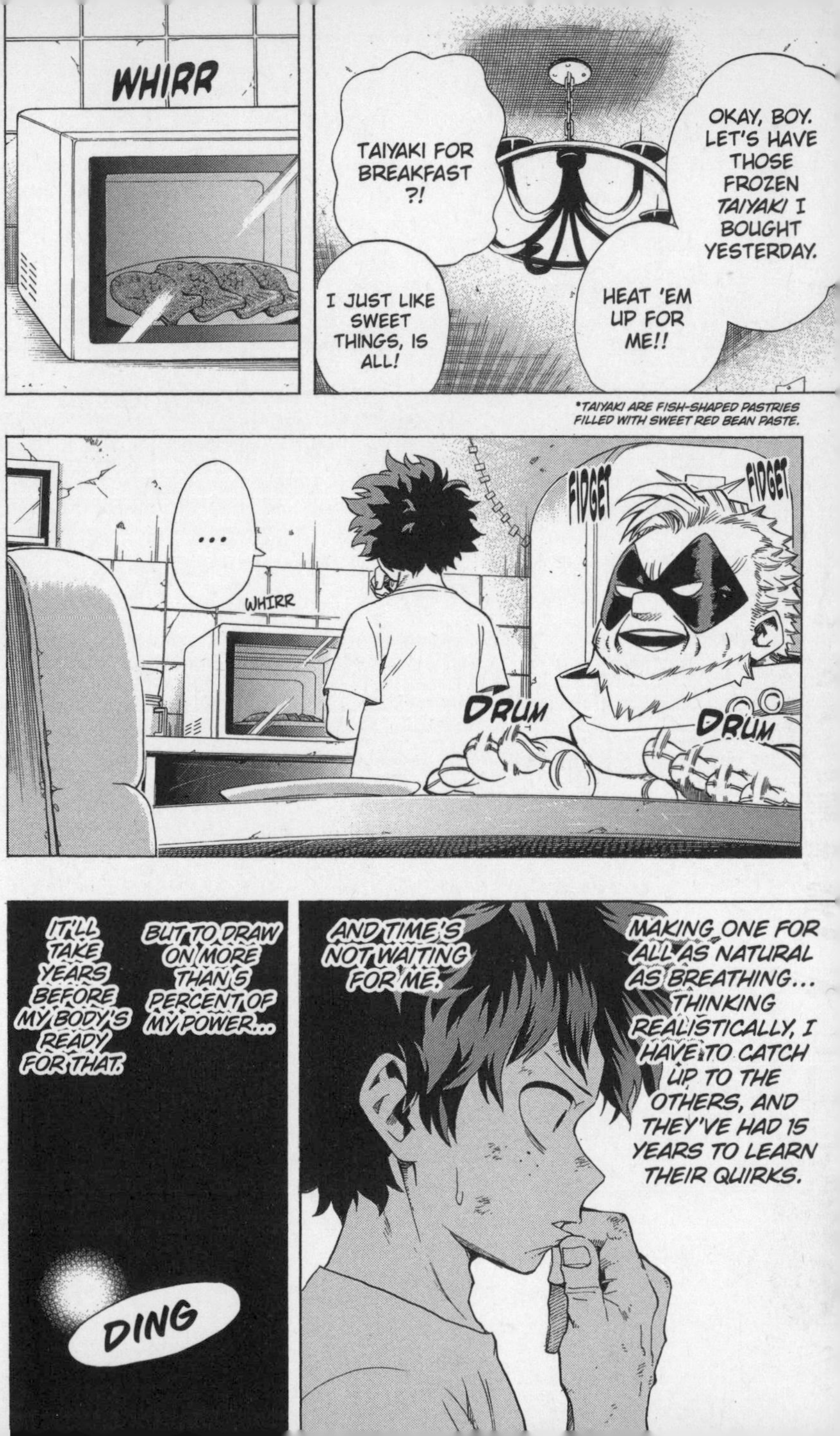
OKAY, BOY. LET'S HAVE THOSE FROZEN *TAIYAKI* I BOUGHT YESTERDAY.
HEAT 'EM UP FOR ME!!
TAIYAKI FOR BREAKFAST?!
I JUST LIKE SWEET THINGS, IS ALL!
WHIRR
FIDGET
FIDGET
DRUM
DRUM
...
WHIRR
MAKING ONE FOR ALL AS NATURAL AS BREATHING... THINKING REALISTICALLY, I HAVE TO CATCH UP TO THE OTHERS, AND THEY'VE HAD 15 YEARS TO LEARN THEIR QUIRKS.
AND TIME'S NOT WAITING FOR ME.
BUT TO DRAW ON MORE THAN 5 PERCENT OF MY POWER...
IT'LL TAKE YEARS BEFORE MY BODY'S READY FOR THAT.
DING
*TAIYAKI ARE FISH-SHAPED PASTRIES FILLED WITH SWEET RED BEAN PASTE.

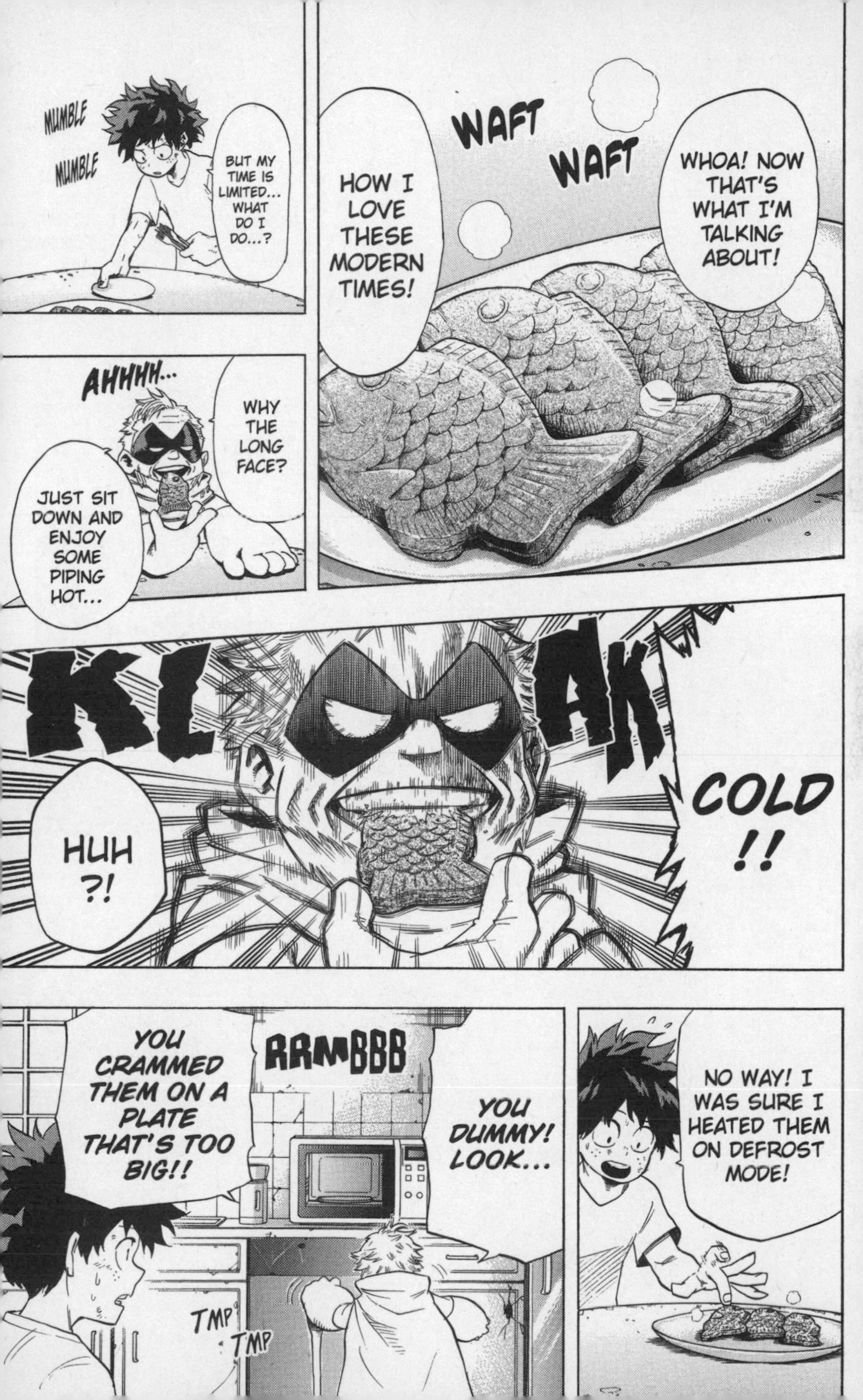
WAFT
WAFT
WHOA! NOW THAT'S WHAT I'M TALKING ABOUT!
HOW I LOVE THESE MODERN TIMES!
MUMBLE
MUMBLE
BUT MY TIME IS LIMITED... WHAT DO I DO...?
AHHHH...
WHY THE LONG FACE?
JUST SIT DOWN AND ENJOY SOME PIPING HOT...
KLAK
COLD!!
HUH?!
NO WAY! I WAS SURE I HEATED THEM ON DEFROST MODE!
RRMBBB
YOU DUMMY! LOOK...
YOU CRAMMED THEM ON A PLATE THAT'S TOO BIG!!
TMP
TMP

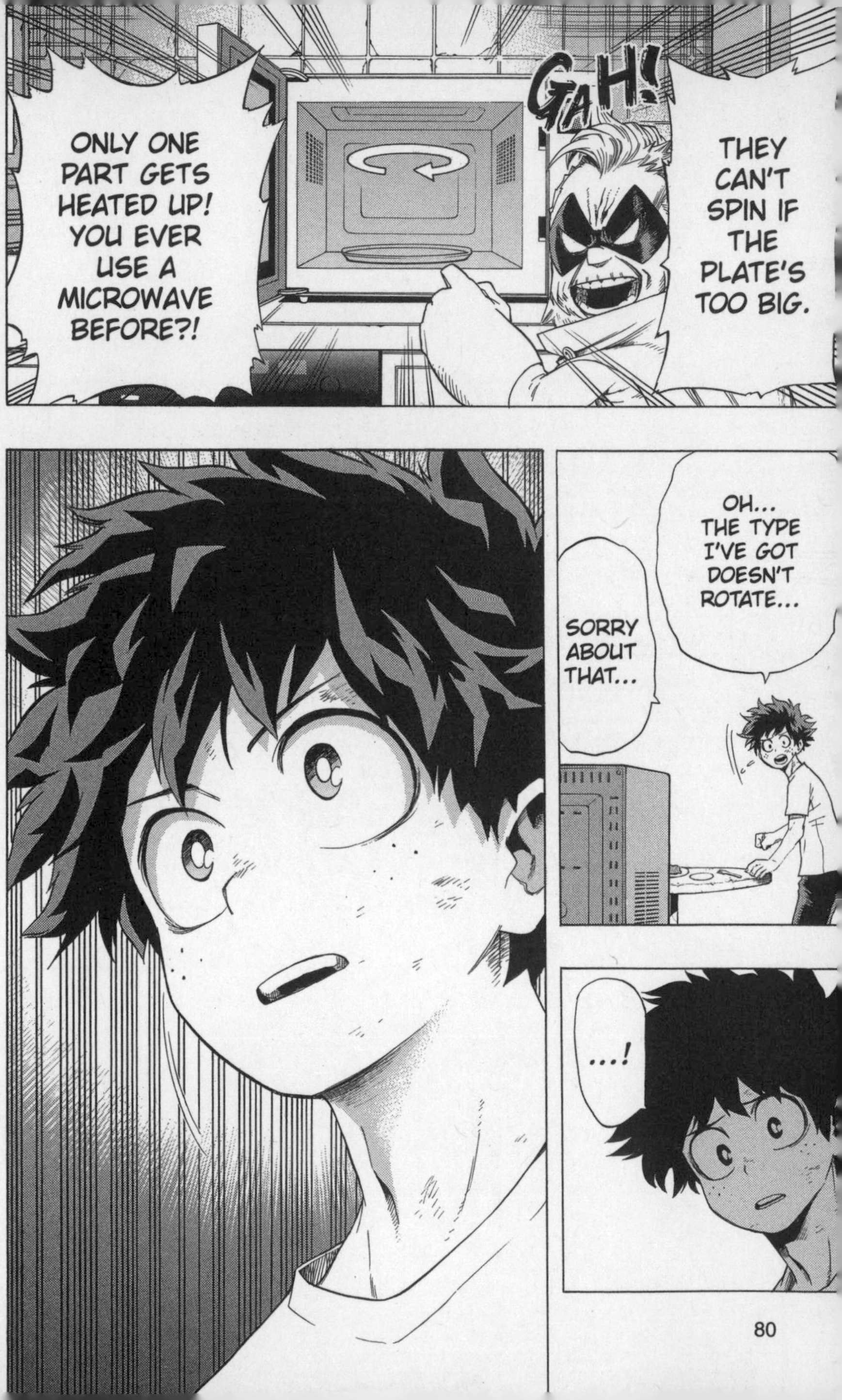
GAH!
THEY CAN'T SPIN IF THE PLATE'S TOO BIG.
ONLY ONE PART GETS HEATED UP! YOU EVER USE A MICROWAVE BEFORE?!
OH... THE TYPE I'VE GOT DOESN'T ROTATE...
SORRY ABOUT THAT...
...!

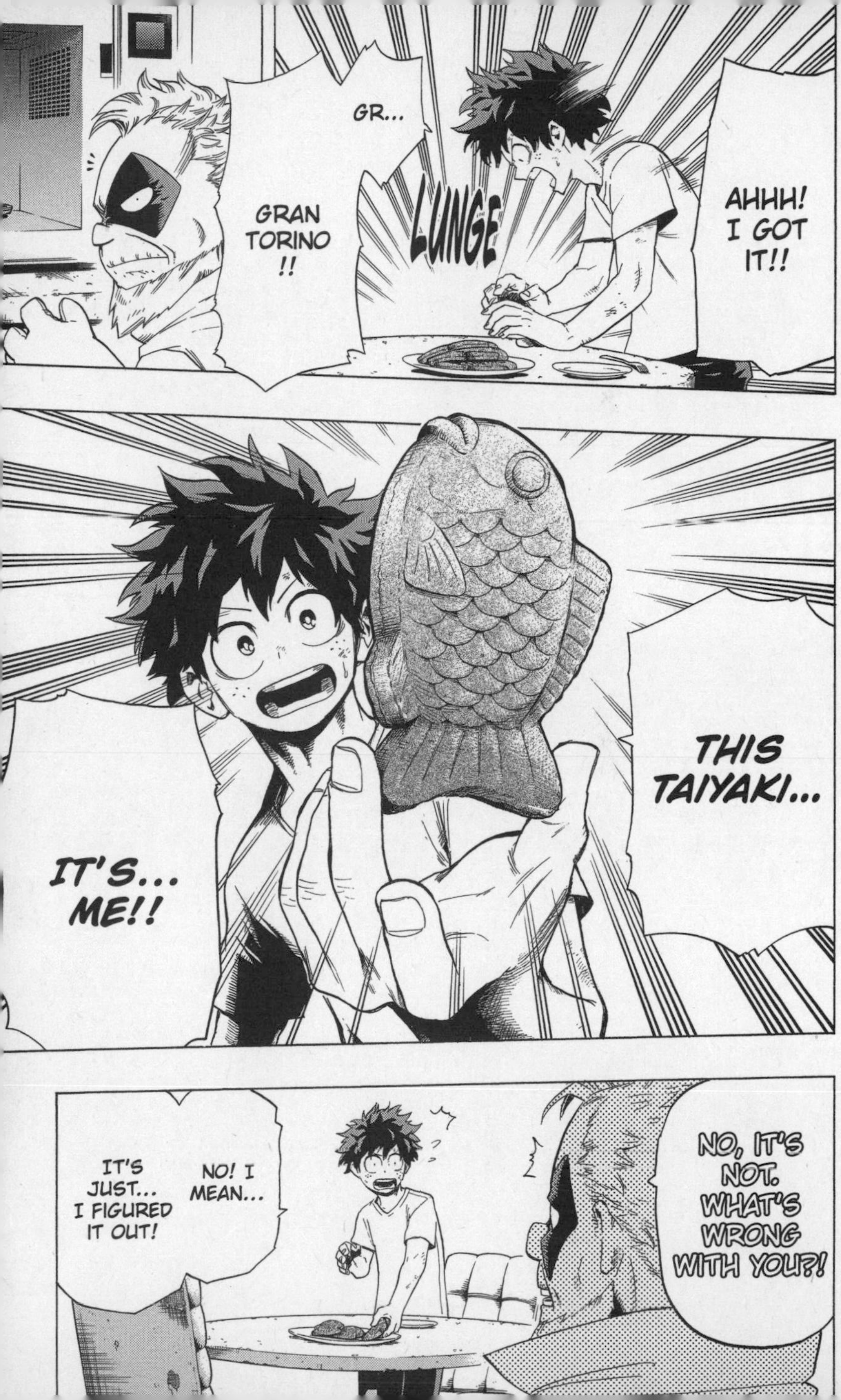
AHHH! I GOT IT!!
GR...
LUNGE
GRAN TORINO !!
THIS TAIYAKI...
IT'S... ME!!
NO, IT'S NOT. WHAT'S WRONG WITH YOU?!
NO! I MEAN...
IT'S JUST... I FIGURED IT OUT!

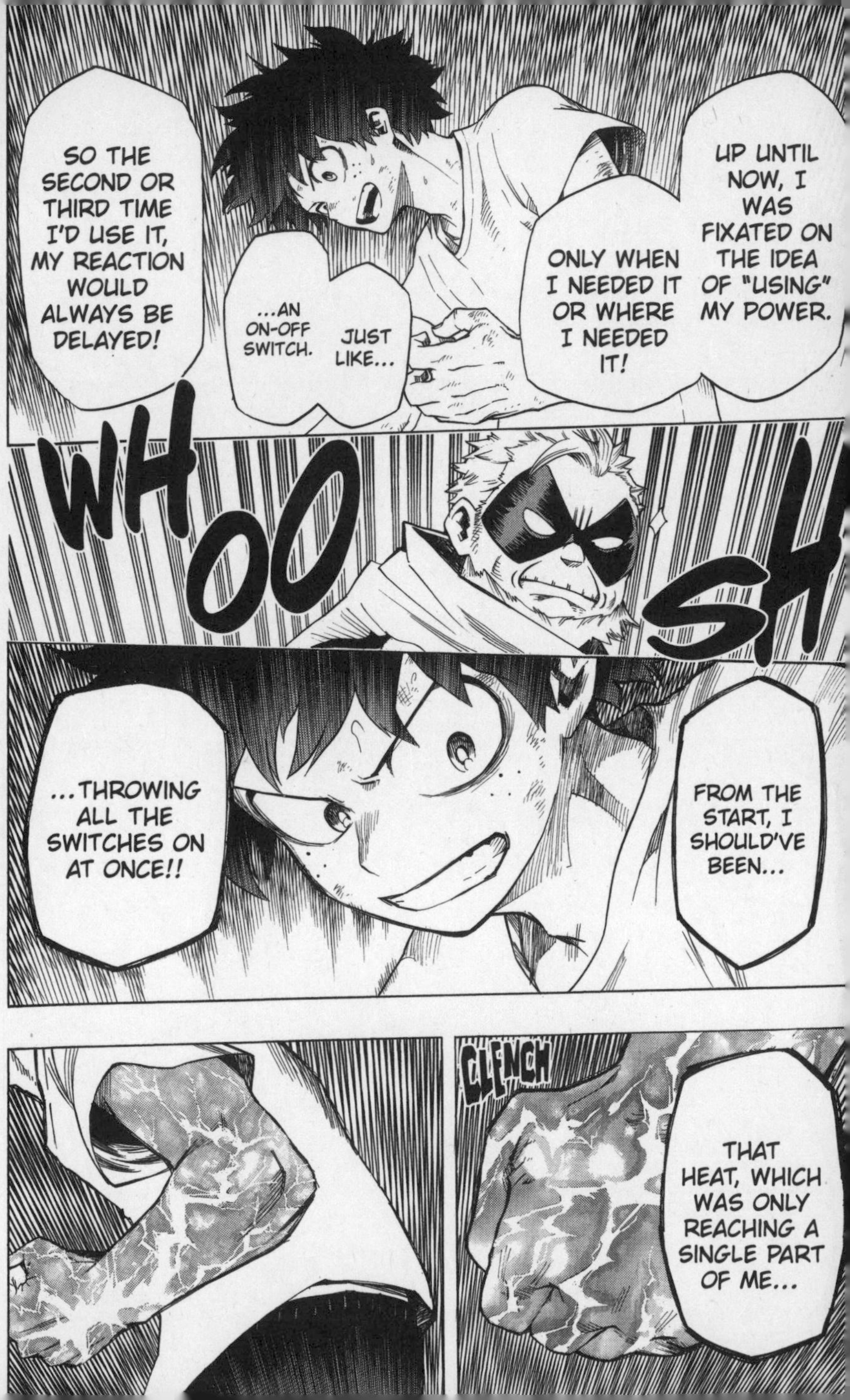
UP UNTIL NOW, I WAS FIXATED ON THE IDEA OF "USING" MY POWER.
ONLY WHEN I NEEDED IT OR WHERE I NEEDED IT!
JUST LIKE...
...AN ON-OFF SWITCH.
SO THE SECOND OR THIRD TIME I'D USE IT, MY REACTION WOULD ALWAYS BE DELAYED!
WHOOSH
FROM THE START, I SHOULD'VE BEEN...
...THROWING ALL THE SWITCHES ON AT ONCE!!
CLENCH
THAT HEAT, WHICH WAS ONLY REACHING A SINGLE PART OF ME...

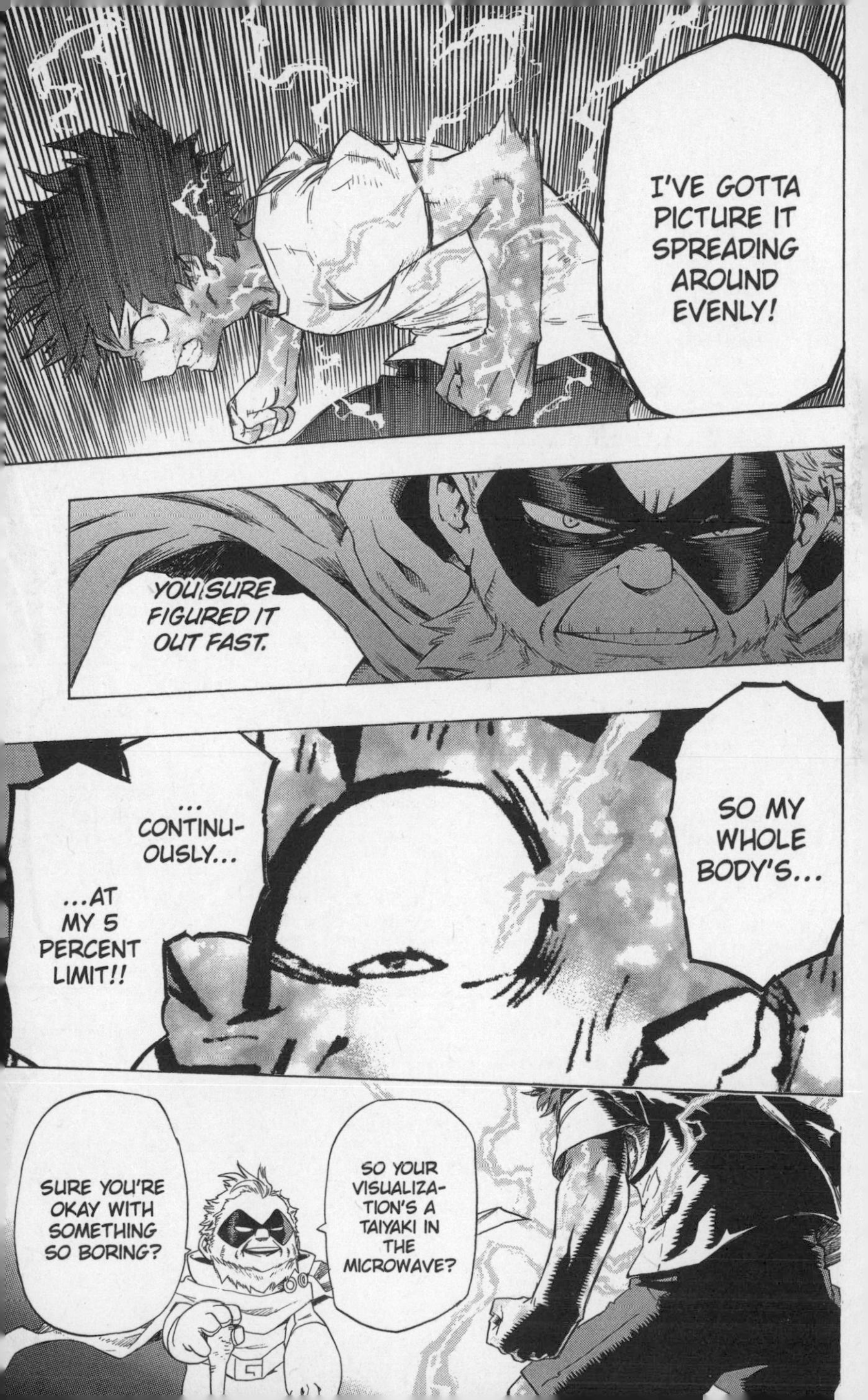
I'VE GOTTA PICTURE IT SPREADING AROUND EVENLY!
YOU SURE FIGURED IT OUT FAST.
SO MY WHOLE BODY'S...
...CONTINUOUSLY...
...AT MY 5 PERCENT LIMIT!!
SO YOUR VISUALIZATION'S A TAIYAKI IN THE MICROWAVE?
SURE YOU'RE OKAY WITH SOMETHING SO BORING?

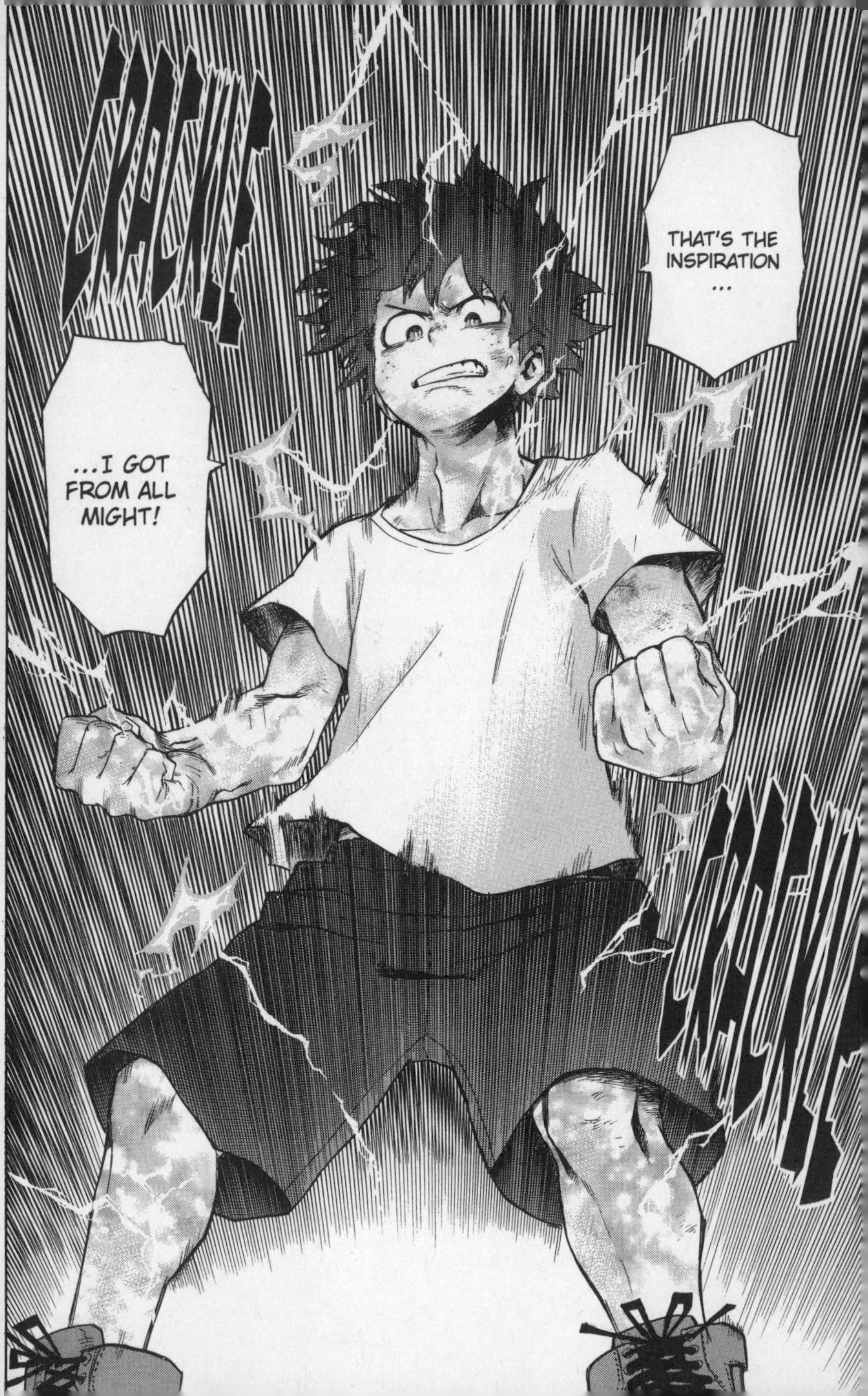
THAT'S THE INSPIRATION ...
...I GOT FROM ALL MIGHT!

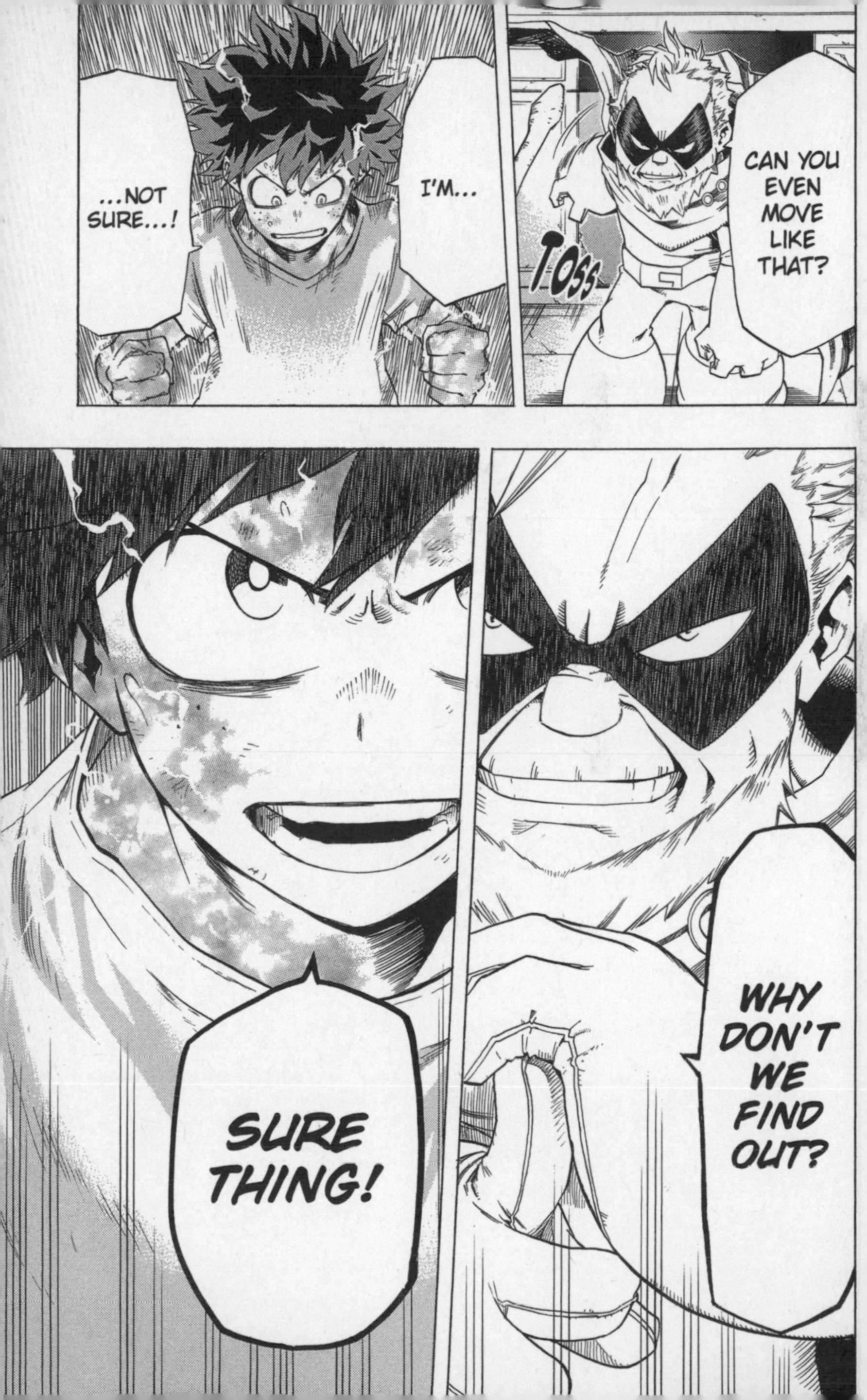
CAN YOU EVEN MOVE LIKE THAT?
TOSS
I'M...
...NOT SURE...!
WHY DON'T WE FIND OUT?
SURE THING!

HERO

BEST JEANIST (35) [TSUNAGU HAKAMADA]

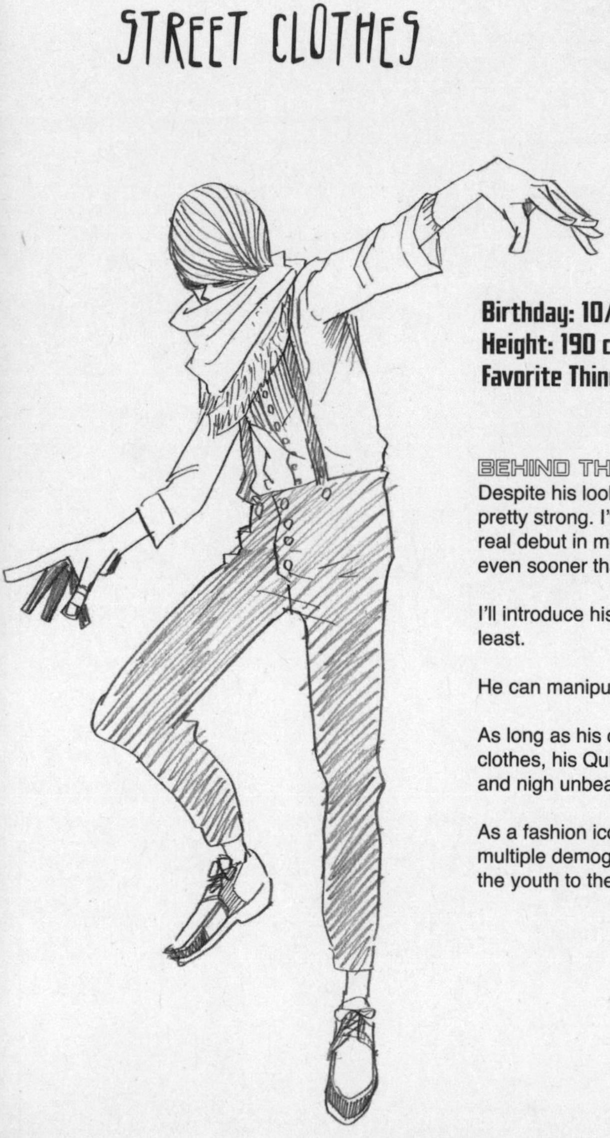
STREET CLOTHES

Birthday: 10/5
Height: 190 cm
Favorite Thing: Wolves

BEHIND THE SCENES

Despite his looks, I'm thinking he's pretty strong. I've got a time for his real debut in mind, but it might come even sooner than that.

I'll introduce his Quirk right here, at least.

He can manipulate textiles at will.

As long as his opponent's wearing clothes, his Quirk is incredibly strong and nigh unbeatable.

As a fashion icon, he's popular with multiple demographics, ranging from the youth to the middle-aged.

No. 49 - Midoriya and Shigaraki

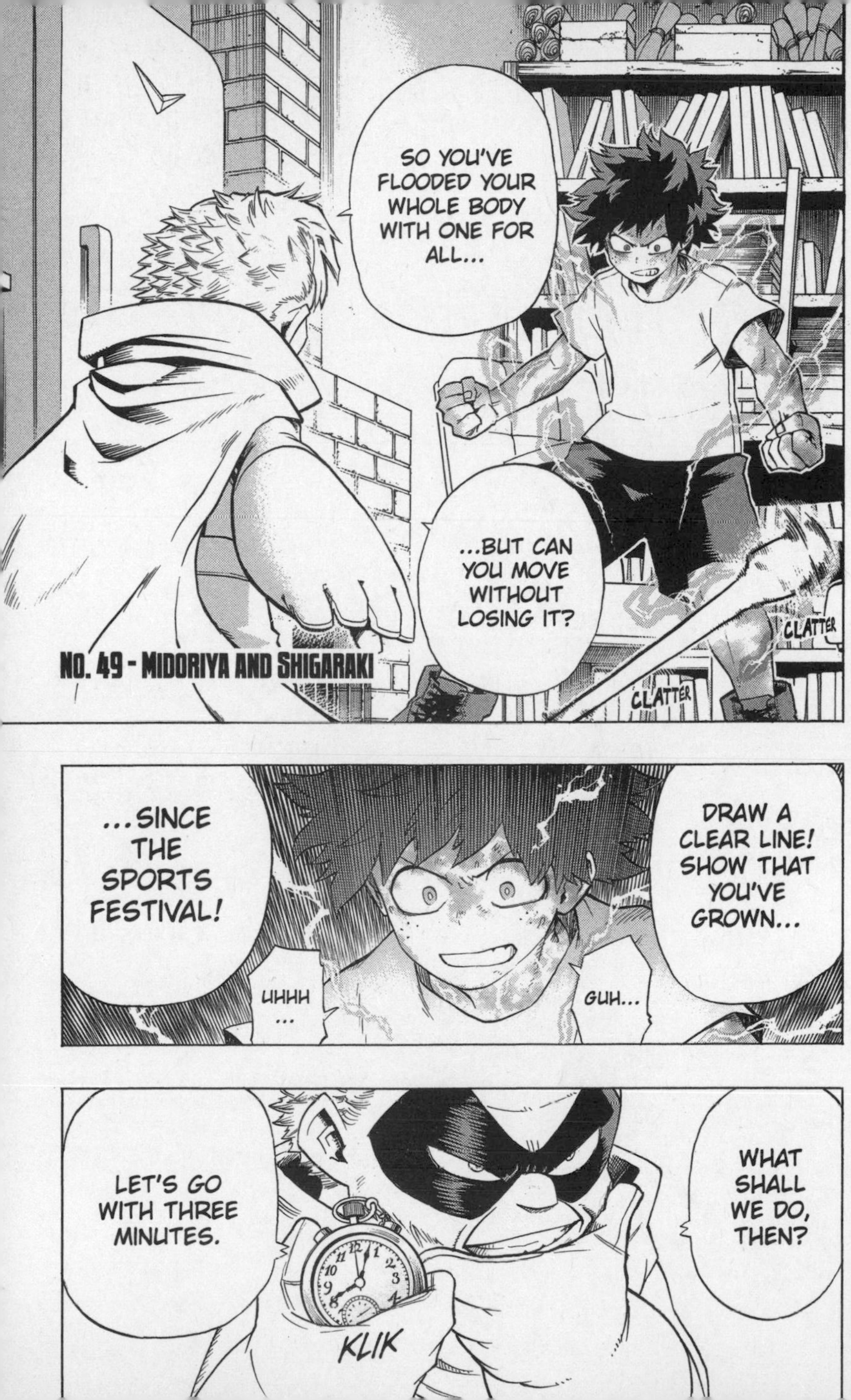
SO YOU'VE FLOODED YOUR WHOLE BODY WITH ONE FOR ALL...
...BUT CAN YOU MOVE WITHOUT LOSING IT?
CLATTER
CLATTER
DRAW A CLEAR LINE! SHOW THAT YOU'VE GROWN...
GUH...
UHHH...
...SINCE THE SPORTS FESTIVAL!
WHAT SHALL WE DO, THEN?
LET'S GO WITH THREE MINUTES.
KLIK

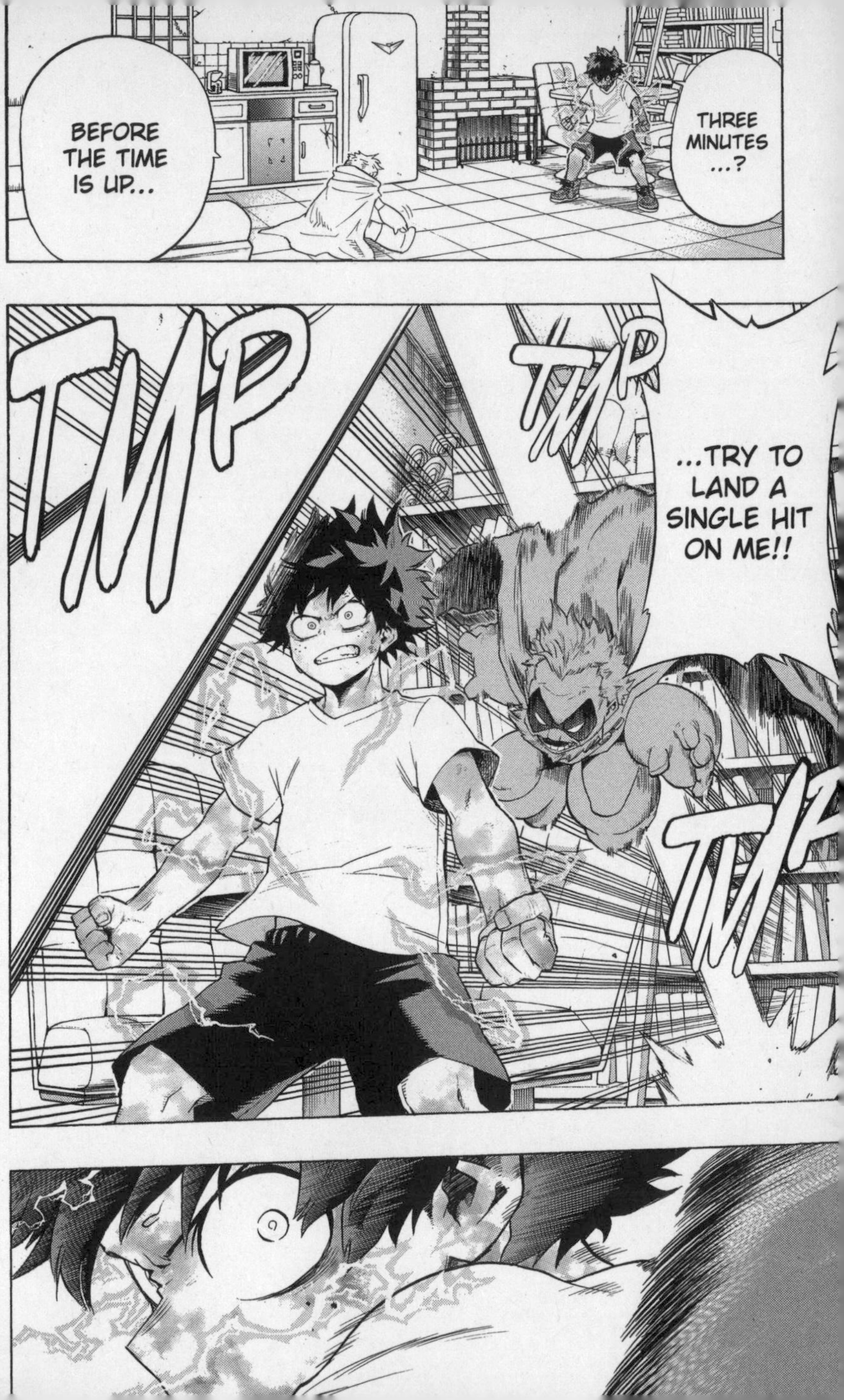
THREE MINUTES ...?
BEFORE THE TIME IS UP...
TMP
...TRY TO LAND A SINGLE HIT ON ME!!
TMP
TMP

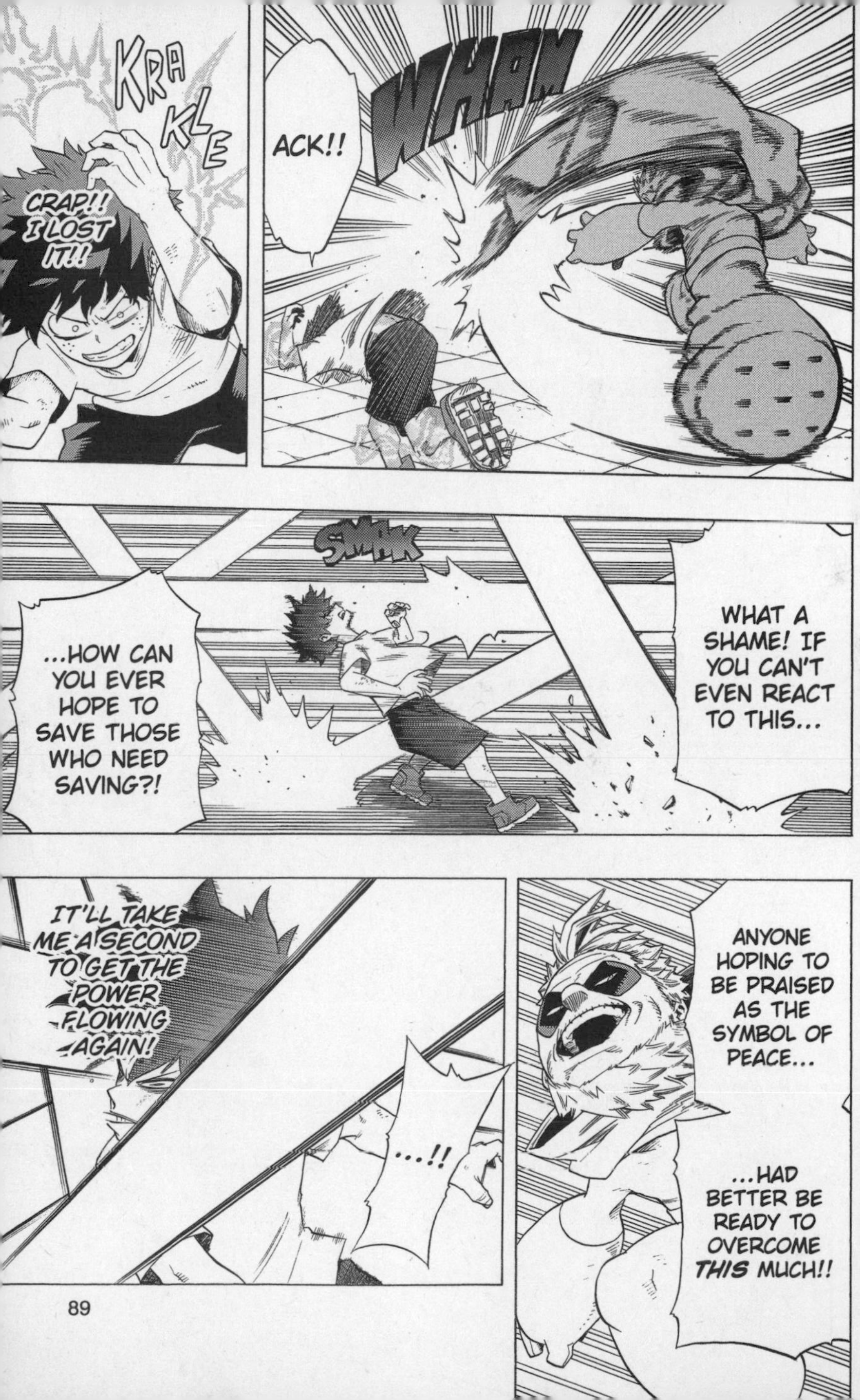
WHAM
ACK!!
KRAKLE
CRAP!! I LOST IT!!
SMAK
WHAT A SHAME! IF YOU CAN'T EVEN REACT TO THIS...
...HOW CAN YOU EVER HOPE TO SAVE THOSE WHO NEED SAVING?!
ANYONE HOPING TO BE PRAISED AS THE SYMBOL OF PEACE...
...HAD BETTER BE READY TO OVERCOME THIS MUCH!!
IT'LL TAKE ME A SECOND TO GET THE POWER FLOWING AGAIN!
...!!

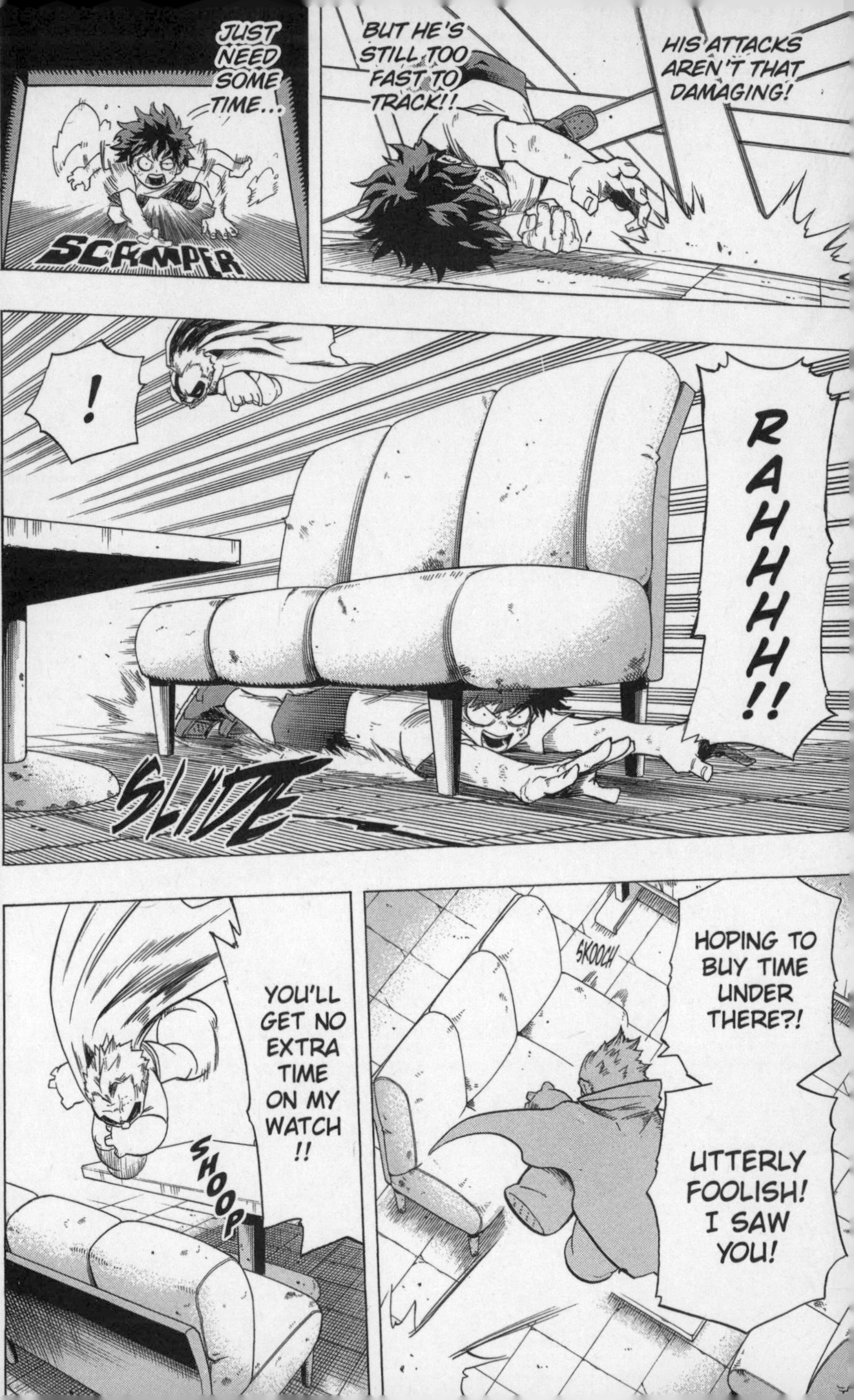
HIS ATTACKS AREN'T THAT DAMAGING!
BUT HE'S STILL TOO FAST TO TRACK!!
JUST NEED SOME TIME...
SCAMPER
RAHHHHH!!
!
SLIDE
HOPING TO BUY TIME UNDER THERE?!
SKOOCH
UTTERLY FOOLISH! I SAW YOU!
YOU'LL GET NO EXTRA TIME ON MY WATCH!!
SHOOP

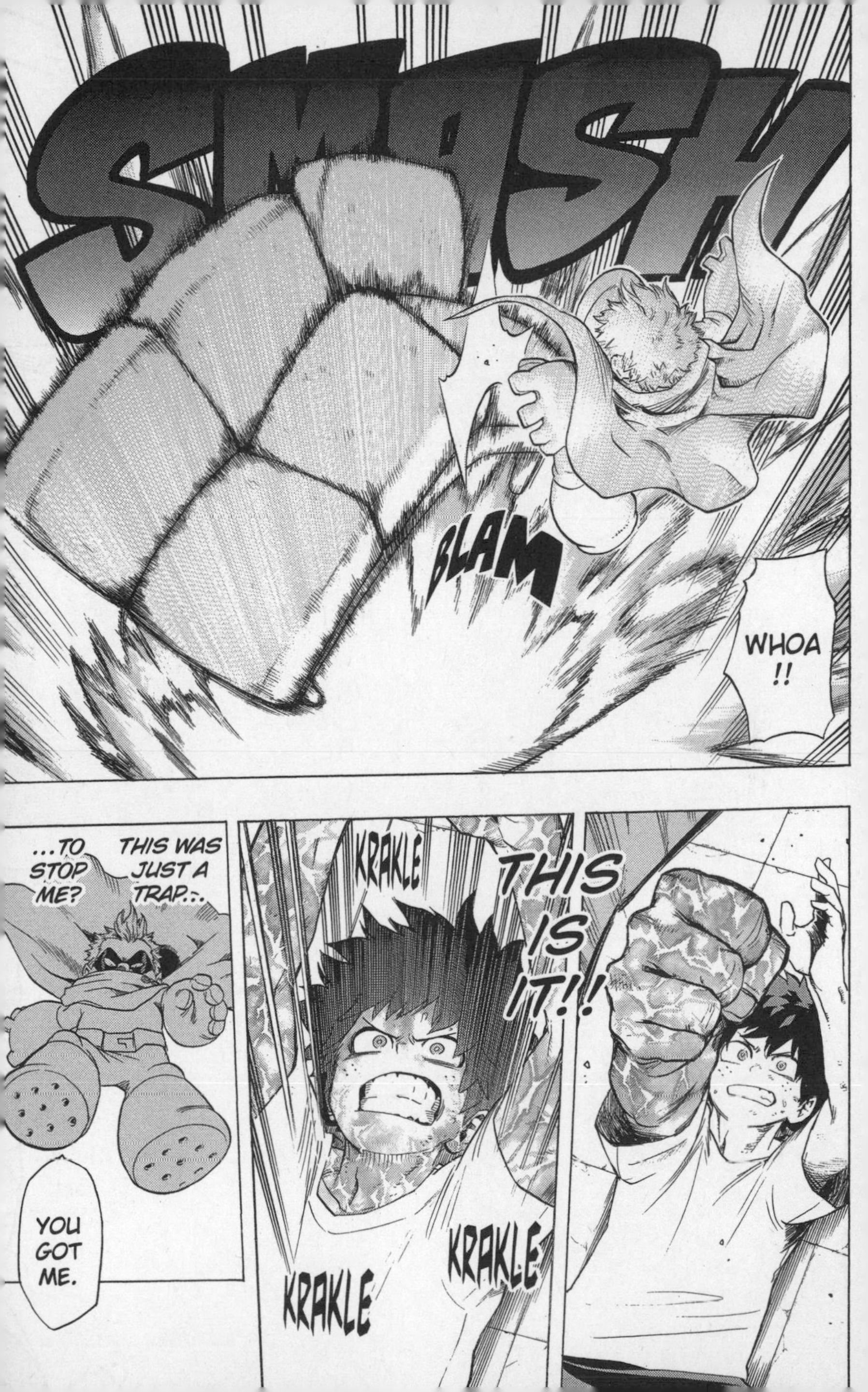
SMASH
BLAM
WHOA !!
THIS IS IT!!
KRAKLE
KRAKLE
KRAKLE
THIS WAS JUST A TRAP...
...TO STOP ME?
YOU GOT ME.

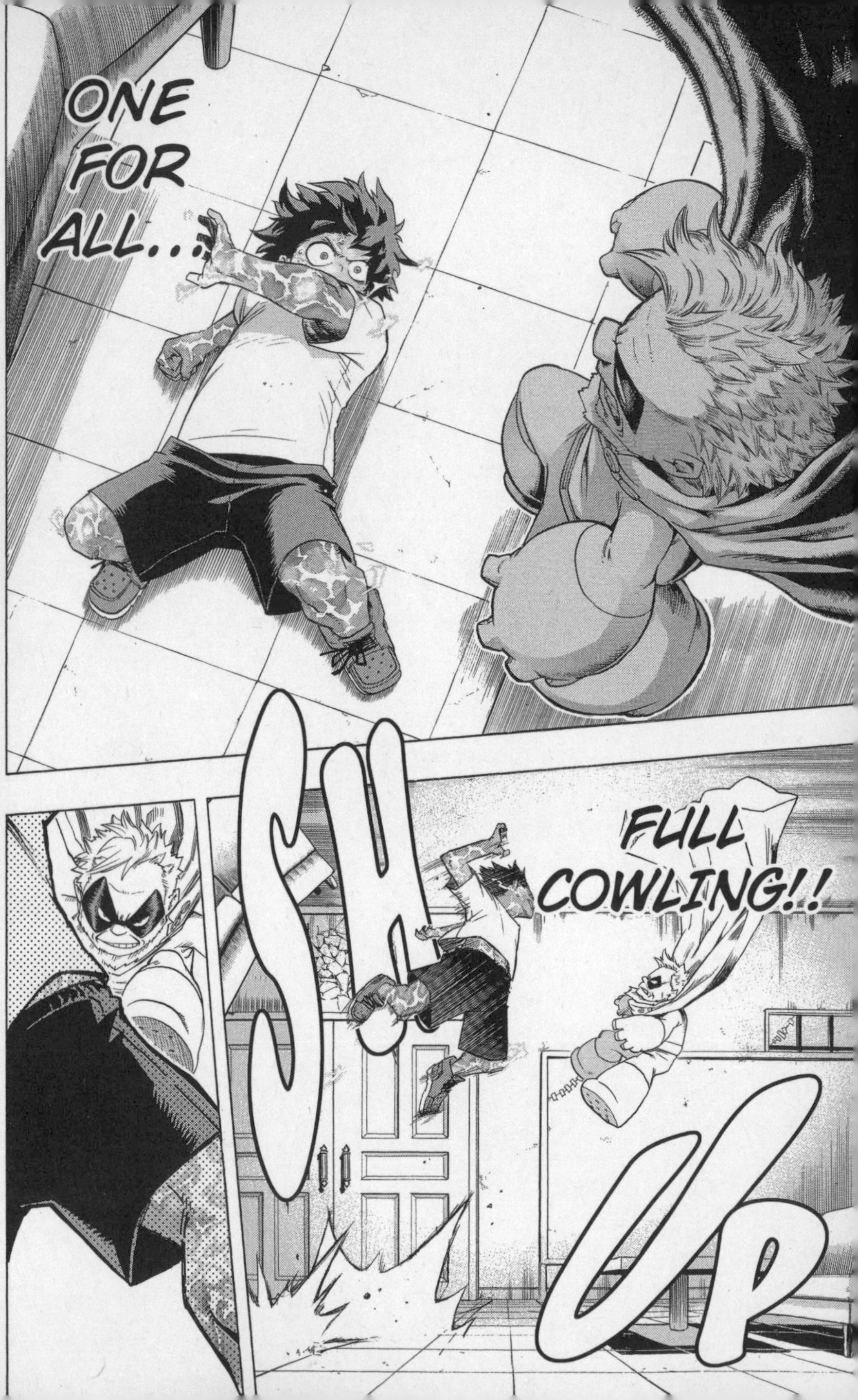
ONE FOR ALL...
FULL COWLING!!
SHUP

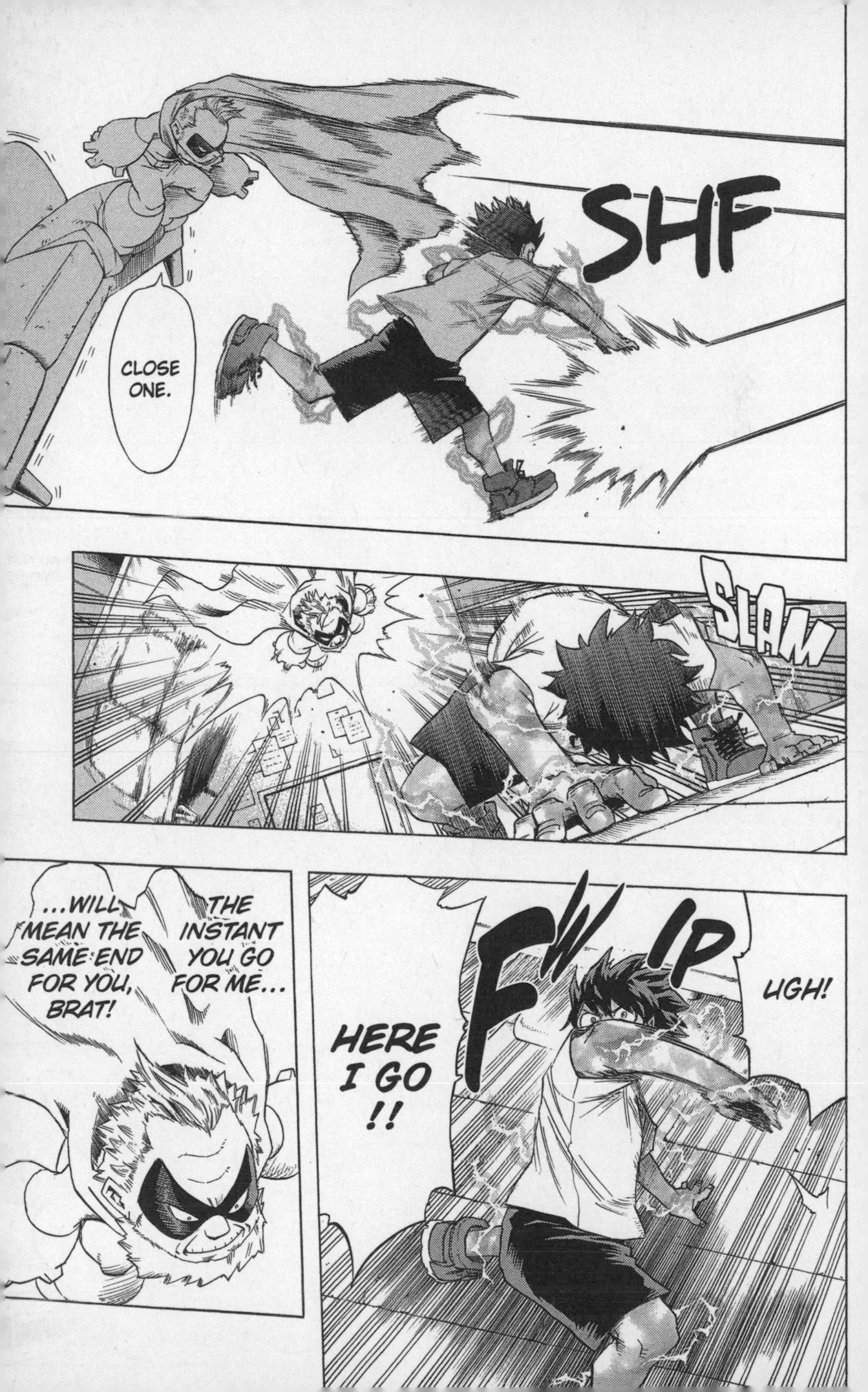
SHF
CLOSE ONE.
SLAM
FWIP
UGH!
HERE I GO!!
THE INSTANT YOU GO FOR ME...
...WILL MEAN THE SAME END FOR YOU, BRAT!

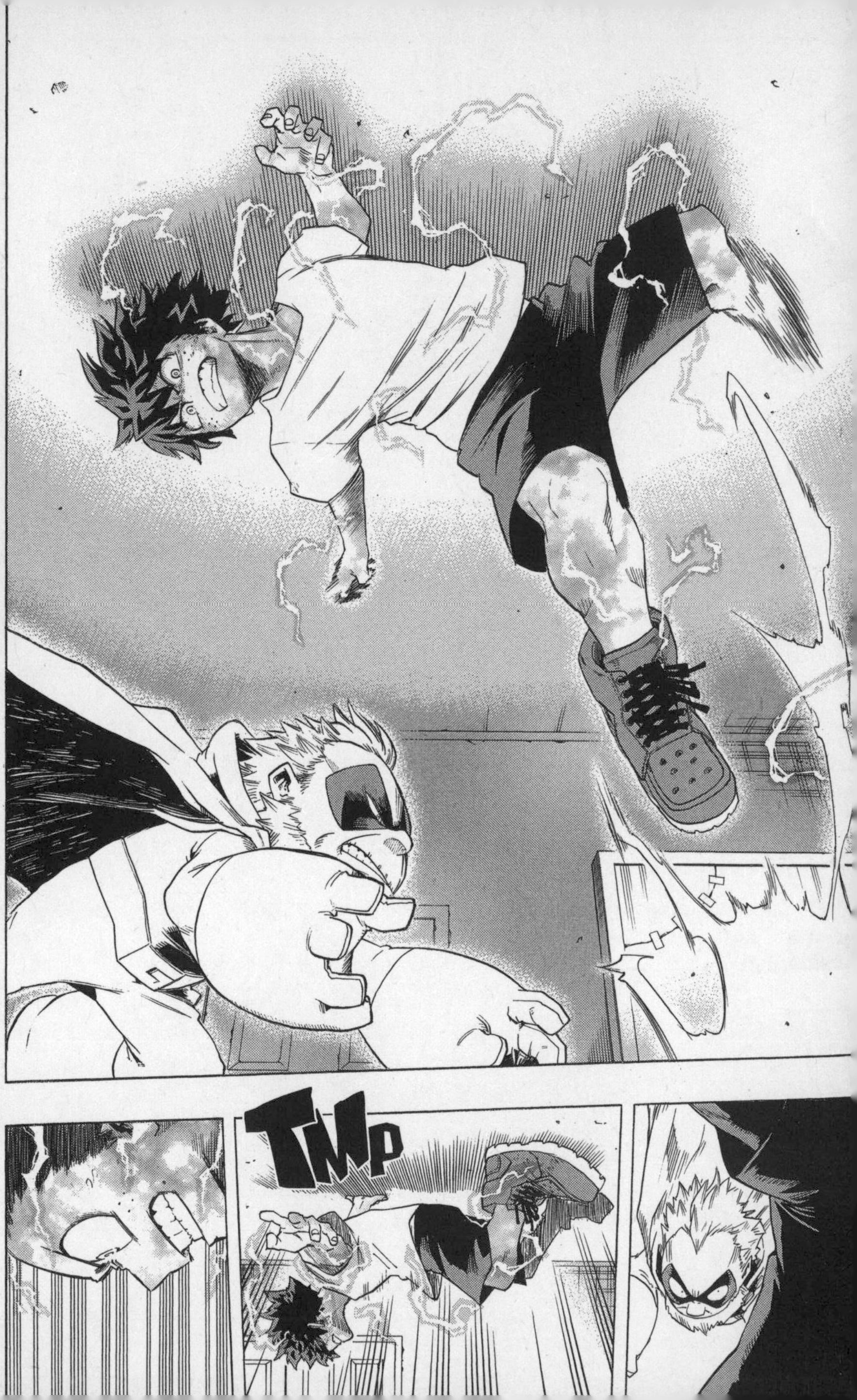
TMP

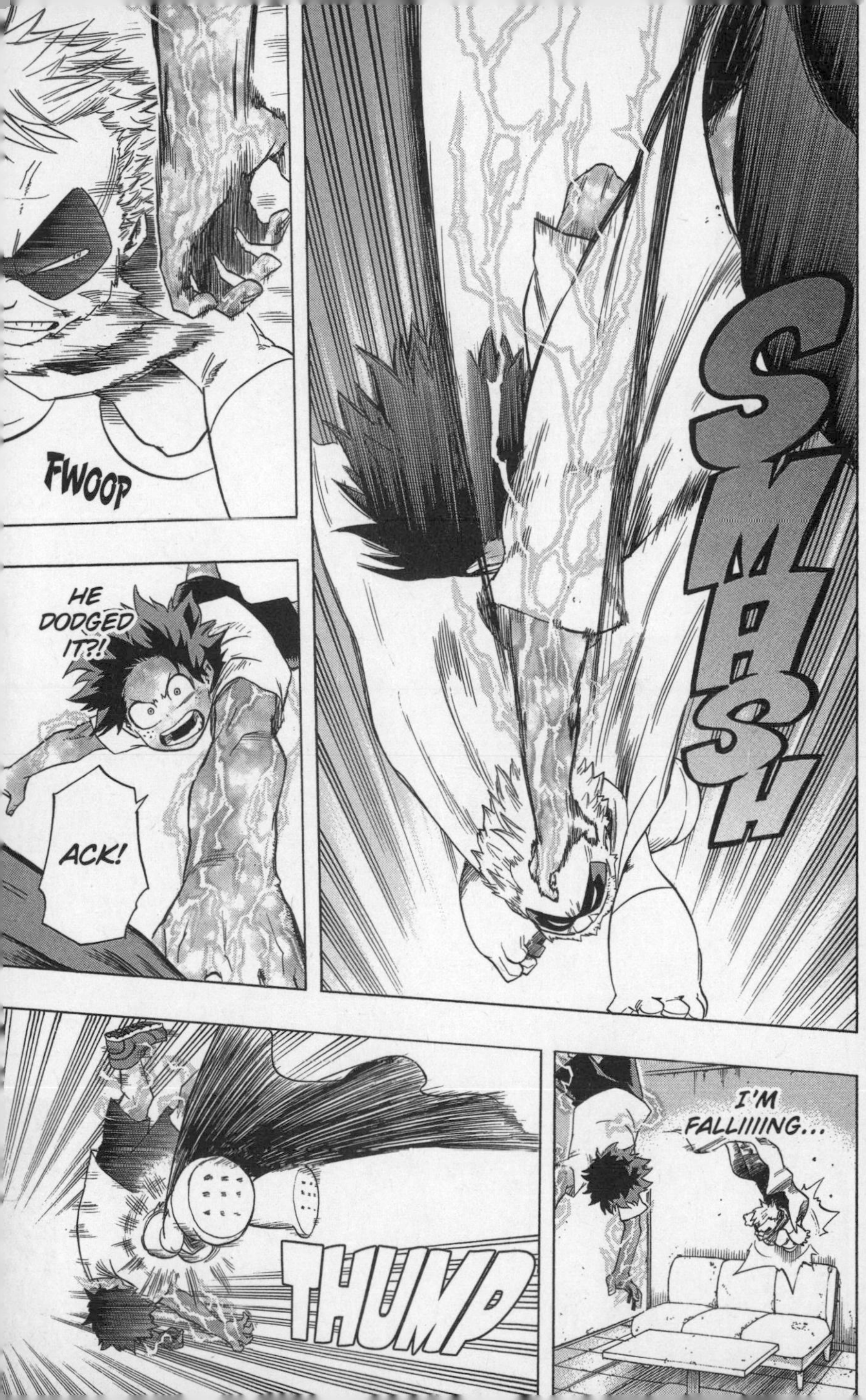
SMASH
FWOOP
HE DODGED IT?!
ACK!
I'M FALLIIIING...
THUMP

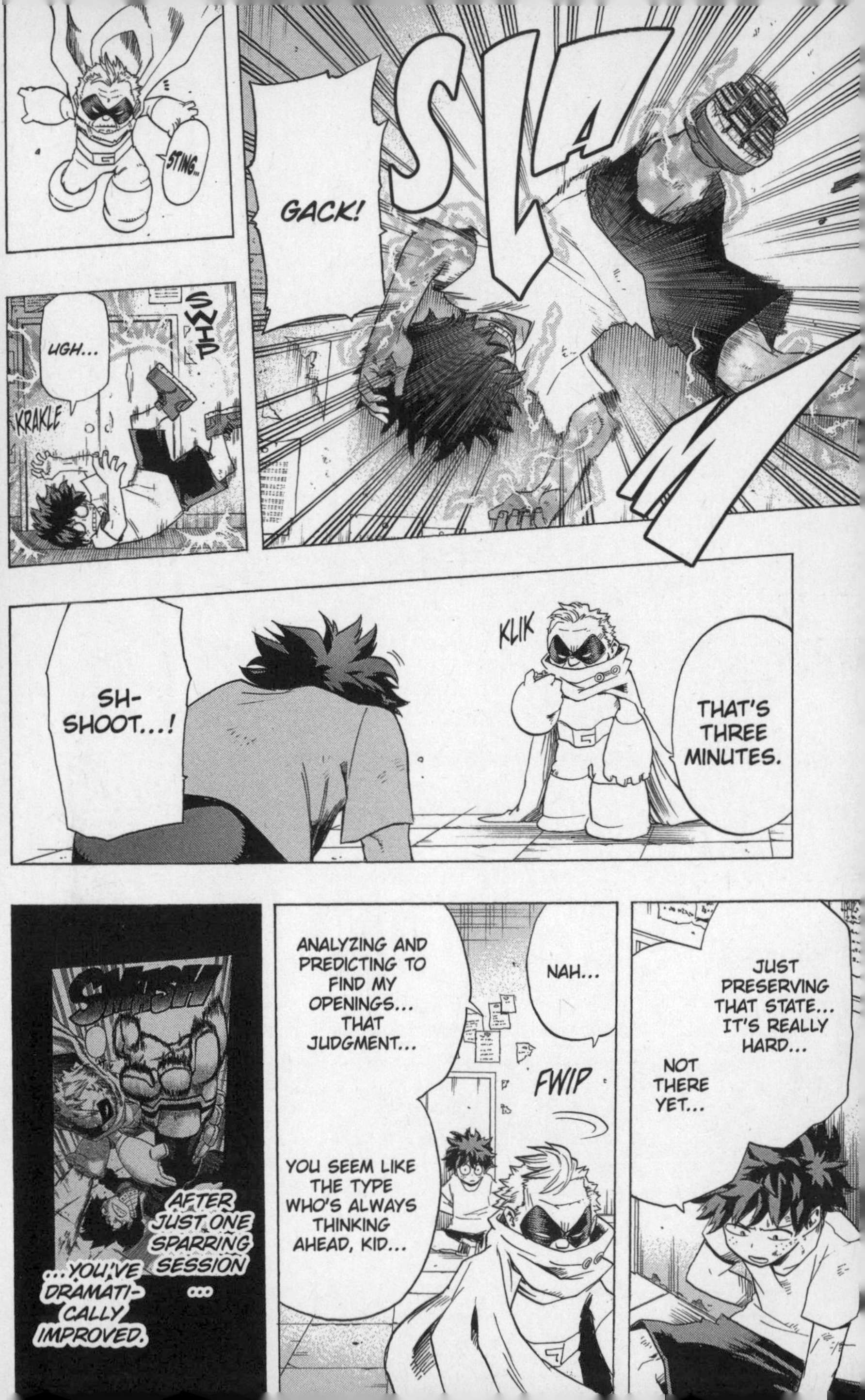
SLAM
GACK!
STING...
UGH...
SWIP
KRAKLE
THAT'S THREE MINUTES.
KLIK
SH- SHOOT...!
JUST PRESERVING THAT STATE... IT'S REALLY HARD...
NOT THERE YET...
NAH...
FWIP
ANALYZING AND PREDICTING TO FIND MY OPENINGS... THAT JUDGMENT...
YOU SEEM LIKE THE TYPE WHO'S ALWAYS THINKING AHEAD, KID...
SMASH
AFTER JUST ONE SPARRING SESSION...
...YOU'VE DRAMATI-CALLY IMPROVED.

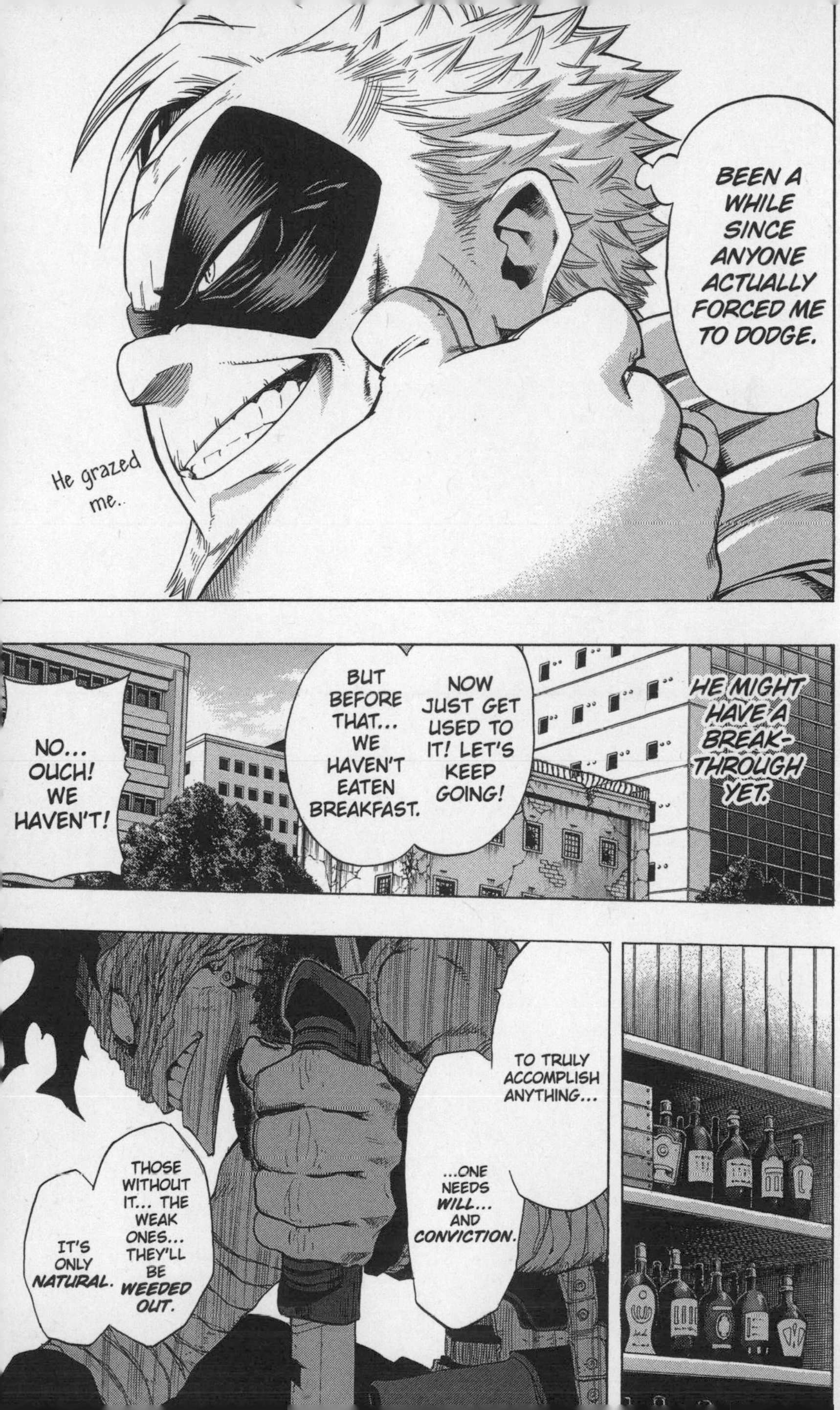

BEEN A WHILE SINCE ANYONE ACTUALLY FORCED ME TO DODGE.
He grazed me..
HE MIGHT HAVE A BREAK-THROUGH YET.
NOW JUST GET USED TO IT! LET'S KEEP GOING!
BUT BEFORE THAT... WE HAVEN'T EATEN BREAKFAST.
NO... OUCH! WE HAVEN'T!
TO TRULY ACCOMPLISH ANYTHING...
...ONE NEEDS WILL... AND CONVICTION.
THOSE WITHOUT IT... THE WEAK ONES... THEY'LL BE WEEDED OUT.
IT'S ONLY NATURAL.

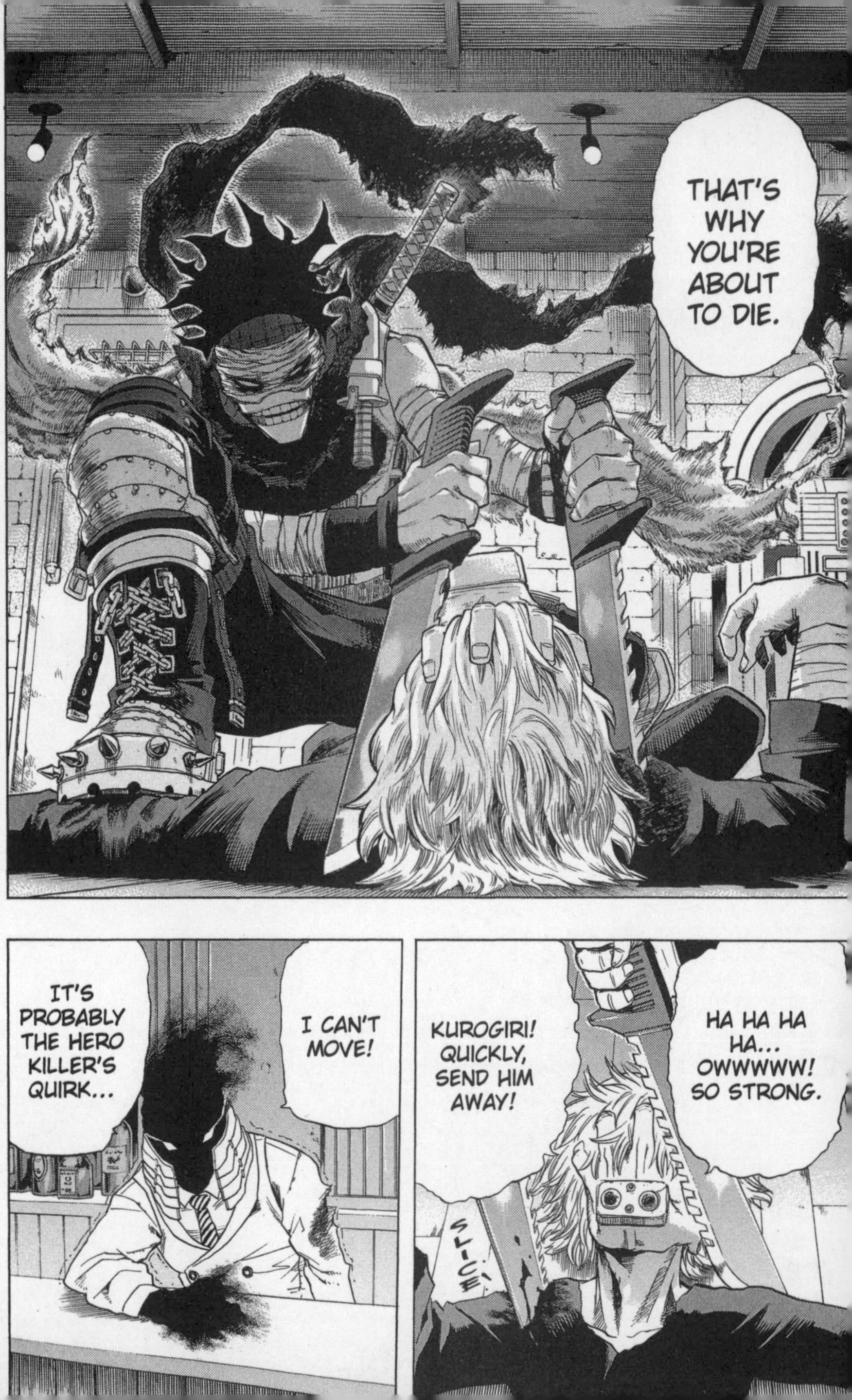
THAT'S WHY YOU'RE ABOUT TO DIE.
HA HA HA HA... OWWWWW! SO STRONG.
KUROGIRI! QUICKLY, SEND HIM AWAY!
SLICE
I CAN'T MOVE!
IT'S PROBABLY THE HERO KILLER'S QUIRK...

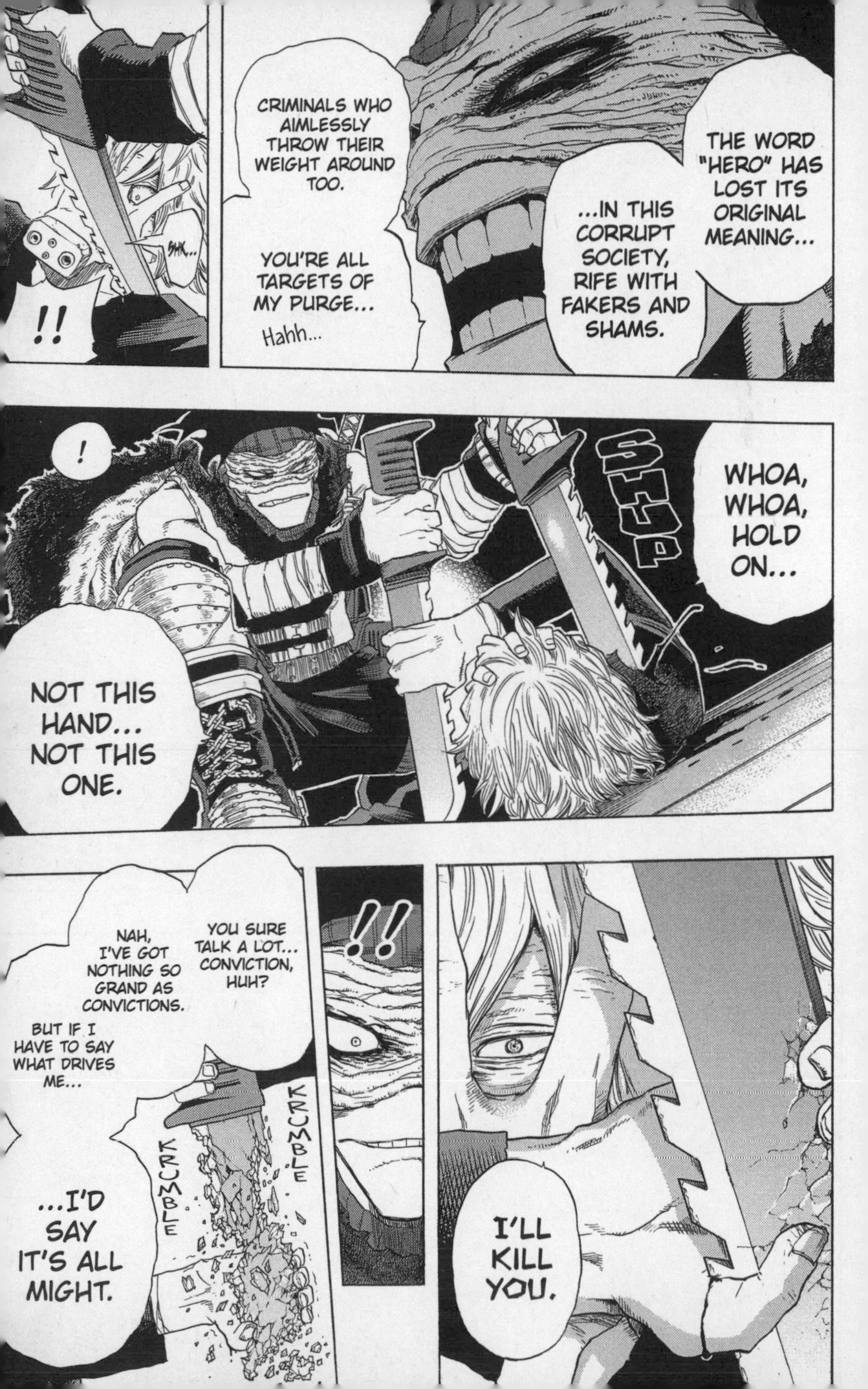
THE WORD "HERO" HAS LOST ITS ORIGINAL MEANING...
...IN THIS CORRUPT SOCIETY, RIFE WITH FAKERS AND SHAMS.
CRIMINALS WHO AIMLESSLY THROW THEIR WEIGHT AROUND TOO.
YOU'RE ALL TARGETS OF MY PURGE...
Hahh...
SHK...
!!
WHOA, WHOA, HOLD ON...
SHUP
!
NOT THIS HAND... NOT THIS ONE.
I'LL KILL YOU.
!!
YOU SURE TALK A LOT... CONVICTION, HUH?
NAH, I'VE GOT NOTHING SO GRAND AS CONVICTIONS.
BUT IF I HAVE TO SAY WHAT DRIVES ME...
KRUMBLE
KRUMBLE
...I'D SAY IT'S ALL MIGHT.

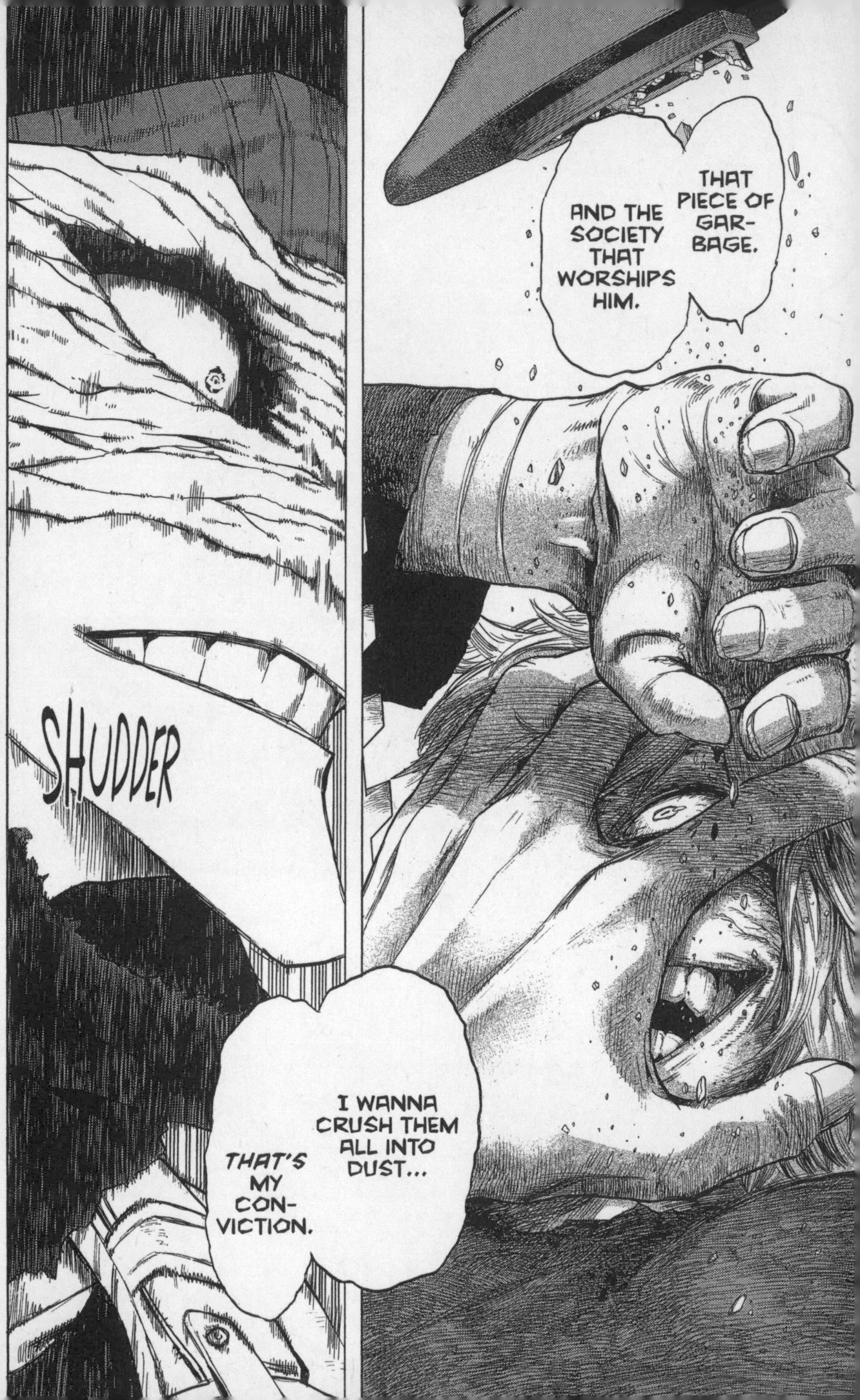
THAT PIECE OF GAR-BAGE.
AND THE SOCIETY THAT WORSHIPS HIM.
I WANNA CRUSH THEM ALL INTO DUST...
THAT'S MY CON-VICTION.
SHUDDER

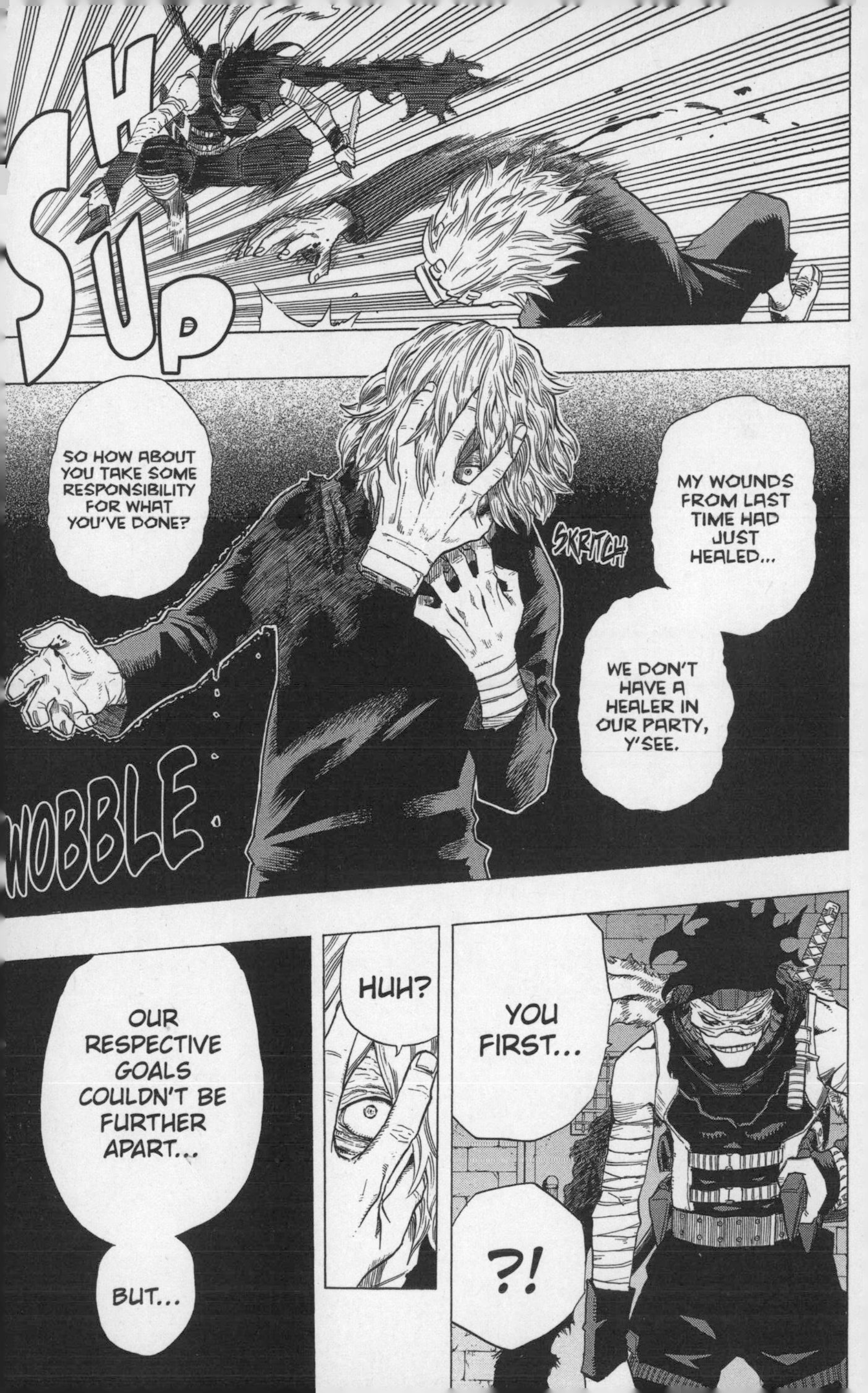
SHUP
MY WOUNDS FROM LAST TIME HAD JUST HEALED...
SKRITCH
WE DON'T HAVE A HEALER IN OUR PARTY, Y'SEE.
SO HOW ABOUT YOU TAKE SOME RESPONSIBILITY FOR WHAT YOU'VE DONE?
WOBBLE
YOU FIRST...
?!
HUH?
OUR RESPECTIVE GOALS COULDN'T BE FURTHER APART...
BUT...

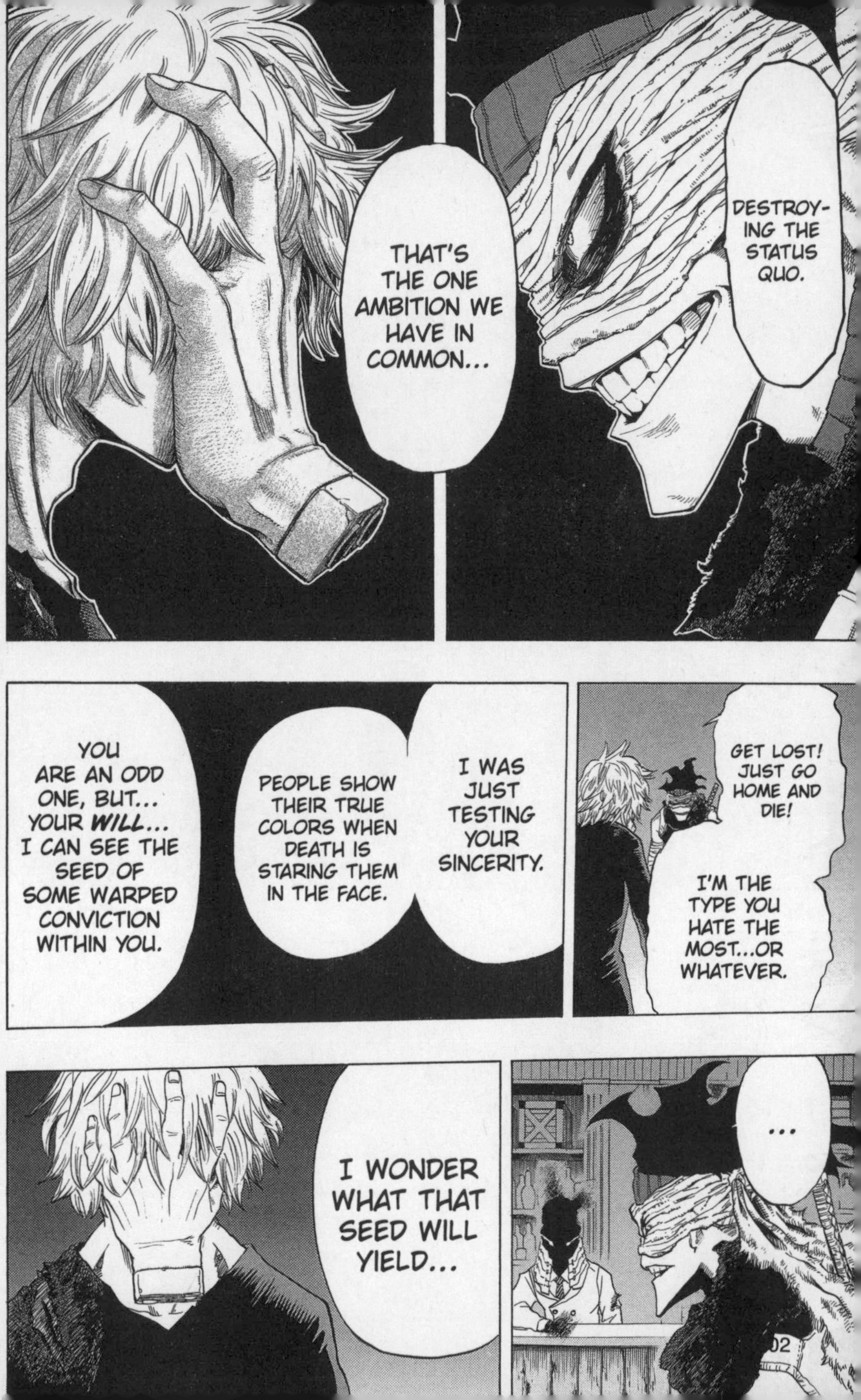
DESTROYING THE STATUS QUO.
THAT'S THE ONE AMBITION WE HAVE IN COMMON...
GET LOST! JUST GO HOME AND DIE!
I'M THE TYPE YOU HATE THE MOST...OR WHATEVER.
I WAS JUST TESTING YOUR SINCERITY.
PEOPLE SHOW THEIR TRUE COLORS WHEN DEATH IS STARING THEM IN THE FACE.
YOU ARE AN ODD ONE, BUT... YOUR *WILL*... I CAN SEE THE SEED OF SOME WARPED CONVICTION WITHIN YOU.
...
I WONDER WHAT THAT SEED WILL YIELD...

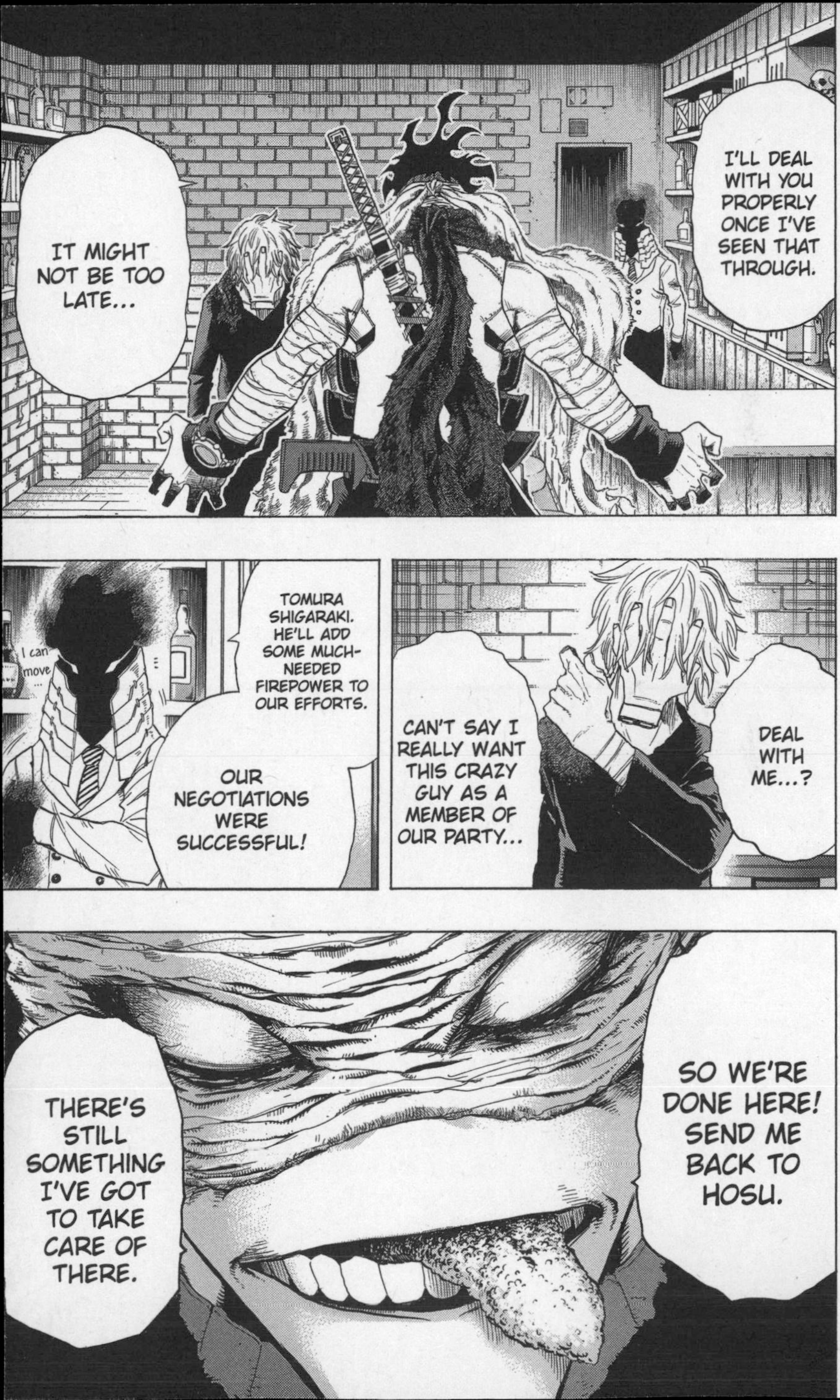
I'LL DEAL WITH YOU PROPERLY ONCE I'VE SEEN THAT THROUGH.
IT MIGHT NOT BE TOO LATE...
DEAL WITH ME...?
CAN'T SAY I REALLY WANT THIS CRAZY GUY AS A MEMBER OF OUR PARTY...
TOMURA SHIGARAKI. HE'LL ADD SOME MUCH-NEEDED FIREPOWER TO OUR EFFORTS.
OUR NEGOTIATIONS WERE SUCCESSFUL!
I can move...
SO WE'RE DONE HERE! SEND ME BACK TO HOSU.
THERE'S STILL SOMETHING I'VE GOT TO TAKE CARE OF THERE.

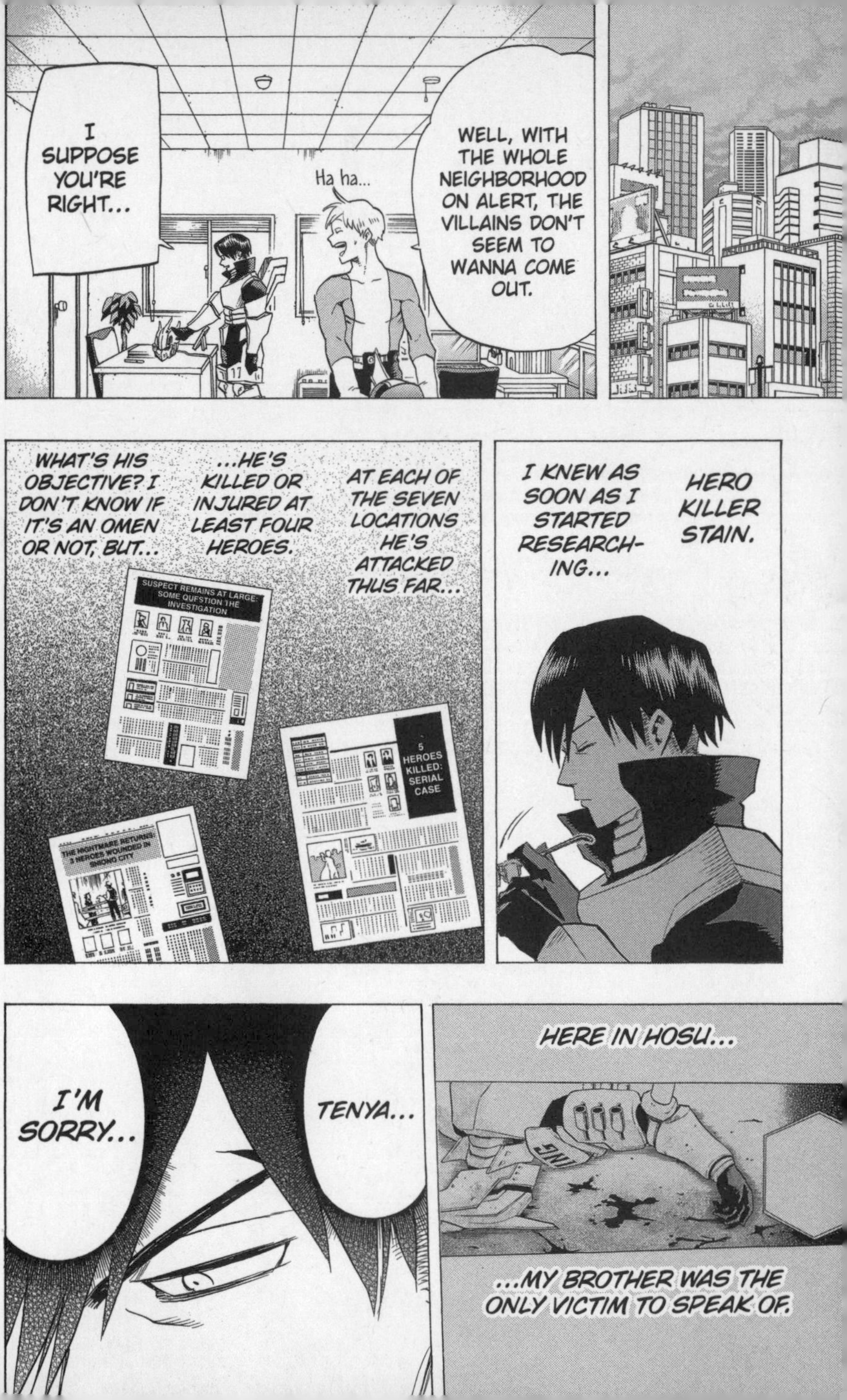
WELL, WITH THE WHOLE NEIGHBORHOOD ON ALERT, THE VILLAINS DON'T SEEM TO WANNA COME OUT.
Ha ha...
I SUPPOSE YOU'RE RIGHT...
HERO KILLER STAIN.
I KNEW AS SOON AS I STARTED RESEARCHING...
AT EACH OF THE SEVEN LOCATIONS HE'S ATTACKED THUS FAR...
...HE'S KILLED OR INJURED AT LEAST FOUR HEROES.
WHAT'S HIS OBJECTIVE? I DON'T KNOW IF IT'S AN OMEN OR NOT, BUT...
SUSPECT REMAINS AT LARGE: SOME QUESTION THE INVESTIGATION
5 HEROES KILLED: SERIAL CASE
THE NIGHTMARE RETURNS: 3 HEROES WOUNDED IN SHIONO CITY
HERE IN HOSU...
...MY BROTHER WAS THE ONLY VICTIM TO SPEAK OF.
TENYA...
I'M SORRY...

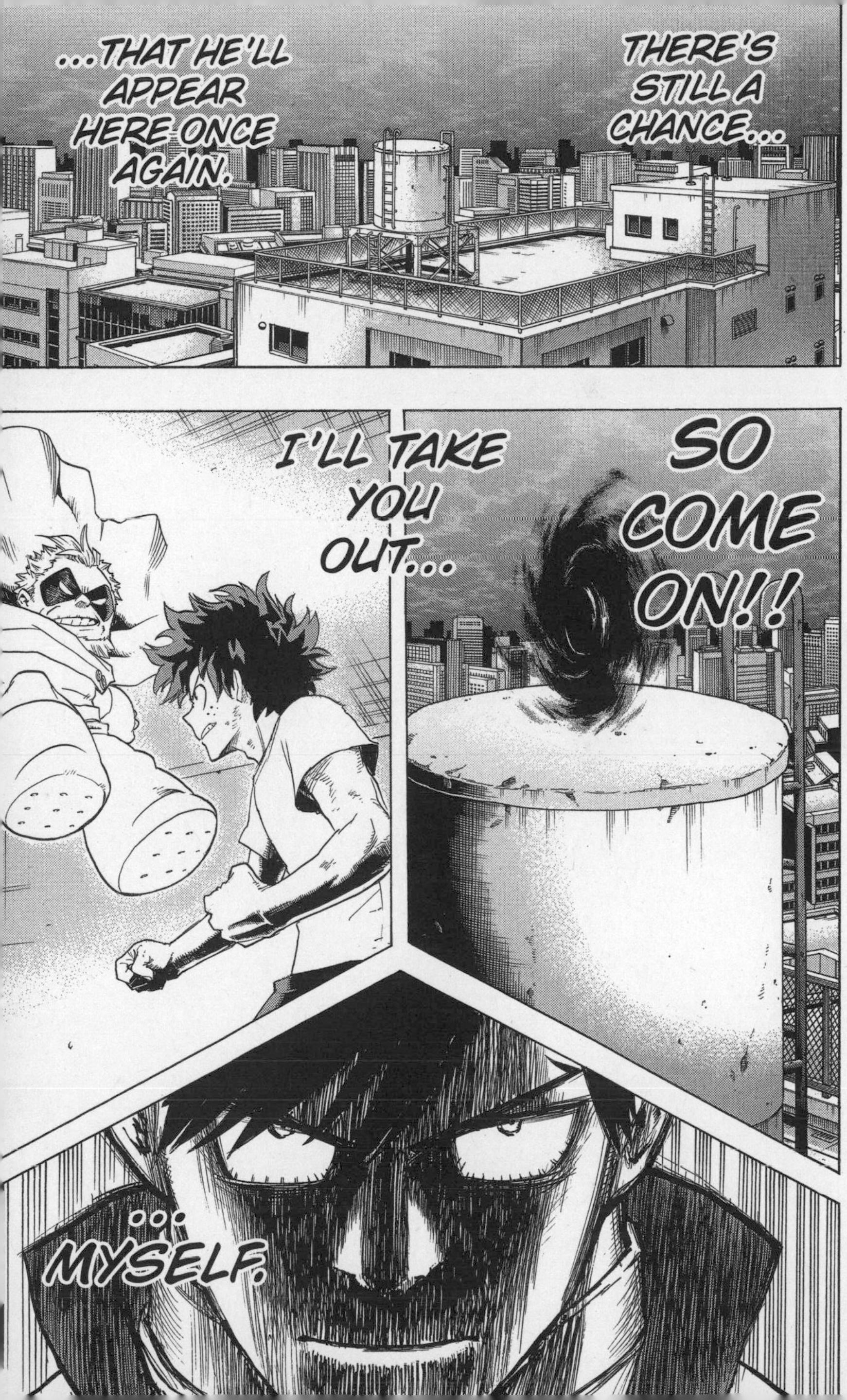
THERE'S STILL A CHANCE...
...THAT HE'LL APPEAR HERE ONCE AGAIN.
SO COME ON!!
I'LL TAKE YOU OUT...
...MYSELF.

THE PROS

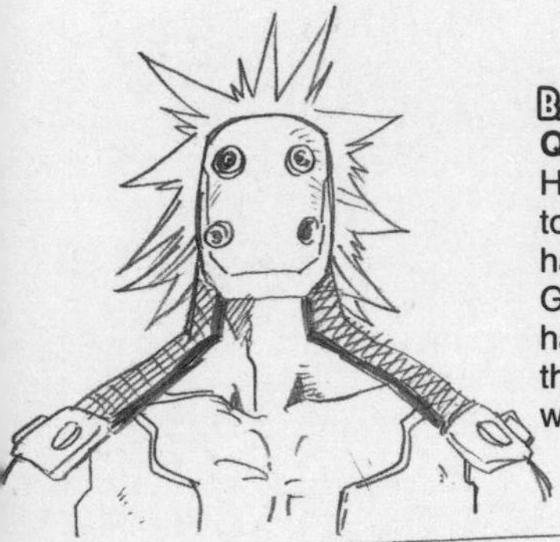

BATTLE HERO: GUNHEAD

QUIRK: GATLING

He's got gun-like devices attached to his arms that can shoot out hardened, keratin-like masses. Gunhead specializes in hand-to-hand combat, so they mostly serve as warning shots.

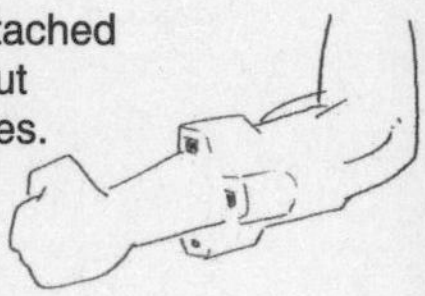

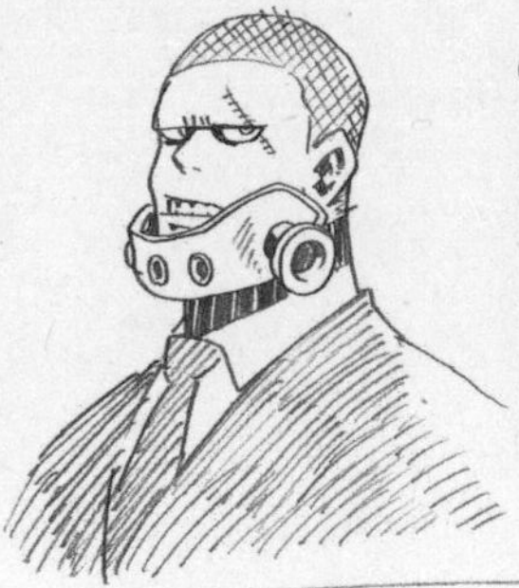

CHIVALROUS HERO: FOURTH KIND

QUIRK: QUAD ARMS

As his Quirk name suggests, he's literally got four arms. Fourth Kind also specializes in hand-to-hand combat, but perhaps more worthy of mention is his calm and collected nature that allows him to come up with battle tactics.

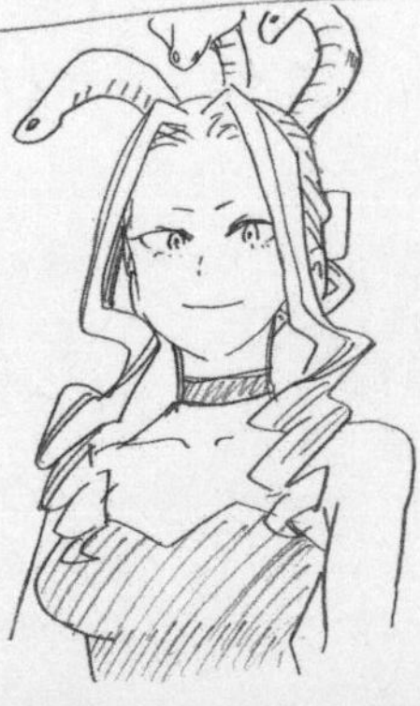

SNAKE HERO: UWABAMI

QUIRK: SERPENTRESS

The ends of her hair are snakes. The snakes are great at seeking out villains who may be fleeing or hiding, allowing for quick capture.

She's not an amazing combatant by any means, but her assistance in arresting villains is undeniable.

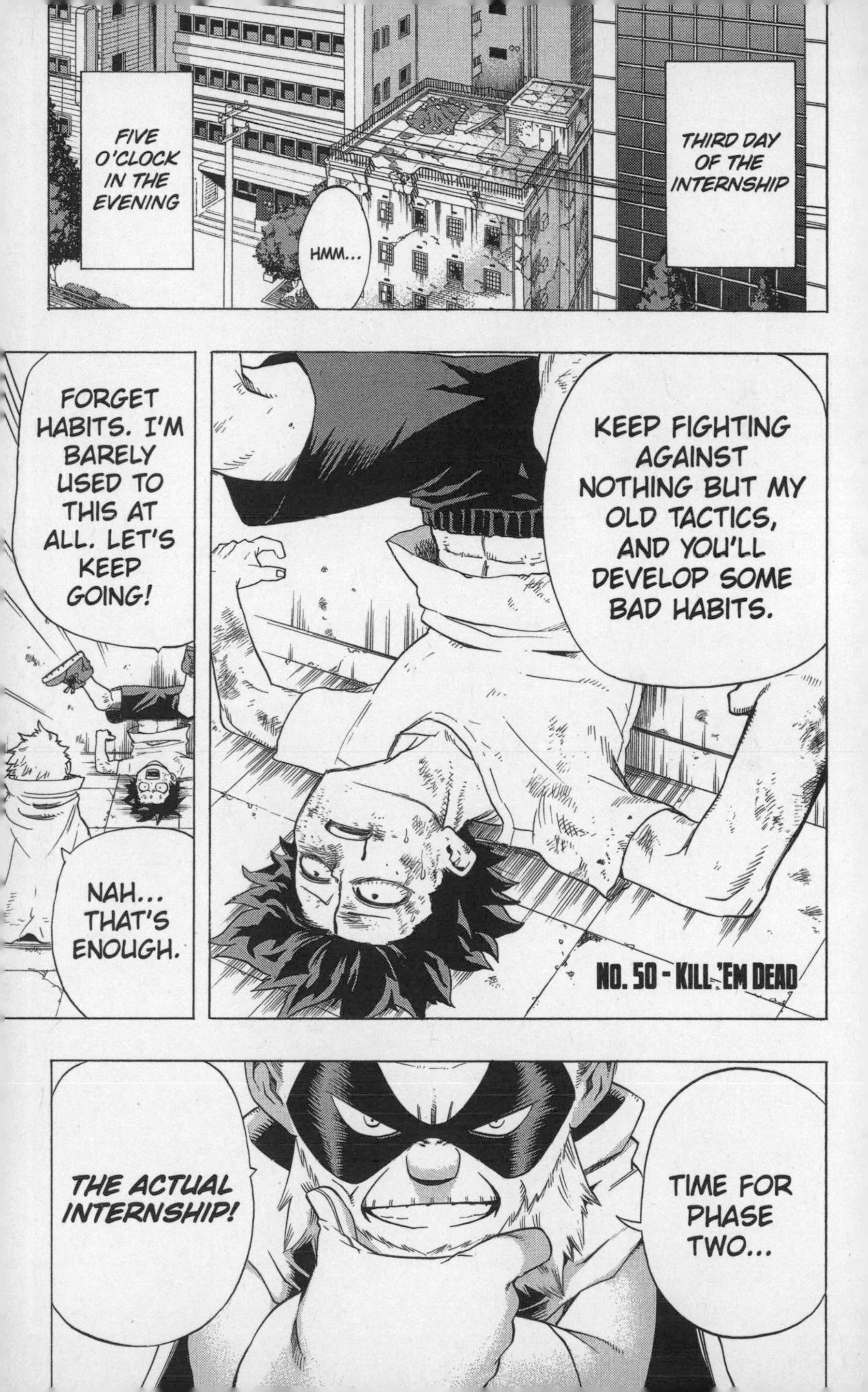
THIRD DAY OF THE INTERNSHIP
FIVE O'CLOCK IN THE EVENING
HMM...
KEEP FIGHTING AGAINST NOTHING BUT MY OLD TACTICS, AND YOU'LL DEVELOP SOME BAD HABITS.
NO. 50 - KILL 'EM DEAD
FORGET HABITS. I'M BARELY USED TO THIS AT ALL. LET'S KEEP GOING!
NAH... THAT'S ENOUGH.
TIME FOR PHASE TWO...
THE ACTUAL INTERNSHIP!

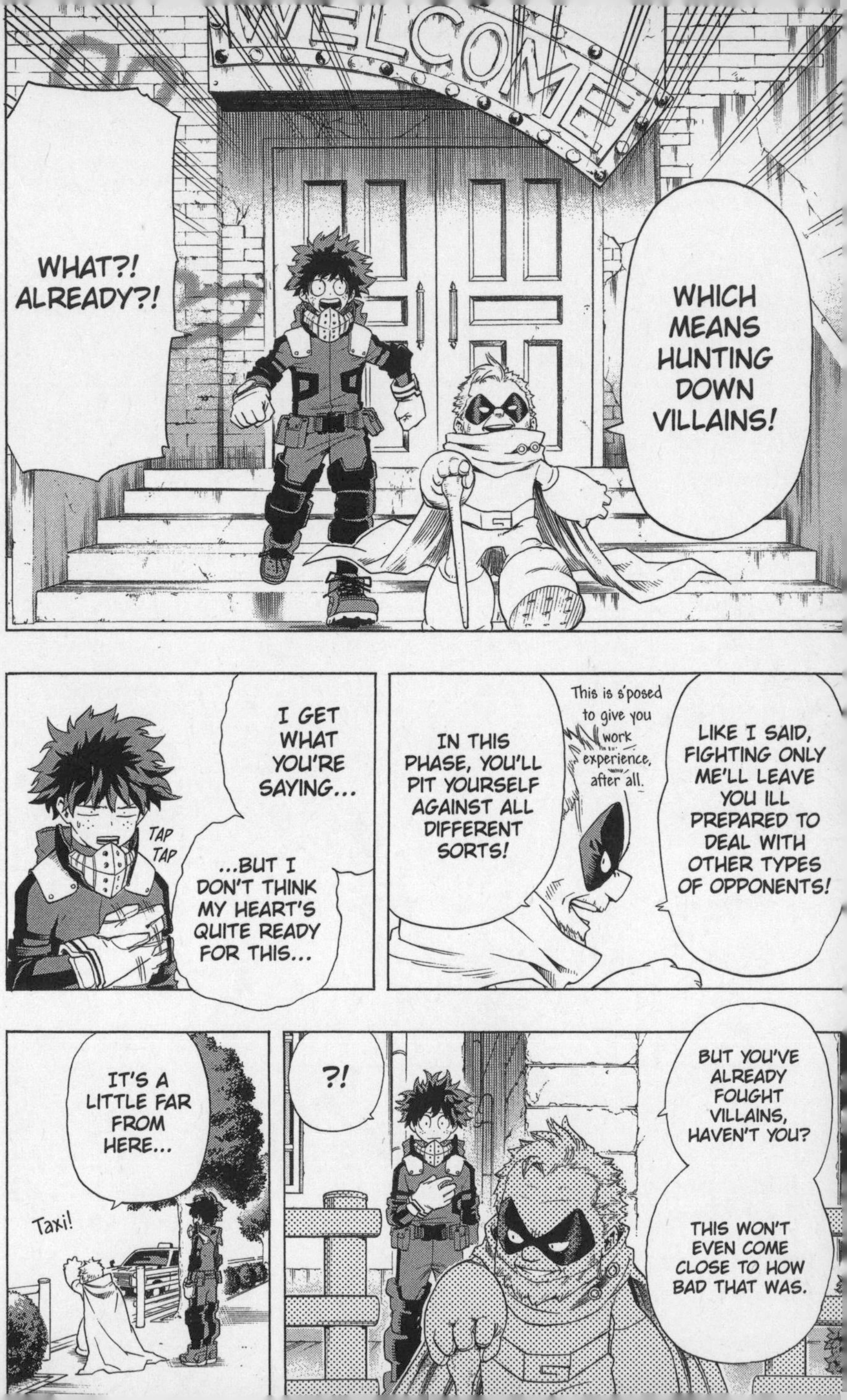
WHICH MEANS HUNTING DOWN VILLAINS!
WHAT?! ALREADY?!
LIKE I SAID, FIGHTING ONLY ME'LL LEAVE YOU ILL PREPARED TO DEAL WITH OTHER TYPES OF OPPONENTS!
This is s'posed to give you work experience, after all.
IN THIS PHASE, YOU'LL PIT YOURSELF AGAINST ALL DIFFERENT SORTS!
I GET WHAT YOU'RE SAYING...
TAP TAP
...BUT I DON'T THINK MY HEART'S QUITE READY FOR THIS...
BUT YOU'VE ALREADY FOUGHT VILLAINS, HAVEN'T YOU?
THIS WON'T EVEN COME CLOSE TO HOW BAD THAT WAS.
?!
IT'S A LITTLE FAR FROM HERE...
Taxi!

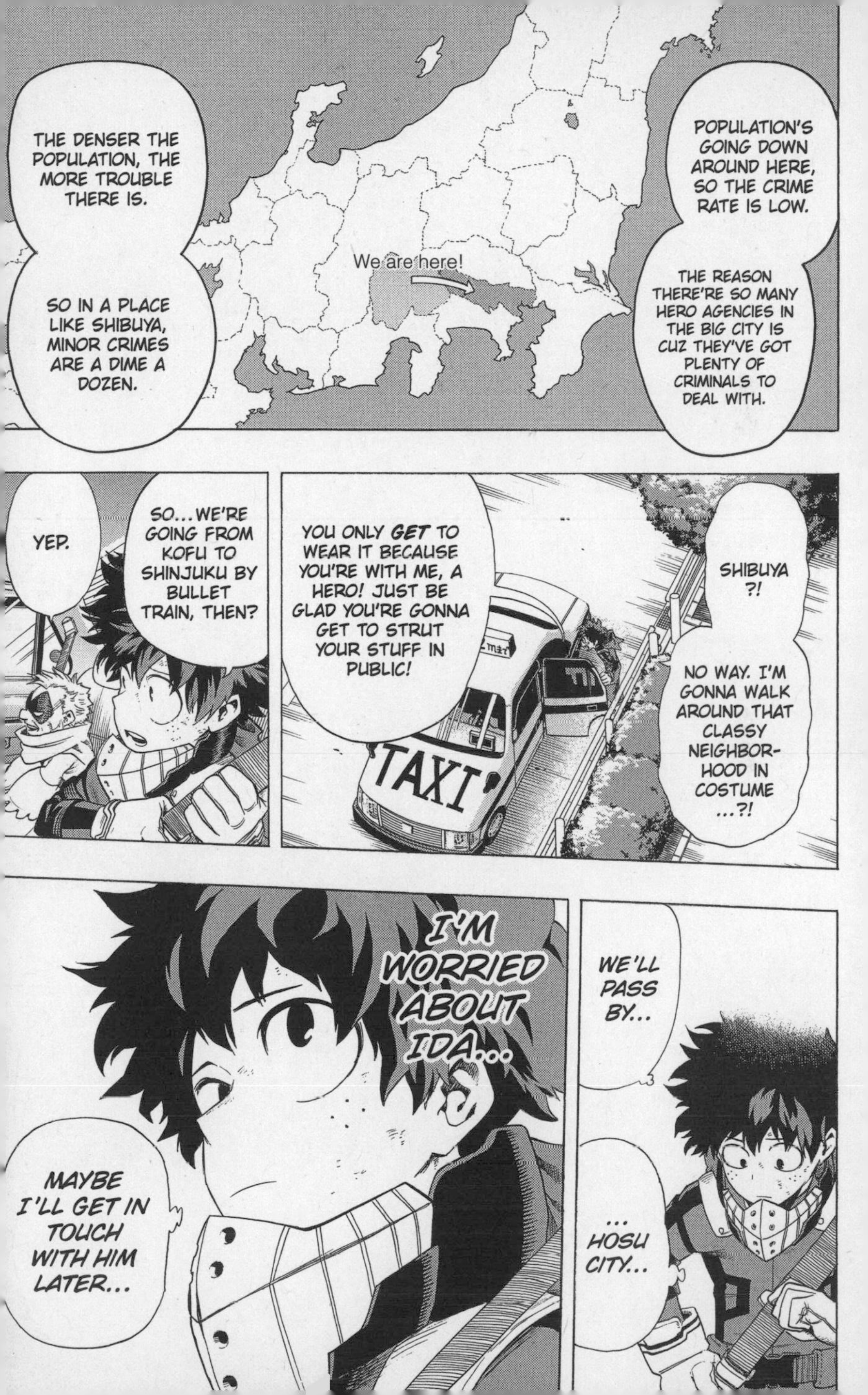
POPULATION'S GOING DOWN AROUND HERE, SO THE CRIME RATE IS LOW.
THE REASON THERE'RE SO MANY HERO AGENCIES IN THE BIG CITY IS CUZ THEY'VE GOT PLENTY OF CRIMINALS TO DEAL WITH.
We are here!
THE DENSER THE POPULATION, THE MORE TROUBLE THERE IS.
SO IN A PLACE LIKE SHIBUYA, MINOR CRIMES ARE A DIME A DOZEN.
SHIBUYA ?!
NO WAY. I'M GONNA WALK AROUND THAT CLASSY NEIGHBOR-HOOD IN COSTUME ...?!
YOU ONLY GET TO WEAR IT BECAUSE YOU'RE WITH ME, A HERO! JUST BE GLAD YOU'RE GONNA GET TO STRUT YOUR STUFF IN PUBLIC!
TAXI
SO...WE'RE GOING FROM KOFU TO SHINJUKU BY BULLET TRAIN, THEN?
YEP.
WE'LL PASS BY...
...HOSU CITY...
I'M WORRIED ABOUT IDA...
MAYBE I'LL GET IN TOUCH WITH HIM LATER...

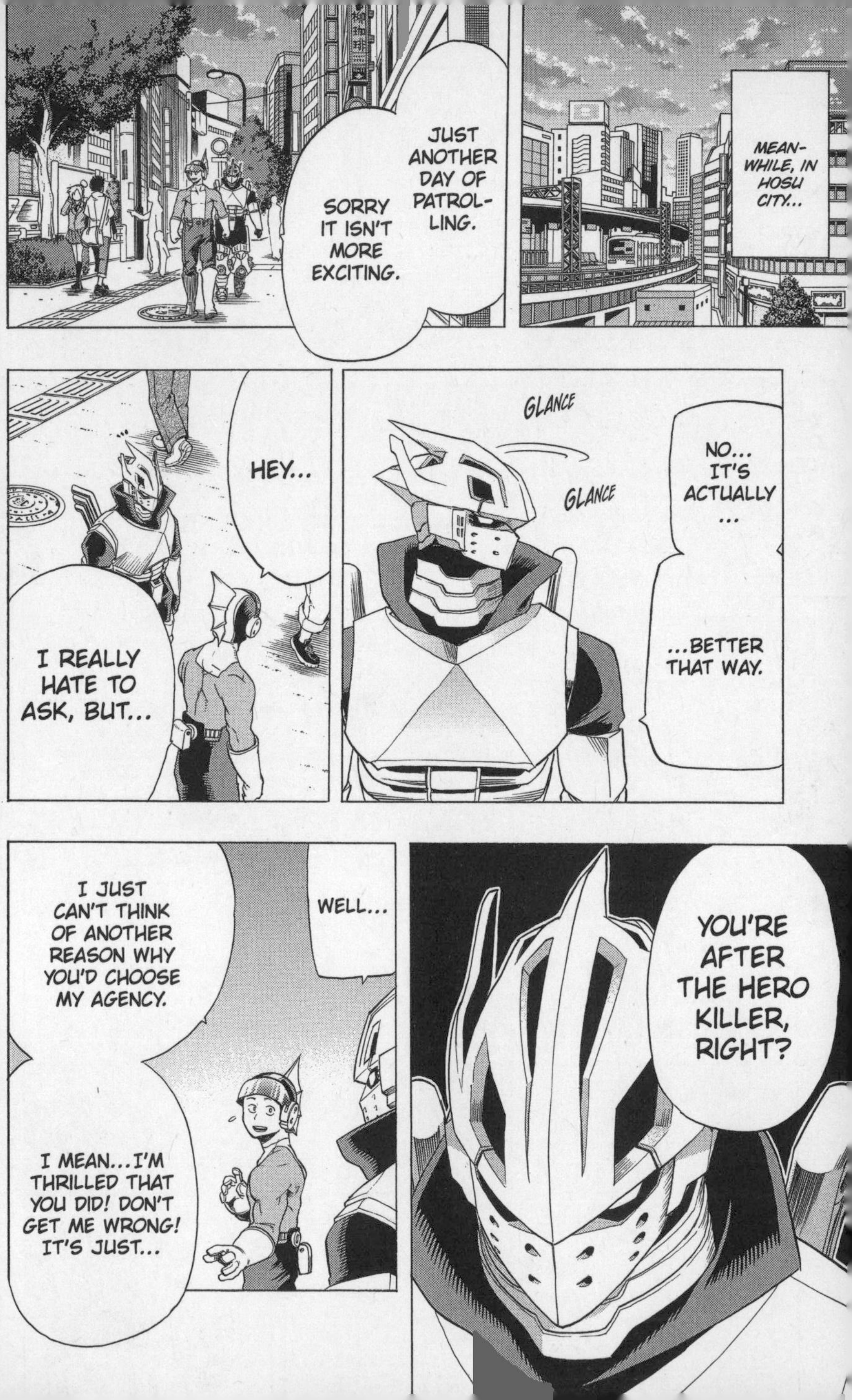
MEAN-WHILE, IN HOSU CITY...
JUST ANOTHER DAY OF PATROL-LING.
SORRY IT ISN'T MORE EXCITING.
GLANCE
GLANCE
NO... IT'S ACTUALLY ...
...BETTER THAT WAY.
HEY...
I REALLY HATE TO ASK, BUT...
YOU'RE AFTER THE HERO KILLER, RIGHT?
WELL...
I JUST CAN'T THINK OF ANOTHER REASON WHY YOU'D CHOOSE MY AGENCY.
I MEAN...I'M THRILLED THAT YOU DID! DON'T GET ME WRONG! IT'S JUST...

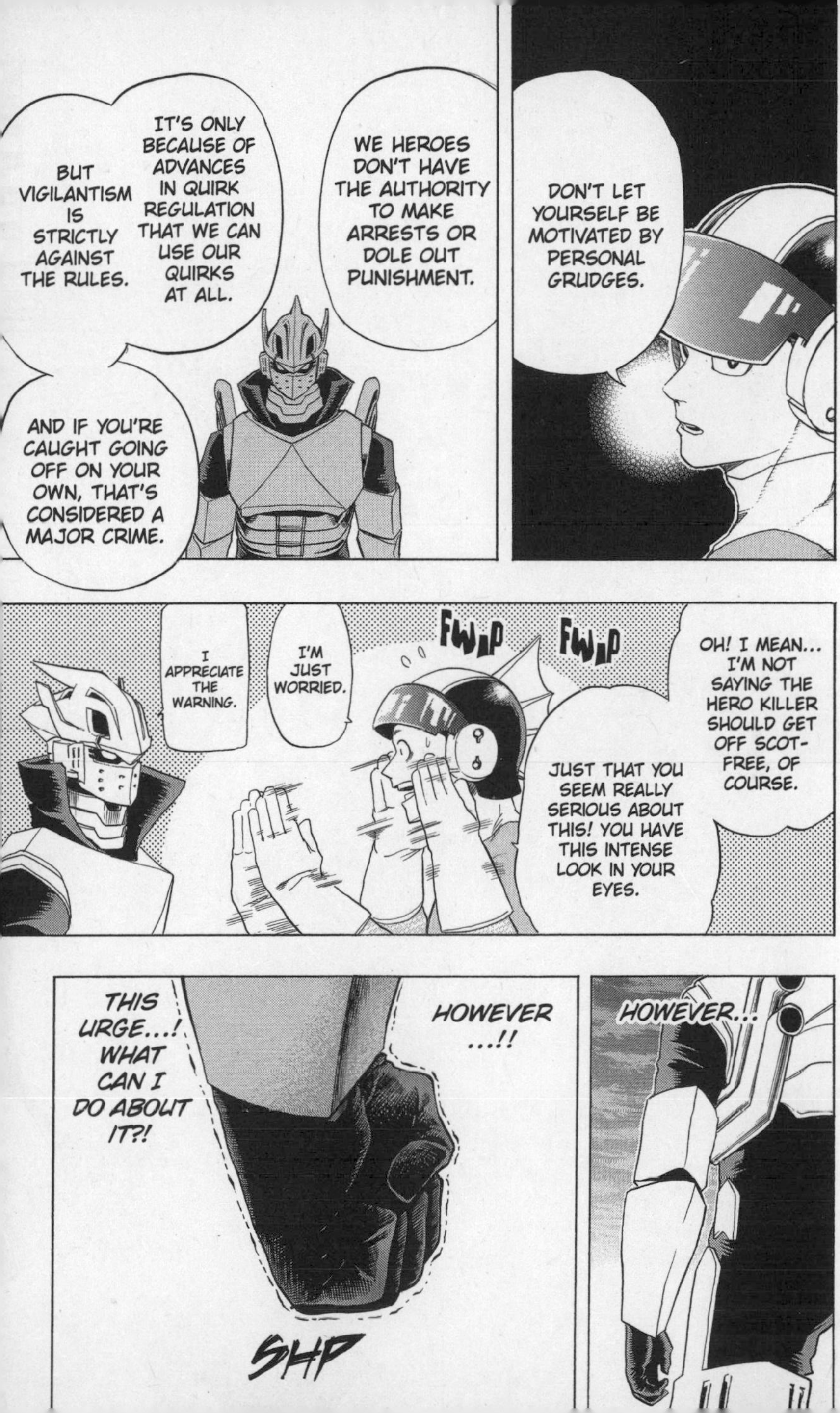
DON'T LET YOURSELF BE MOTIVATED BY PERSONAL GRUDGES.
WE HEROES DON'T HAVE THE AUTHORITY TO MAKE ARRESTS OR DOLE OUT PUNISHMENT.
IT'S ONLY BECAUSE OF ADVANCES IN QUIRK REGULATION THAT WE CAN USE OUR QUIRKS AT ALL.
BUT VIGILANTISM IS STRICTLY AGAINST THE RULES.
AND IF YOU'RE CAUGHT GOING OFF ON YOUR OWN, THAT'S CONSIDERED A MAJOR CRIME.
FWIP
FWIP
OH! I MEAN... I'M NOT SAYING THE HERO KILLER SHOULD GET OFF SCOT-FREE, OF COURSE.
JUST THAT YOU SEEM REALLY SERIOUS ABOUT THIS! YOU HAVE THIS INTENSE LOOK IN YOUR EYES.
I'M JUST WORRIED.
I APPRECIATE THE WARNING.
HOWEVER...
HOWEVER ...!!
THIS URGE...! WHAT CAN I DO ABOUT IT?!
SHP

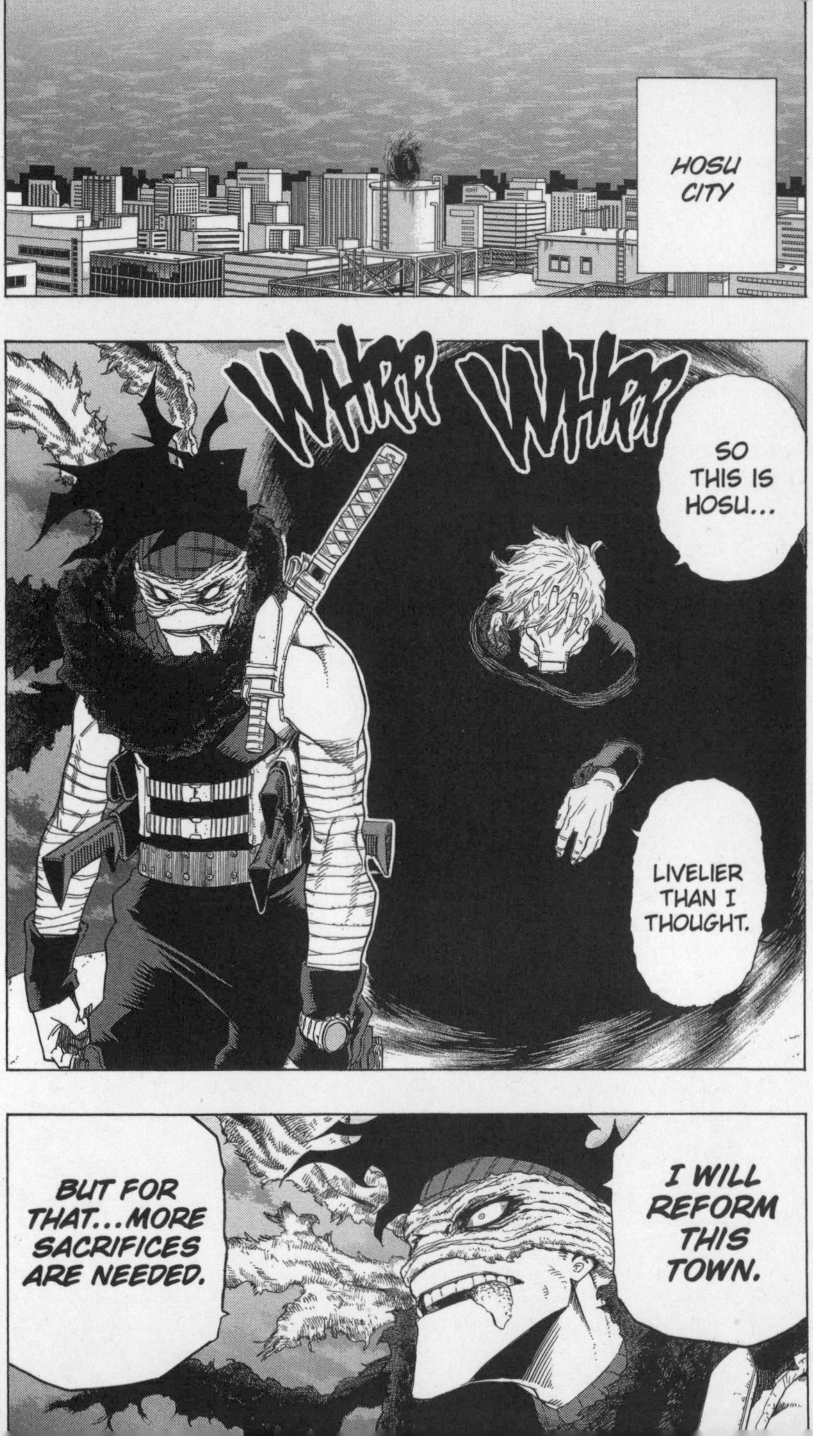
HOSU CITY
WHRRR WHRRR
SO THIS IS HOSU...
LIVELIER THAN I THOUGHT.
I WILL REFORM THIS TOWN.
BUT FOR THAT...MORE SACRIFICES ARE NEEDED.

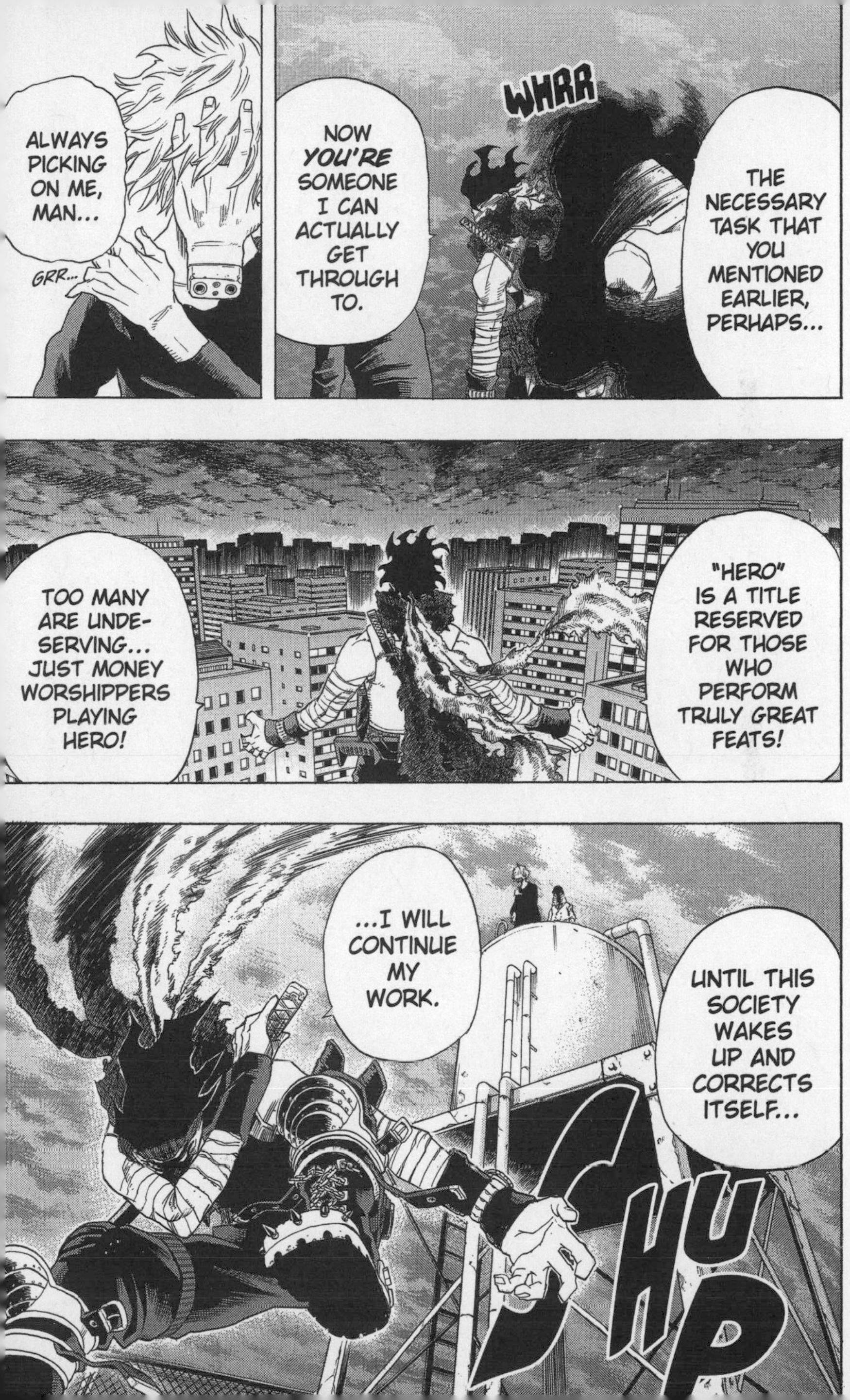
WHRR
THE NECESSARY TASK THAT YOU MENTIONED EARLIER, PERHAPS...
NOW *YOU'RE* SOMEONE I CAN ACTUALLY GET THROUGH TO.
ALWAYS PICKING ON ME, MAN...
GRR...
"HERO" IS A TITLE RESERVED FOR THOSE WHO PERFORM TRULY GREAT FEATS!
TOO MANY ARE UNDE-SERVING... JUST MONEY WORSHIPPERS PLAYING HERO!
UNTIL THIS SOCIETY WAKES UP AND CORRECTS ITSELF...
...I WILL CONTINUE MY WORK.
SHUP

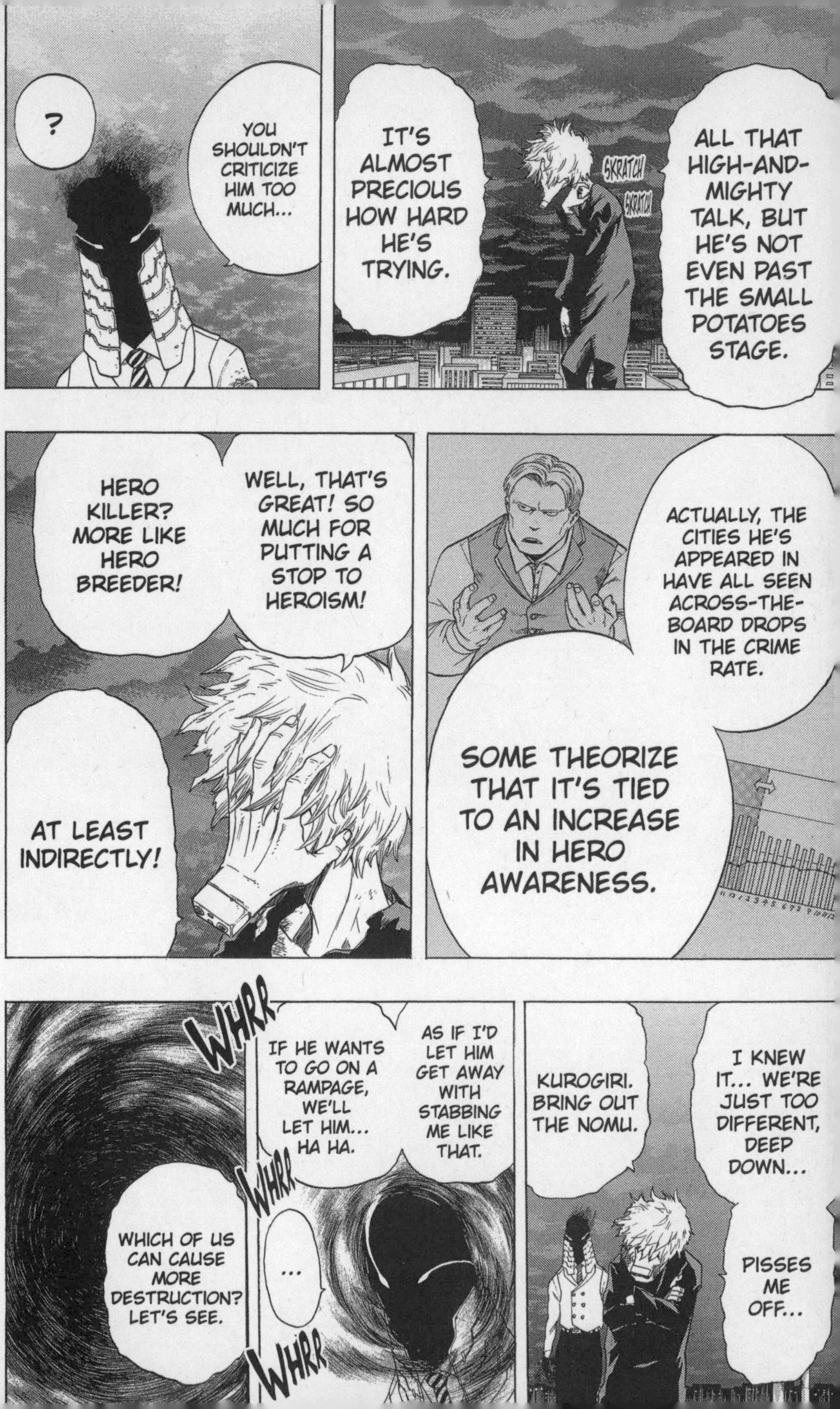

ALL THAT HIGH-AND-MIGHTY TALK, BUT HE'S NOT EVEN PAST THE SMALL POTATOES STAGE.
SKRATCH
SKRATCH
IT'S ALMOST PRECIOUS HOW HARD HE'S TRYING.
YOU SHOULDN'T CRITICIZE HIM TOO MUCH...
?
ACTUALLY, THE CITIES HE'S APPEARED IN HAVE ALL SEEN ACROSS-THE-BOARD DROPS IN THE CRIME RATE.
SOME THEORIZE THAT IT'S TIED TO AN INCREASE IN HERO AWARENESS.
WELL, THAT'S GREAT! SO MUCH FOR PUTTING A STOP TO HEROISM!
HERO KILLER? MORE LIKE HERO BREEDER!
AT LEAST INDIRECTLY!
I KNEW IT... WE'RE JUST TOO DIFFERENT, DEEP DOWN...
PISSES ME OFF...
KUROGIRI. BRING OUT THE NOMU.
AS IF I'D LET HIM GET AWAY WITH STABBING ME LIKE THAT.
IF HE WANTS TO GO ON A RAMPAGE, WE'LL LET HIM... HA HA.
WHRR
WHRR
...
WHICH OF US CAN CAUSE MORE DESTRUCTION? LET'S SEE.
WHRR

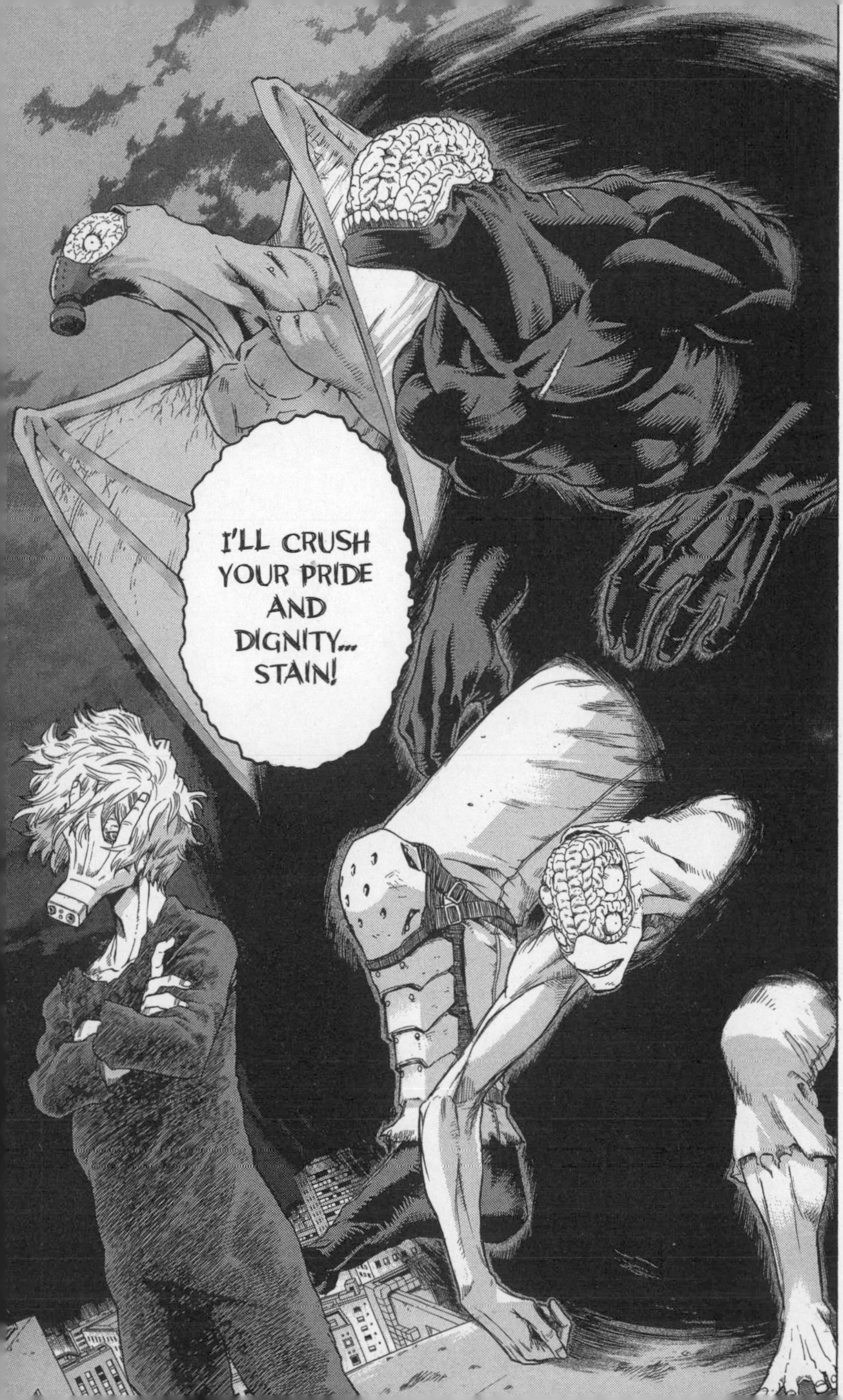
I'LL CRUSH YOUR PRIDE AND DIGNITY... STAIN!

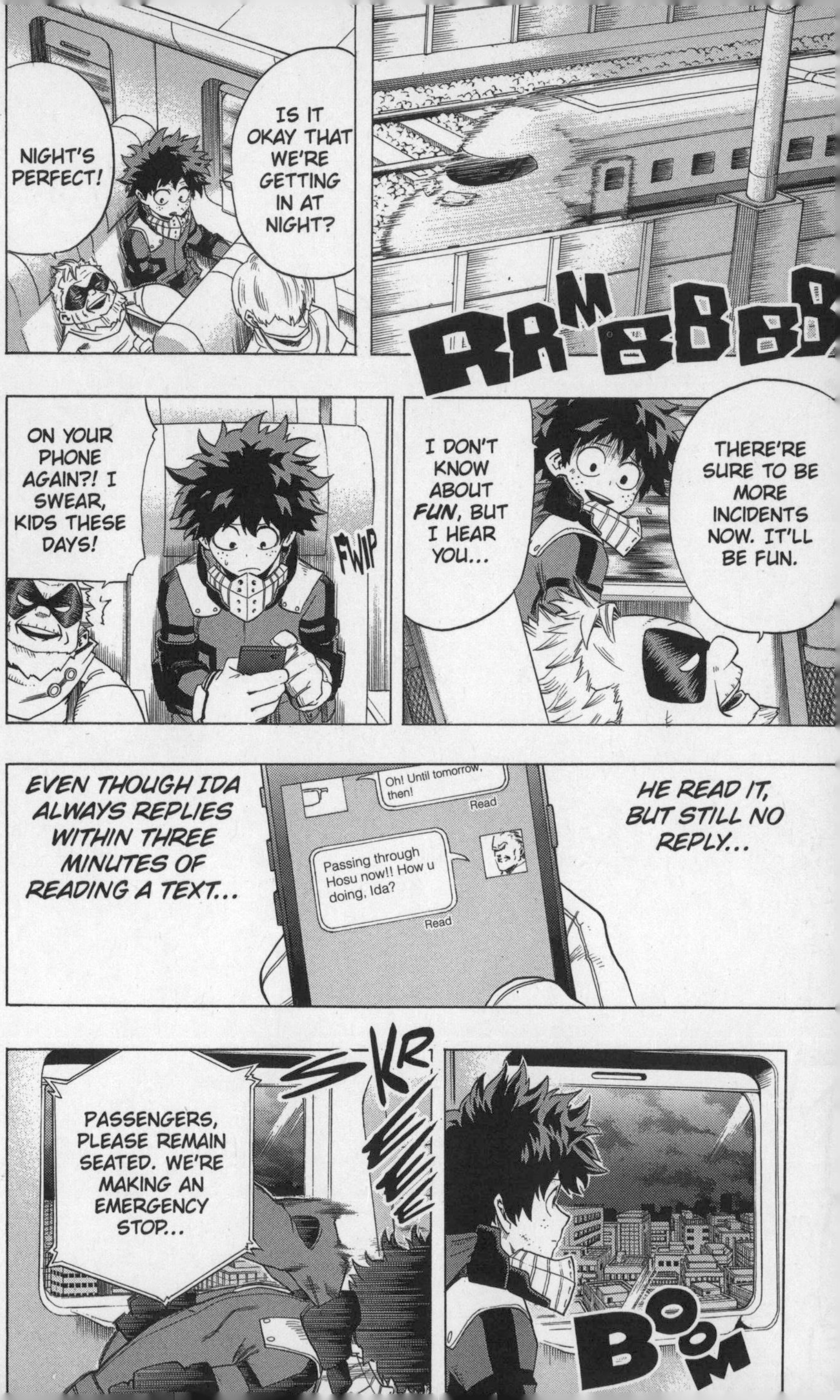
RRMBBB
IS IT OKAY THAT WE'RE GETTING IN AT NIGHT?
NIGHT'S PERFECT!
THERE'RE SURE TO BE MORE INCIDENTS NOW. IT'LL BE FUN.
I DON'T KNOW ABOUT FUN, BUT I HEAR YOU...
FWIP
ON YOUR PHONE AGAIN?! I SWEAR, KIDS THESE DAYS!
EVEN THOUGH IDA ALWAYS REPLIES WITHIN THREE MINUTES OF READING A TEXT...
Oh! Until tomorrow, then!
Read
Passing through Hosu now!! How u doing, Ida?
Read
HE READ IT, BUT STILL NO REPLY...
BOOM
SKR
PASSENGERS, PLEASE REMAIN SEATED. WE'RE MAKING AN EMERGENCY STOP...

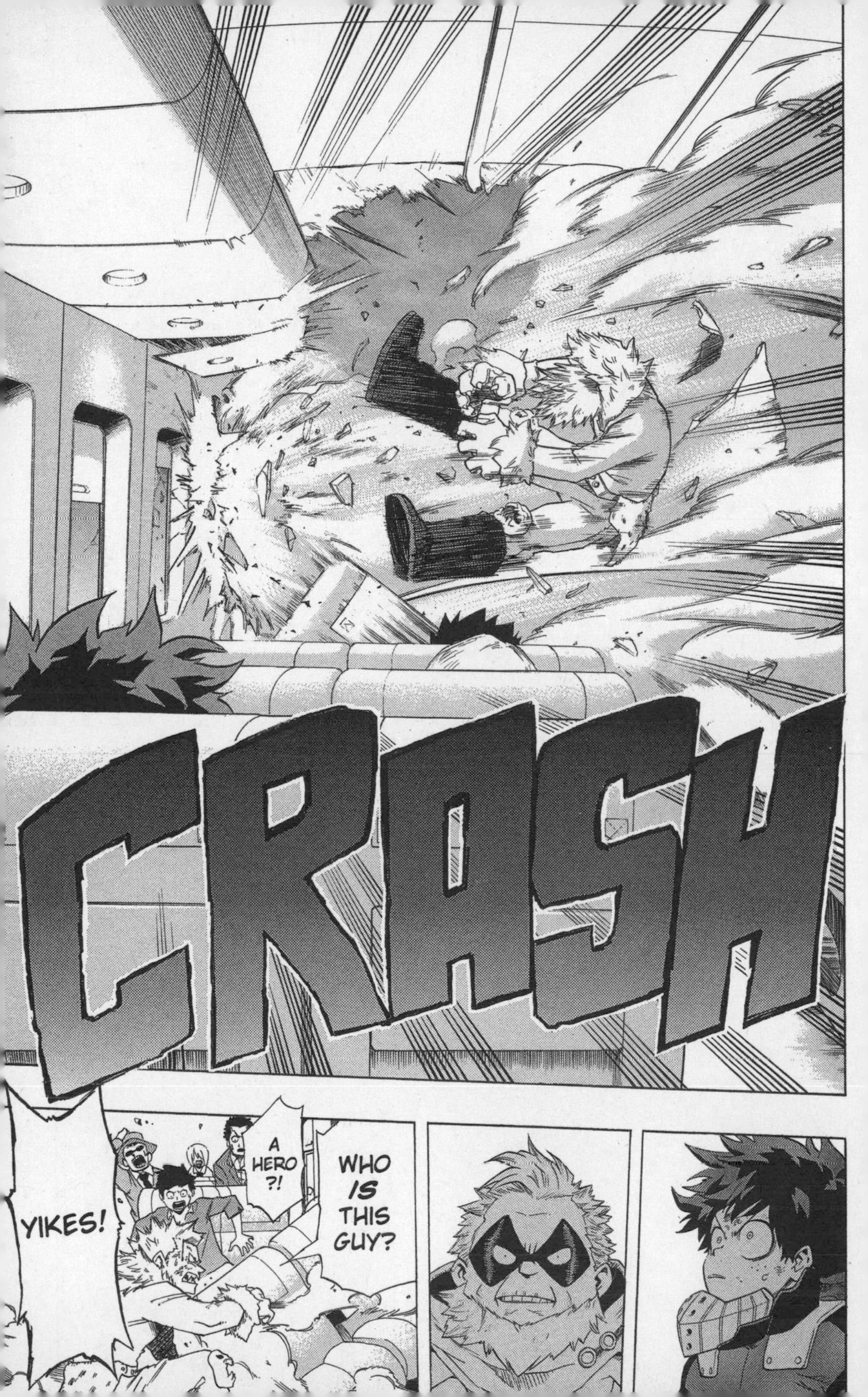
CRASH
WHO IS THIS GUY?
A HERO ?!
YIKES!

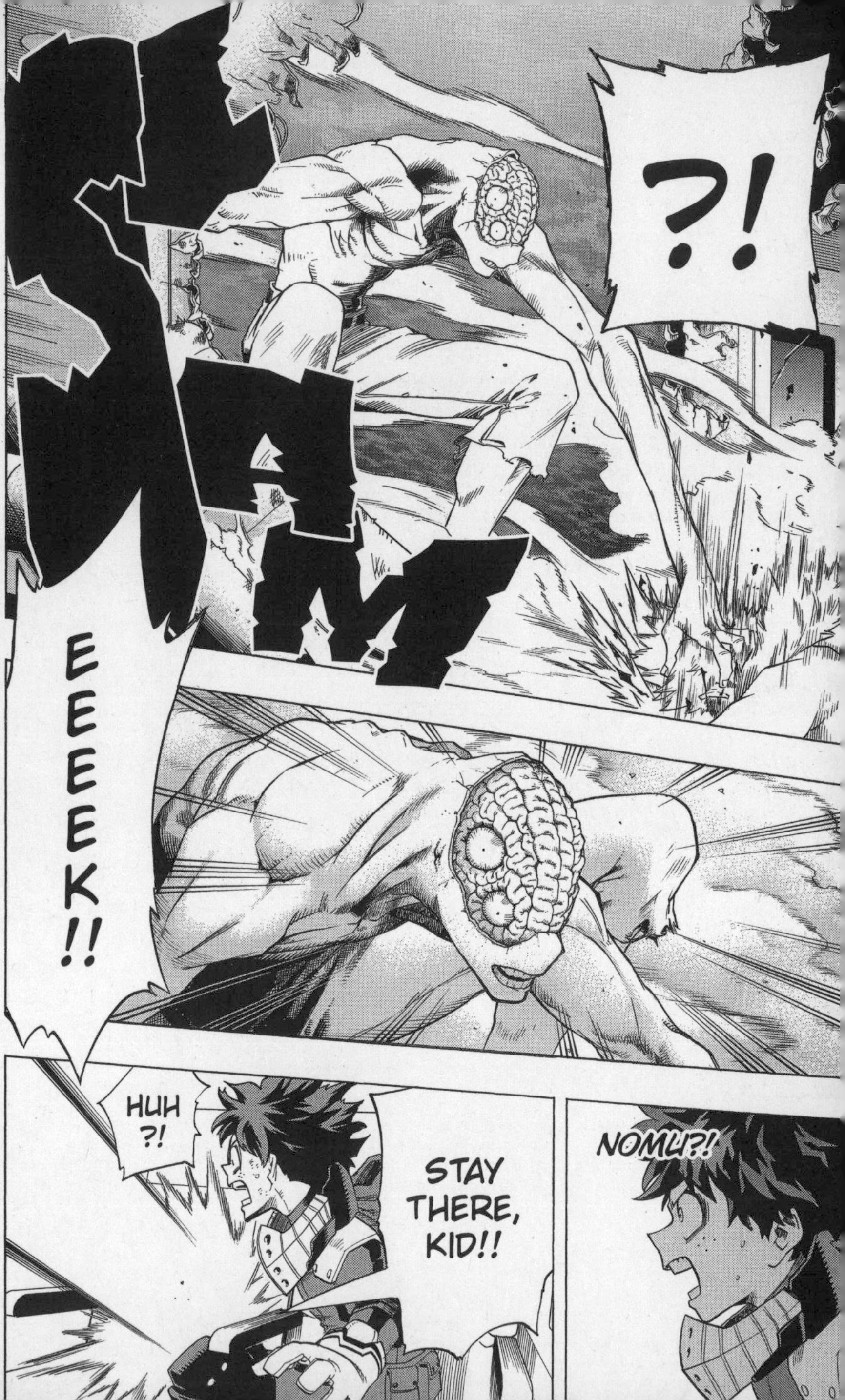
?!
EEEEK!!
NOMU?!
HUH ?!
STAY THERE, KID!!

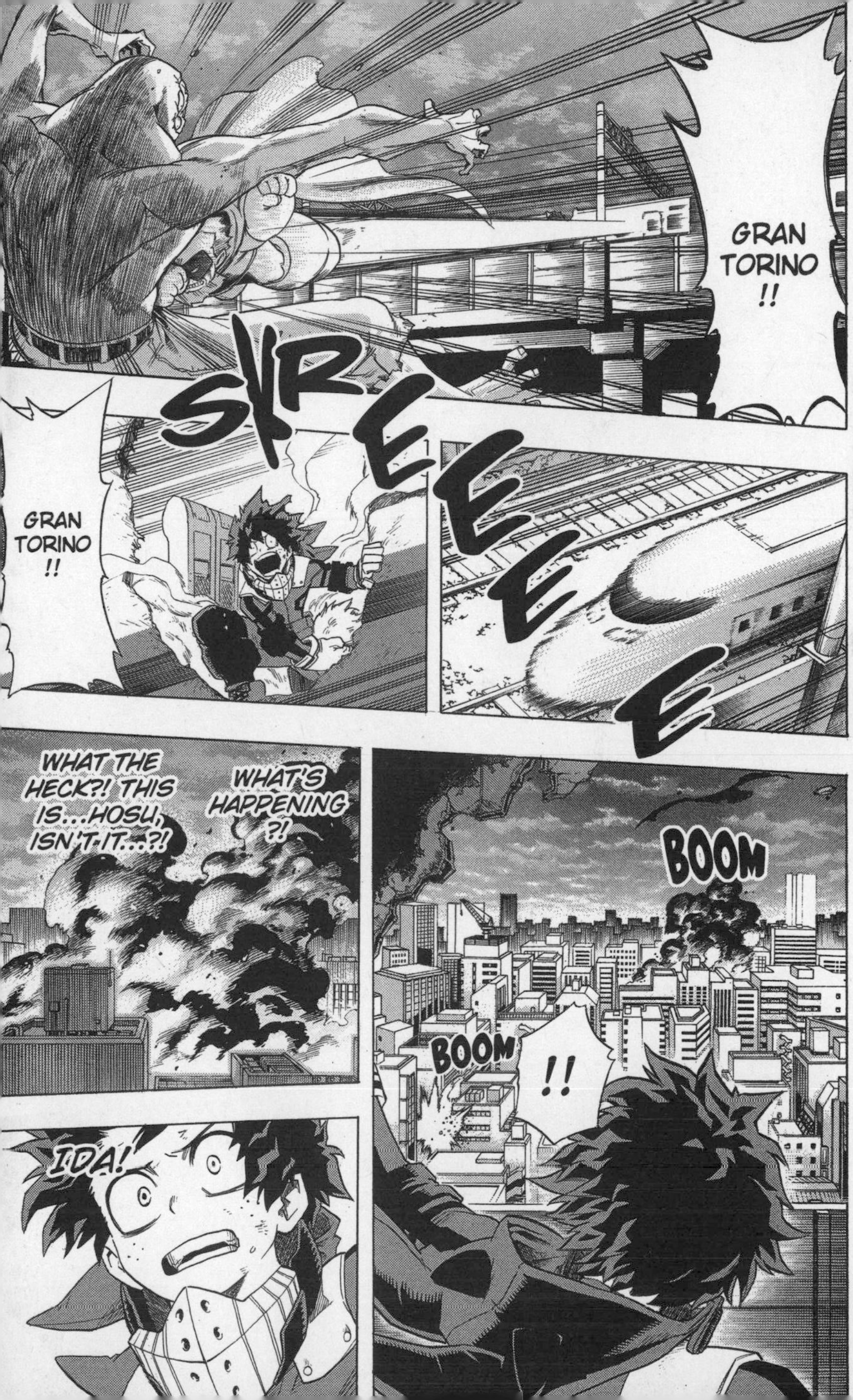
GRAN TORINO !!
SKREEEEE
GRAN TORINO !!
BOOM
BOOM
!!
WHAT'S HAPPENING ?!
WHAT THE HECK?! THIS IS...HOSU, ISN'T IT...?!
IDA!

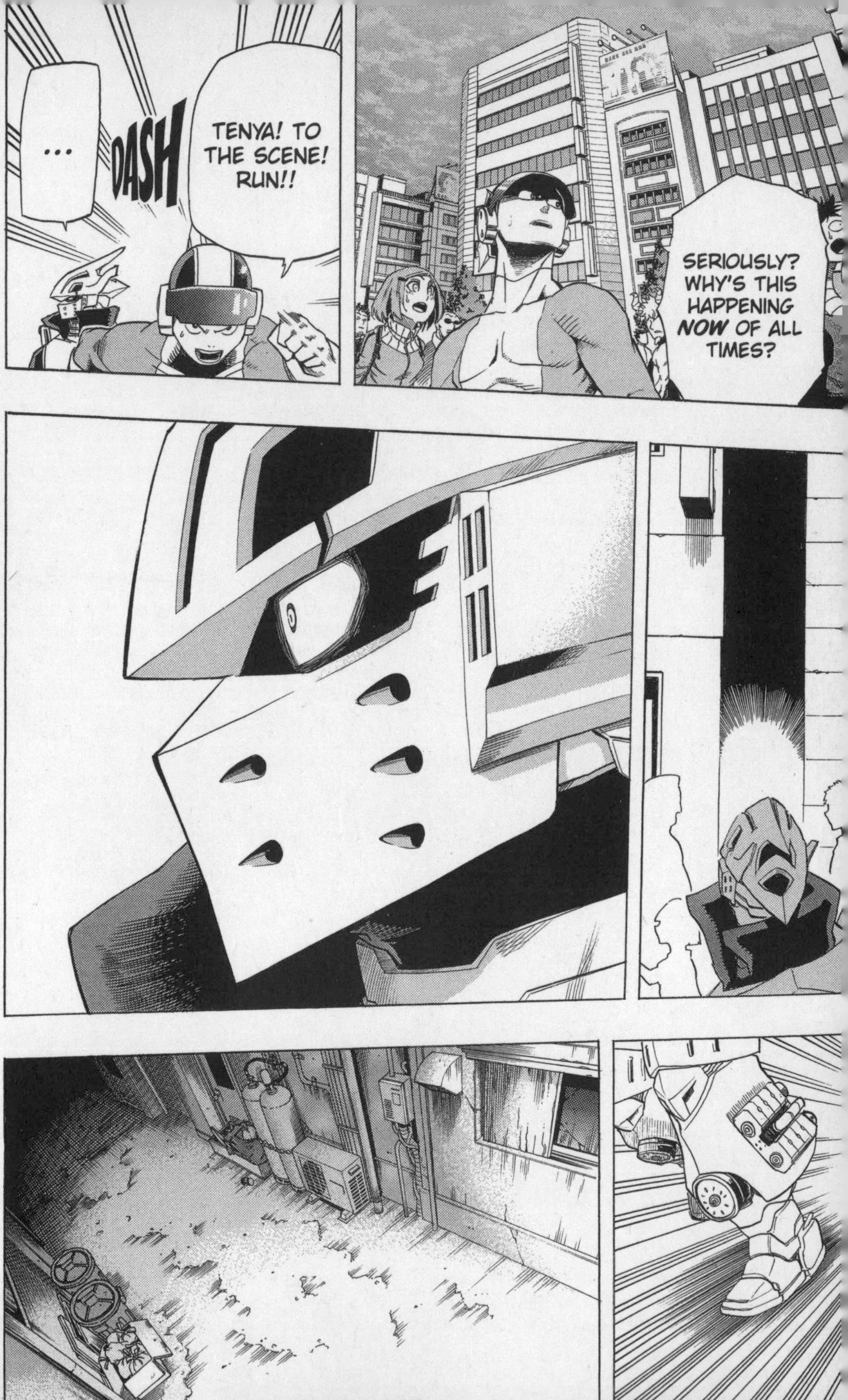
SERIOUSLY? WHY'S THIS HAPPENING NOW OF ALL TIMES?
TENYA! TO THE SCENE! RUN!!
DASH
...

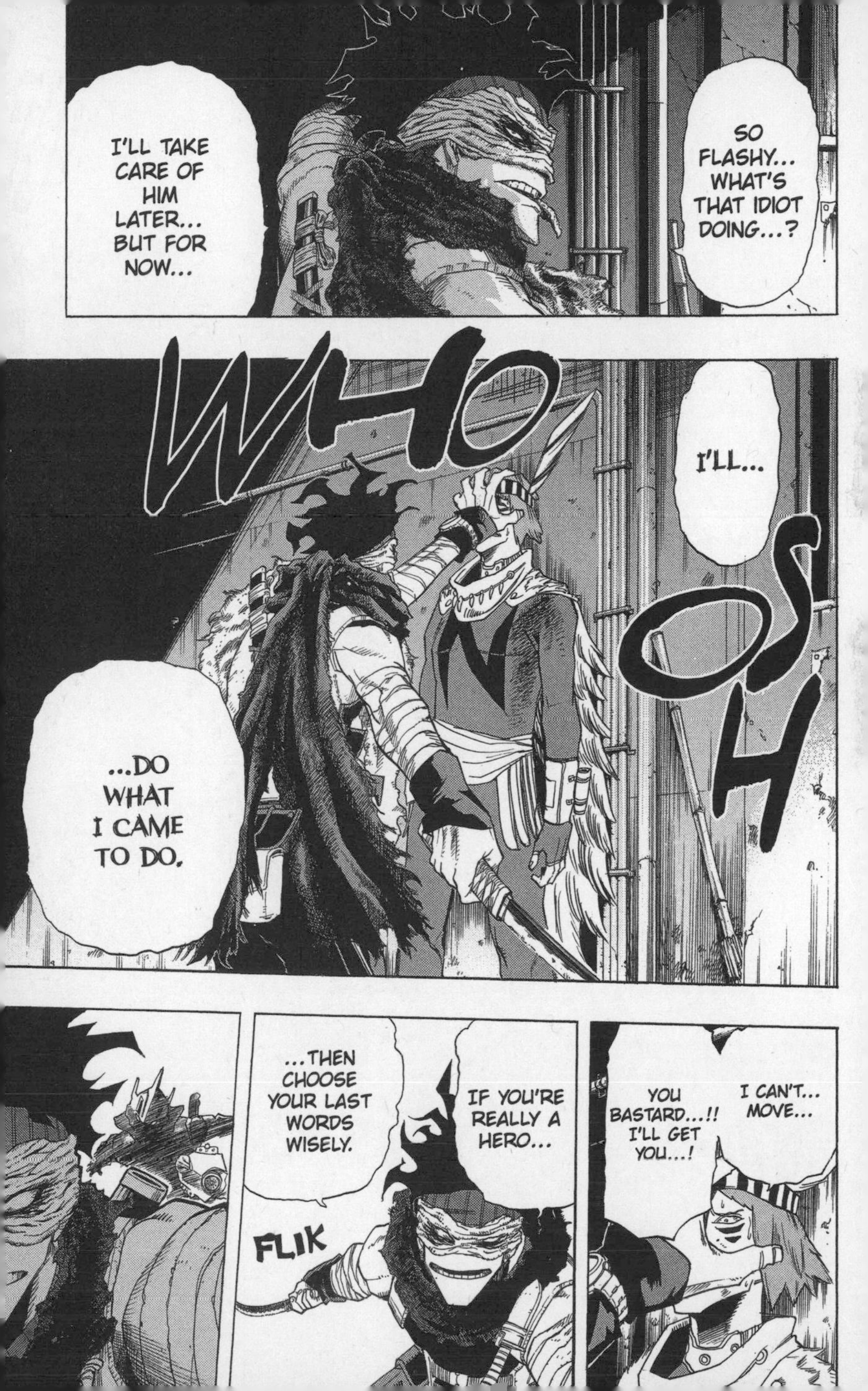
SO FLASHY... WHAT'S THAT IDIOT DOING...?
I'LL TAKE CARE OF HIM LATER... BUT FOR NOW...
I'LL...
WHOOSH
...DO WHAT I CAME TO DO.
I CAN'T... MOVE...
YOU BASTARD...!! I'LL GET YOU...!
IF YOU'RE REALLY A HERO...
...THEN CHOOSE YOUR LAST WORDS WISELY.
FLIK

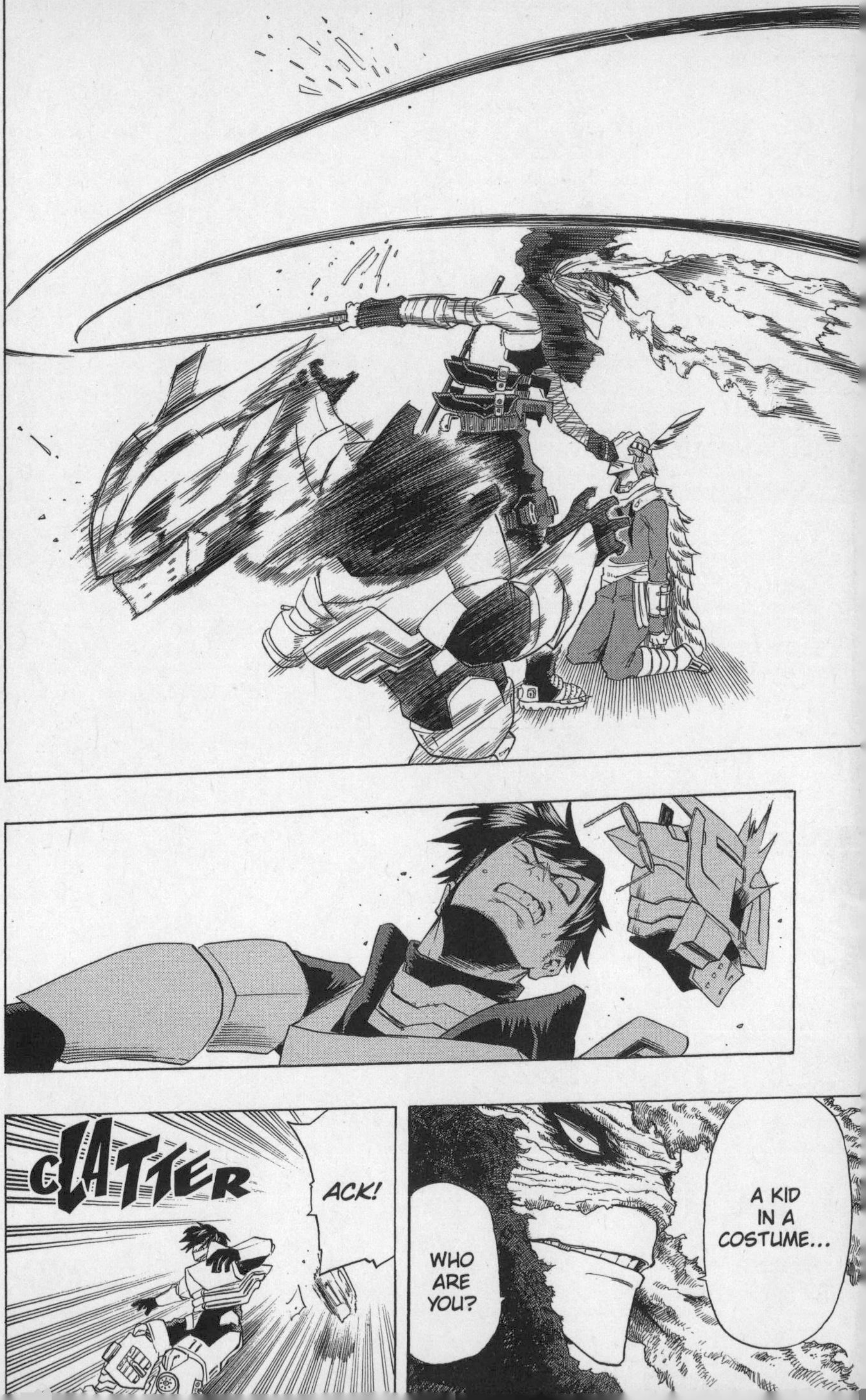
A KID IN A COSTUME...
WHO ARE YOU?
ACK!
CLATTER

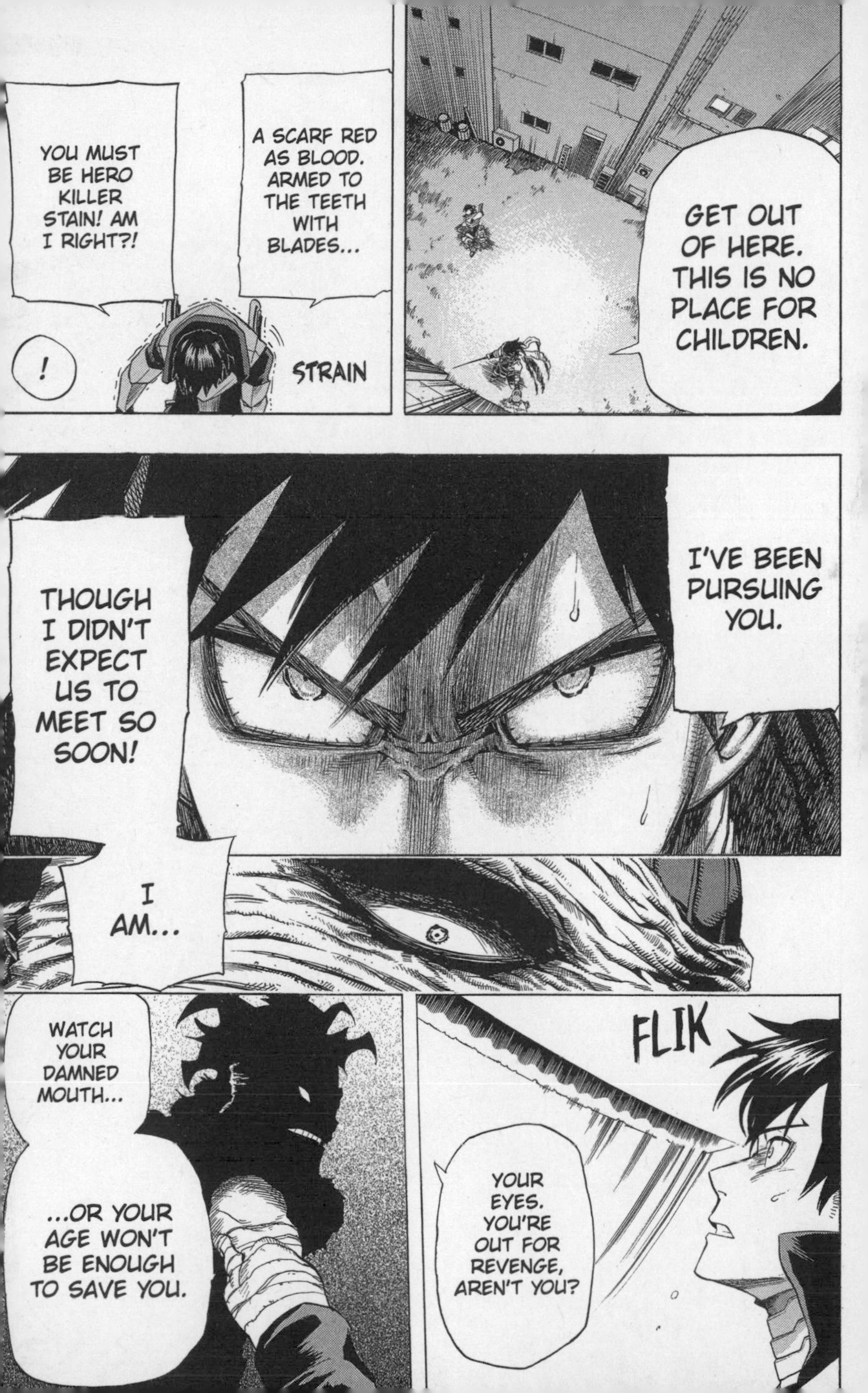
GET OUT OF HERE. THIS IS NO PLACE FOR CHILDREN.
A SCARF RED AS BLOOD. ARMED TO THE TEETH WITH BLADES...
YOU MUST BE HERO KILLER STAIN! AM I RIGHT?!
STRAIN
!
I'VE BEEN PURSUING YOU.
THOUGH I DIDN'T EXPECT US TO MEET SO SOON!
I AM...
FLIK
YOUR EYES. YOU'RE OUT FOR REVENGE, AREN'T YOU?
WATCH YOUR DAMNED MOUTH...
...OR YOUR AGE WON'T BE ENOUGH TO SAVE YOU.

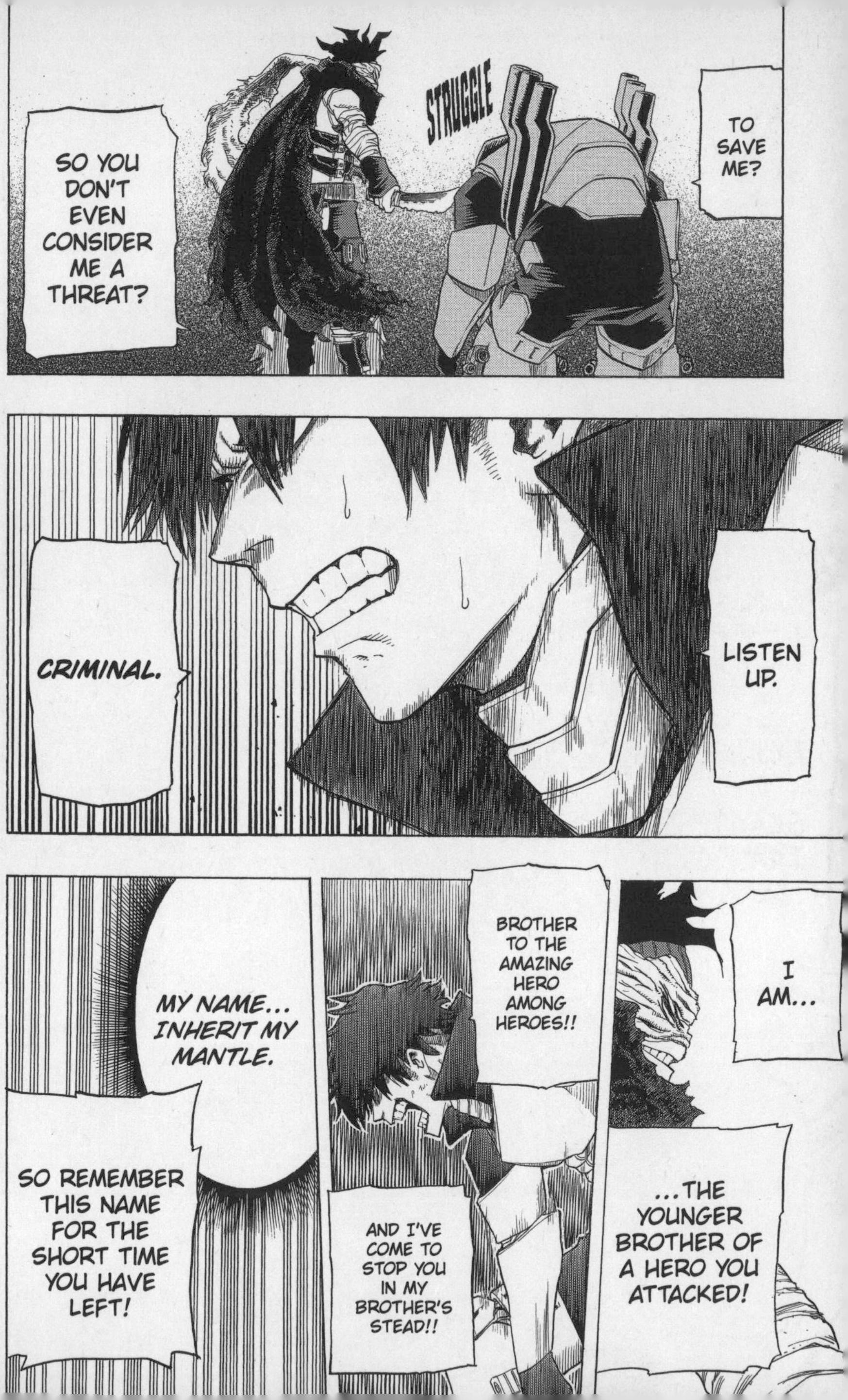
TO SAVE ME?
STRUGGLE
SO YOU DON'T EVEN CONSIDER ME A THREAT?
LISTEN UP.
CRIMINAL.
I AM...
...THE YOUNGER BROTHER OF A HERO YOU ATTACKED!
BROTHER TO THE AMAZING HERO AMONG HEROES!!
AND I'VE COME TO STOP YOU IN MY BROTHER'S STEAD!!
MY NAME... INHERIT MY MANTLE.
SO REMEMBER THIS NAME FOR THE SHORT TIME YOU HAVE LEFT!

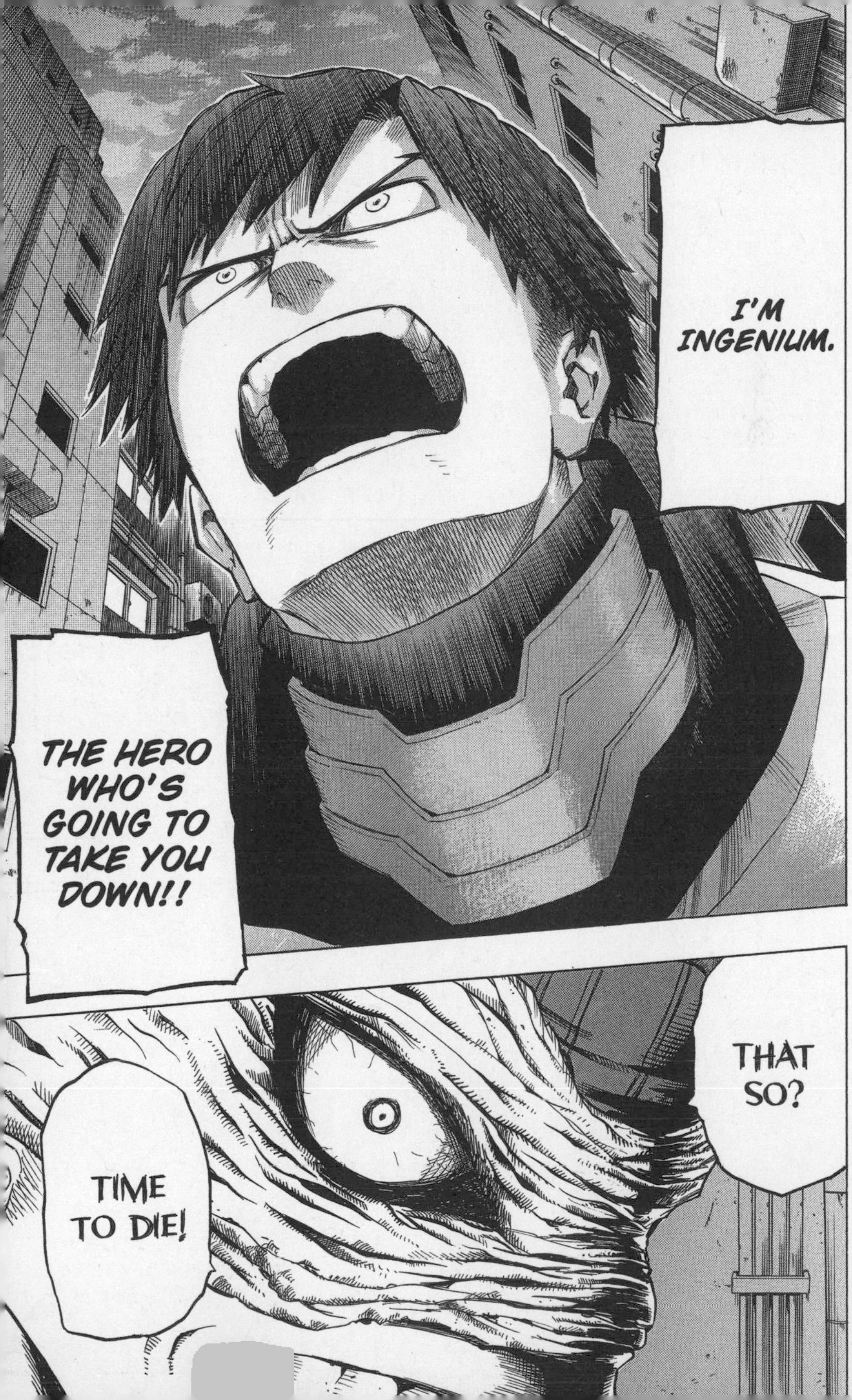
I'M INGENIUM.
THE HERO WHO'S GOING TO TAKE YOU DOWN!!
THAT SO?
TIME TO DIE!

HERO

NORMAL HERO: MANUAL [28] [MASAKI MIZUSHIMA]

STREET CLOTHES

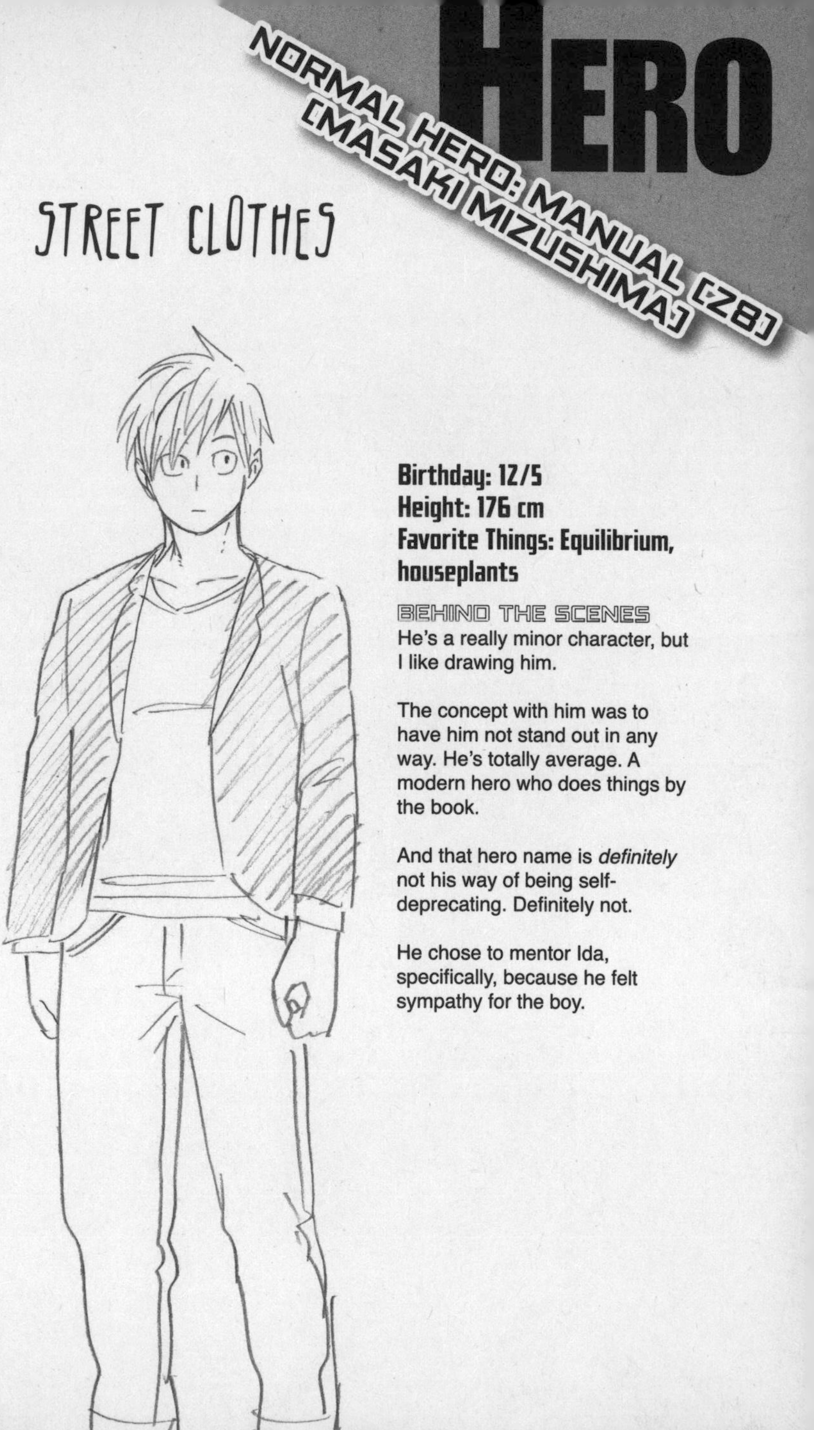

Birthday: 12/5
Height: 176 cm
Favorite Things: Equilibrium, houseplants

BEHIND THE SCENES

He's a really minor character, but I like drawing him.

The concept with him was to have him not stand out in any way. He's totally average. A modern hero who does things by the book.

And that hero name is *definitely* not his way of being self-deprecating. Definitely not.

He chose to mentor Ida, specifically, because he felt sympathy for the boy.

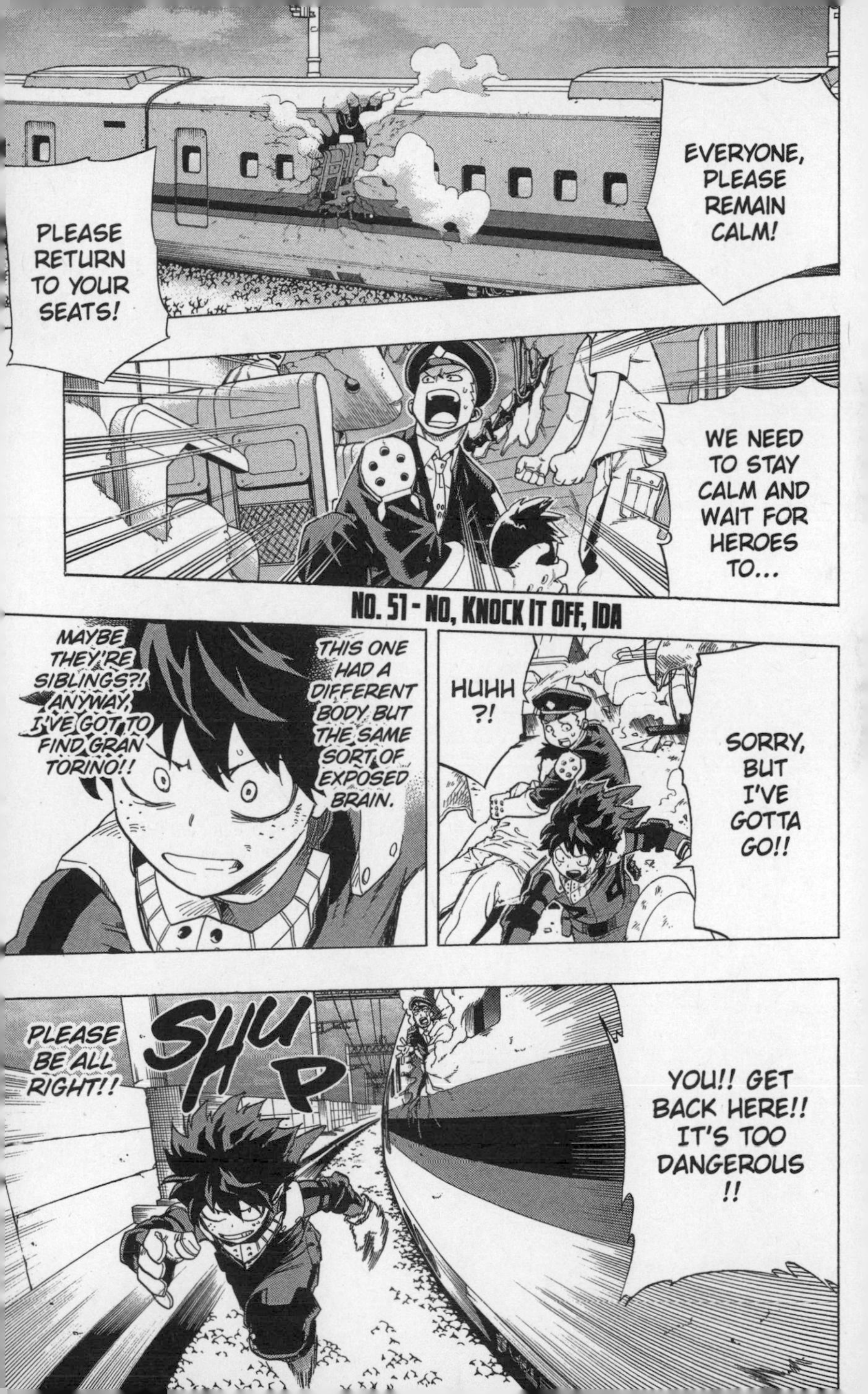
EVERYONE, PLEASE REMAIN CALM!
PLEASE RETURN TO YOUR SEATS!
WE NEED TO STAY CALM AND WAIT FOR HEROES TO...
NO. 51 - NO, KNOCK IT OFF, IDA
SORRY, BUT I'VE GOTTA GO!!
HUHH ?!
THIS ONE HAD A DIFFERENT BODY BUT THE SAME SORT OF EXPOSED BRAIN.
MAYBE THEY'RE SIBLINGS?! ANYWAY, I'VE GOT TO FIND GRAN TORINO!!
YOU!! GET BACK HERE!! IT'S TOO DANGEROUS !!
SHUP
PLEASE BE ALL RIGHT!!

No. 51 - No, Knock It Off, Ida

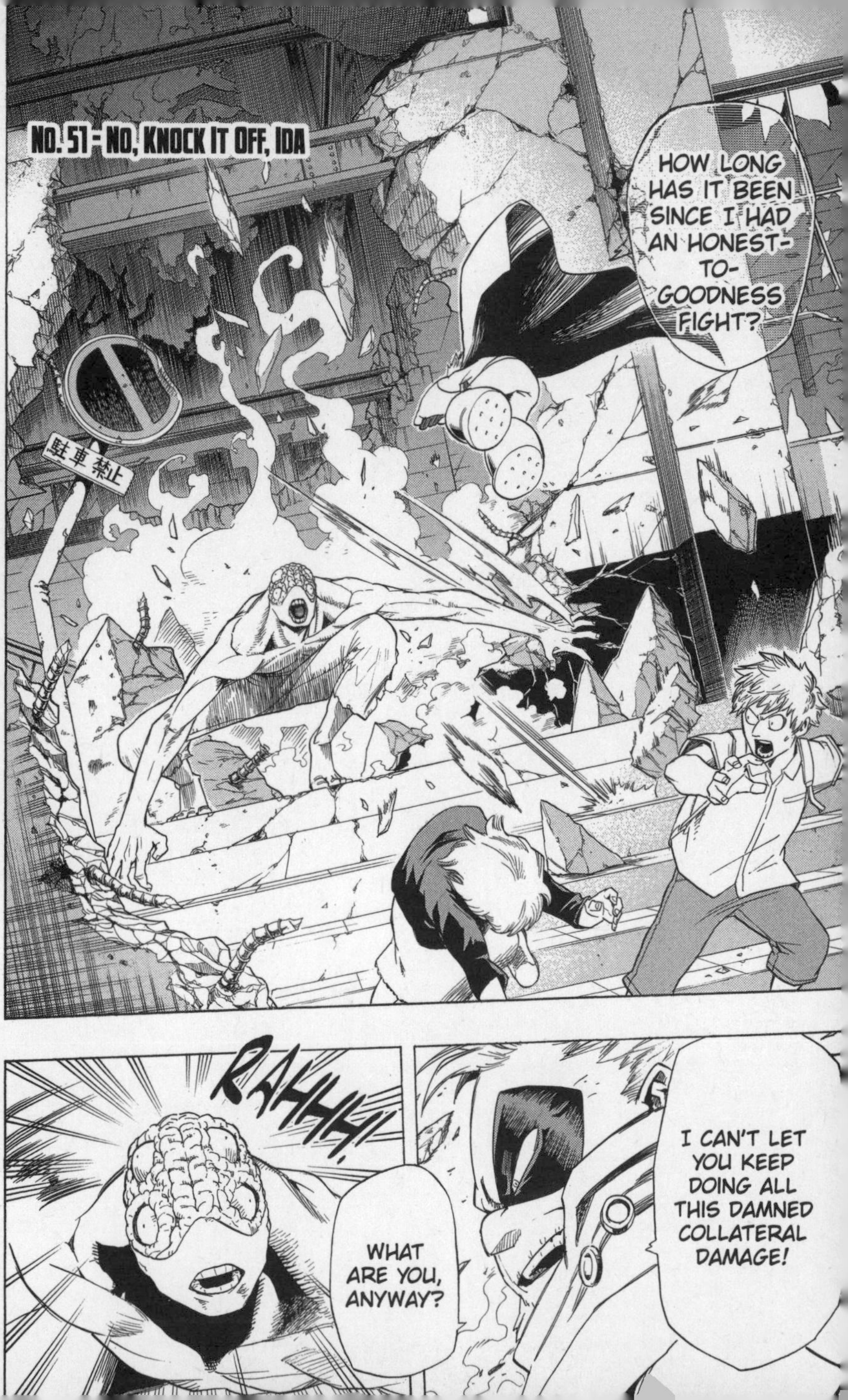
HOW LONG HAS IT BEEN SINCE I HAD AN HONEST-TO-GOODNESS FIGHT?
駐車禁止
I CAN'T LET YOU KEEP DOING ALL THIS DAMNED COLLATERAL DAMAGE!
RAHHH!
WHAT ARE YOU, ANYWAY?

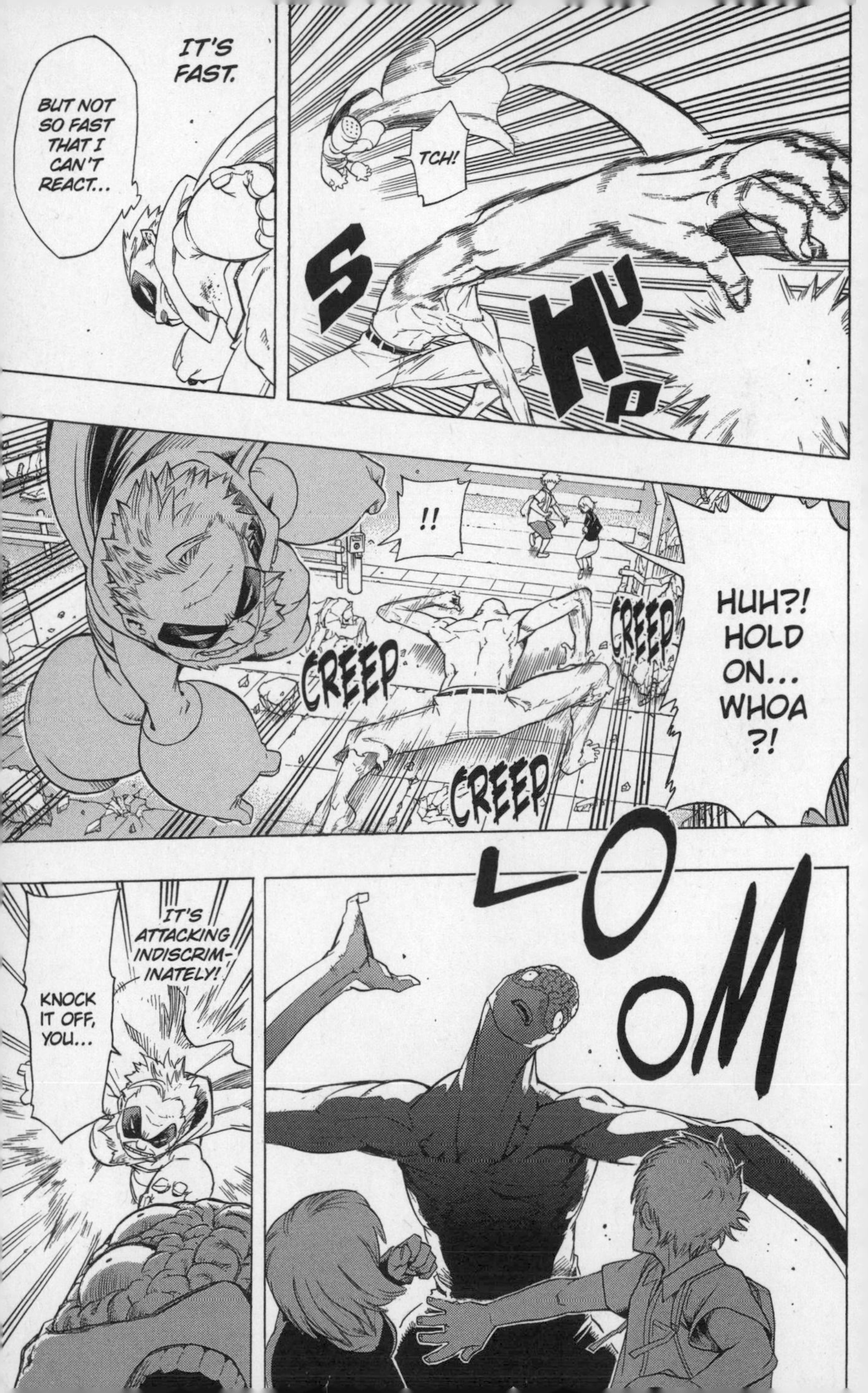
TCH!
SHUP
IT'S FAST.
BUT NOT SO FAST THAT I CAN'T REACT...
HUH?! HOLD ON... WHOA?!
!!
CREEP
CREEP
CREEP
VOOM
IT'S ATTACKING INDISCRIMINATELY!
KNOCK IT OFF, YOU...

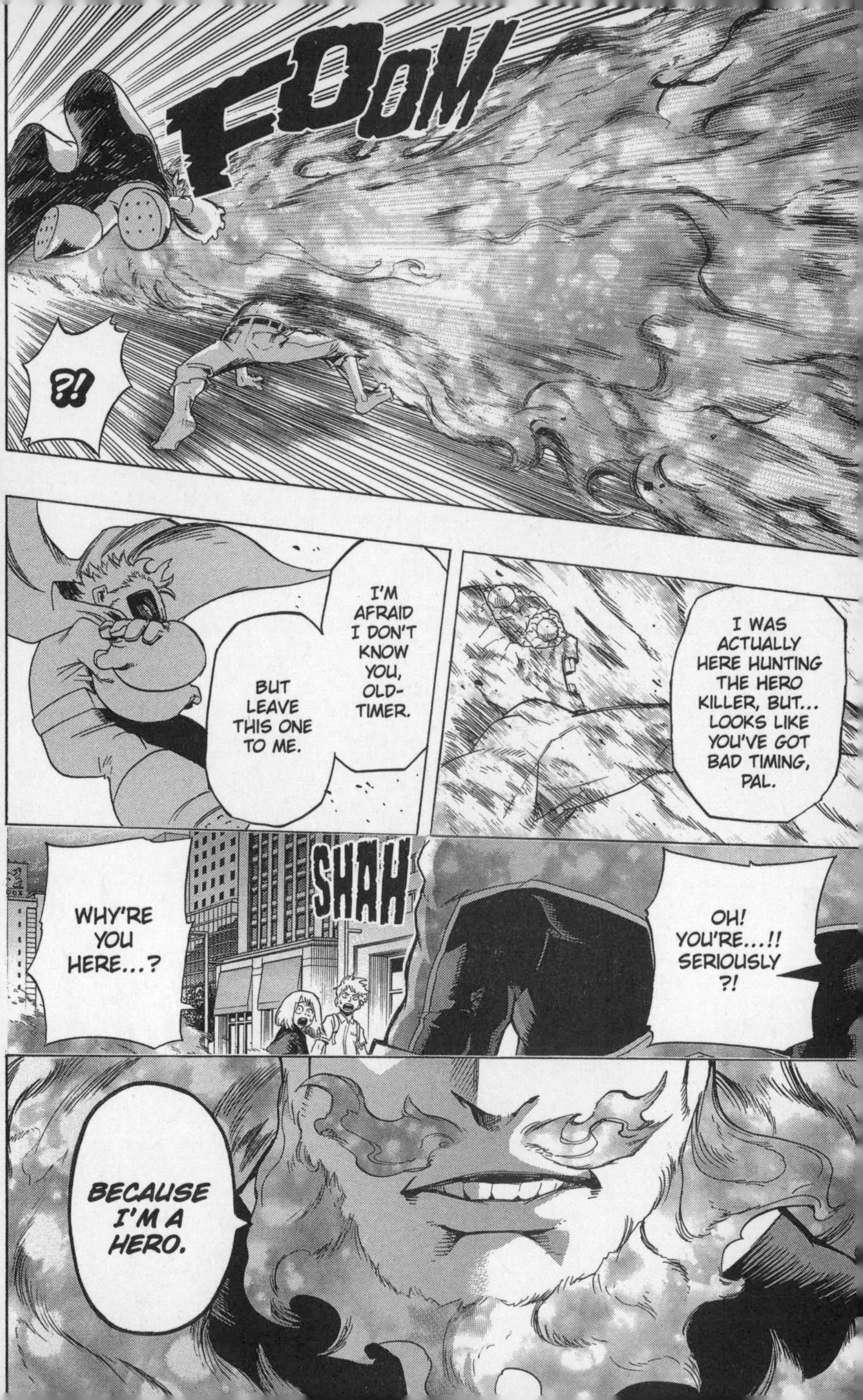
FOOM
?!
I WAS ACTUALLY HERE HUNTING THE HERO KILLER, BUT... LOOKS LIKE YOU'VE GOT BAD TIMING, PAL.
I'M AFRAID I DON'T KNOW YOU, OLD-TIMER.
BUT LEAVE THIS ONE TO ME.
OH! YOU'RE...!! SERIOUSLY ?!
SHAH
WHY'RE YOU HERE...?
BECAUSE I'M A HERO.

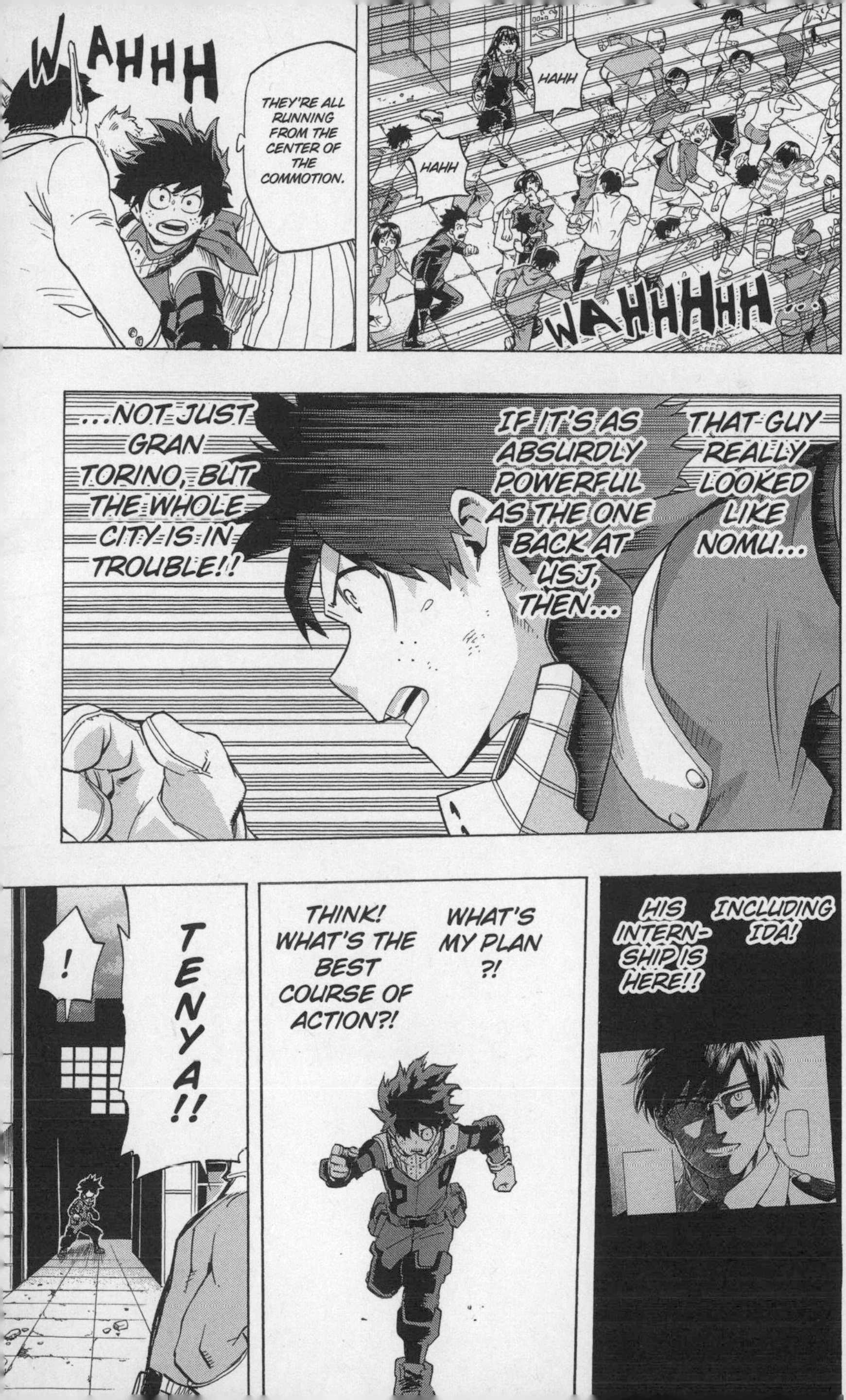
HAHH
HAHH
WAHHHHH
THEY'RE ALL RUNNING FROM THE CENTER OF THE COMMOTION.
WAHHH
THAT GUY REALLY LOOKED LIKE NOMU...
IF IT'S AS ABSURDLY POWERFUL AS THE ONE BACK AT USJ, THEN...
...NOT JUST GRAN TORINO, BUT THE WHOLE CITY IS IN TROUBLE!!
INCLUDING IDA!
HIS INTERN-SHIP IS HERE!!
WHAT'S MY PLAN ?!
THINK! WHAT'S THE BEST COURSE OF ACTION?!
TENYA!!
!

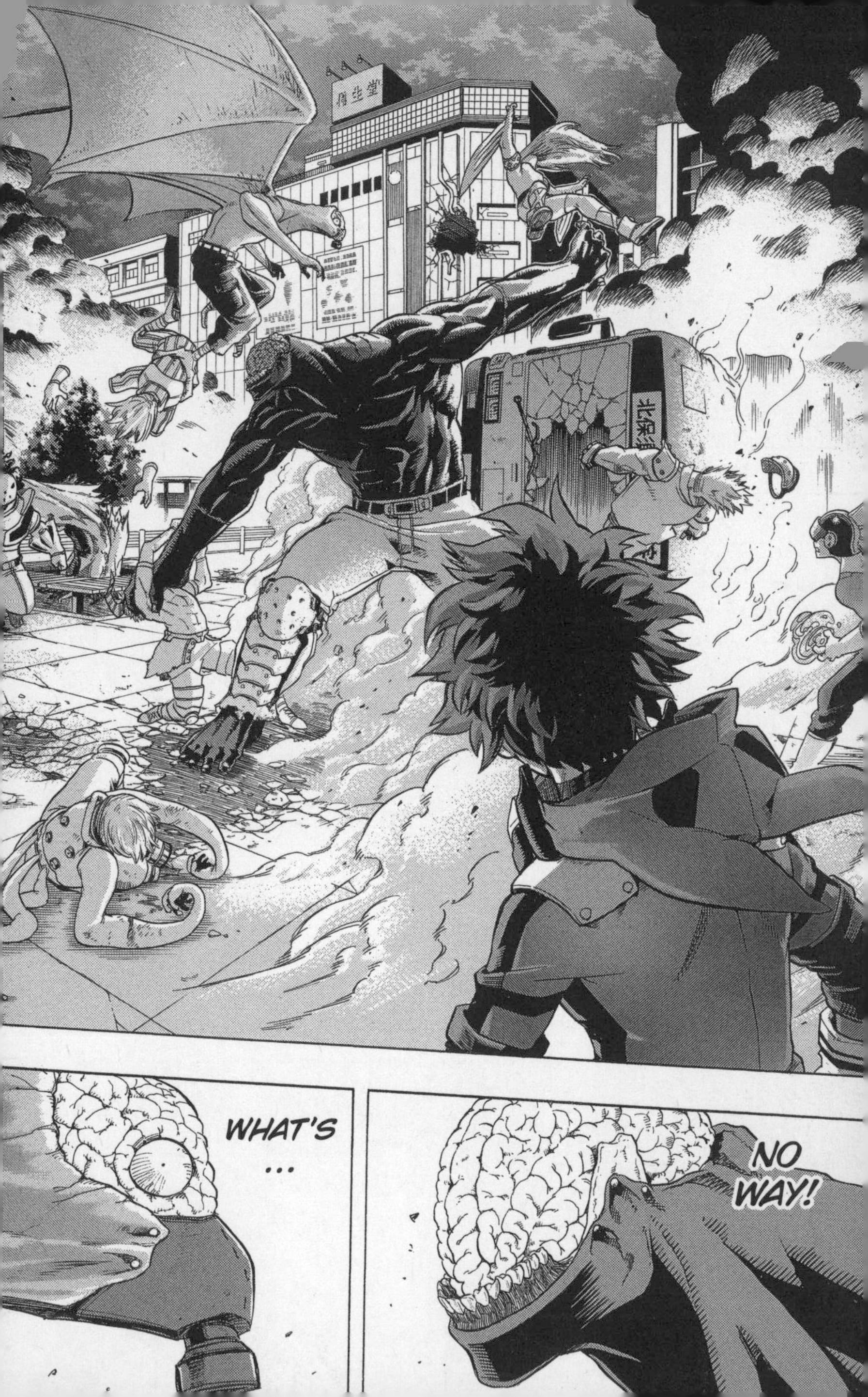
NO WAY!
WHAT'S ...

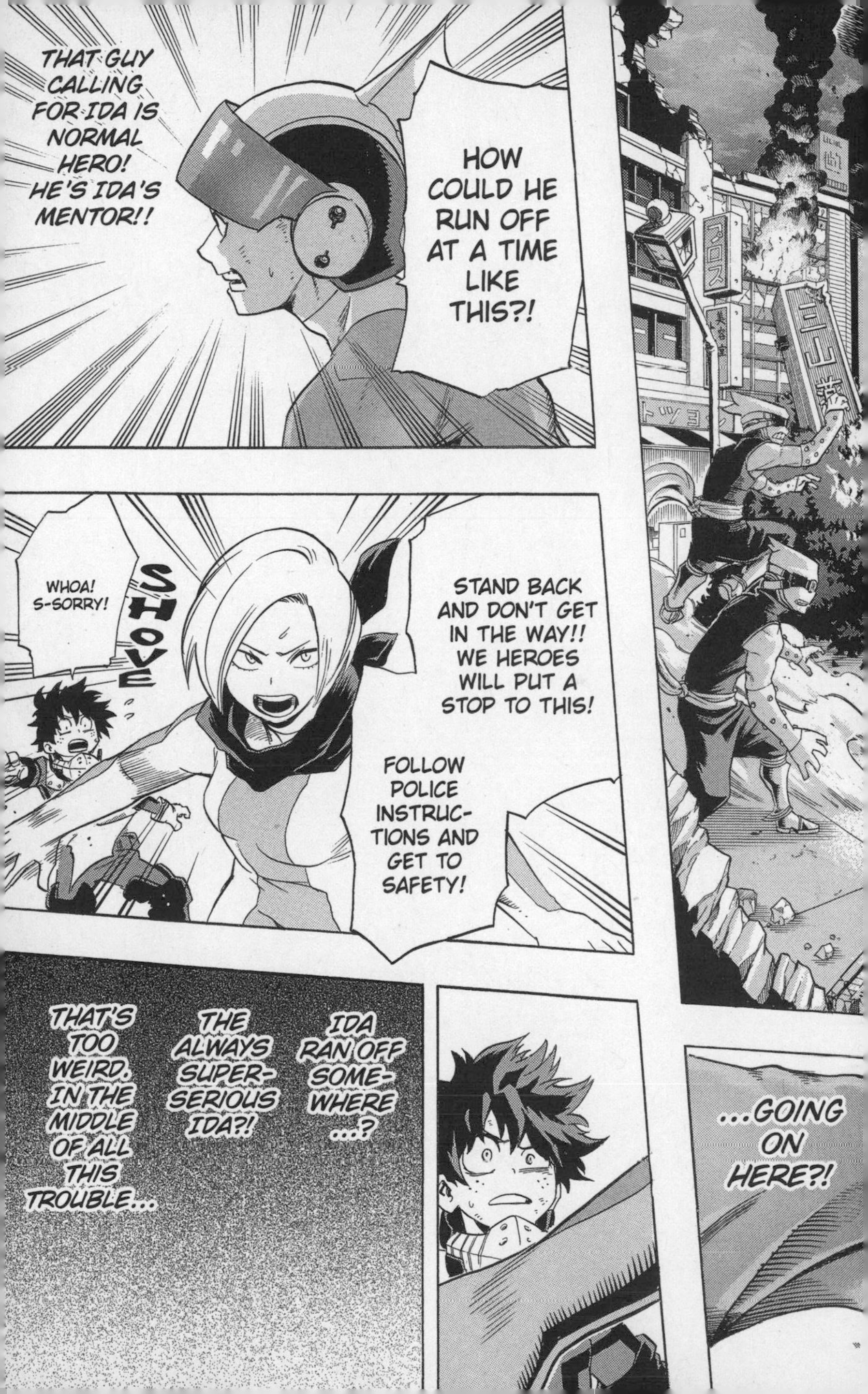
HOW COULD HE RUN OFF AT A TIME LIKE THIS?!
THAT GUY CALLING FOR IDA IS NORMAL HERO! HE'S IDA'S MENTOR!!
STAND BACK AND DON'T GET IN THE WAY!! WE HEROES WILL PUT A STOP TO THIS!
FOLLOW POLICE INSTRUC-TIONS AND GET TO SAFETY!
SHOVE
WHOA! S-SORRY!
...GOING ON HERE?!
IDA RAN OFF SOME-WHERE ...?
THE ALWAYS SUPER-SERIOUS IDA?!
THAT'S TOO WEIRD. IN THE MIDDLE OF ALL THIS TROUBLE...

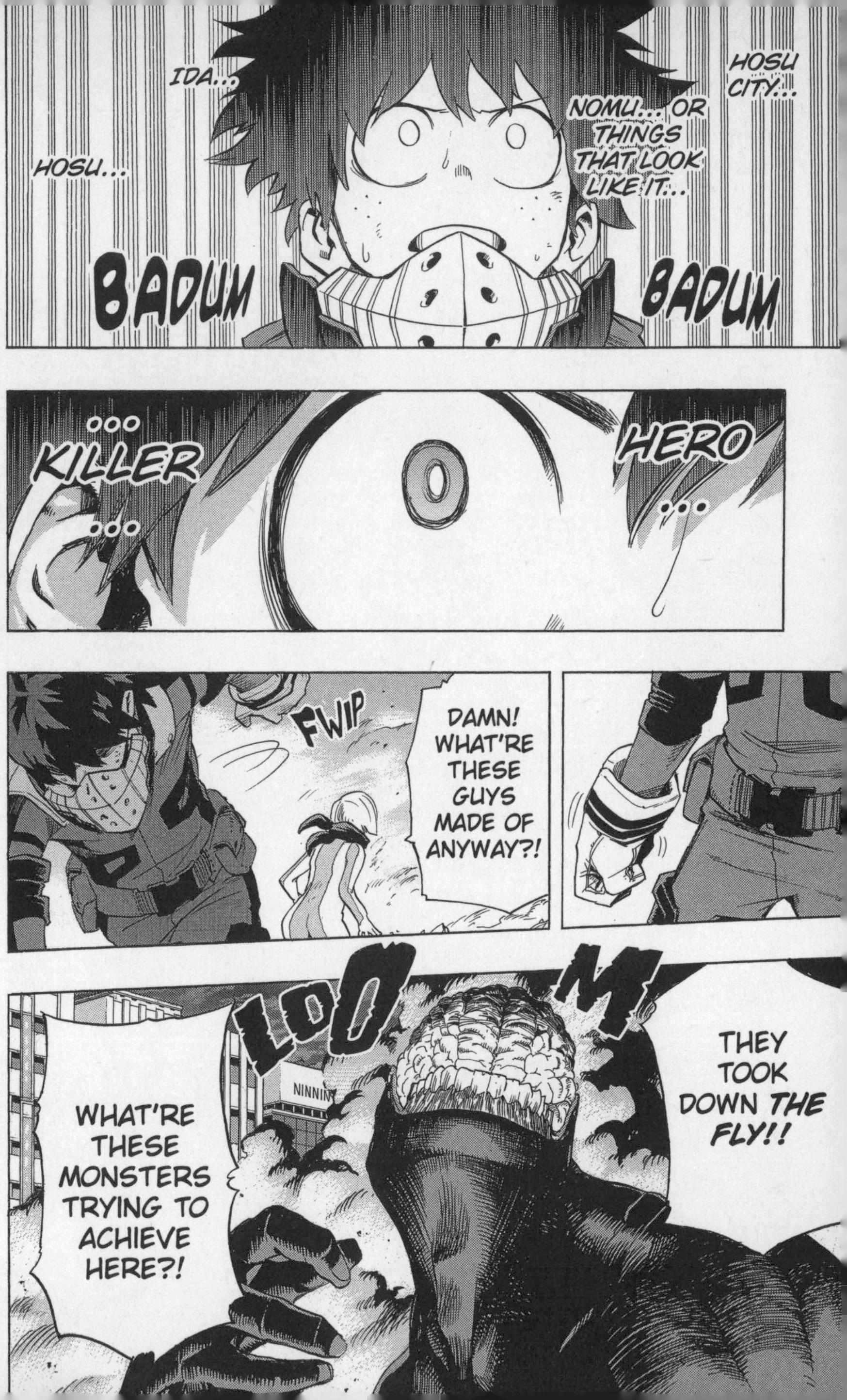
HOSU CITY...
NOMU... OR THINGS THAT LOOK LIKE IT...
IDA...
HOSU...
BADUM
BADUM
HERO ...
... KILLER ...
FWIP
DAMN! WHAT'RE THESE GUYS MADE OF ANYWAY?!
LOOM
THEY TOOK DOWN *THE FLY*!!
WHAT'RE THESE MONSTERS TRYING TO ACHIEVE HERE?!

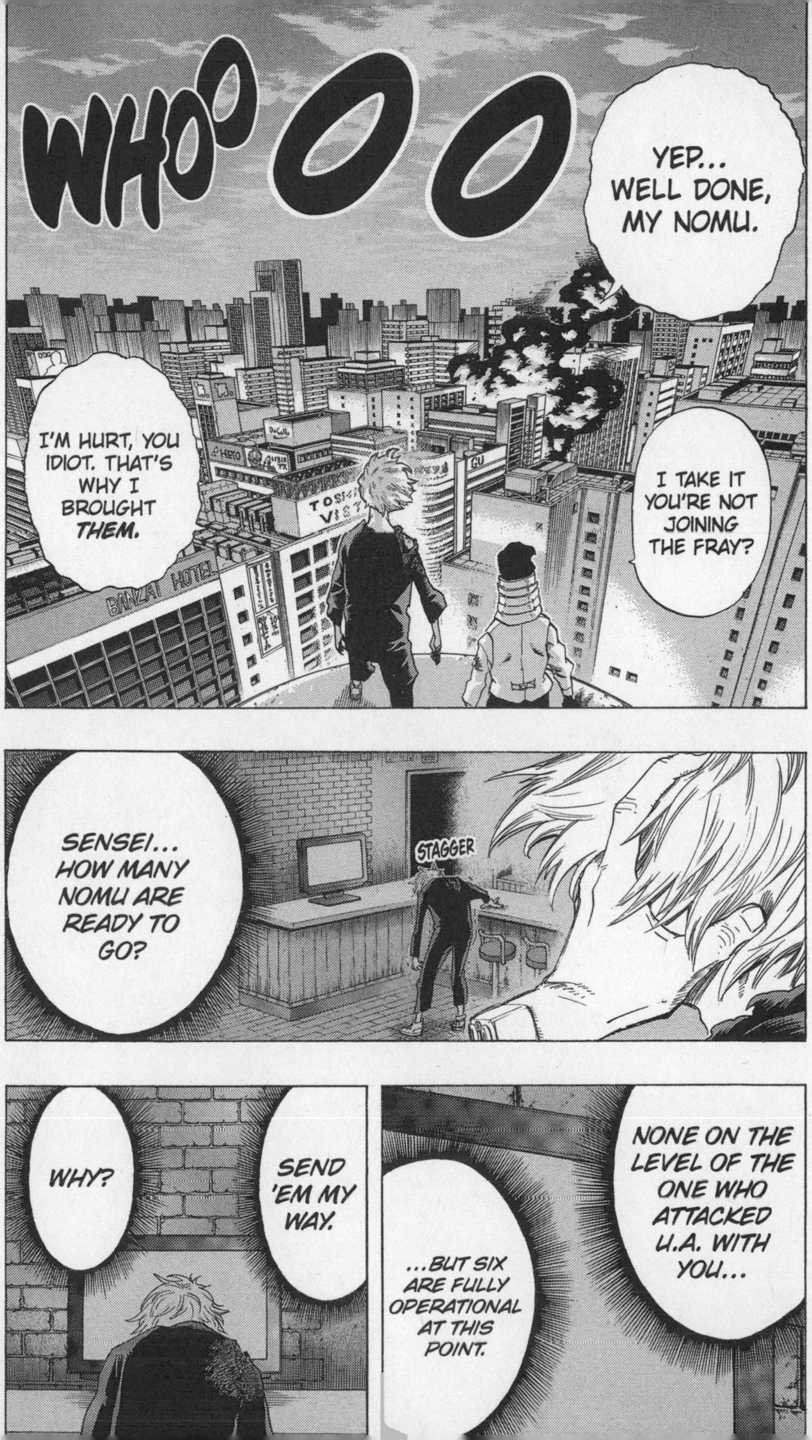
WHOOOO
YEP... WELL DONE, MY NOMU.
I TAKE IT YOU'RE NOT JOINING THE FRAY?
I'M HURT, YOU IDIOT. THAT'S WHY I BROUGHT THEM.
BANZAI HOTEL
STAGGER
SENSEI... HOW MANY NOMU ARE READY TO GO?
NONE ON THE LEVEL OF THE ONE WHO ATTACKED U.A. WITH YOU...
...BUT SIX ARE FULLY OPERATIONAL AT THIS POINT.
SEND 'EM MY WAY.
WHY?

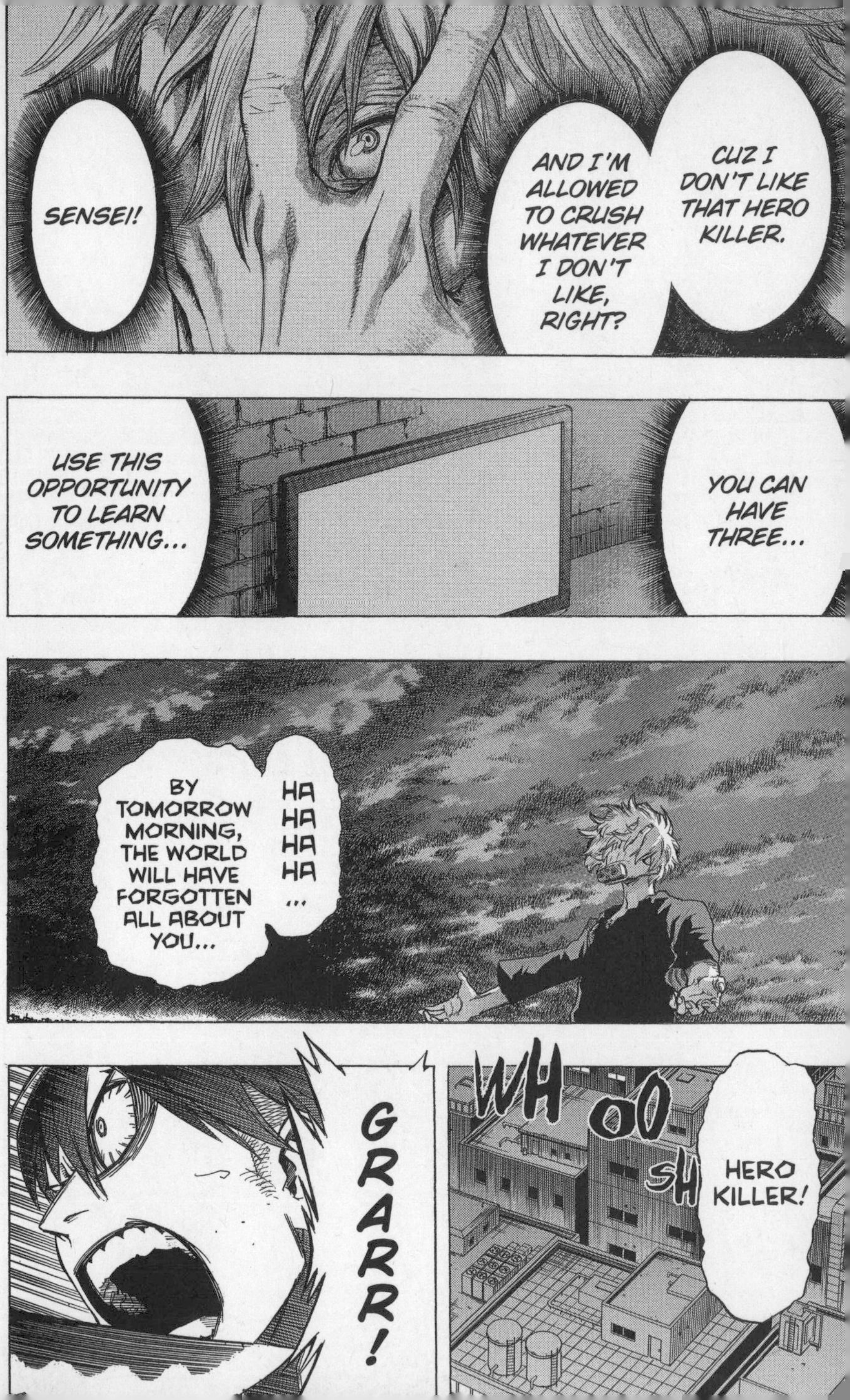
CUZ I DON'T LIKE THAT HERO KILLER.
AND I'M ALLOWED TO CRUSH WHATEVER I DON'T LIKE, RIGHT?
SENSEI!
YOU CAN HAVE THREE...
USE THIS OPPORTUNITY TO LEARN SOMETHING...
HA HA HA HA ...
BY TOMORROW MORNING, THE WORLD WILL HAVE FORGOTTEN ALL ABOUT YOU...
WHOOSH
HERO KILLER!
GRARR!

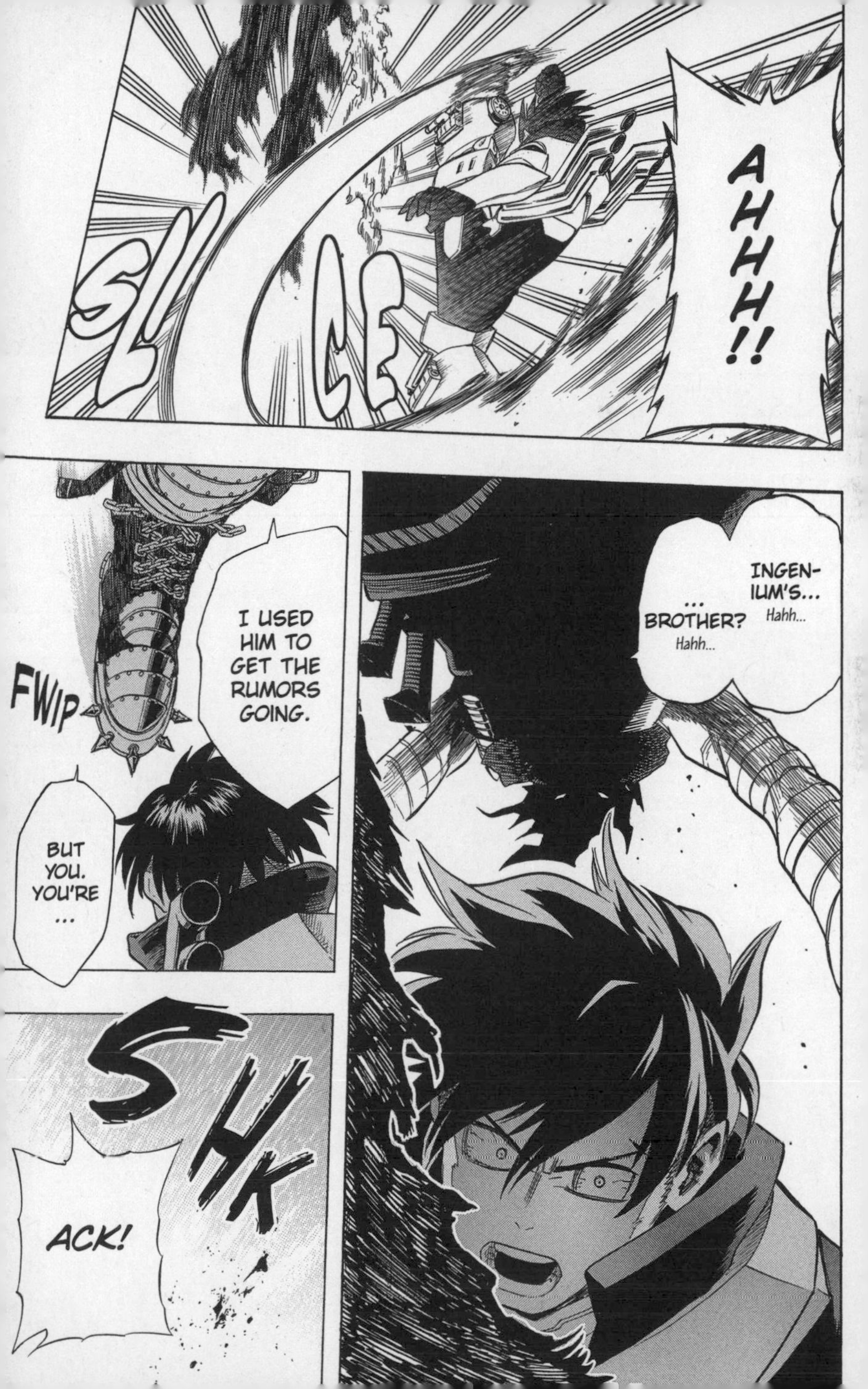
AHHHH!!
SLICE
INGEN-
IUM'S...
Hahh...
... BROTHER?
Hahh...
I USED HIM TO GET THE RUMORS GOING.
FWIP
BUT YOU. YOU'RE ...
SHK
ACK!

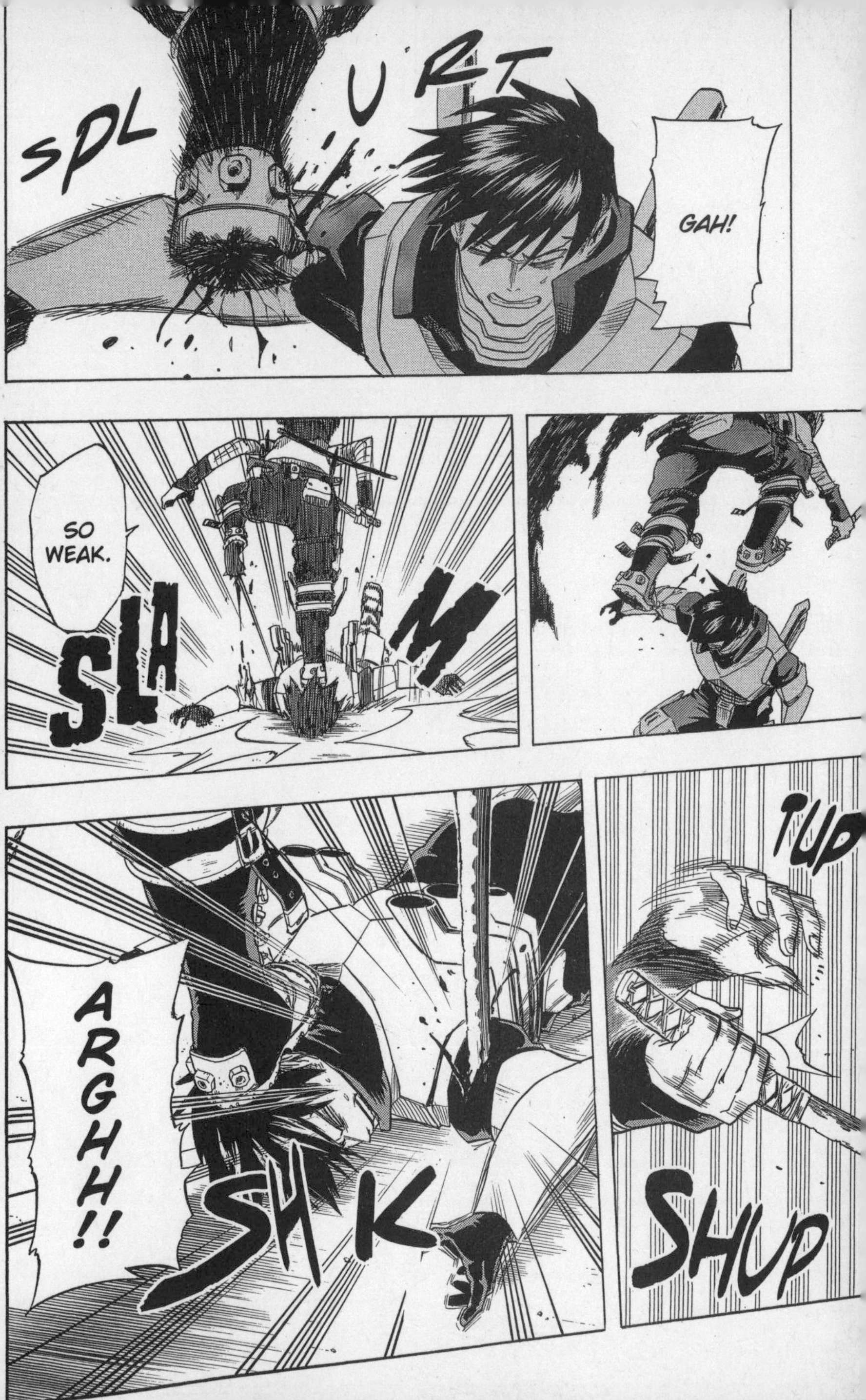
SPLURT
GAH!
SO WEAK.
SLAM
TUD
SHUP
ARGHH!!
SHK

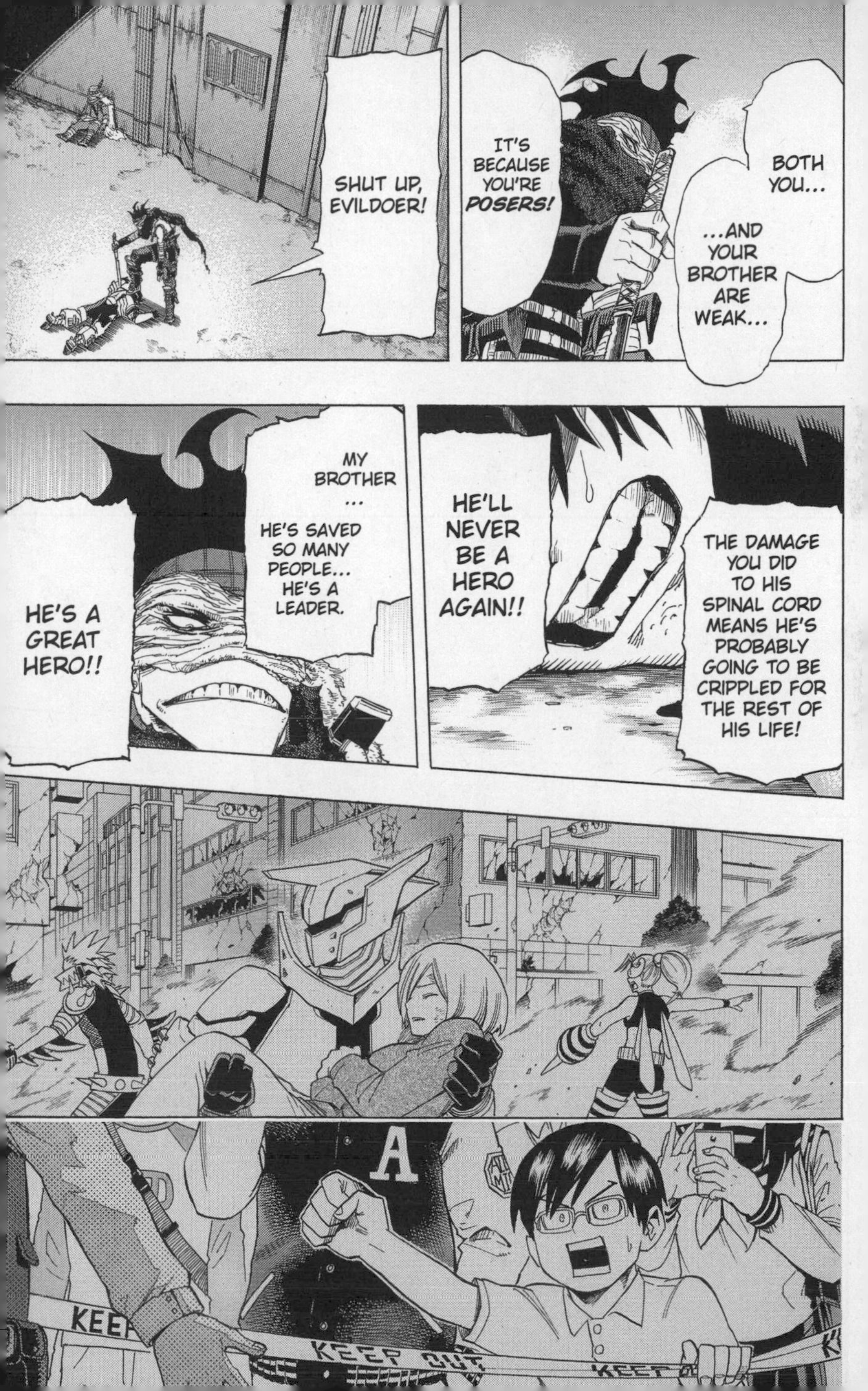
BOTH YOU...
...AND YOUR BROTHER ARE WEAK...
IT'S BECAUSE YOU'RE *POSERS!*
SHUT UP, EVILDOER!
THE DAMAGE YOU DID TO HIS SPINAL CORD MEANS HE'S PROBABLY GOING TO BE CRIPPLED FOR THE REST OF HIS LIFE!
HE'LL NEVER BE A HERO AGAIN!!
MY BROTHER ...
HE'S SAVED SO MANY PEOPLE... HE'S A LEADER.
HE'S A GREAT HERO!!
KEEP OUT
KEEP

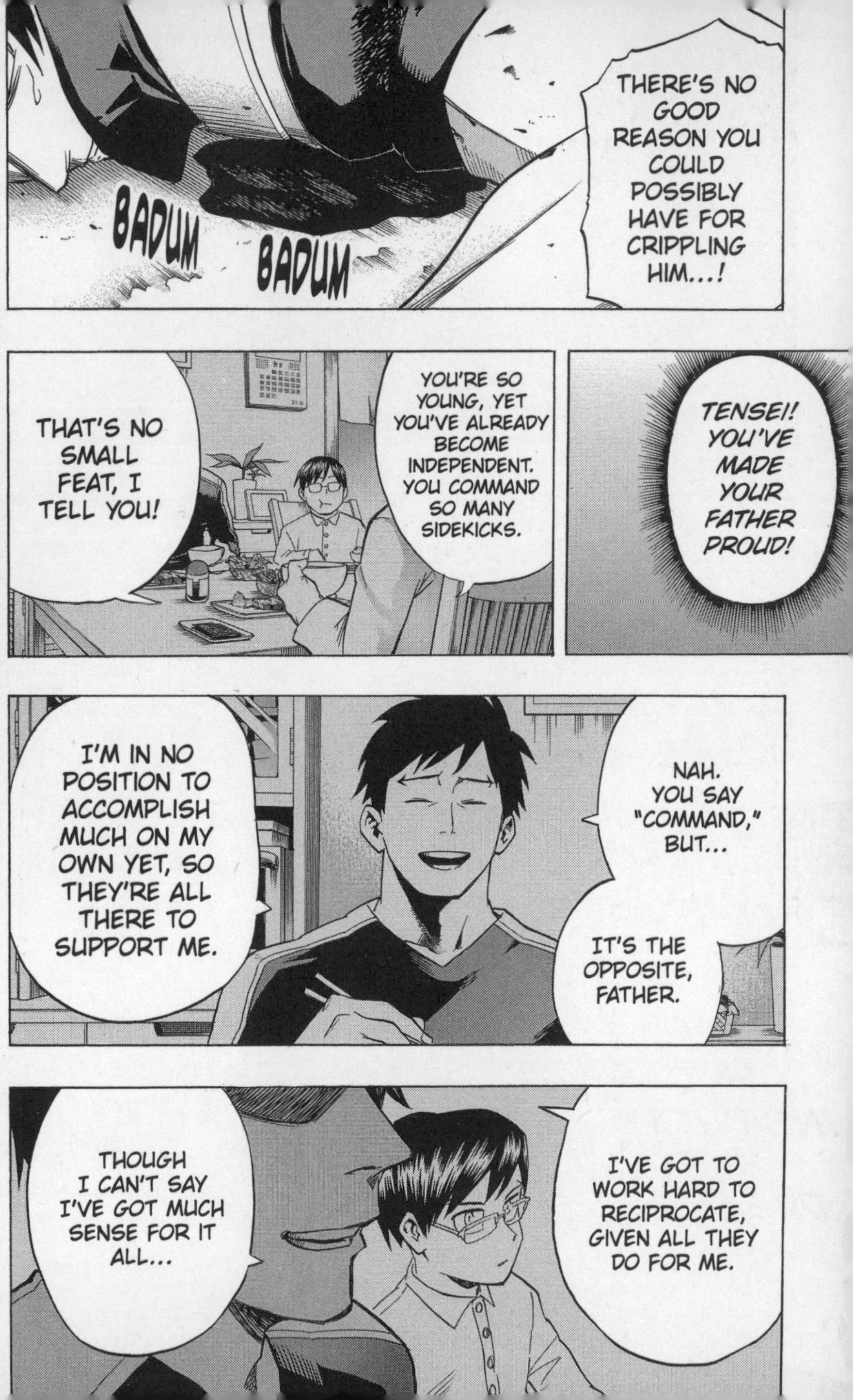
THERE'S NO GOOD REASON YOU COULD POSSIBLY HAVE FOR CRIPPLING HIM...!
BADUM
BADUM
TENSEI! YOU'VE MADE YOUR FATHER PROUD!
YOU'RE SO YOUNG, YET YOU'VE ALREADY BECOME INDEPENDENT. YOU COMMAND SO MANY SIDEKICKS.
THAT'S NO SMALL FEAT, I TELL YOU!
NAH. YOU SAY "COMMAND," BUT...
IT'S THE OPPOSITE, FATHER.
I'M IN NO POSITION TO ACCOMPLISH MUCH ON MY OWN YET, SO THEY'RE ALL THERE TO SUPPORT ME.
I'VE GOT TO WORK HARD TO RECIPROCATE, GIVEN ALL THEY DO FOR ME.
THOUGH I CAN'T SAY I'VE GOT MUCH SENSE FOR IT ALL...

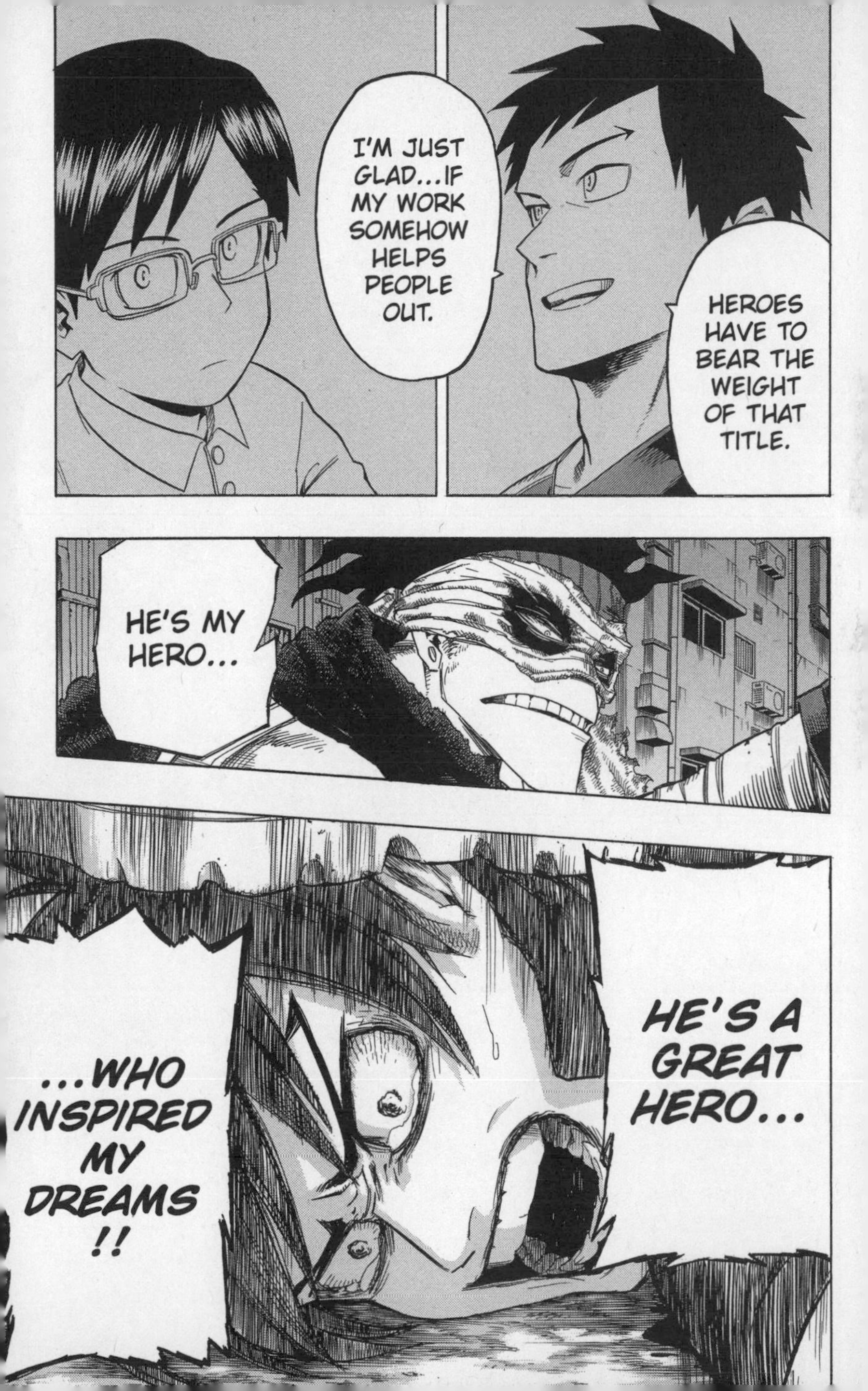
HEROES HAVE TO BEAR THE WEIGHT OF THAT TITLE.
I'M JUST GLAD...IF MY WORK SOMEHOW HELPS PEOPLE OUT.
HE'S MY HERO...
HE'S A GREAT HERO...
...WHO INSPIRED MY DREAMS!!

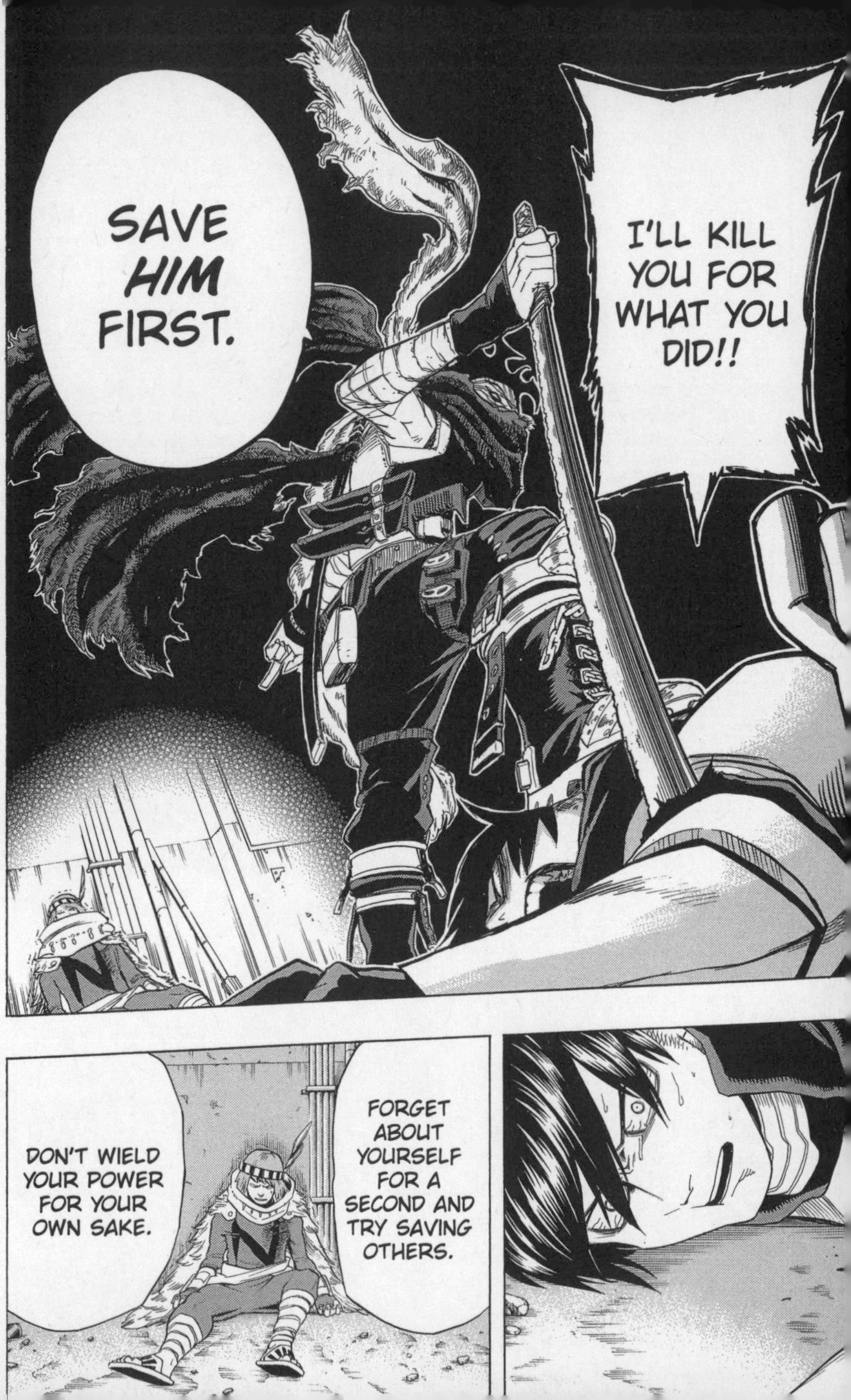
I'LL KILL YOU FOR WHAT YOU DID!!
SAVE *HIM* FIRST.
FORGET ABOUT YOURSELF FOR A SECOND AND TRY SAVING OTHERS.
DON'T WIELD YOUR POWER FOR YOUR OWN SAKE.

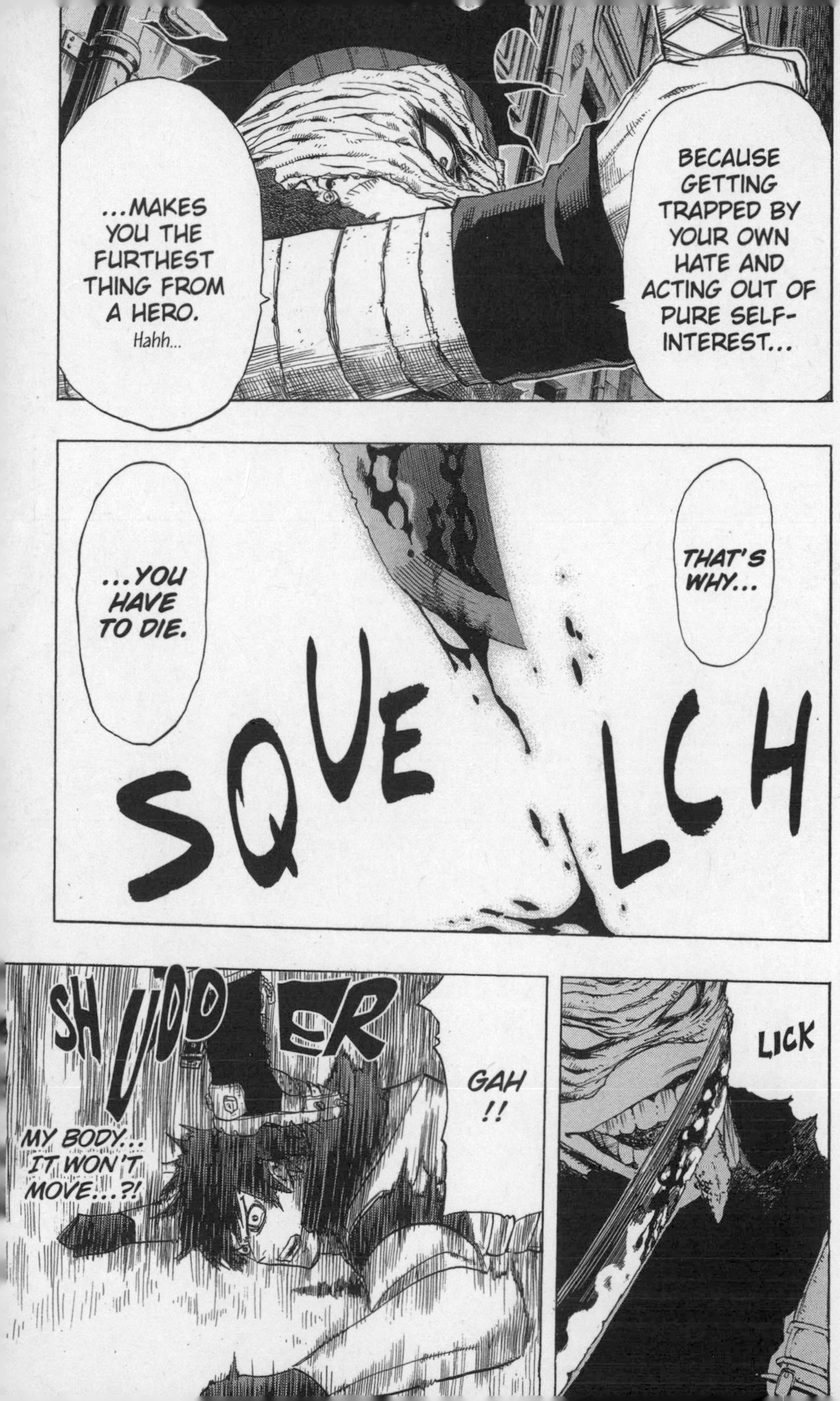
BECAUSE GETTING TRAPPED BY YOUR OWN HATE AND ACTING OUT OF PURE SELF-INTEREST...
...MAKES YOU THE FURTHEST THING FROM A HERO.
Hahh...
THAT'S WHY...
...YOU HAVE TO DIE.
SQUELCH
LICK
GAH !!
SHUDDER
MY BODY... IT WON'T MOVE...?!

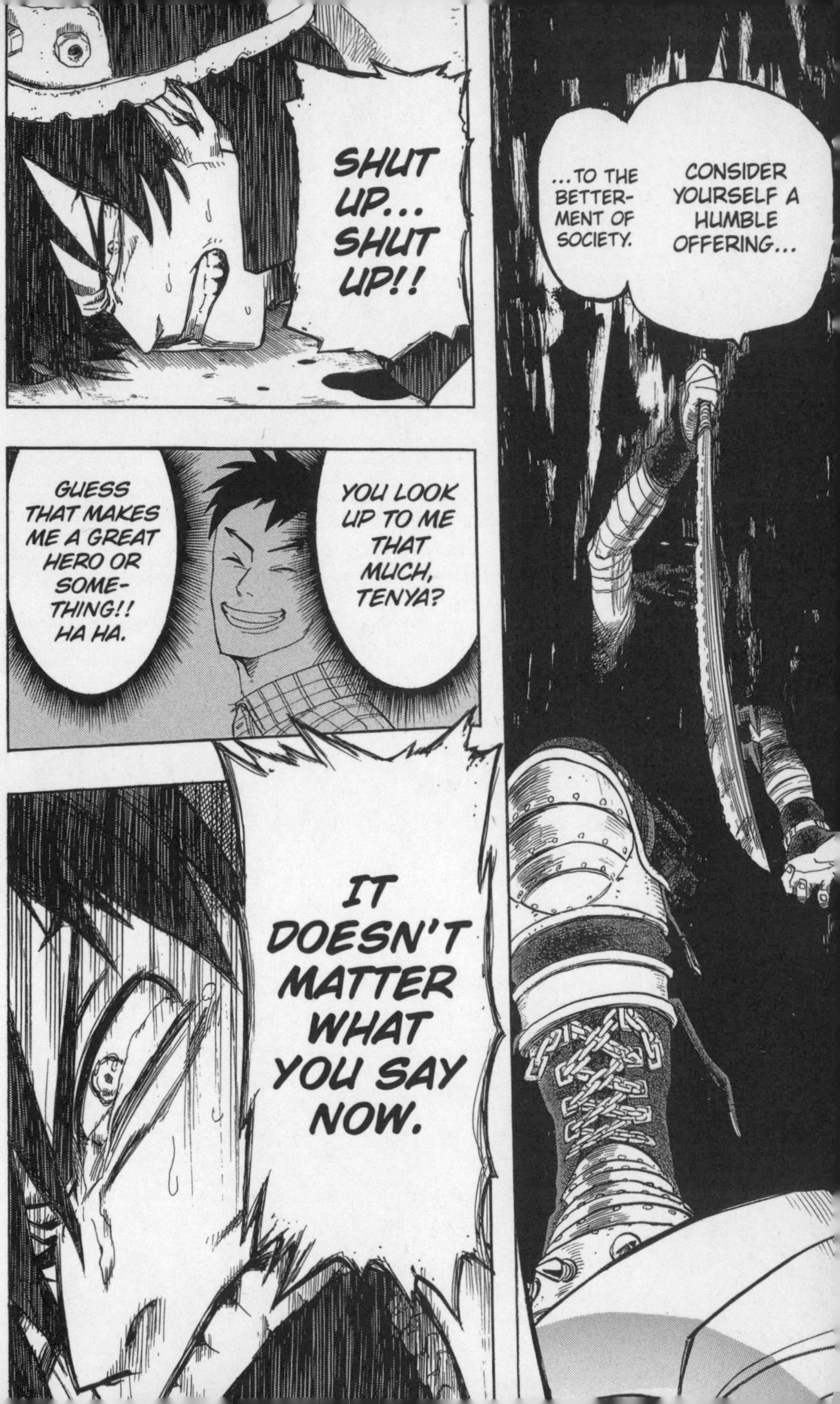

CONSIDER YOURSELF A HUMBLE OFFERING...
...TO THE BETTERMENT OF SOCIETY.
SHUT UP... SHUT UP!!
YOU LOOK UP TO ME THAT MUCH, TENYA?
GUESS THAT MAKES ME A GREAT HERO OR SOMETHING!! HA HA.
IT DOESN'T MATTER WHAT YOU SAY NOW.

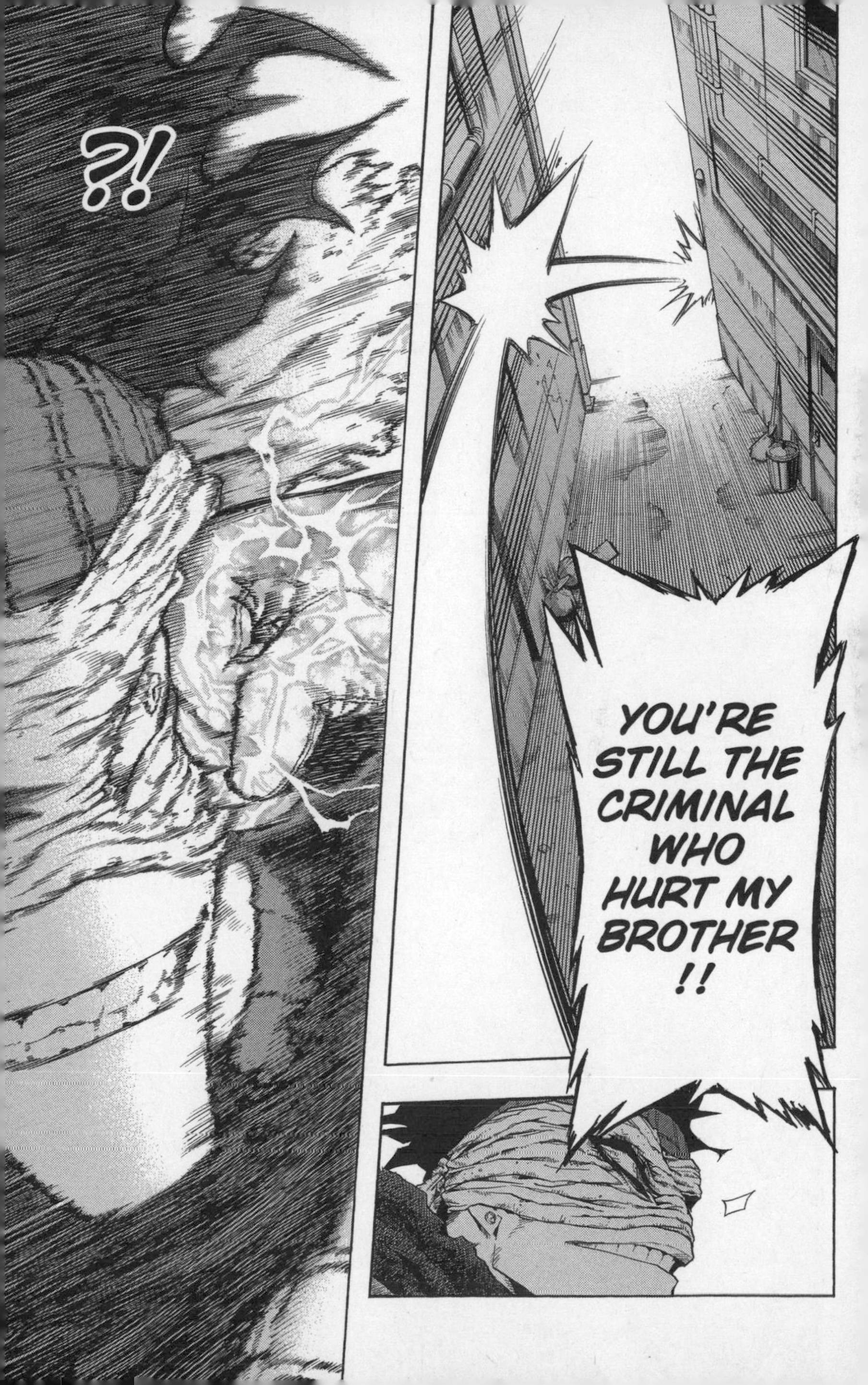
YOU'RE STILL THE CRIMINAL WHO HURT MY BROTHER !!
?!

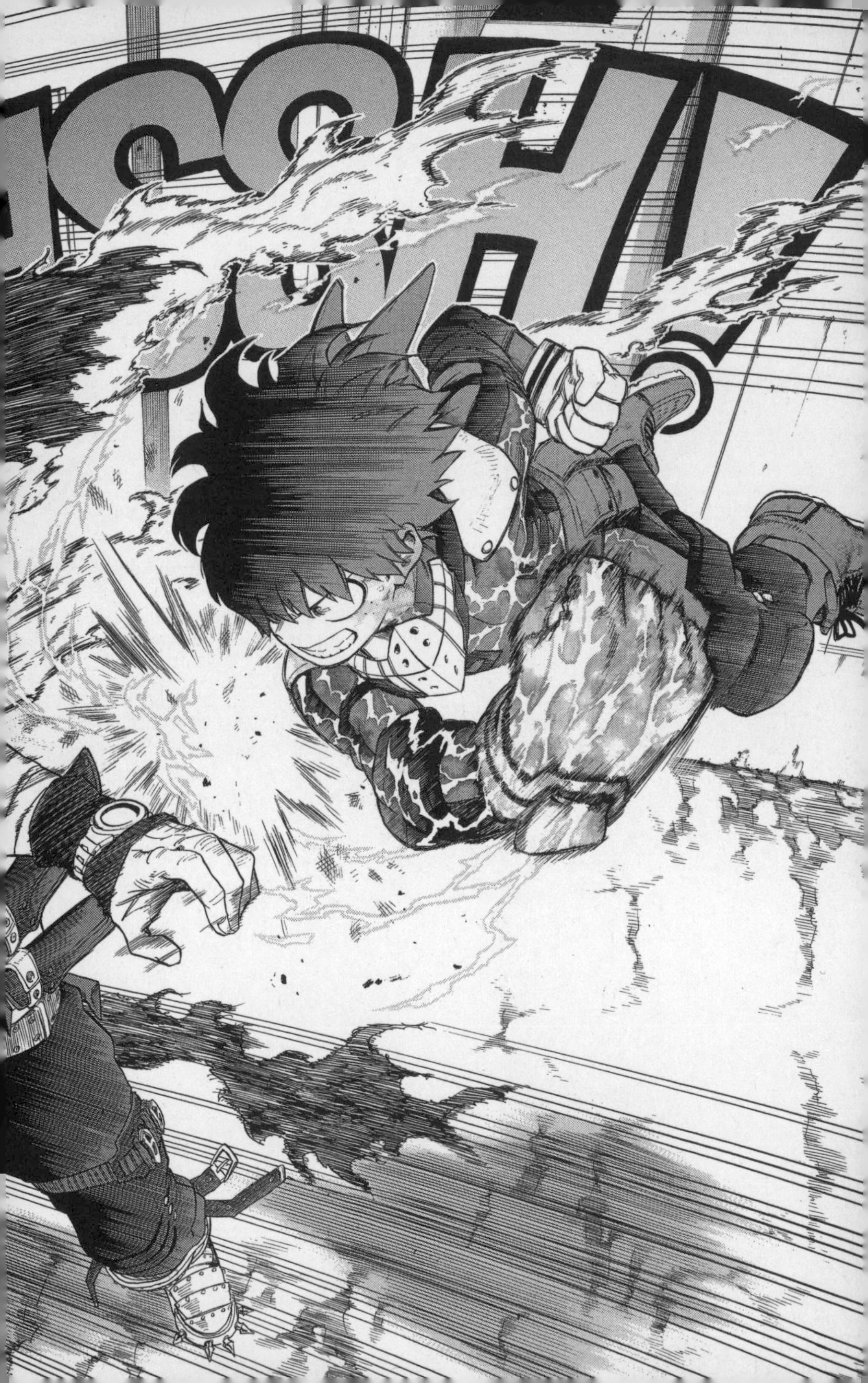

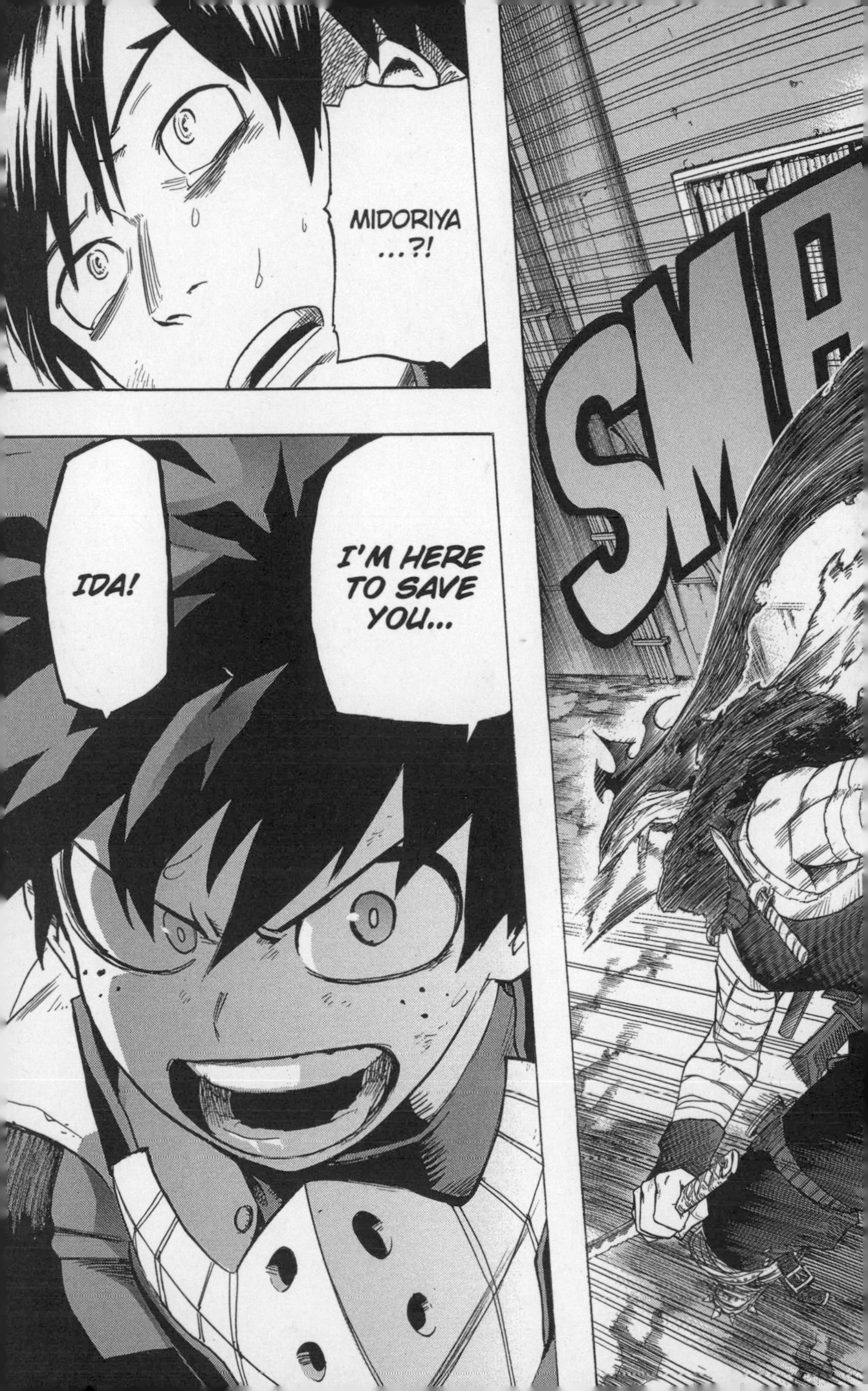
MIDORIYA ...?!
I'M HERE TO SAVE YOU...
IDA!

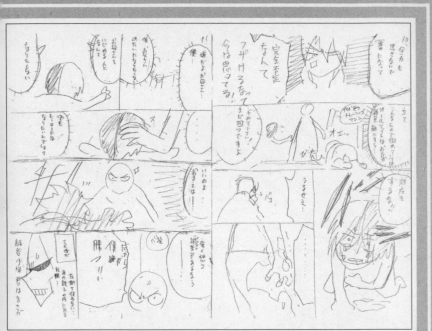

THE "SUDDENLY, A ROUGH DRAFT" CORNER
("FILLING IN BLANK PAGES" CORNER)

This is a rough draft of pages from volume 5's "Deku vs. Todoroki" (No. 39). If you compare with the graphic novel release, you'll notice that the panel placements are slightly different (the middle section of the left page, in particular). That's because when you have a double-page spread, you want the four rows of panels to line up on each side. It's a matter of presentation, not just the panel placement. Once I get the green light for the rough draft, I go ahead and fiddle with the composition and dialogue too.

I'm always in a battle against deadlines, so the purpose of the rough draft is to give a quick and dirty presentation of the flow of the chapter, with less room for details.

So once I get that green light, I'll self-edit certain spots for the final draft.

Sometimes, my editor tells me a chapter came out better than in the rough draft, which is a thrill—though it's only happened once or twice.

In summary, time doesn't grow on trees.

End of lesson!

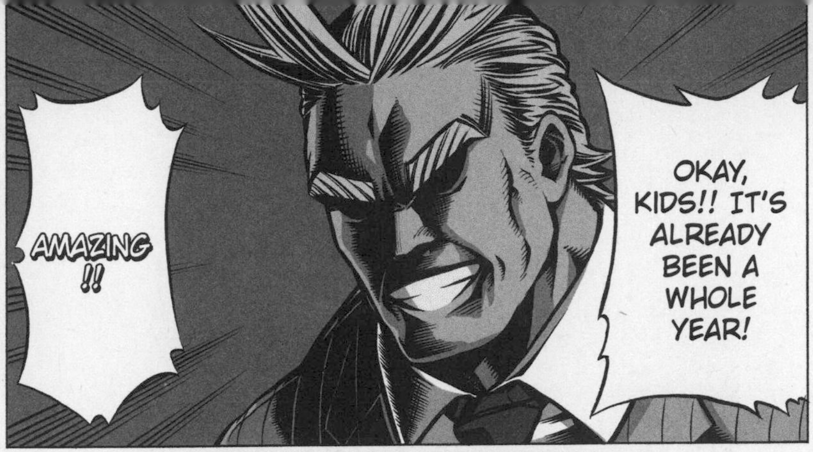
OKAY, KIDS!! IT'S ALREADY BEEN A WHOLE YEAR!
AMAZING!!

No. 52 - Hero Killer Stain vs. U.A. Students

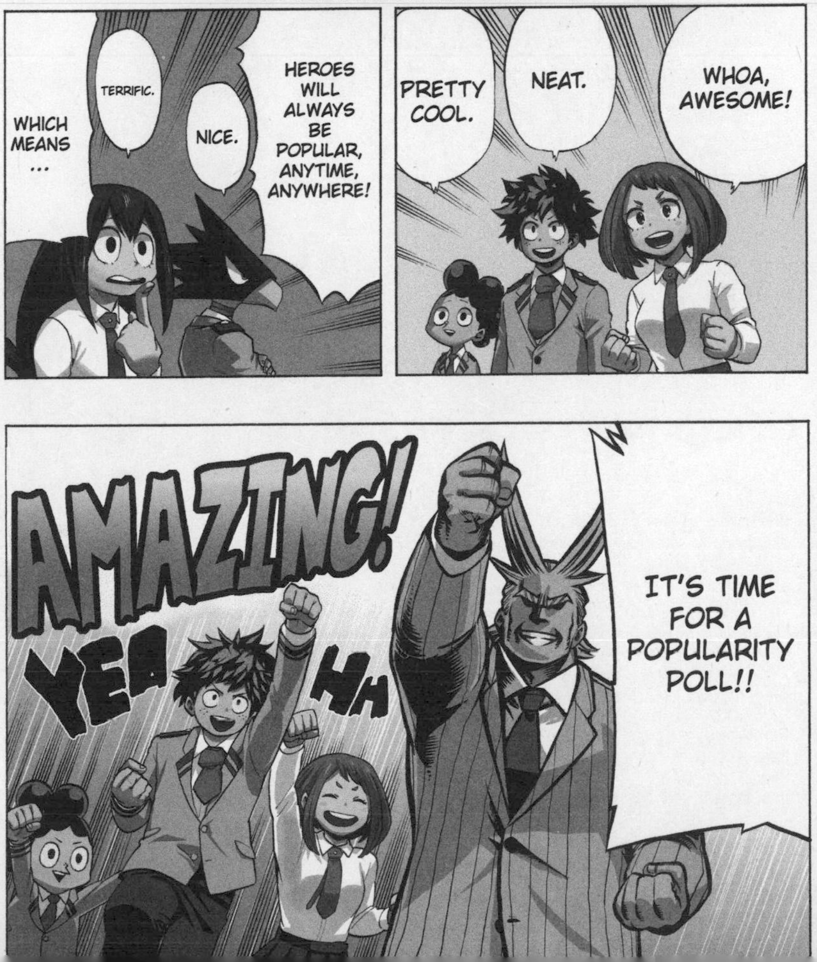
WHOA, AWESOME!
NEAT.
PRETTY COOL.
HEROES WILL ALWAYS BE POPULAR, ANYTIME, ANYWHERE!
NICE.
TERRIFIC.
WHICH MEANS...
IT'S TIME FOR A POPULARITY POLL!!
AMAZING!
YEAHH

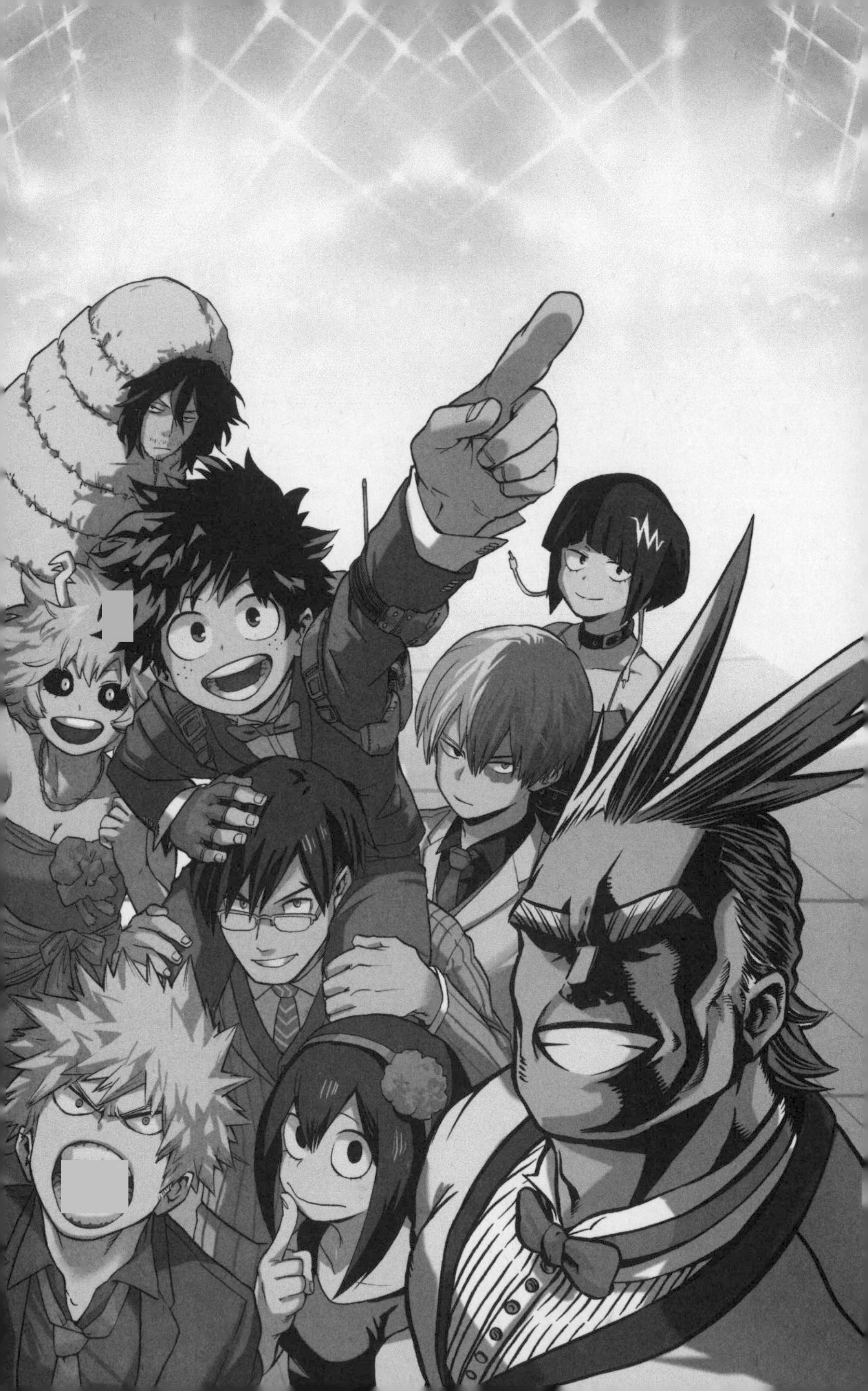

No. 52 - Hero Killer Stain vs. U.A. Students

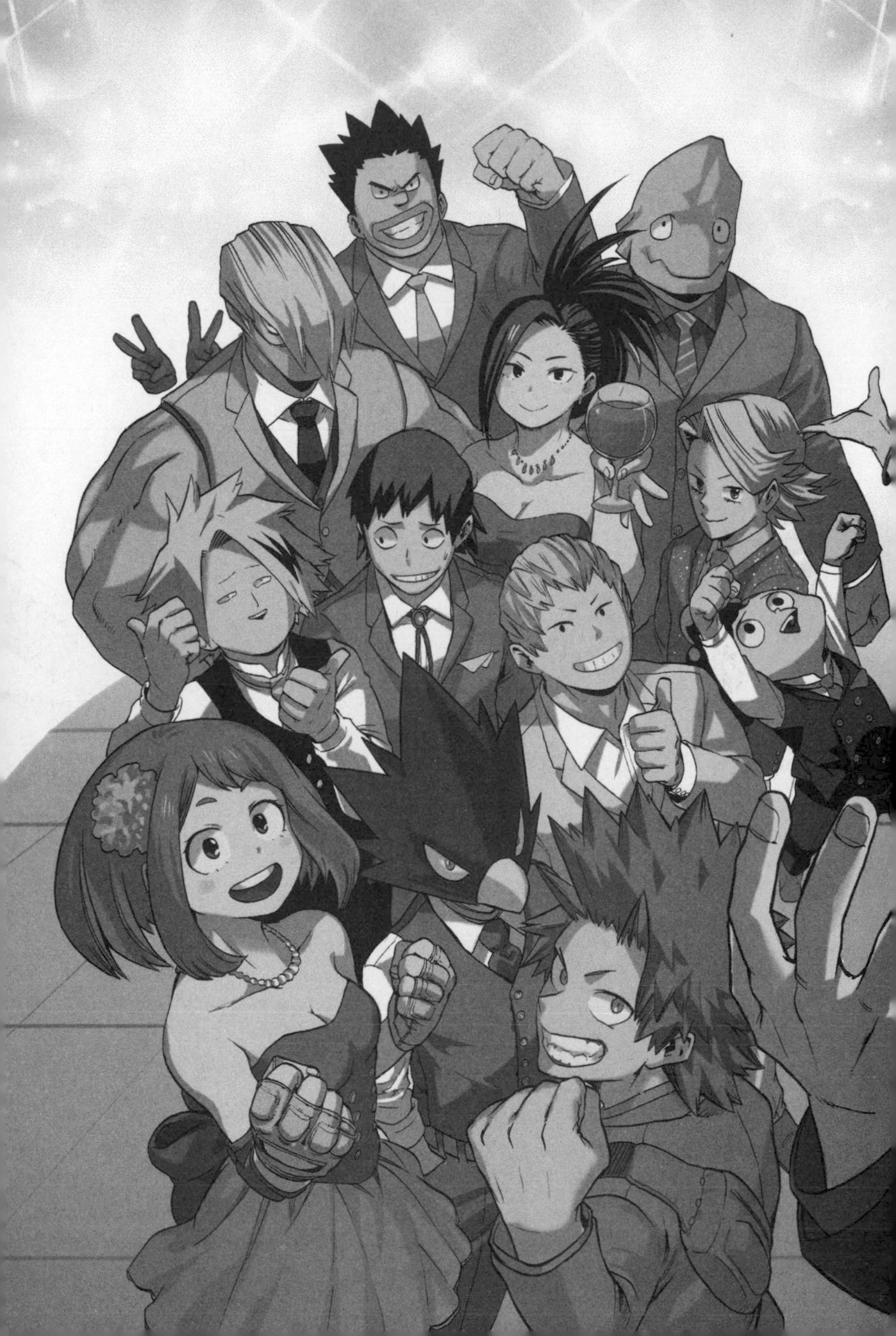

MY HERO ACADEMIA

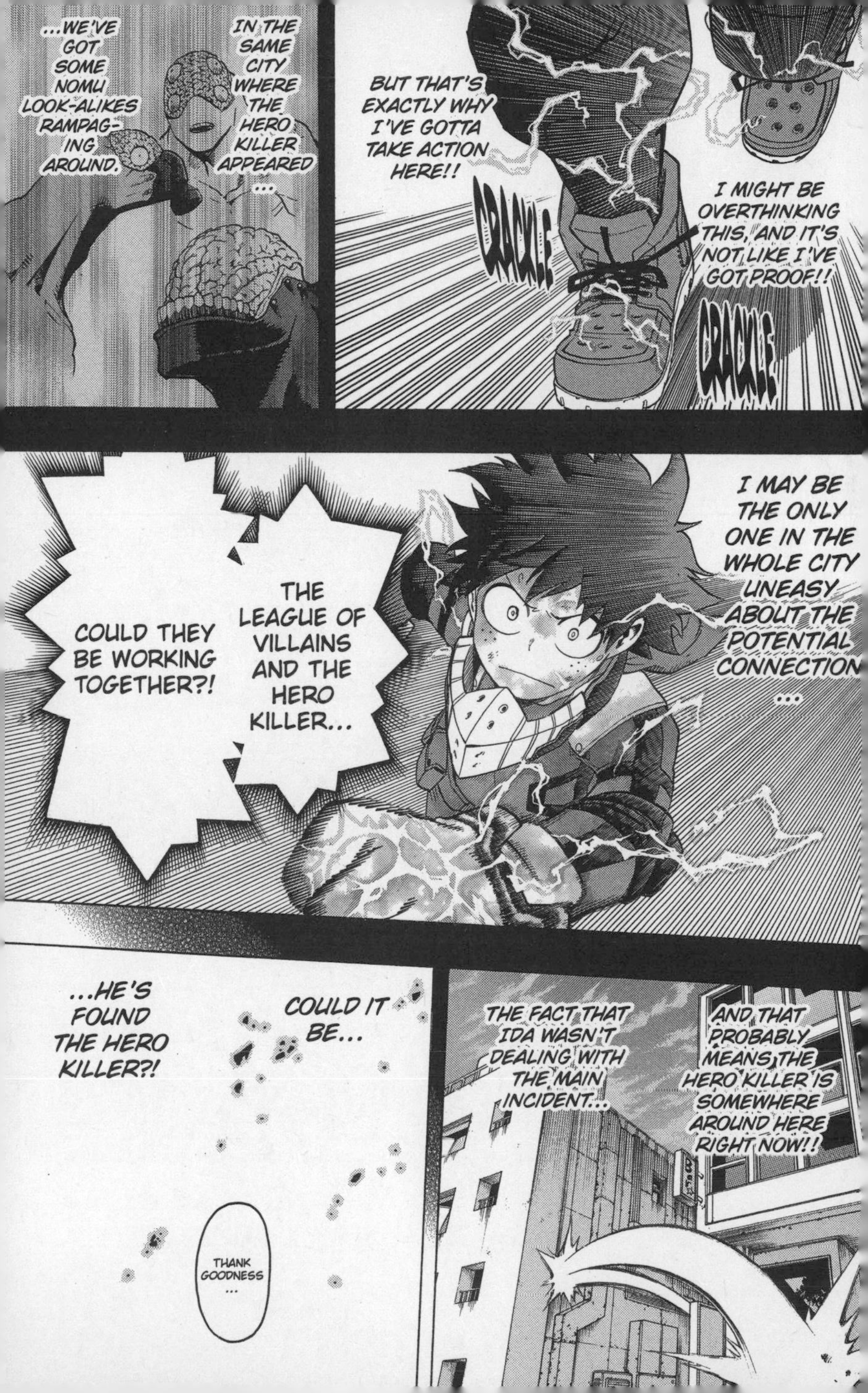
I MIGHT BE OVERTHINKING THIS, AND IT'S NOT LIKE I'VE GOT PROOF!!
CRACKLE
BUT THAT'S EXACTLY WHY I'VE GOTTA TAKE ACTION HERE!!
CRACKLE
IN THE SAME CITY WHERE THE HERO KILLER APPEARED...
...WE'VE GOT SOME NOMU LOOK-ALIKES RAMPAG-ING AROUND.
I MAY BE THE ONLY ONE IN THE WHOLE CITY UNEASY ABOUT THE POTENTIAL CONNECTION...
THE LEAGUE OF VILLAINS AND THE HERO KILLER...
COULD THEY BE WORKING TOGETHER?!
AND THAT PROBABLY MEANS THE HERO KILLER IS SOMEWHERE AROUND HERE RIGHT NOW!!
THE FACT THAT IDA WASN'T DEALING WITH THE MAIN INCIDENT...
COULD IT BE...
...HE'S FOUND THE HERO KILLER?!
THANK GOODNESS...

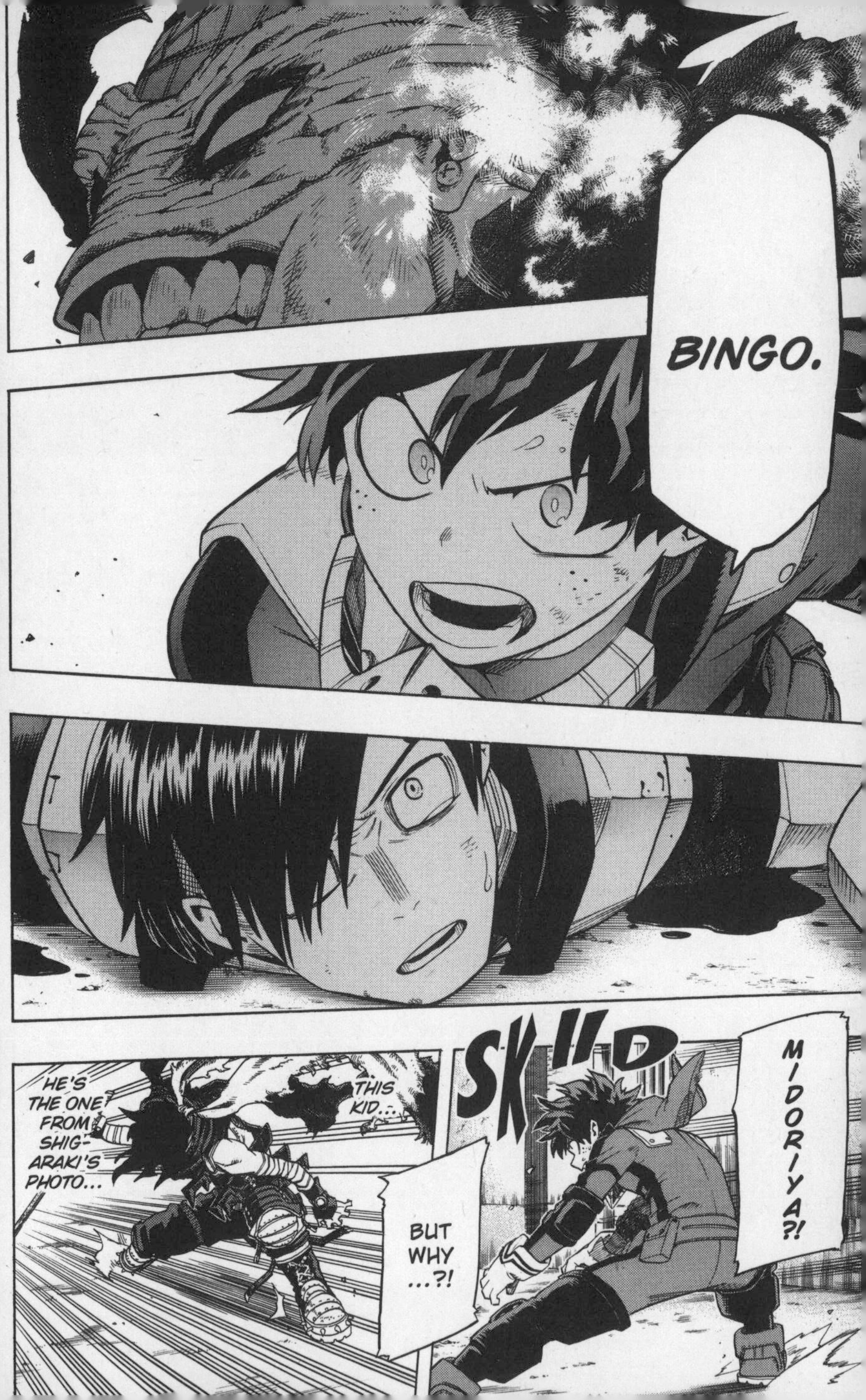
BINGO.
MIDORIYA?!
SKID
THIS KID...
HE'S THE ONE FROM SHIGARAKI'S PHOTO...
BUT WHY ...?!

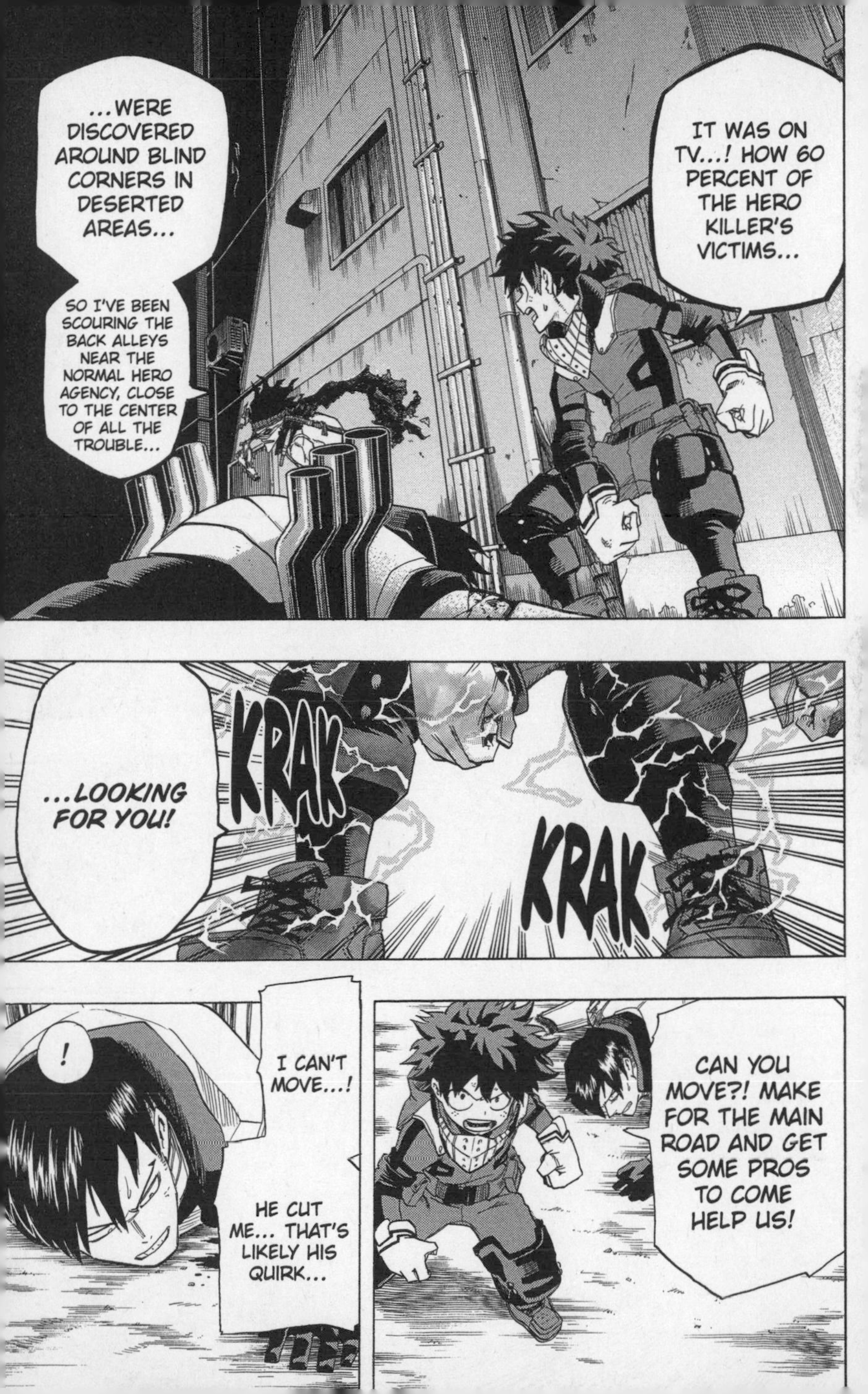
IT WAS ON TV...! HOW 60 PERCENT OF THE HERO KILLER'S VICTIMS...
...WERE DISCOVERED AROUND BLIND CORNERS IN DESERTED AREAS...
SO I'VE BEEN SCOURING THE BACK ALLEYS NEAR THE NORMAL HERO AGENCY, CLOSE TO THE CENTER OF ALL THE TROUBLE...
KRAK
KRAK
...LOOKING FOR YOU!
CAN YOU MOVE?! MAKE FOR THE MAIN ROAD AND GET SOME PROS TO COME HELP US!
!
I CAN'T MOVE...!
HE CUT ME... THAT'S LIKELY HIS QUIRK...

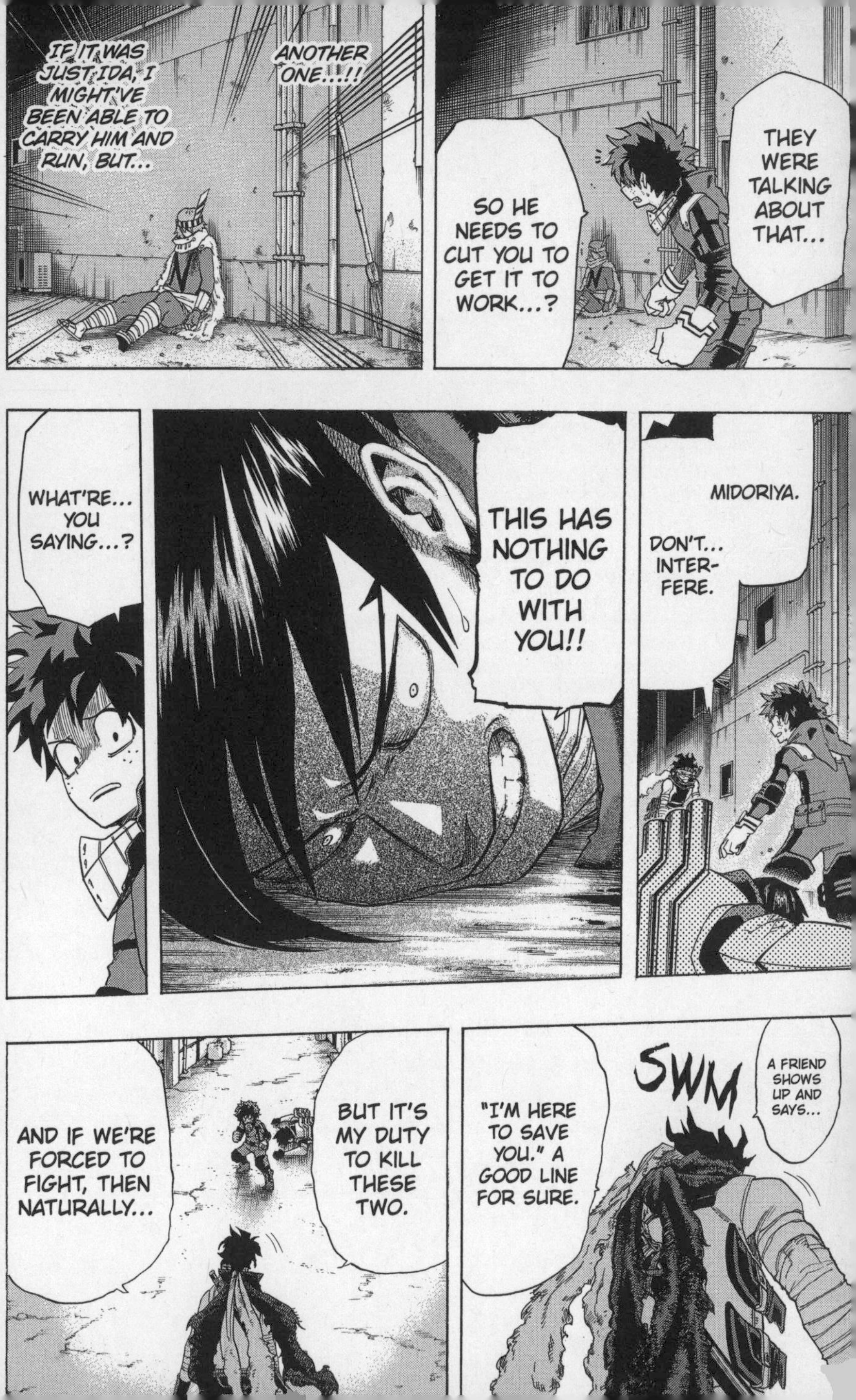
THEY WERE TALKING ABOUT THAT...
SO HE NEEDS TO CUT YOU TO GET IT TO WORK...?
ANOTHER ONE...!!
IF IT WAS JUST IDA, I MIGHT'VE BEEN ABLE TO CARRY HIM AND RUN, BUT...
MIDORIYA.
DON'T... INTER-FERE.
THIS HAS NOTHING TO DO WITH YOU!!
WHAT'RE... YOU SAYING...?
A FRIEND SHOWS UP AND SAYS...
SWM
"I'M HERE TO SAVE YOU." A GOOD LINE FOR SURE.
BUT IT'S MY DUTY TO KILL THESE TWO.
AND IF WE'RE FORCED TO FIGHT, THEN NATURALLY...

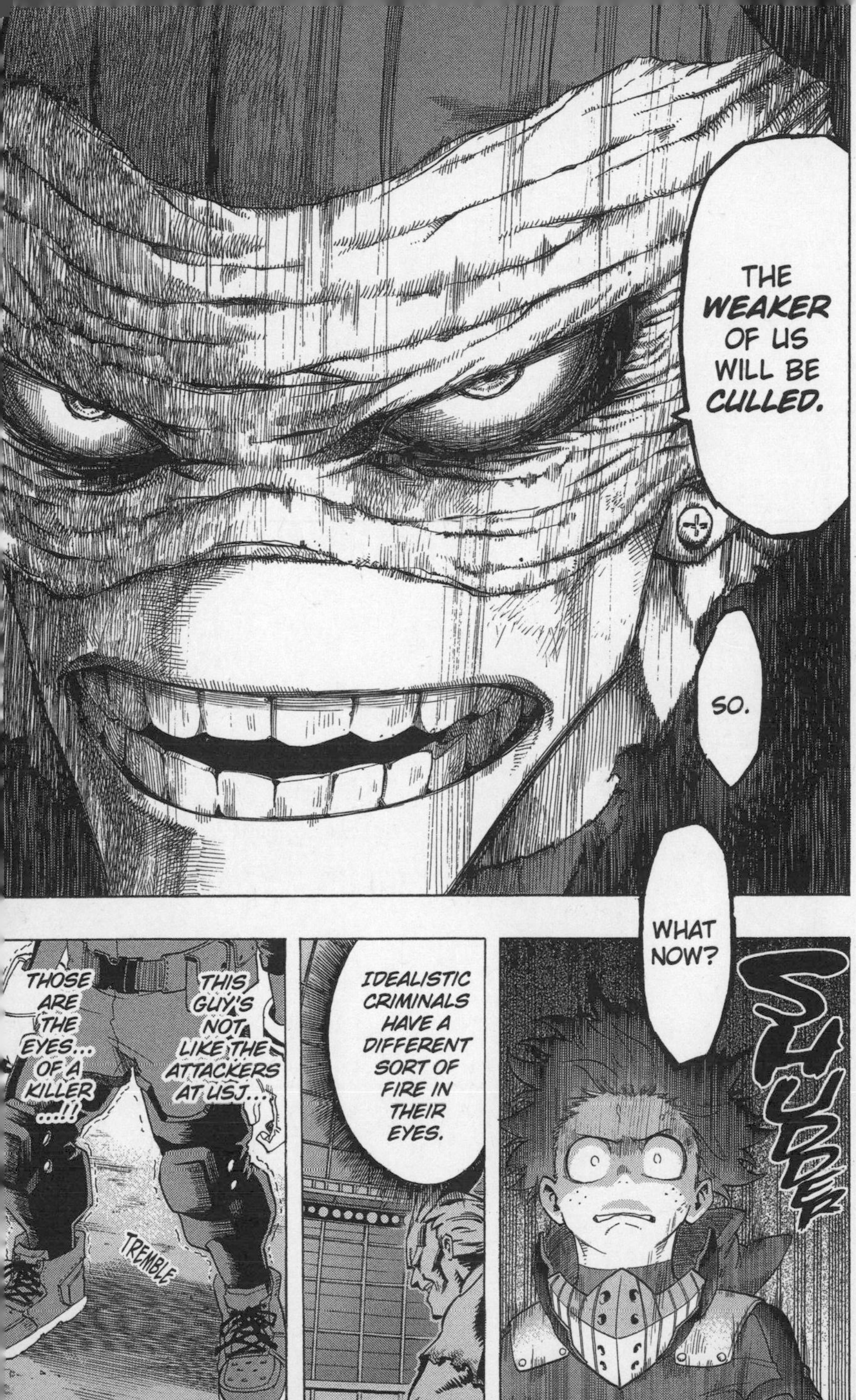
THE WEAKER OF US WILL BE CULLED.
SO.
WHAT NOW?
SHUDDER
IDEALISTIC CRIMINALS HAVE A DIFFERENT SORT OF FIRE IN THEIR EYES.
THIS GUY'S NOT LIKE THE ATTACKERS AT USJ...
THOSE ARE THE EYES... OF A KILLER ...!!
TREMBLE

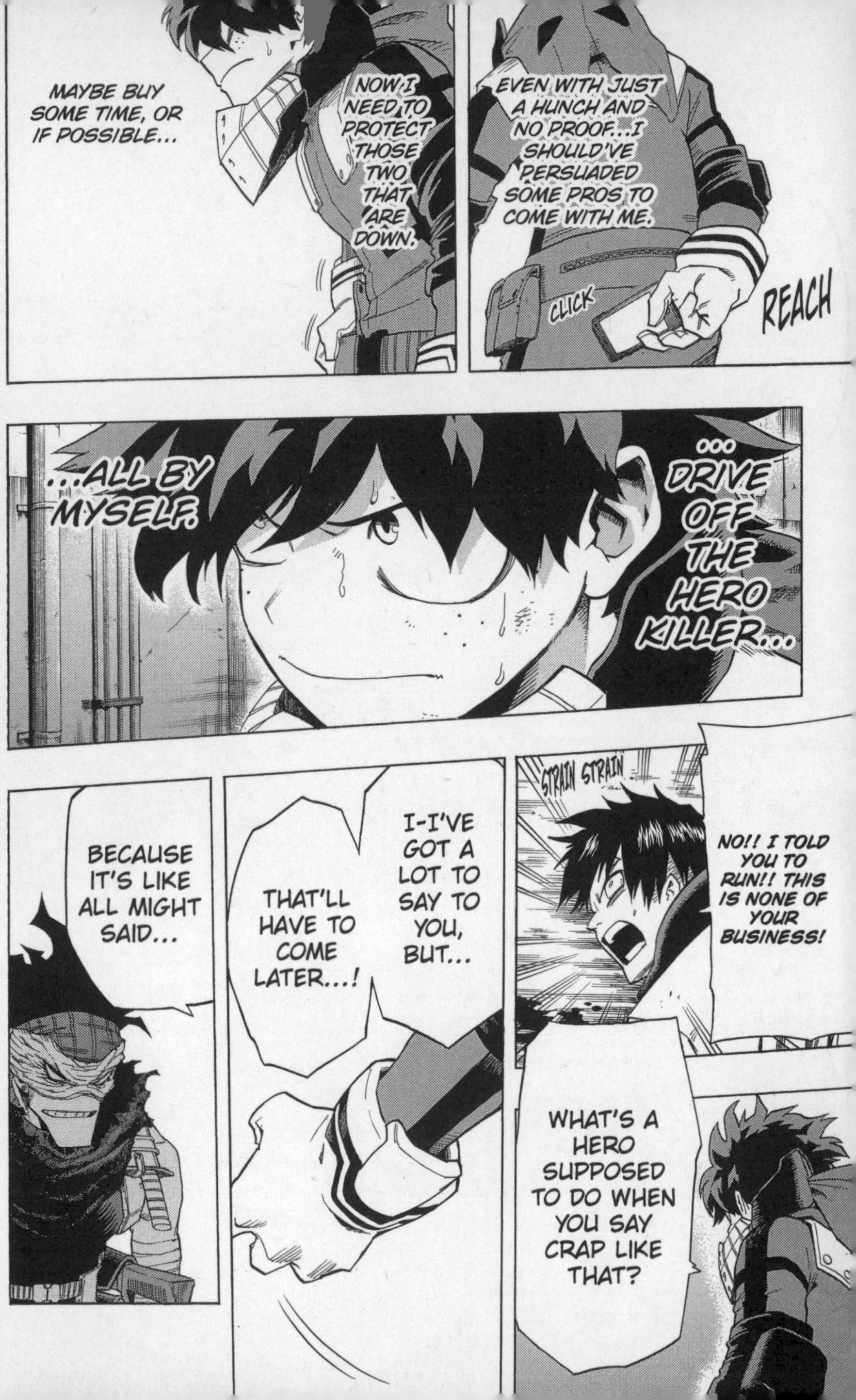
EVEN WITH JUST A HUNCH AND NO PROOF...I SHOULD'VE PERSUADED SOME PROS TO COME WITH ME.
REACH
CLICK
NOW I NEED TO PROTECT THOSE TWO THAT ARE DOWN.
MAYBE BUY SOME TIME, OR IF POSSIBLE...
...DRIVE OFF THE HERO KILLER...
...ALL BY MYSELF.
STRAIN STRAIN
NO!! I TOLD YOU TO RUN!! THIS IS NONE OF YOUR BUSINESS!
WHAT'S A HERO SUPPOSED TO DO WHEN YOU SAY CRAP LIKE THAT?
I-I'VE GOT A LOT TO SAY TO YOU, BUT...
THAT'LL HAVE TO COME LATER...!
BECAUSE IT'S LIKE ALL MIGHT SAID...

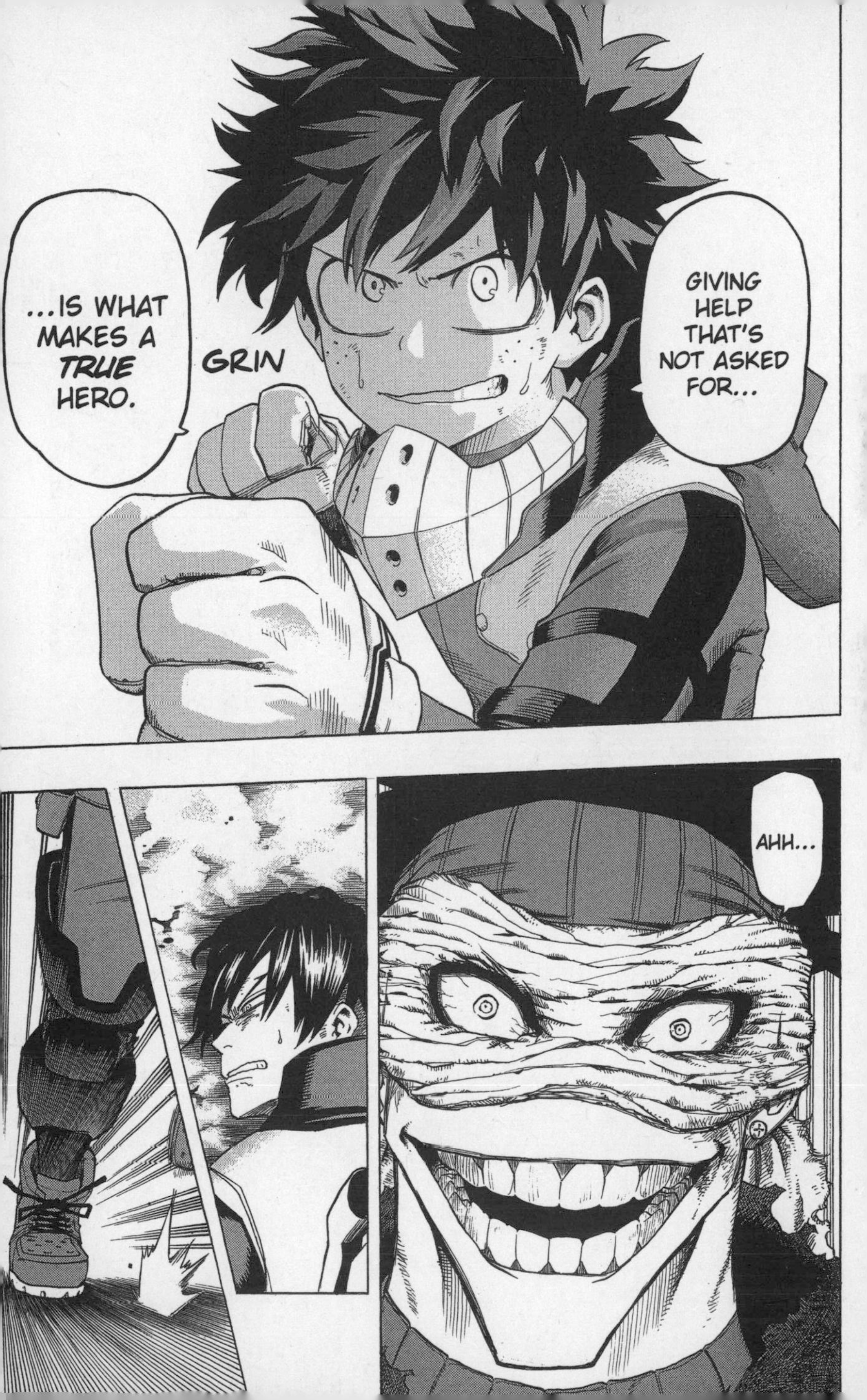
GIVING HELP THAT'S NOT ASKED FOR...
GRIN
...IS WHAT MAKES A *TRUE* HERO.
AHH...

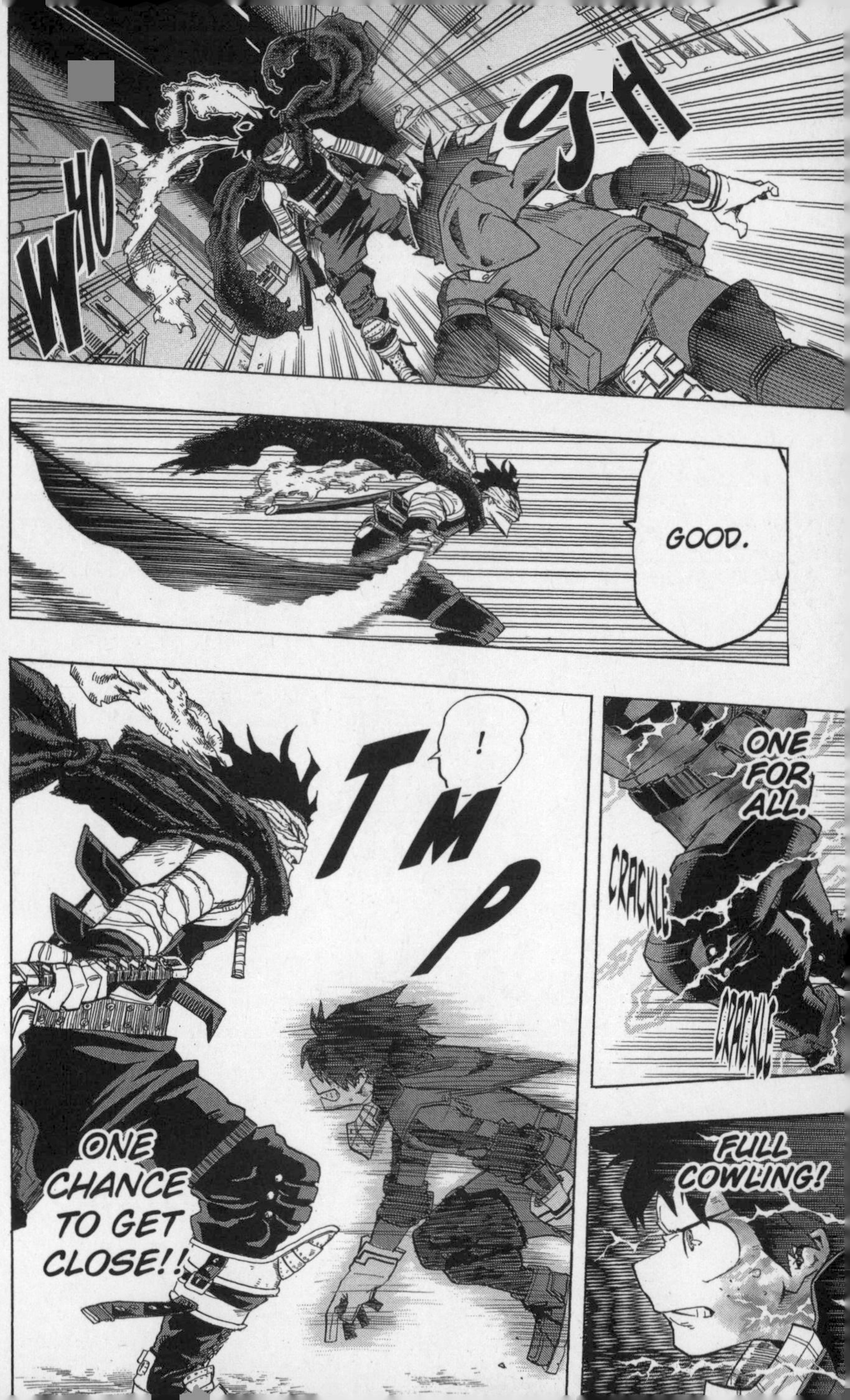
WHOOSH
GOOD.
ONE FOR ALL.
CRACKLE
CRACKLE
FULL COWLING!
!
TMP
ONE CHANCE TO GET CLOSE!!

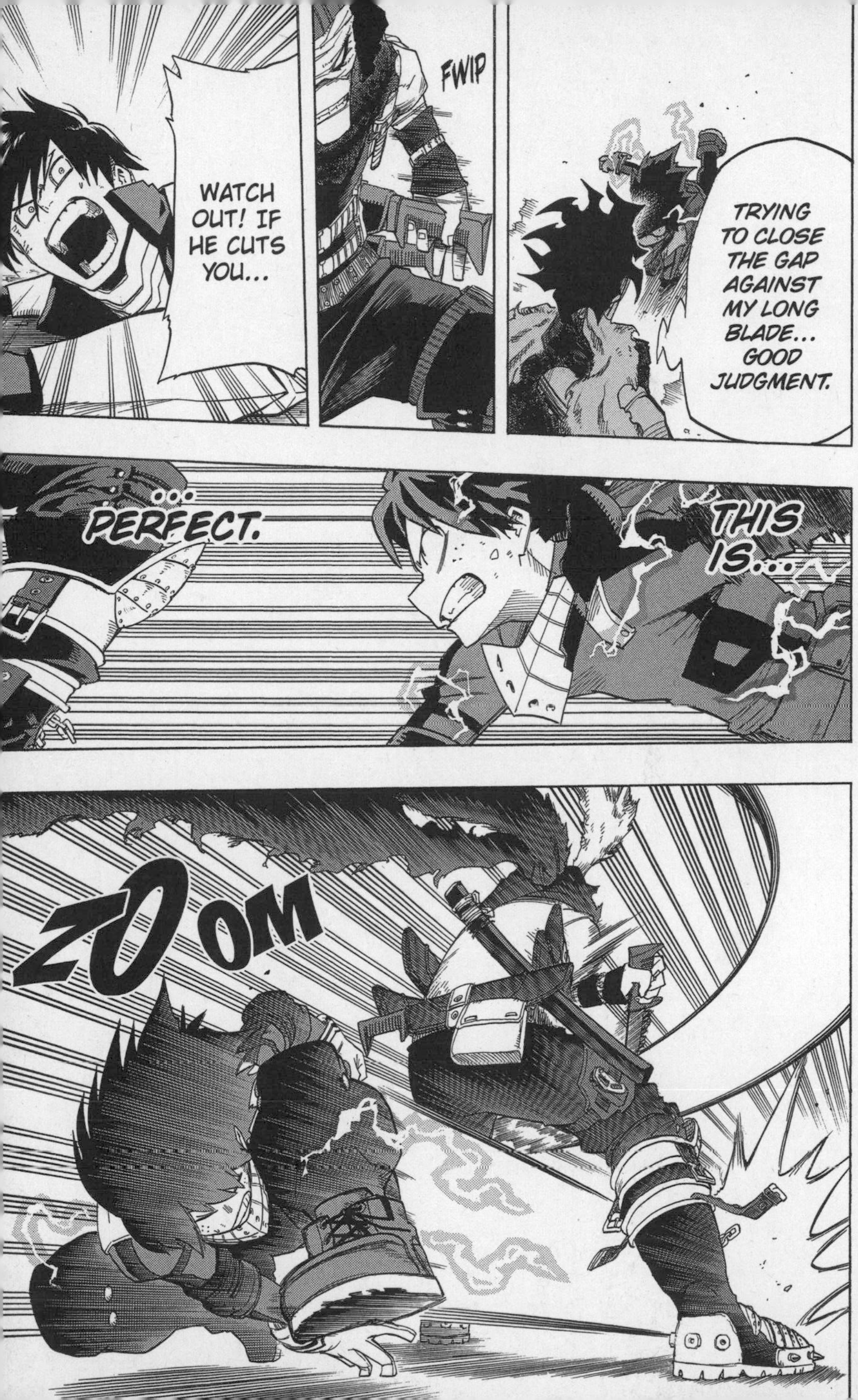
TRYING TO CLOSE THE GAP AGAINST MY LONG BLADE... GOOD JUDGMENT.
FWIP
WATCH OUT! IF HE CUTS YOU...
THIS IS...
...PERFECT.
ZOOM

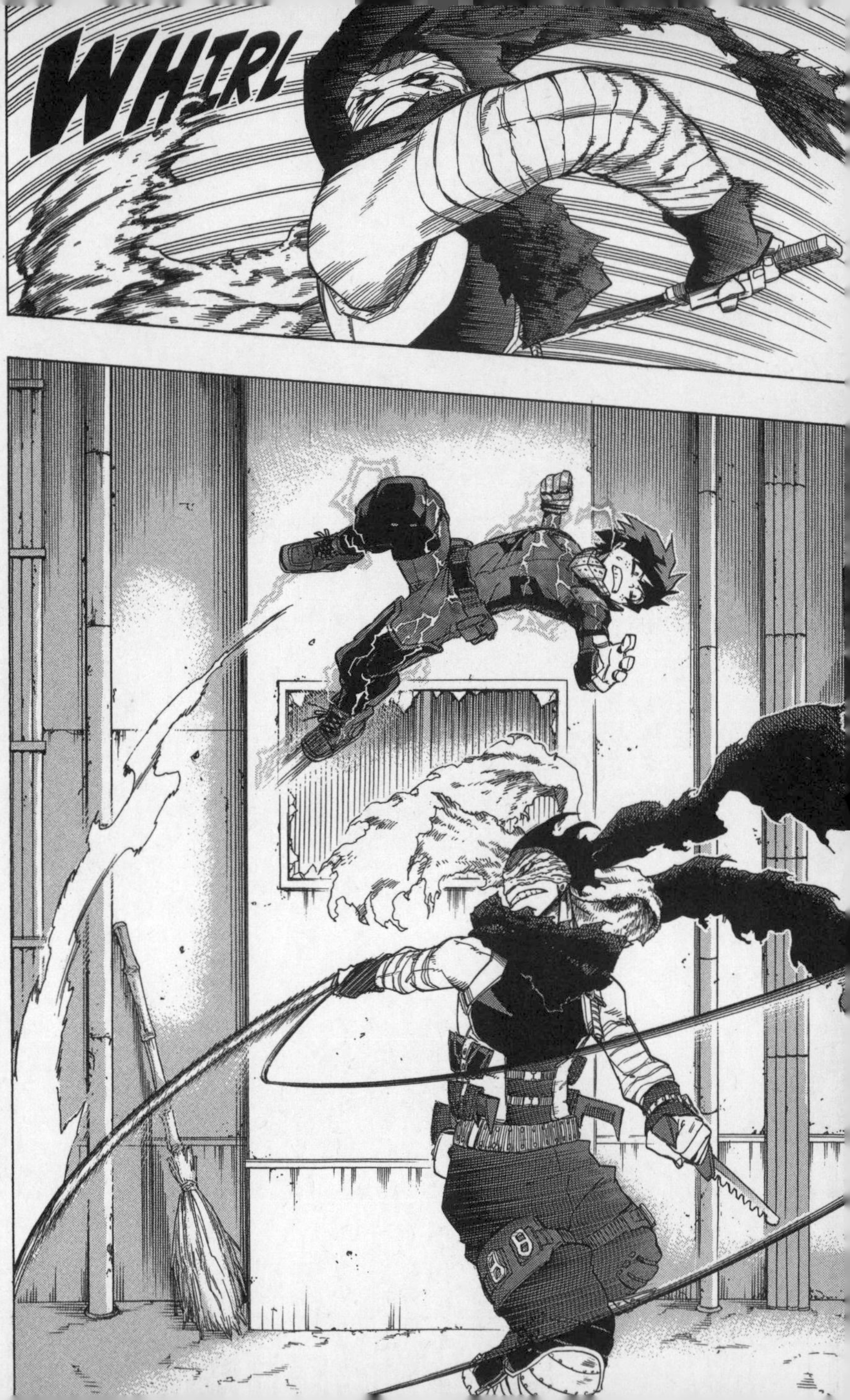
WHIRL

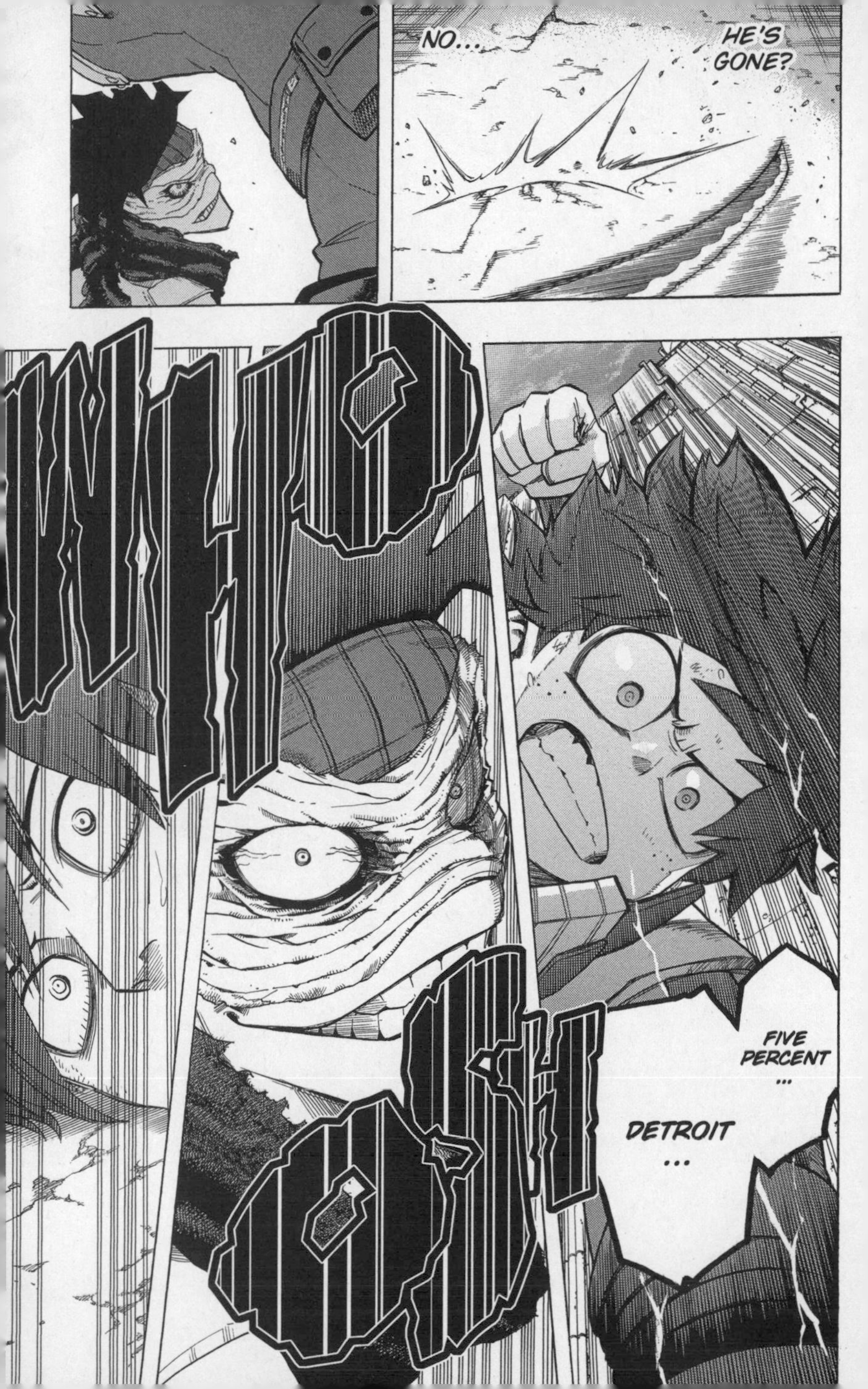
HE'S GONE?
NO...
FIVE PERCENT ...
DETROIT ...

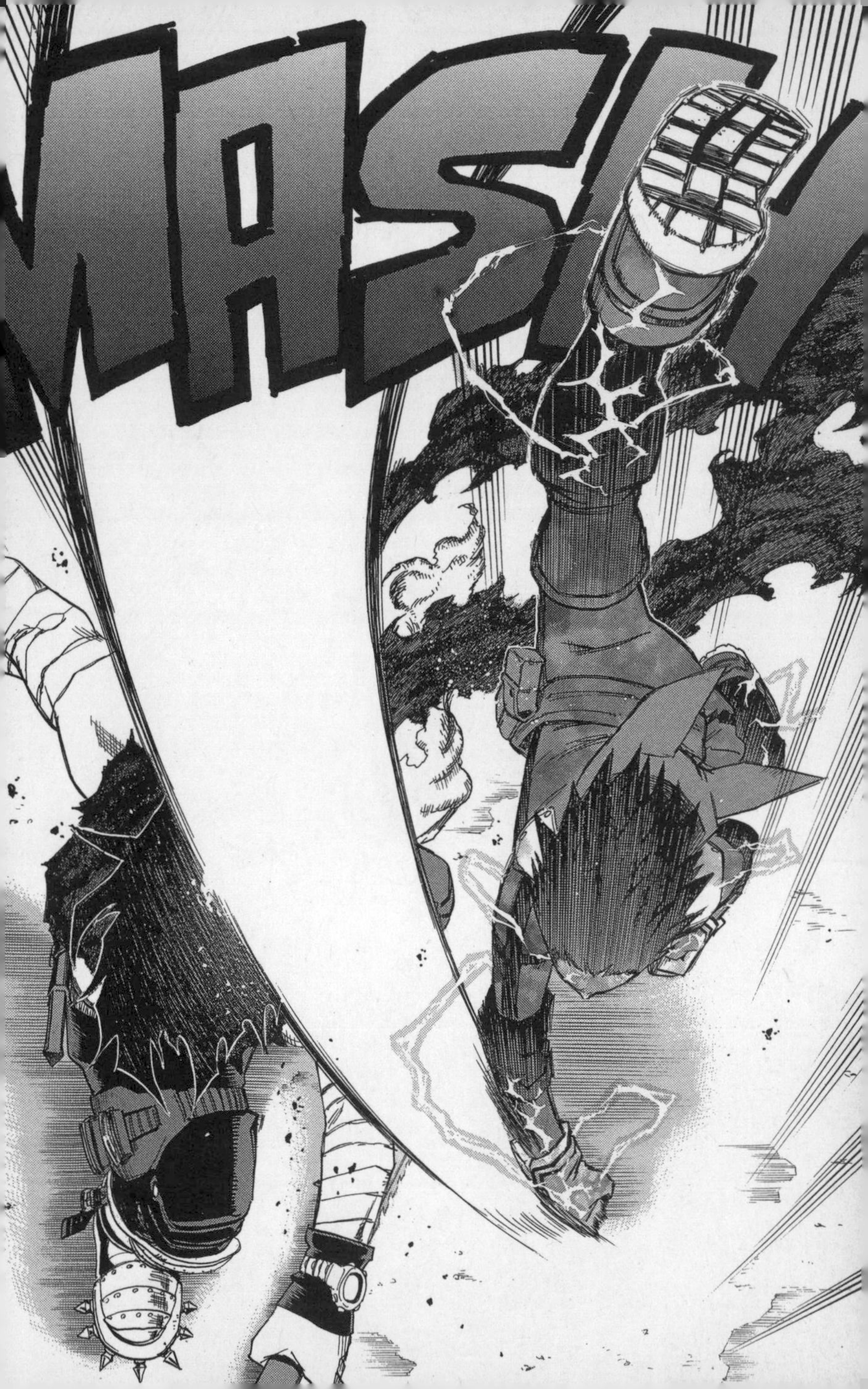

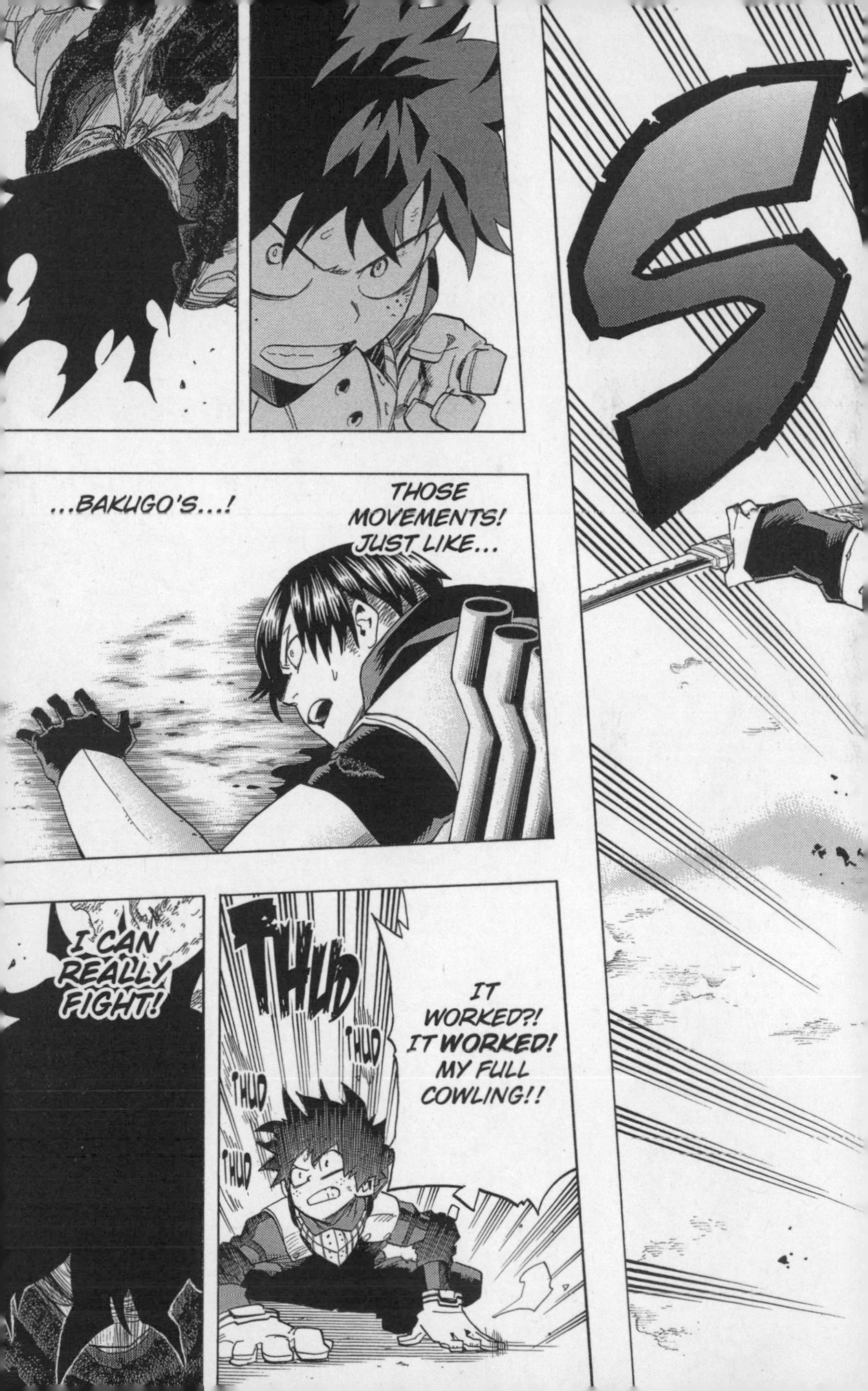
S
THOSE MOVEMENTS! JUST LIKE...
...BAKUGO'S...!
THUD
IT WORKED?! IT WORKED! MY FULL COWLING!!
THUD
THUD
THUD
I CAN REALLY FIGHT!

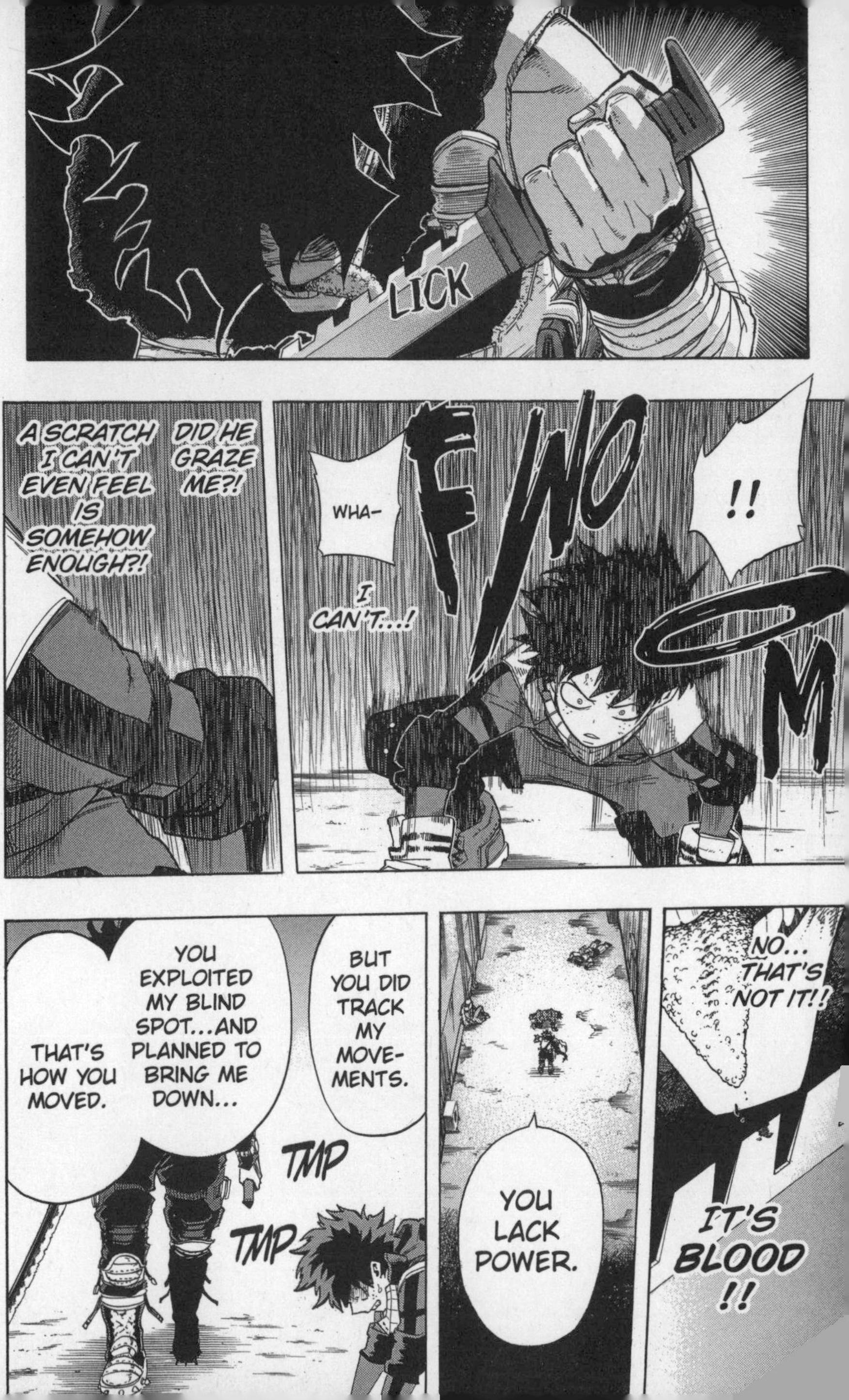
LICK
!!
WHA-
FWOOM
I CAN'T...!
DID HE GRAZE ME?!
A SCRATCH I CAN'T EVEN FEEL IS SOMEHOW ENOUGH?!
NO... THAT'S NOT IT!!
IT'S BLOOD!!
YOU LACK POWER.
BUT YOU DID TRACK MY MOVEMENTS.
YOU EXPLOITED MY BLIND SPOT...AND PLANNED TO BRING ME DOWN...
THAT'S HOW YOU MOVED.
TMP
TMP

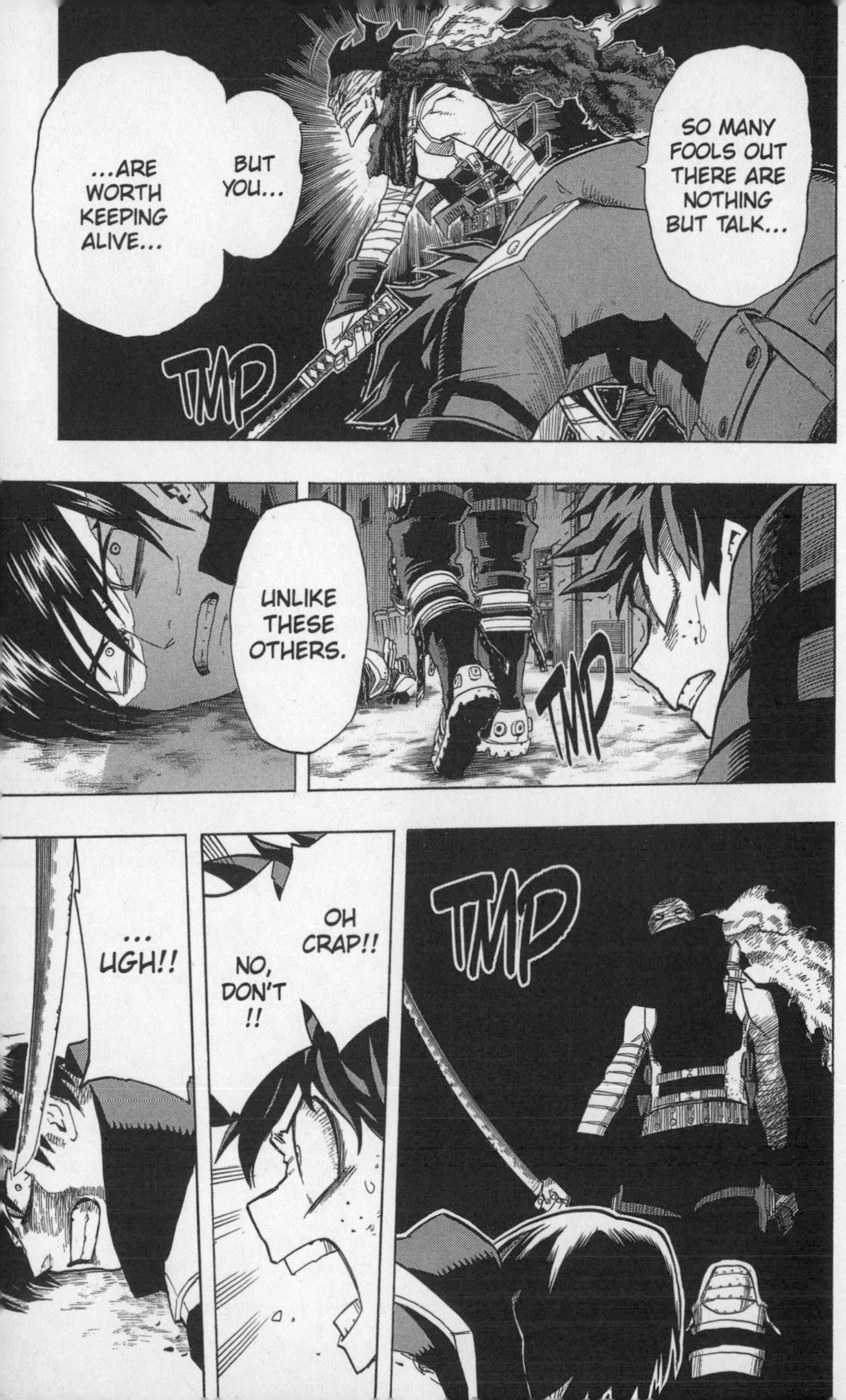
SO MANY FOOLS OUT THERE ARE NOTHING BUT TALK...
BUT YOU...
...ARE WORTH KEEPING ALIVE...
TMP
UNLIKE THESE OTHERS.
TMP
TMP
OH CRAP!!
NO, DON'T !!
... UGH!!

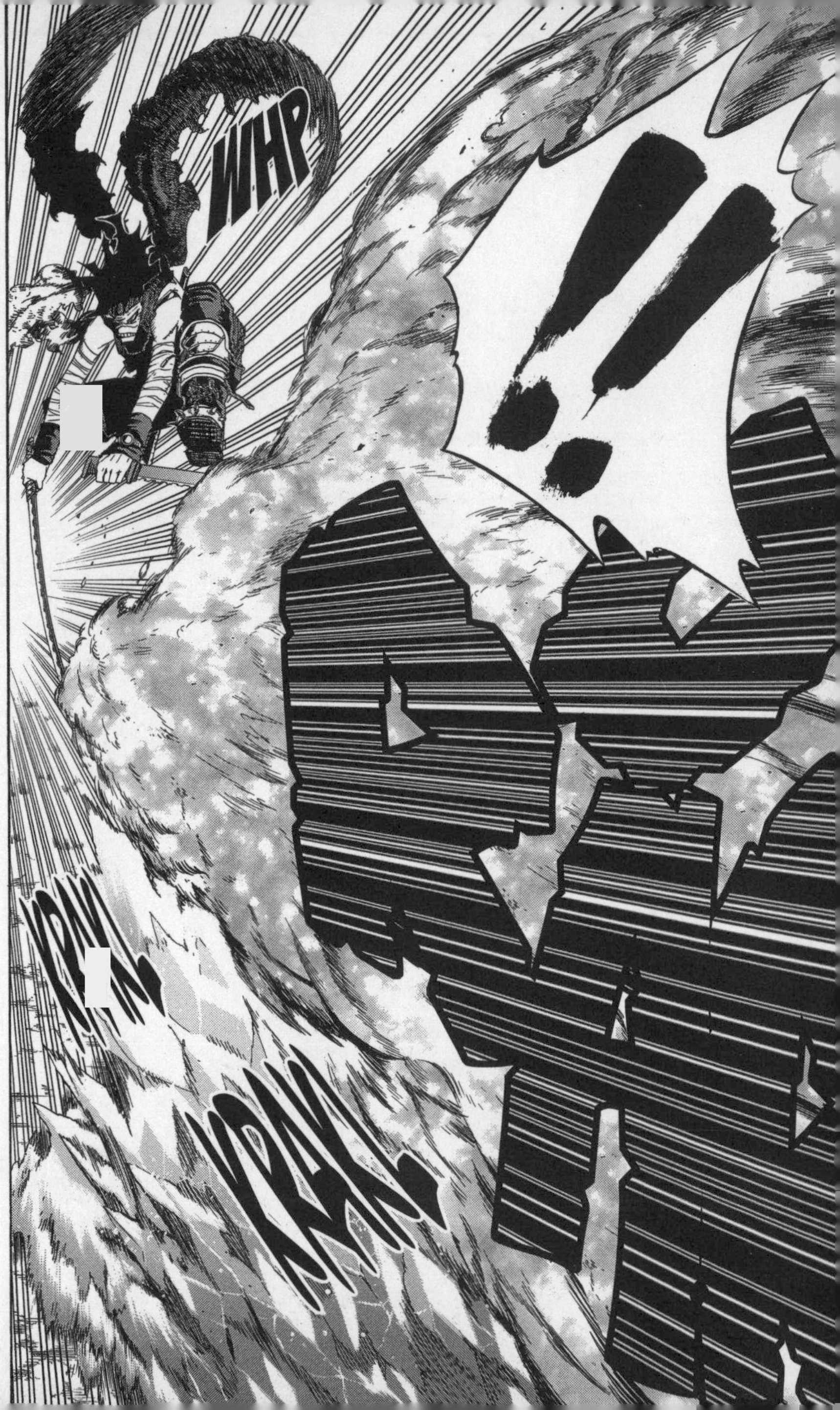
WHP
!!
KRAK
KRAK

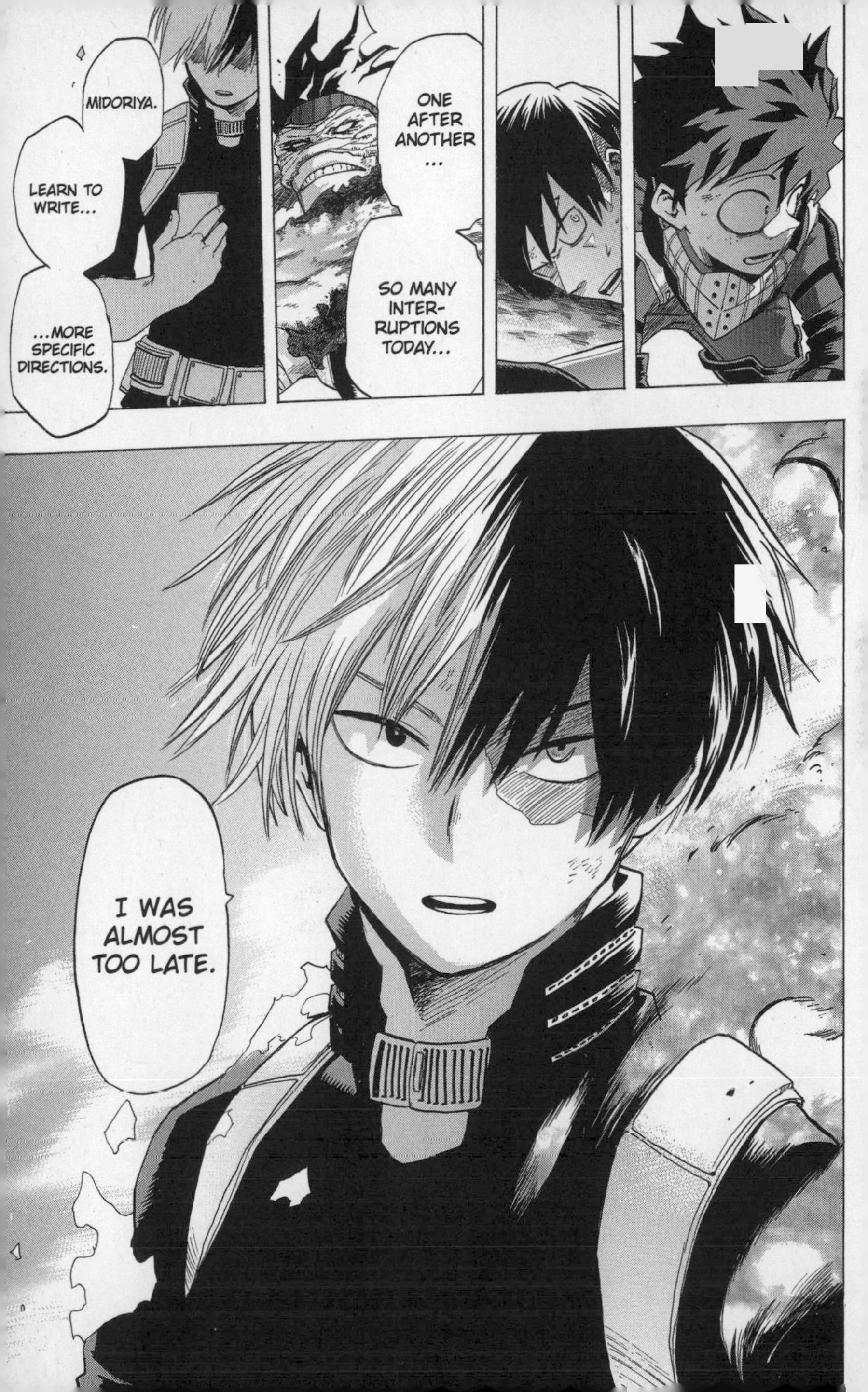
ONE AFTER ANOTHER...
SO MANY INTER-RUPTIONS TODAY...
MIDORIYA.
LEARN TO WRITE...
...MORE SPECIFIC DIRECTIONS.
I WAS ALMOST TOO LATE.

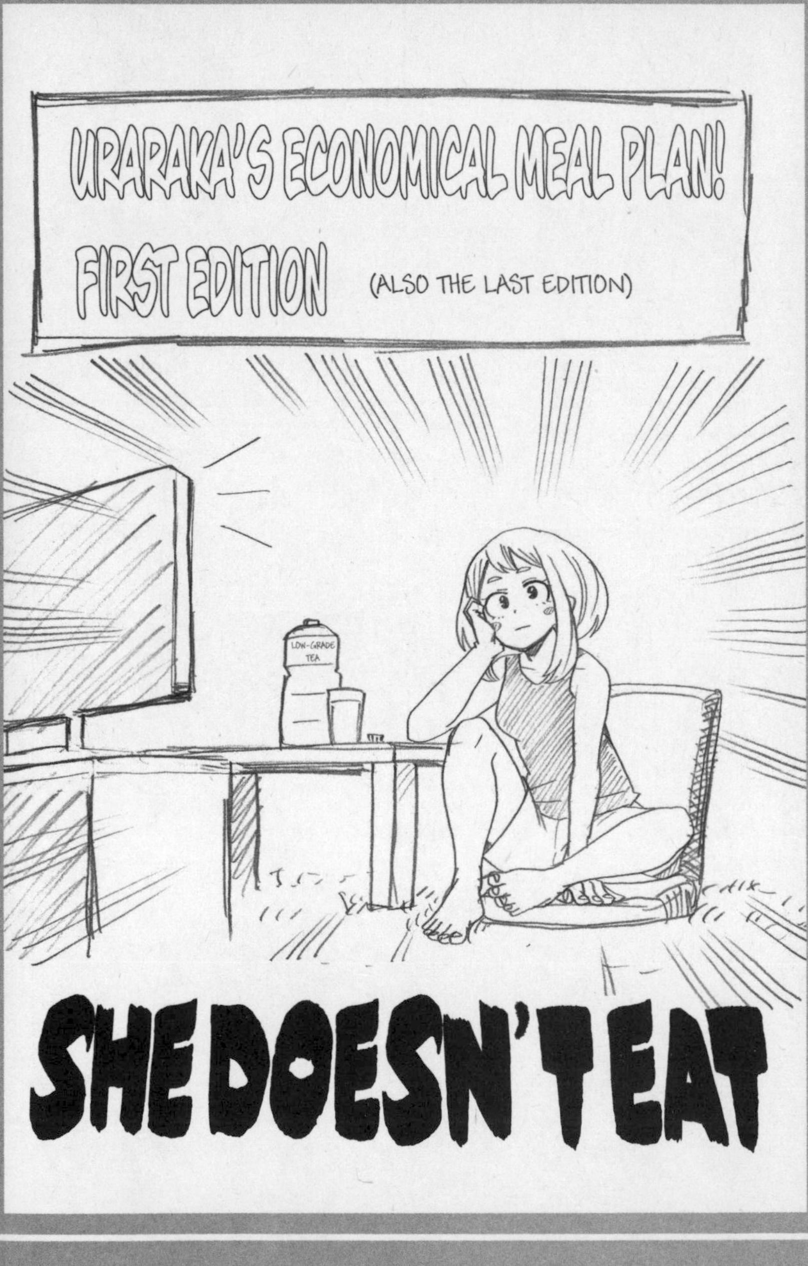
URARAKA'S ECONOMICAL MEAL PLAN!
FIRST EDITION
(ALSO THE LAST EDITION)
LOW-GRADE TEA
SHE DOESN'T EAT

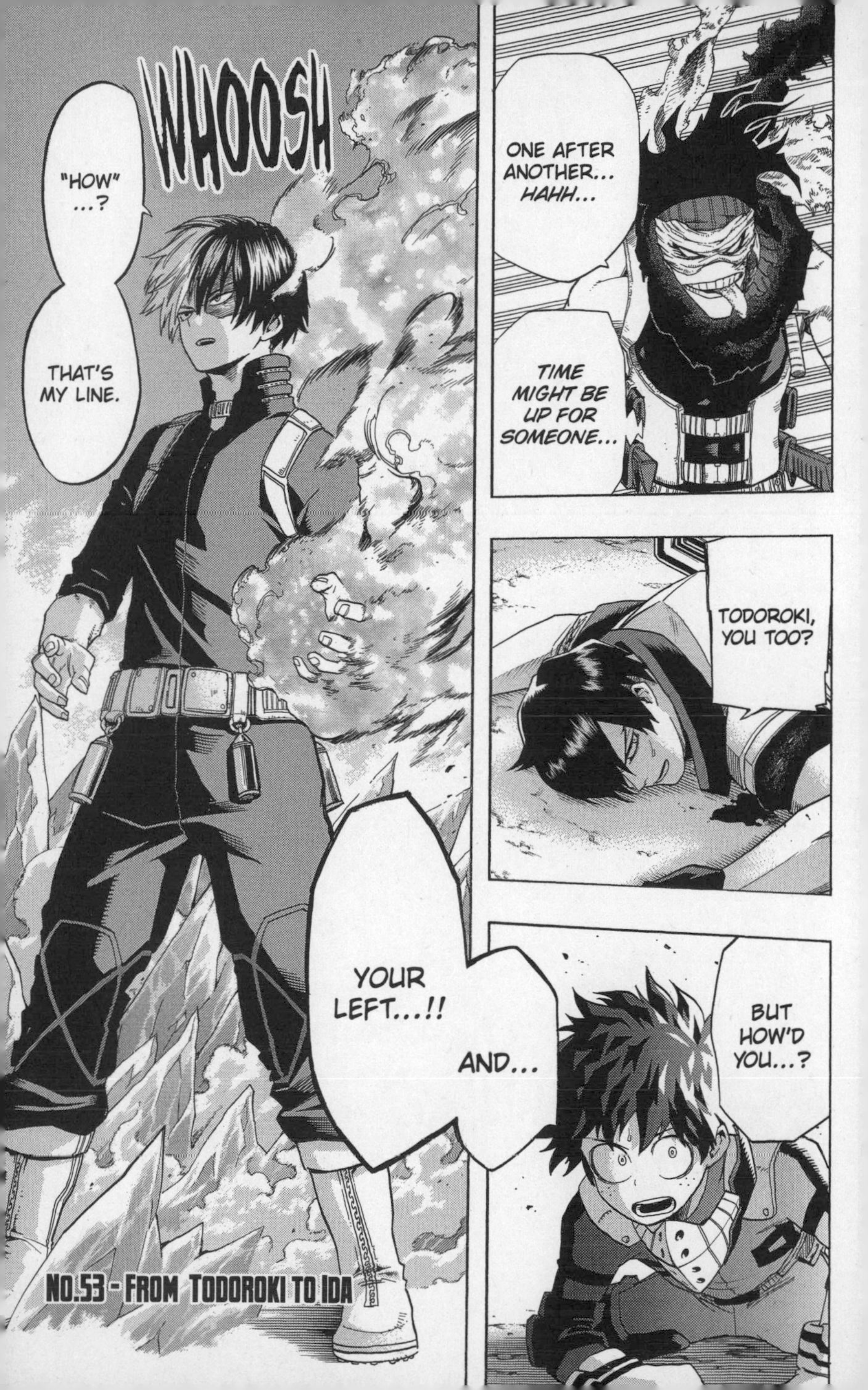
ONE AFTER ANOTHER... HAHH...
TIME MIGHT BE UP FOR SOMEONE...
TODOROKI, YOU TOO?
BUT HOW'D YOU...?
YOUR LEFT...!!
AND...
WHOOSH
"HOW" ...?
THAT'S MY LINE.
NO.53 - FROM TODOROKI TO IDA

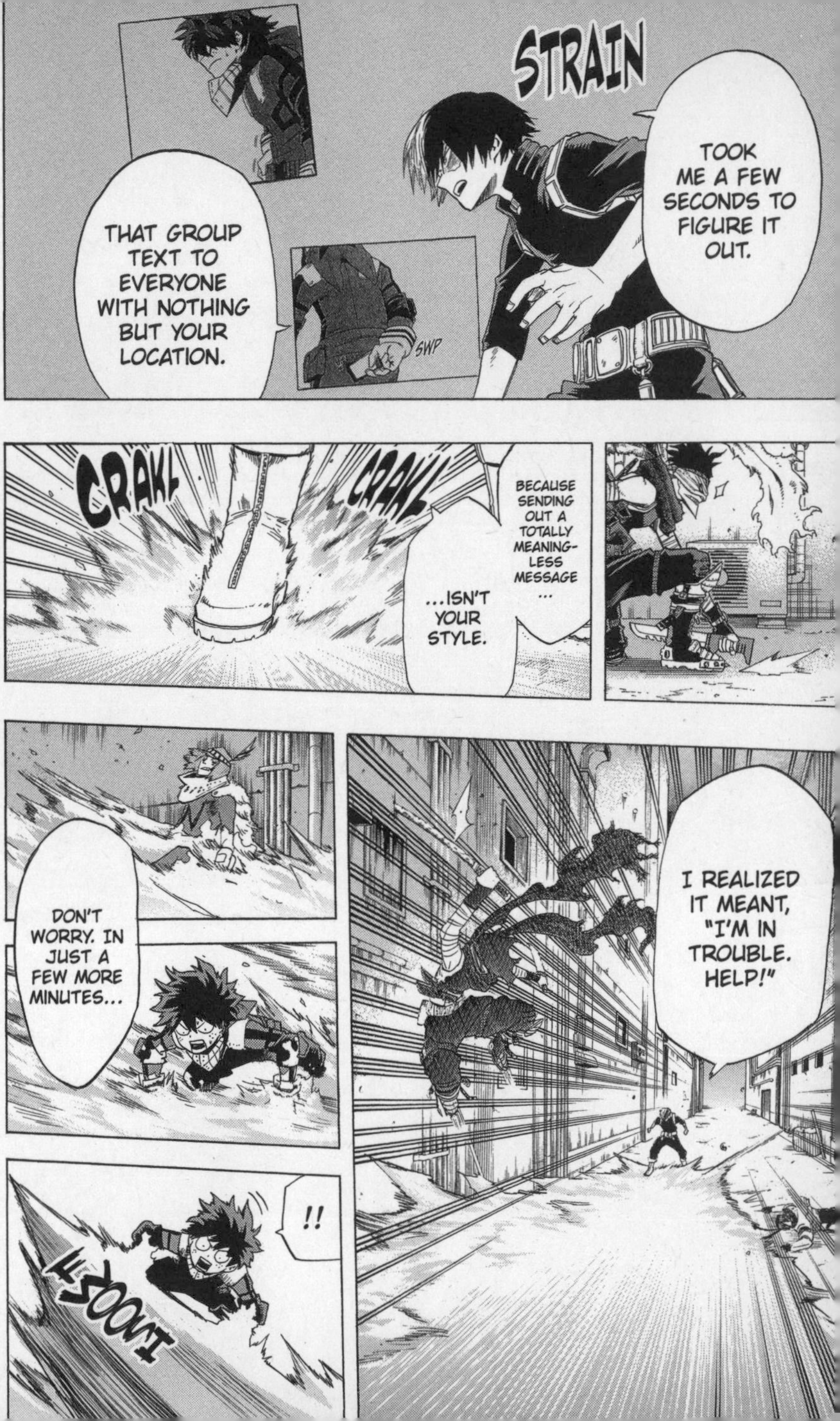
STRAIN
TOOK ME A FEW SECONDS TO FIGURE IT OUT.
THAT GROUP TEXT TO EVERYONE WITH NOTHING BUT YOUR LOCATION.
SWP
BECAUSE SENDING OUT A TOTALLY MEANING-LESS MESSAGE...
...ISN'T YOUR STYLE.
CRAKL
CRAKL
I REALIZED IT MEANT, "I'M IN TROUBLE. HELP!"
DON'T WORRY. IN JUST A FEW MORE MINUTES...
!!
FSOOM!

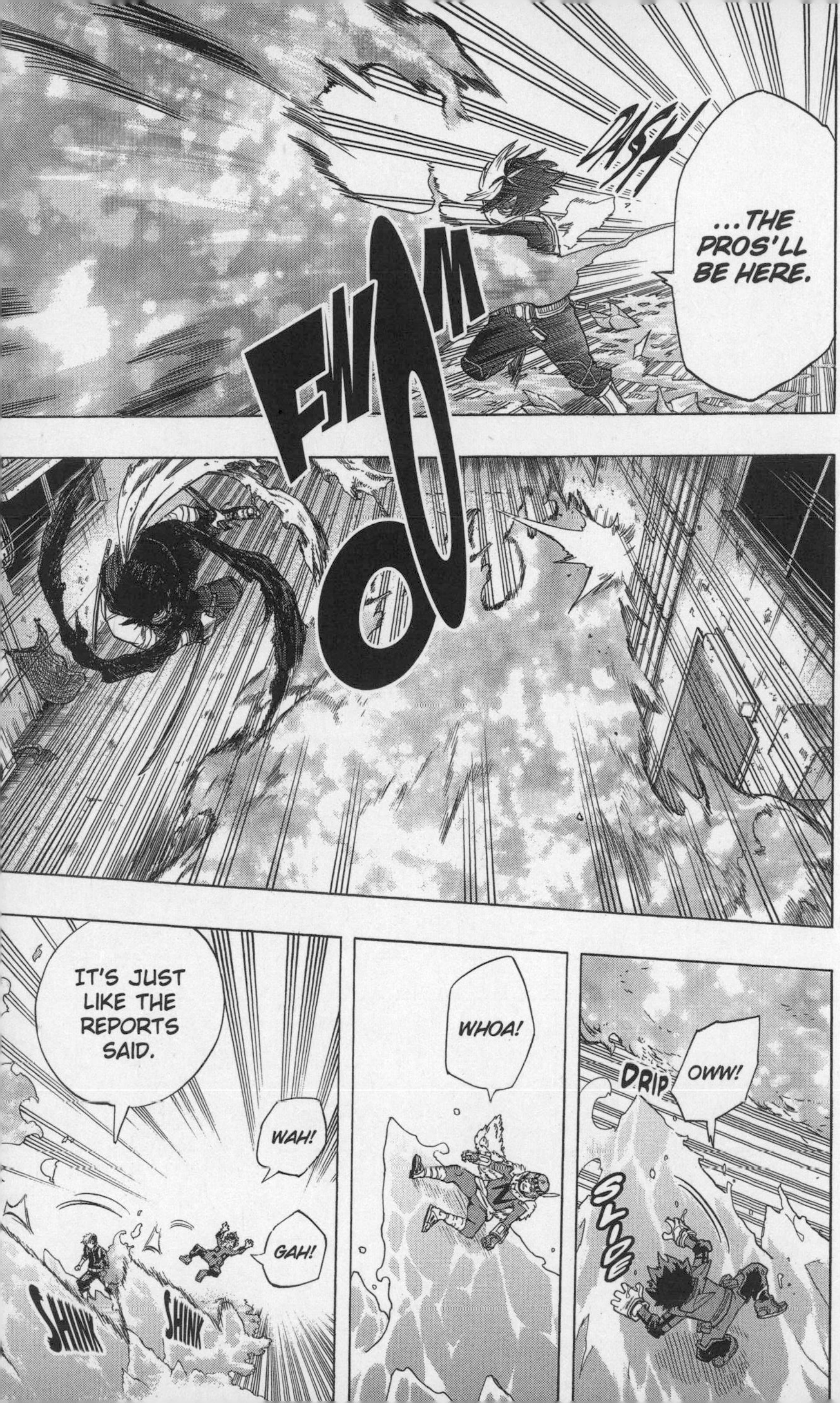
...THE PROS'LL BE HERE.
DASH
FWOOM
IT'S JUST LIKE THE REPORTS SAID.
WAH!
GAH!
SHINK
SHINK
WHOA!
OWW!
DRIP
SLIDE

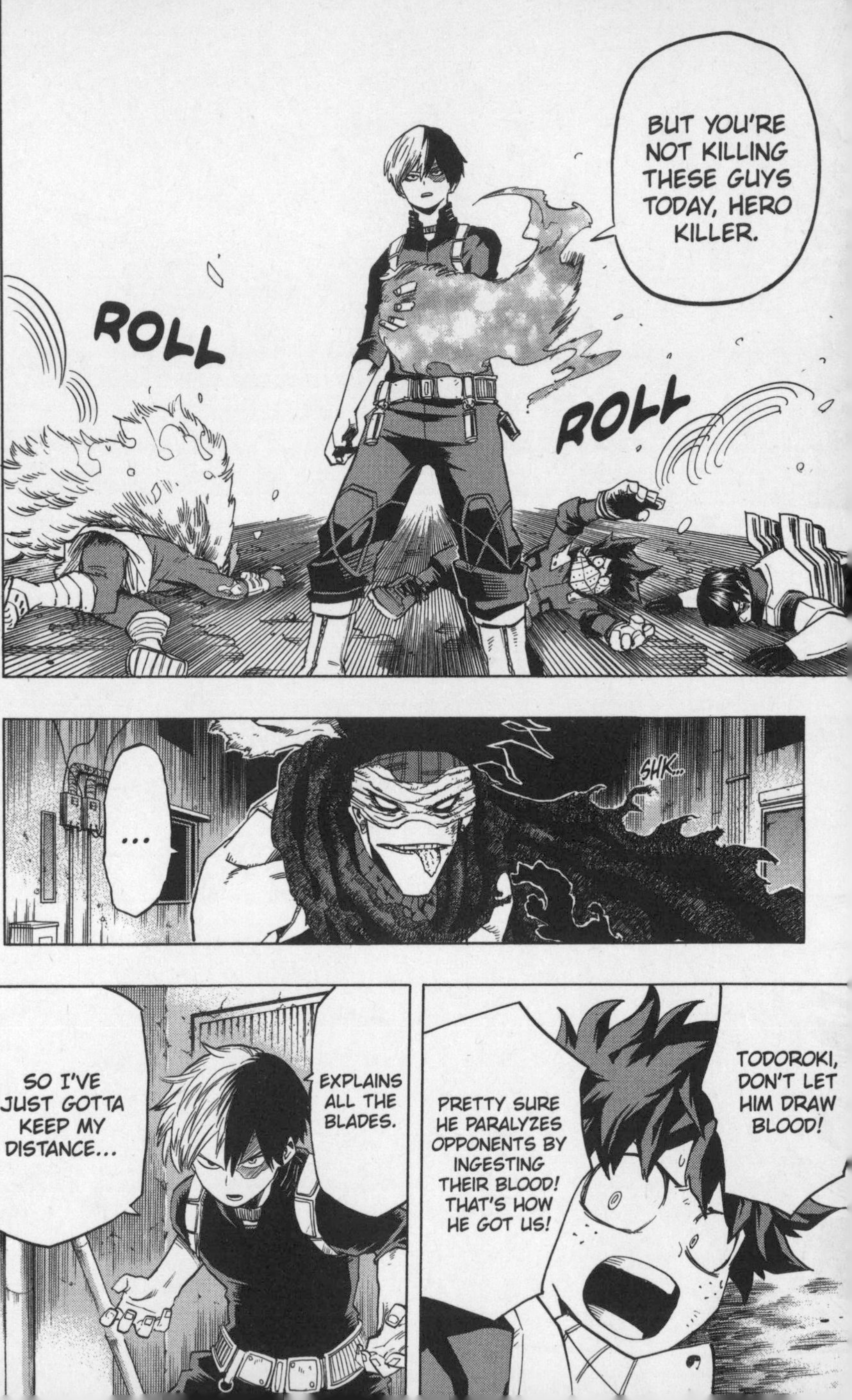
BUT YOU'RE NOT KILLING THESE GUYS TODAY, HERO KILLER.
ROLL
ROLL
SHK..
...
TODOROKI, DON'T LET HIM DRAW BLOOD!
PRETTY SURE HE PARALYZES OPPONENTS BY INGESTING THEIR BLOOD! THAT'S HOW HE GOT US!
EXPLAINS ALL THE BLADES.
SO I'VE JUST GOTTA KEEP MY DISTANCE...

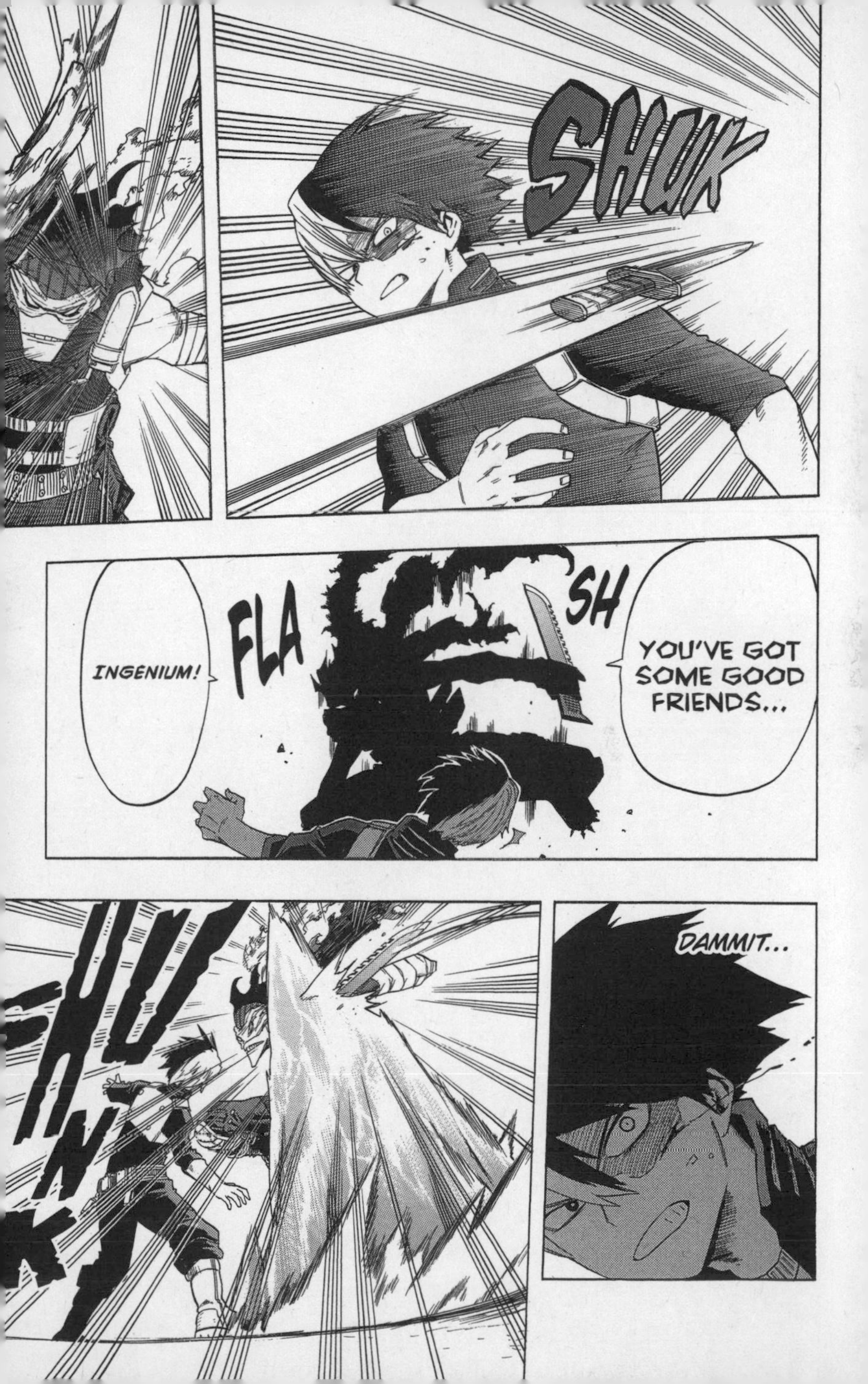
SHUK
YOU'VE GOT SOME GOOD FRIENDS...
FLASH
INGENIUM!
DAMMIT...
SHUNK

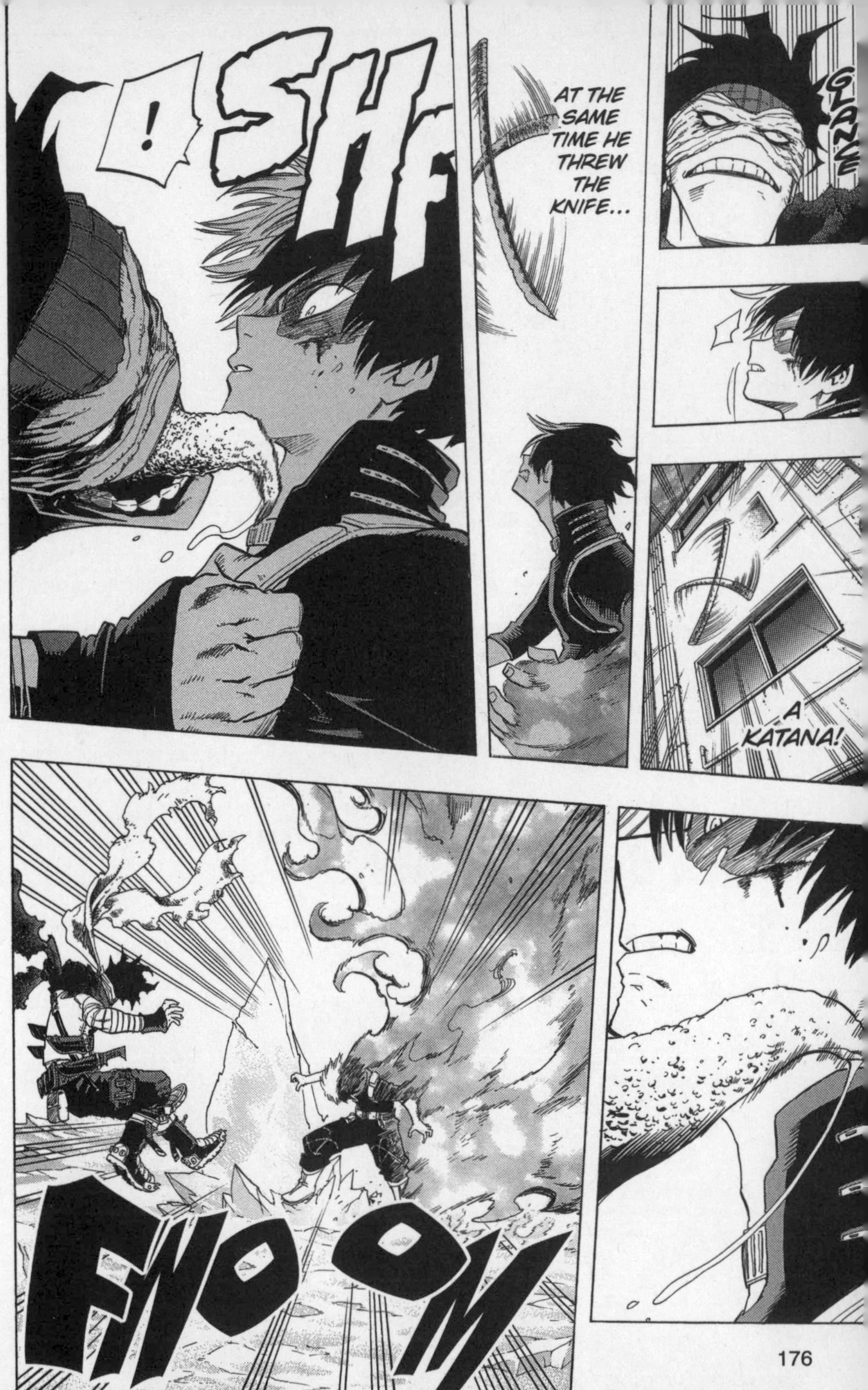
GLANCE
A KATANA!
AT THE SAME TIME HE THREW THE KNIFE...
!
SHF
FWOOM

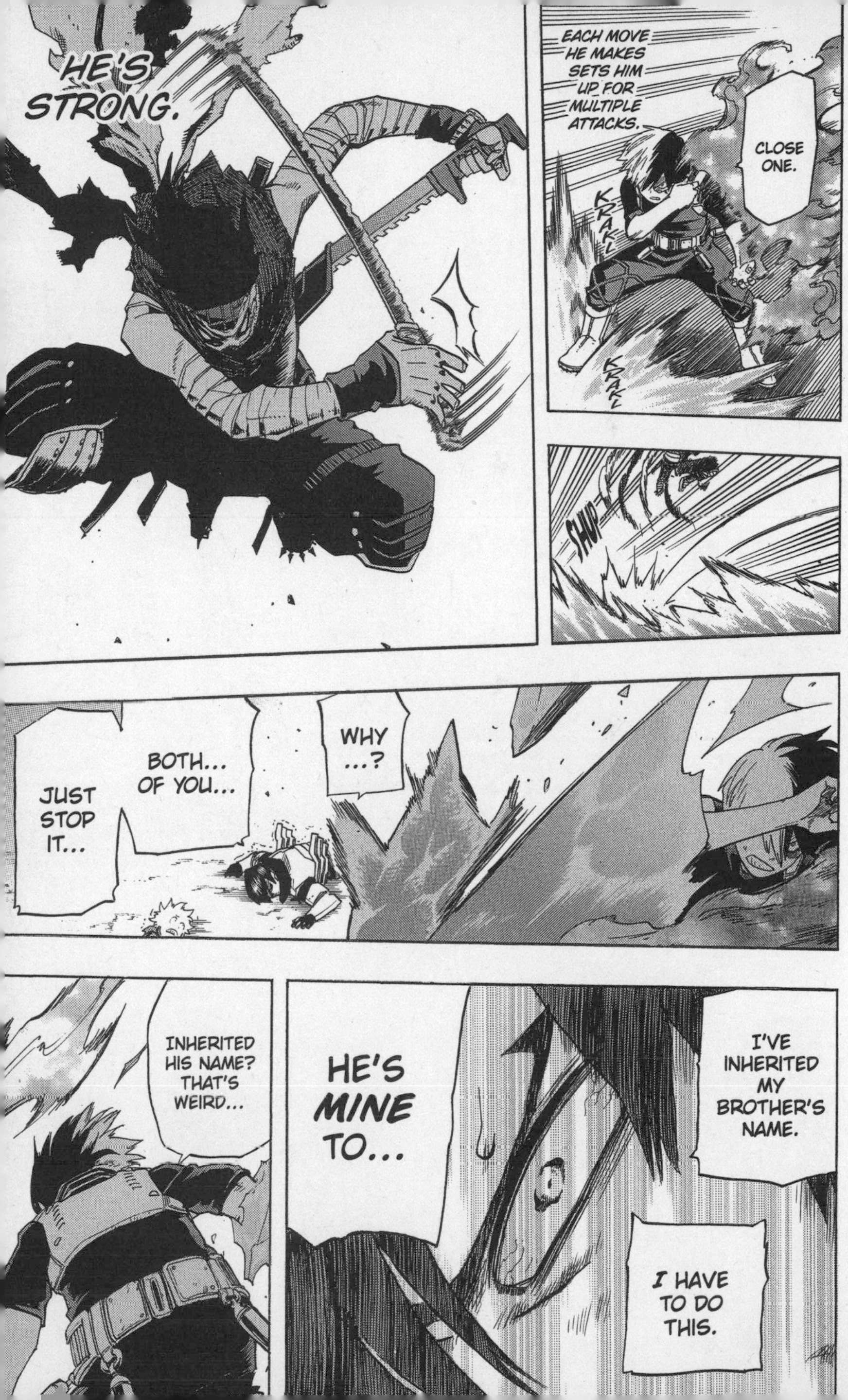

CLOSE ONE.
EACH MOVE HE MAKES SETS HIM UP FOR MULTIPLE ATTACKS.
KRAKL
KRAKL
SHUP
HE'S STRONG.
WHY ...?
BOTH... OF YOU...
JUST STOP IT...
I'VE INHERITED MY BROTHER'S NAME.
HE'S *MINE* TO...
I HAVE TO DO THIS.
INHERITED HIS NAME? THAT'S WEIRD...

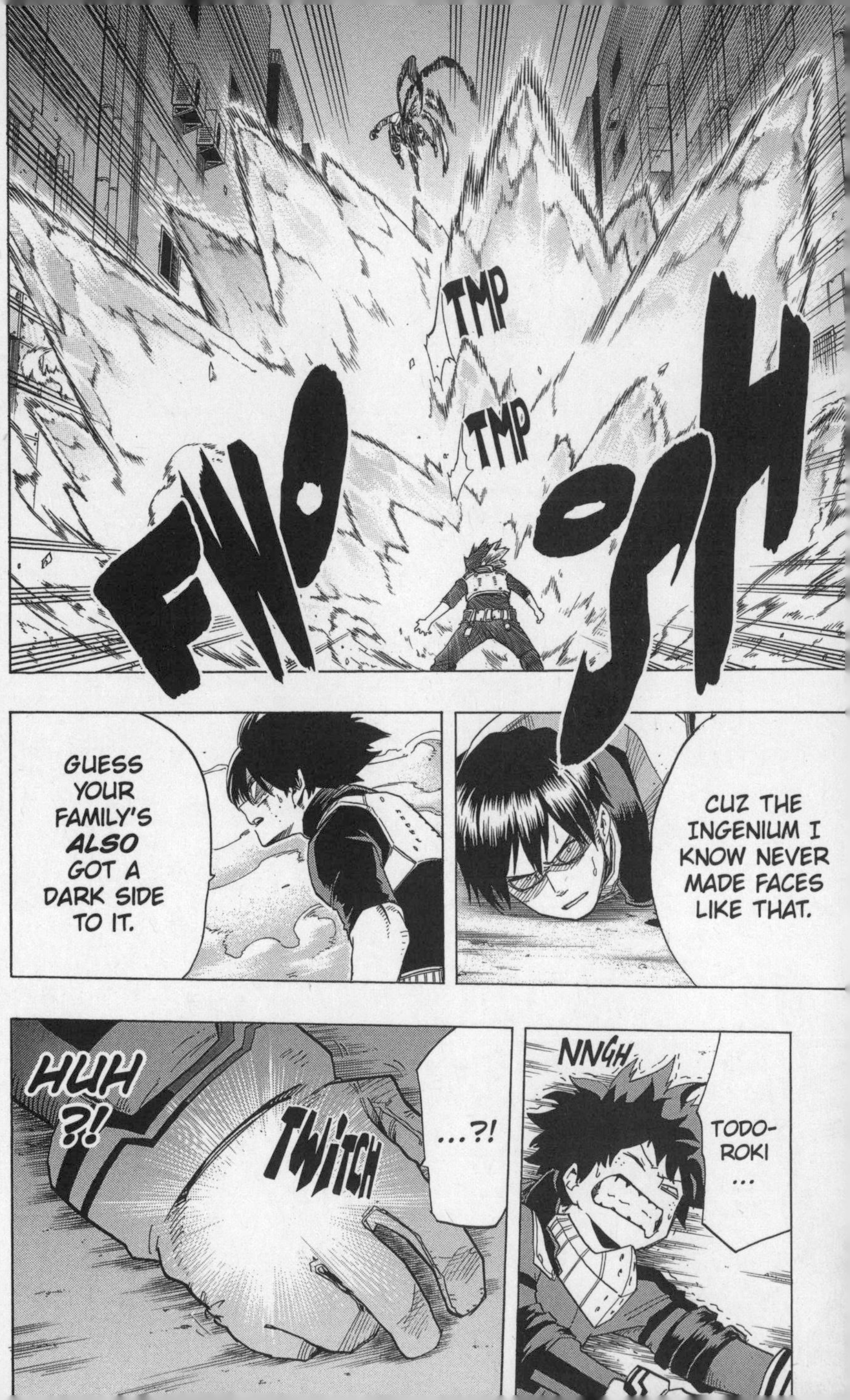
FWOOSH
TMP
TMP
CUZ THE INGENIUM I KNOW NEVER MADE FACES LIKE THAT.
GUESS YOUR FAMILY'S **ALSO** GOT A DARK SIDE TO IT.
NNGH
TODO-ROKI ...
...?!
TWITCH
HUH ?!

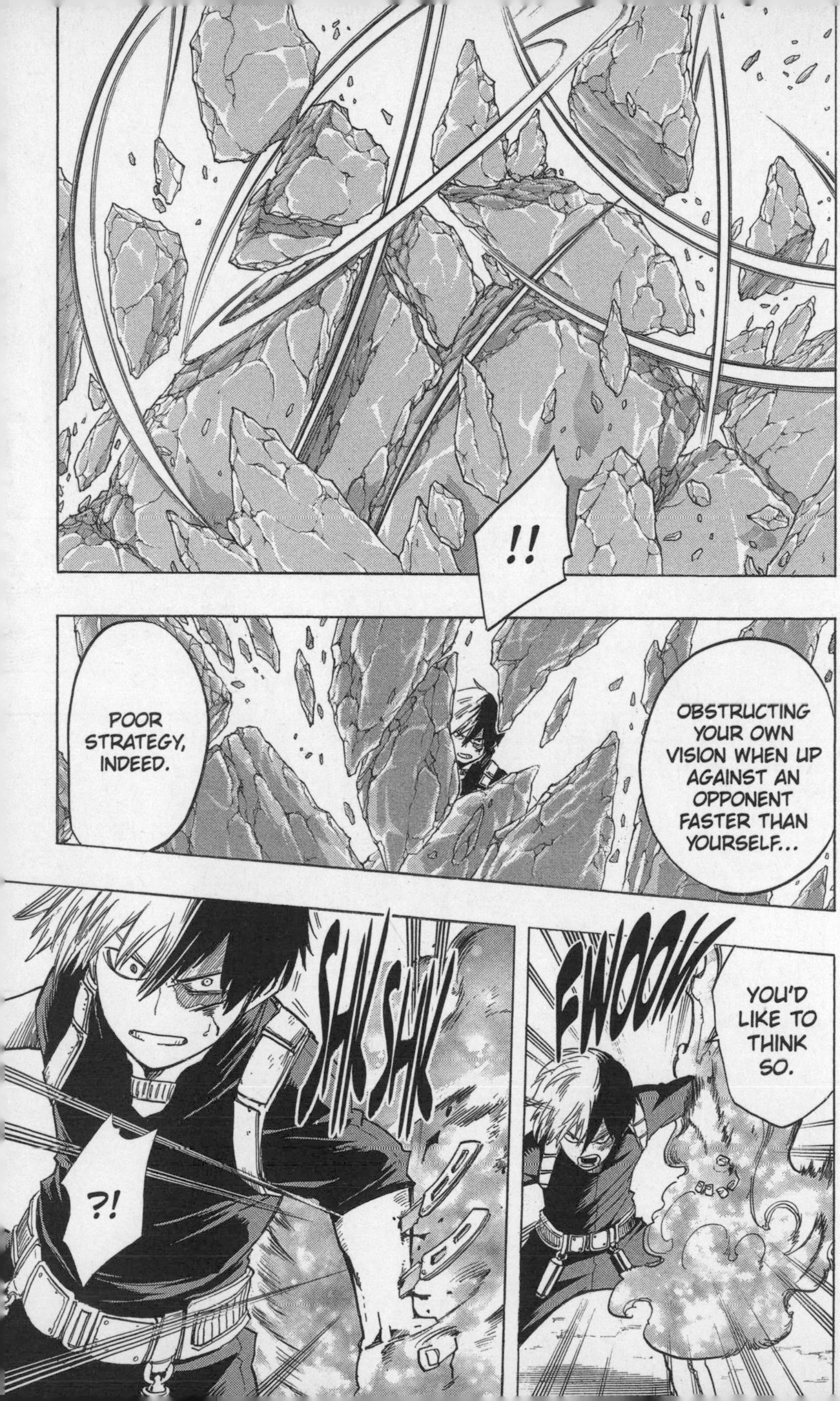
!!
OBSTRUCTING YOUR OWN VISION WHEN UP AGAINST AN OPPONENT FASTER THAN YOURSELF...
POOR STRATEGY, INDEED.
FWOOM
YOU'D LIKE TO THINK SO.
?!

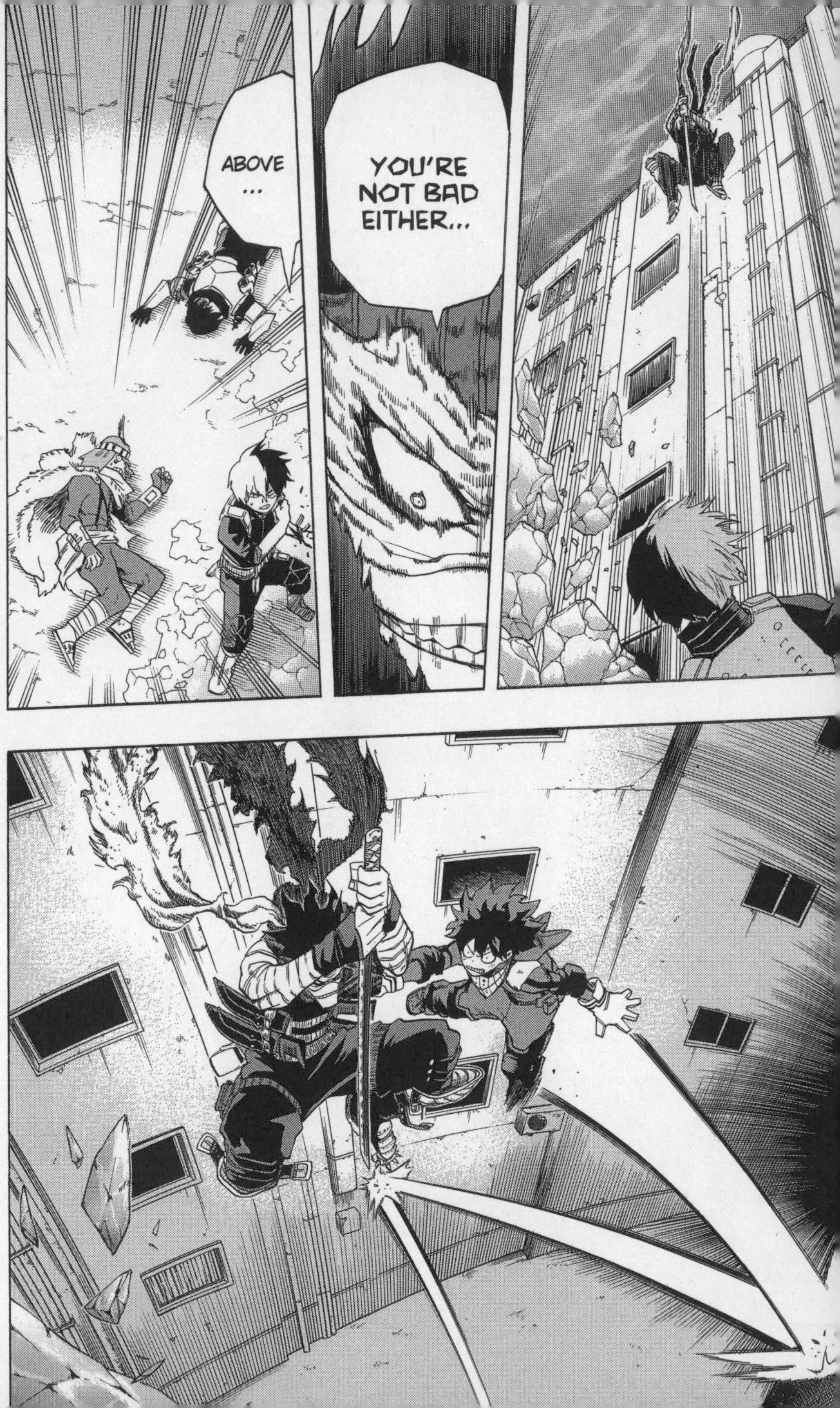
YOU'RE NOT BAD EITHER...
ABOVE ...

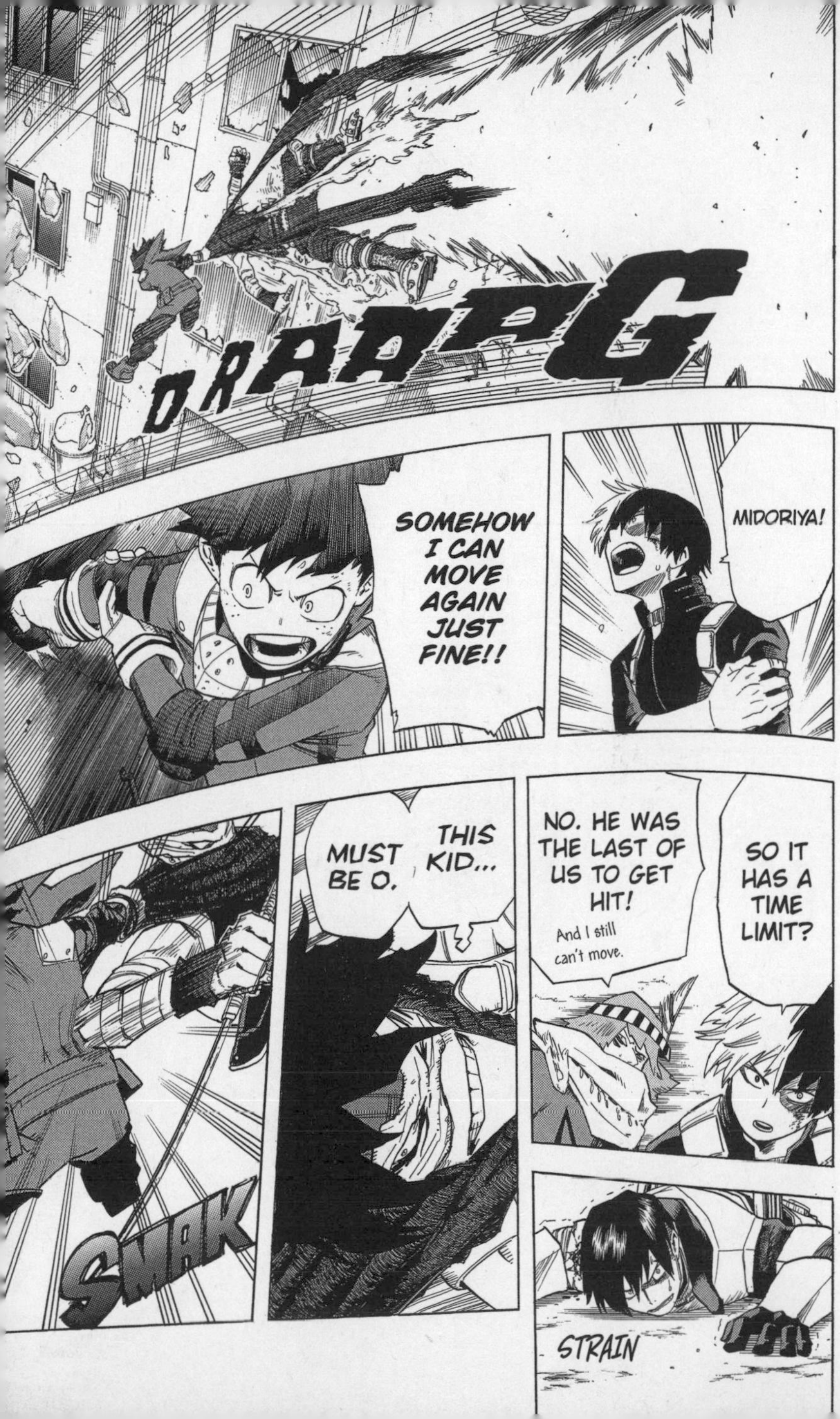
DRAAAG
MIDORIYA!
SOMEHOW I CAN MOVE AGAIN JUST FINE!!
SO IT HAS A TIME LIMIT?
NO. HE WAS THE LAST OF US TO GET HIT!
And I still can't move.
STRAIN
THIS KID...
MUST BE O.
SMAK

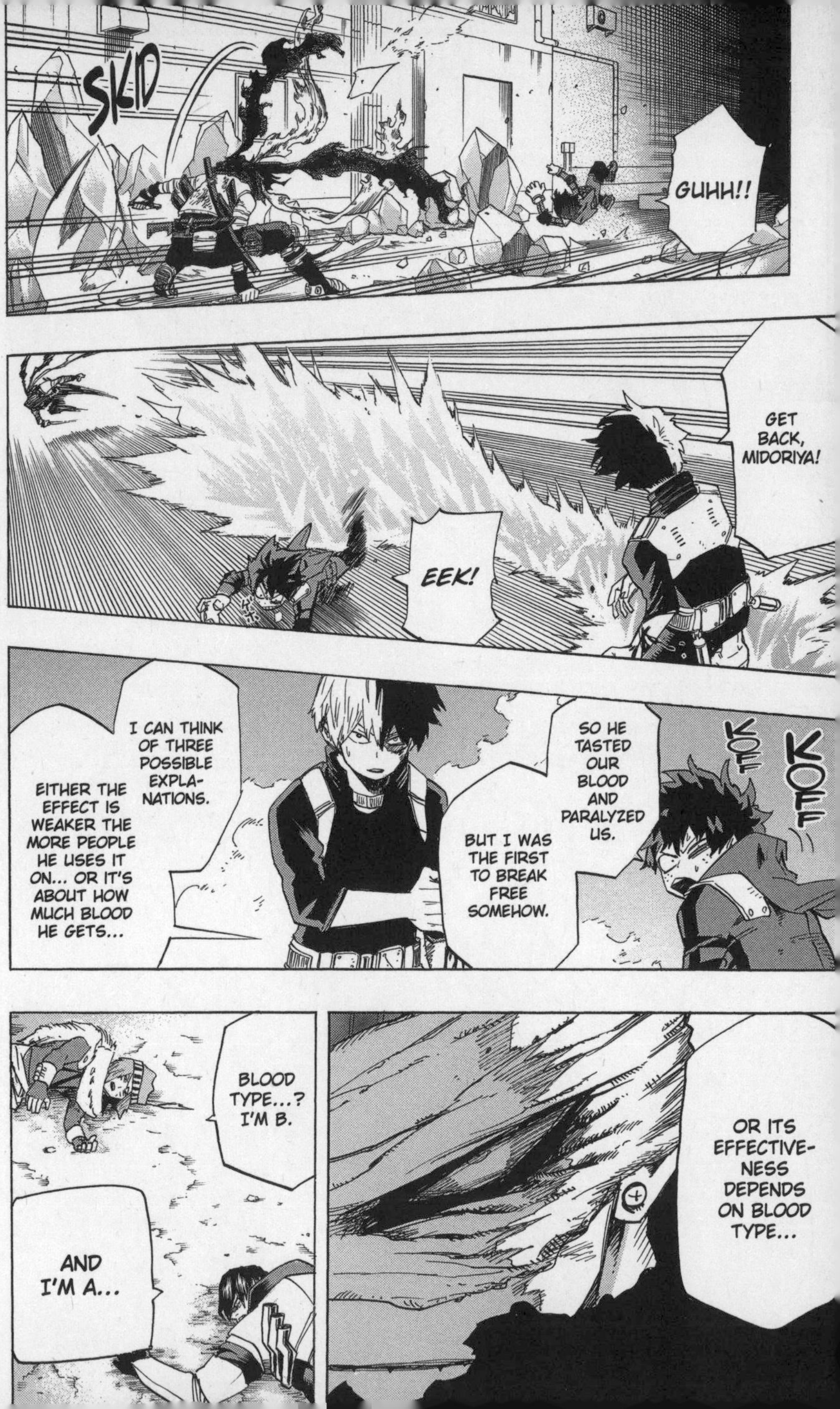
GUHH!!
SKID
GET BACK, MIDORIYA!
EEK!
KOFF
KOFF
SO HE TASTED OUR BLOOD AND PARALYZED US.
BUT I WAS THE FIRST TO BREAK FREE SOMEHOW.
I CAN THINK OF THREE POSSIBLE EXPLANATIONS.
EITHER THE EFFECT IS WEAKER THE MORE PEOPLE HE USES IT ON... OR IT'S ABOUT HOW MUCH BLOOD HE GETS...
OR ITS EFFECTIVENESS DEPENDS ON BLOOD TYPE...
BLOOD TYPE...? I'M B.
AND I'M A...

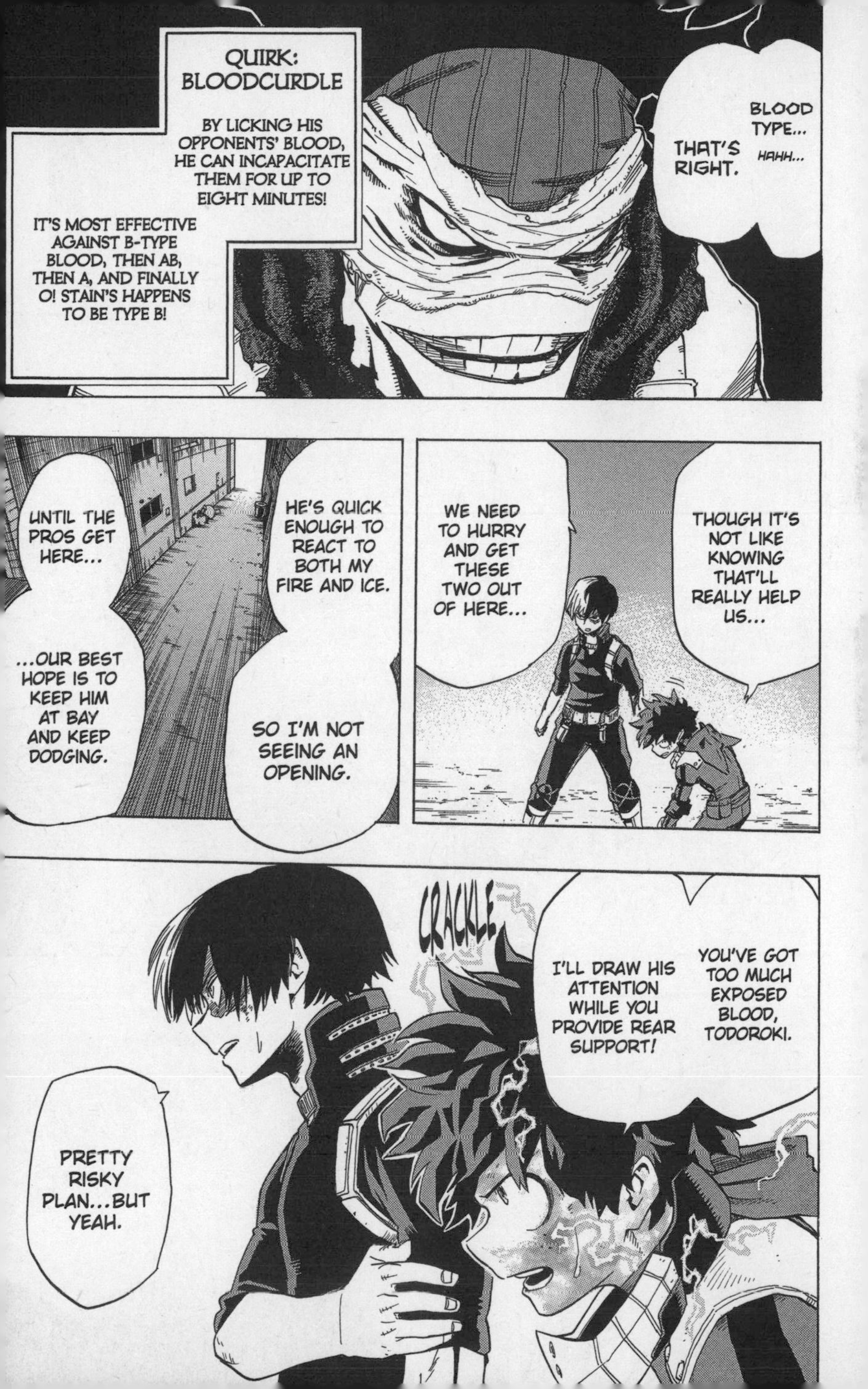
BLOOD TYPE...
HAHH...
THAT'S RIGHT.
QUIRK: BLOODCURDLE
BY LICKING HIS OPPONENTS' BLOOD, HE CAN INCAPACITATE THEM FOR UP TO EIGHT MINUTES!
IT'S MOST EFFECTIVE AGAINST B-TYPE BLOOD, THEN AB, THEN A, AND FINALLY O! STAIN'S HAPPENS TO BE TYPE B!
THOUGH IT'S NOT LIKE KNOWING THAT'LL REALLY HELP US...
WE NEED TO HURRY AND GET THESE TWO OUT OF HERE...
HE'S QUICK ENOUGH TO REACT TO BOTH MY FIRE AND ICE.
SO I'M NOT SEEING AN OPENING.
UNTIL THE PROS GET HERE...
...OUR BEST HOPE IS TO KEEP HIM AT BAY AND KEEP DODGING.
YOU'VE GOT TOO MUCH EXPOSED BLOOD, TODOROKI.
I'LL DRAW HIS ATTENTION WHILE YOU PROVIDE REAR SUPPORT!
CRACKLE
PRETTY RISKY PLAN...BUT YEAH.

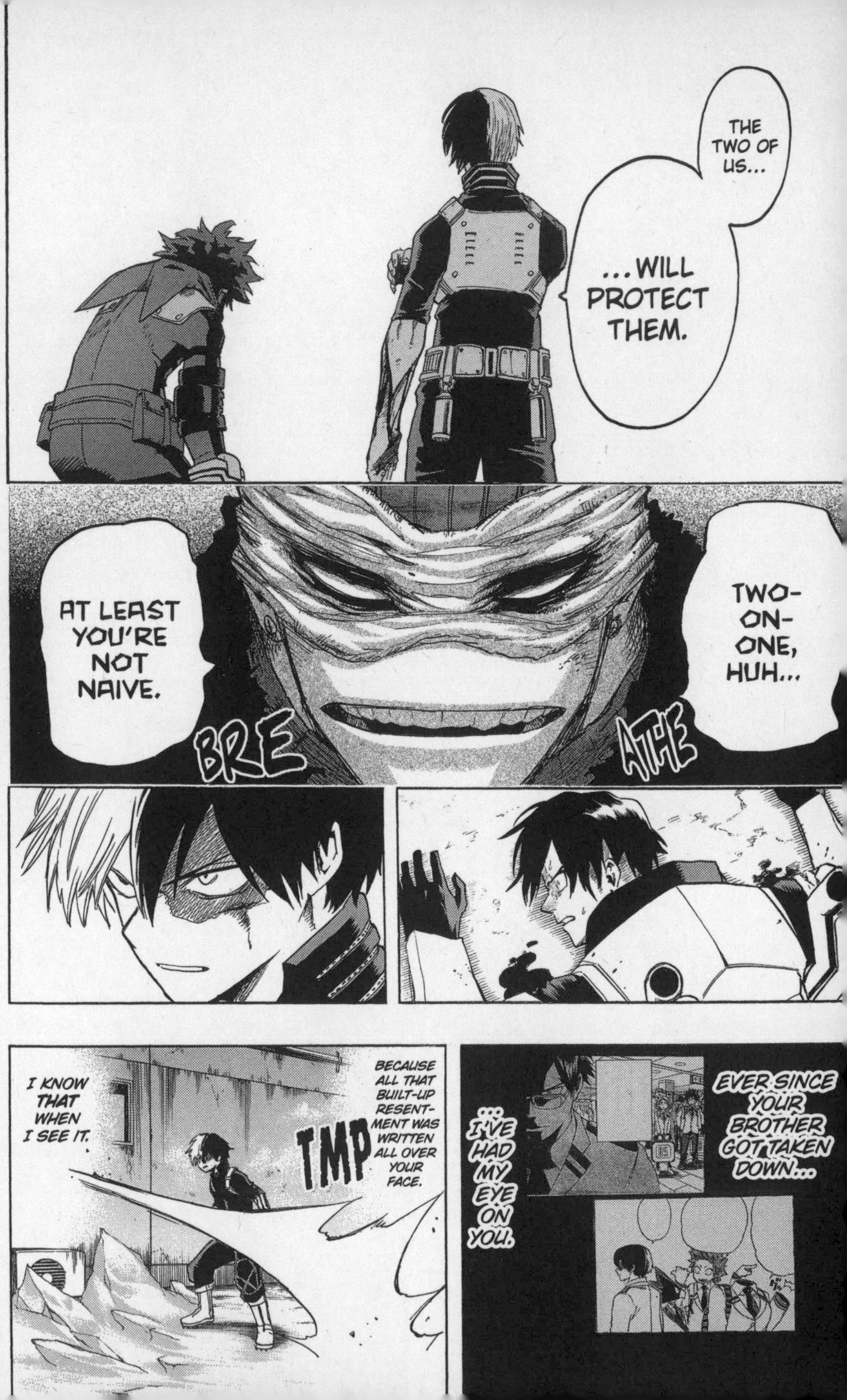
THE TWO OF US...
...WILL PROTECT THEM.
TWO-ON-ONE, HUH...
AT LEAST YOU'RE NOT NAIVE.
BREATHE
EVER SINCE YOUR BROTHER GOT TAKEN DOWN...
...I'VE HAD MY EYE ON YOU.
BECAUSE ALL THAT BUILT-UP RESENTMENT WAS WRITTEN ALL OVER YOUR FACE.
TMP
I KNOW THAT WHEN I SEE IT.

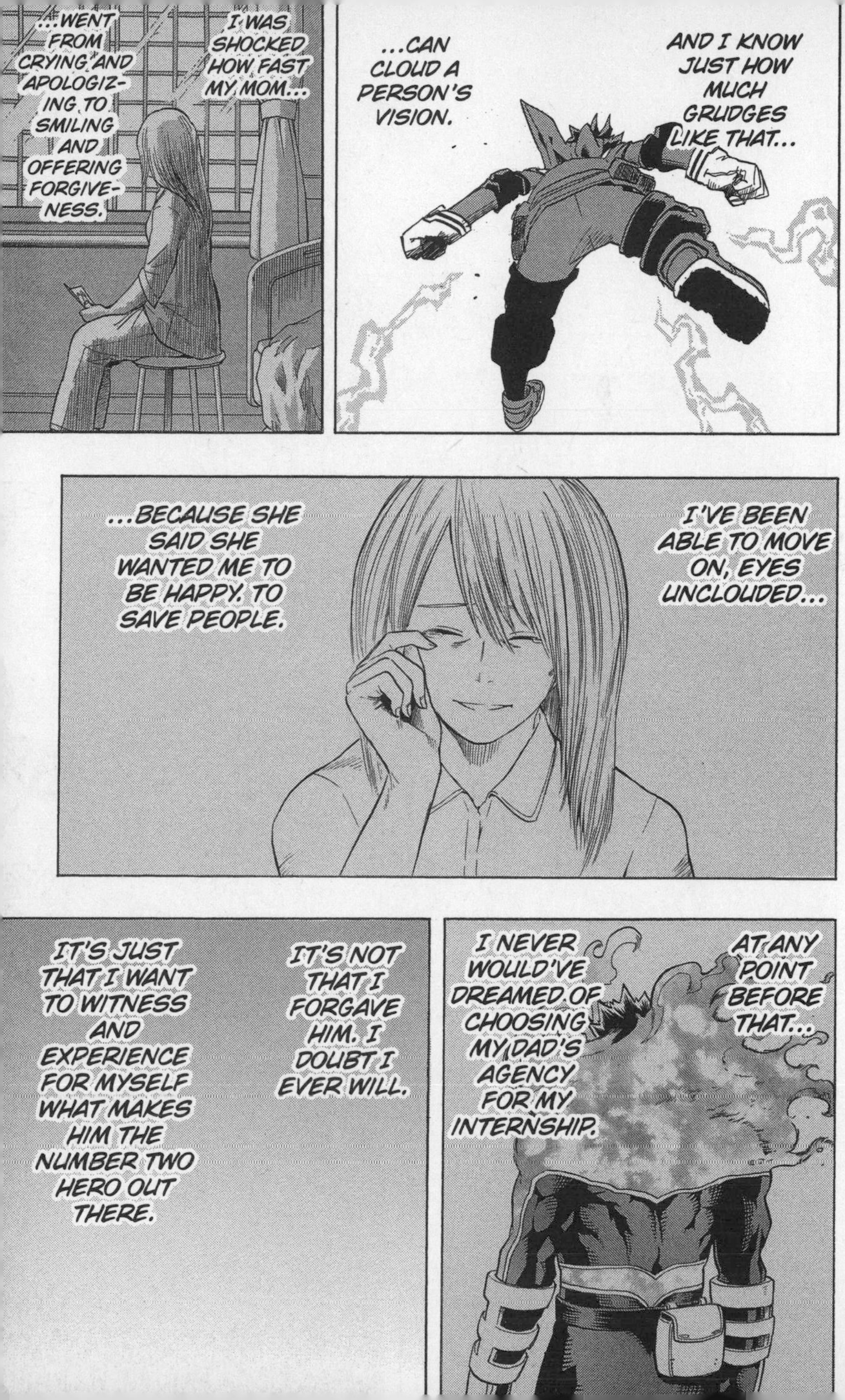
AND I KNOW JUST HOW MUCH GRUDGES LIKE THAT...
...CAN CLOUD A PERSON'S VISION.
I WAS SHOCKED HOW FAST MY MOM...
...WENT FROM CRYING AND APOLOGIZING TO SMILING AND OFFERING FORGIVENESS.
I'VE BEEN ABLE TO MOVE ON, EYES UNCLOUDED...
...BECAUSE SHE SAID SHE WANTED ME TO BE HAPPY. TO SAVE PEOPLE.
AT ANY POINT BEFORE THAT...
I NEVER WOULD'VE DREAMED OF CHOOSING MY DAD'S AGENCY FOR MY INTERNSHIP.
IT'S NOT THAT I FORGAVE HIM. I DOUBT I EVER WILL.
IT'S JUST THAT I WANT TO WITNESS AND EXPERIENCE FOR MYSELF WHAT MAKES HIM THE NUMBER TWO HERO OUT THERE.

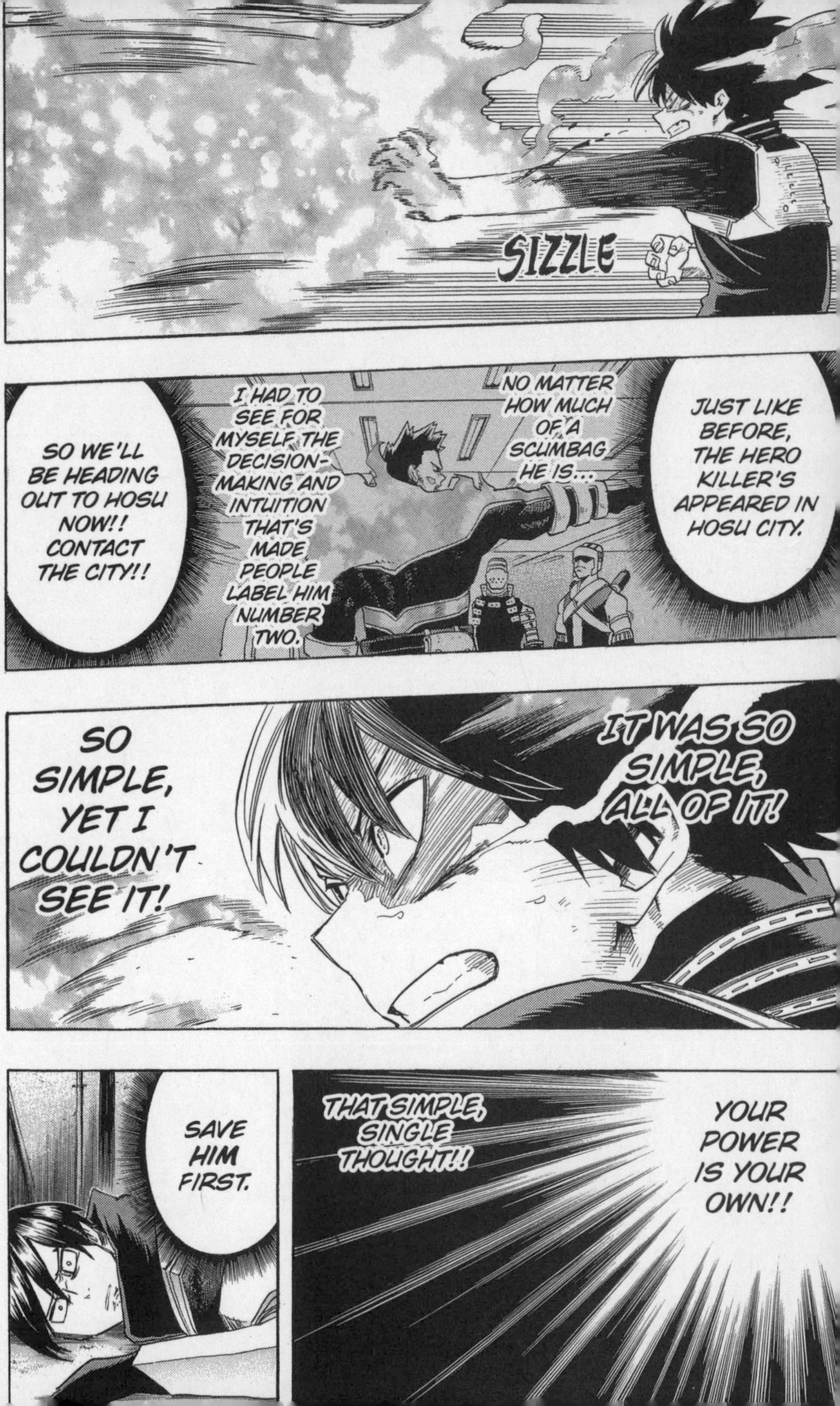
SIZZLE
JUST LIKE BEFORE, THE HERO KILLER'S APPEARED IN HOSU CITY.
NO MATTER HOW MUCH OF A SCUMBAG HE IS...
I HAD TO SEE FOR MYSELF THE DECISION-MAKING AND INTUITION THAT'S MADE PEOPLE LABEL HIM NUMBER TWO.
SO WE'LL BE HEADING OUT TO HOSU NOW!! CONTACT THE CITY!!
IT WAS SO SIMPLE, ALL OF IT!
SO SIMPLE, YET I COULDN'T SEE IT!
YOUR POWER IS YOUR OWN!!
THAT SIMPLE, SINGLE THOUGHT!!
SAVE HIM FIRST.

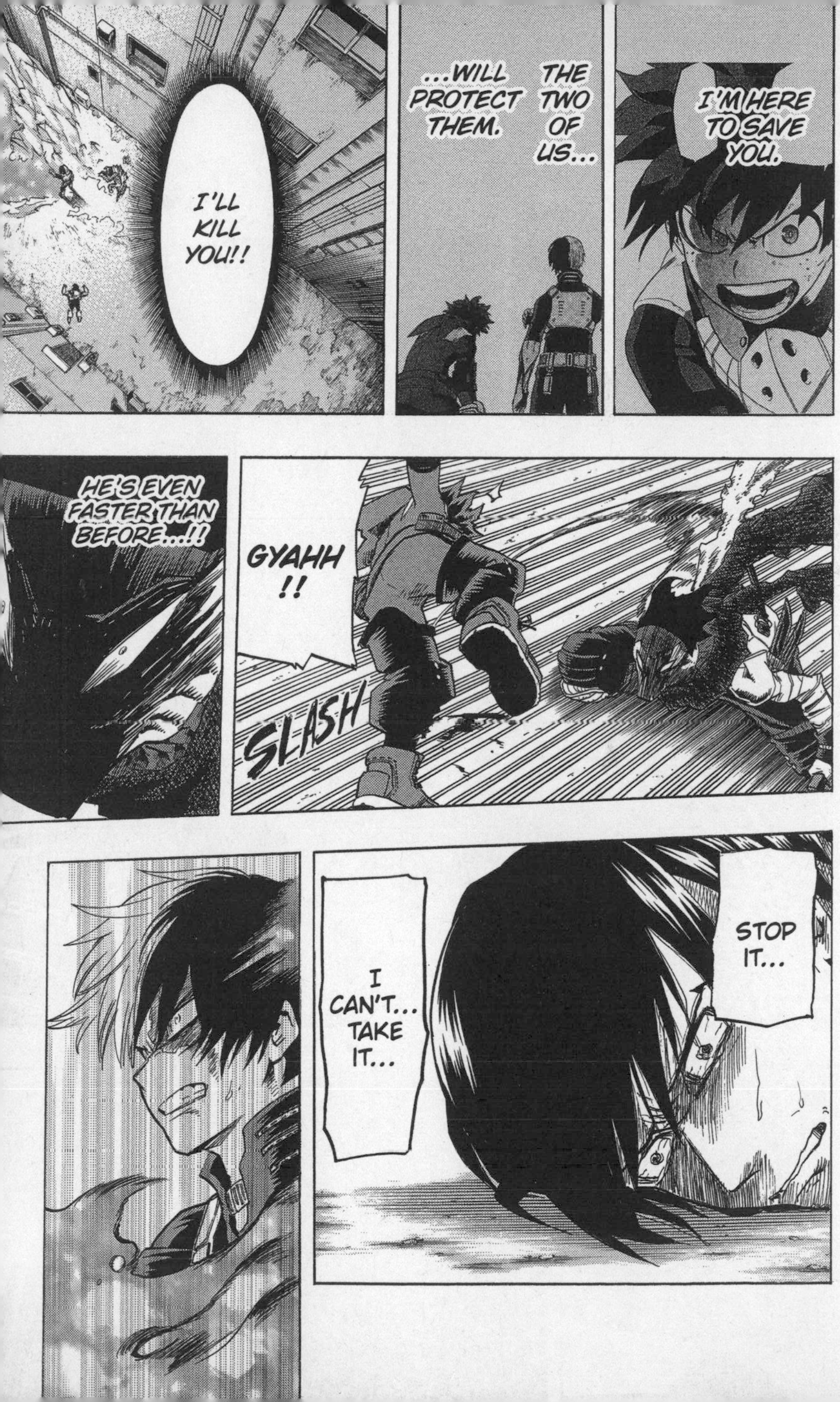
I'M HERE TO SAVE YOU.
THE TWO OF US...
...WILL PROTECT THEM.
I'LL KILL YOU!!
GYAHH !!
SLASH
HE'S EVEN FASTER THAN BEFORE...!!
STOP IT...
I CAN'T... TAKE IT...

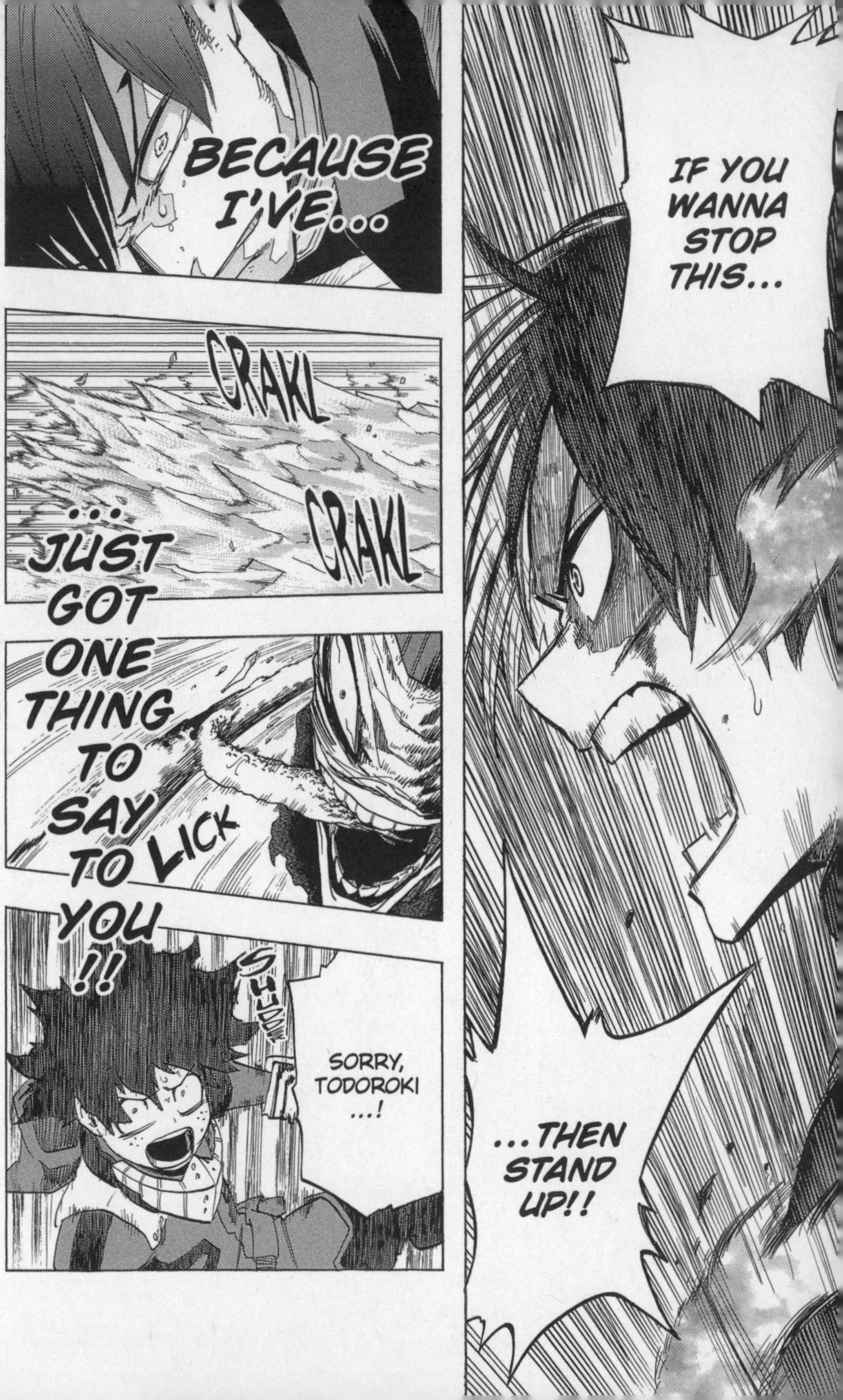
IF YOU WANNA STOP THIS...
...THEN STAND UP!!
BECAUSE I'VE...
CRAKL
CRAKL
...JUST GOT ONE THING TO SAY TO YOU!!
LICK
SHUD
SORRY, TODOROKI ...!

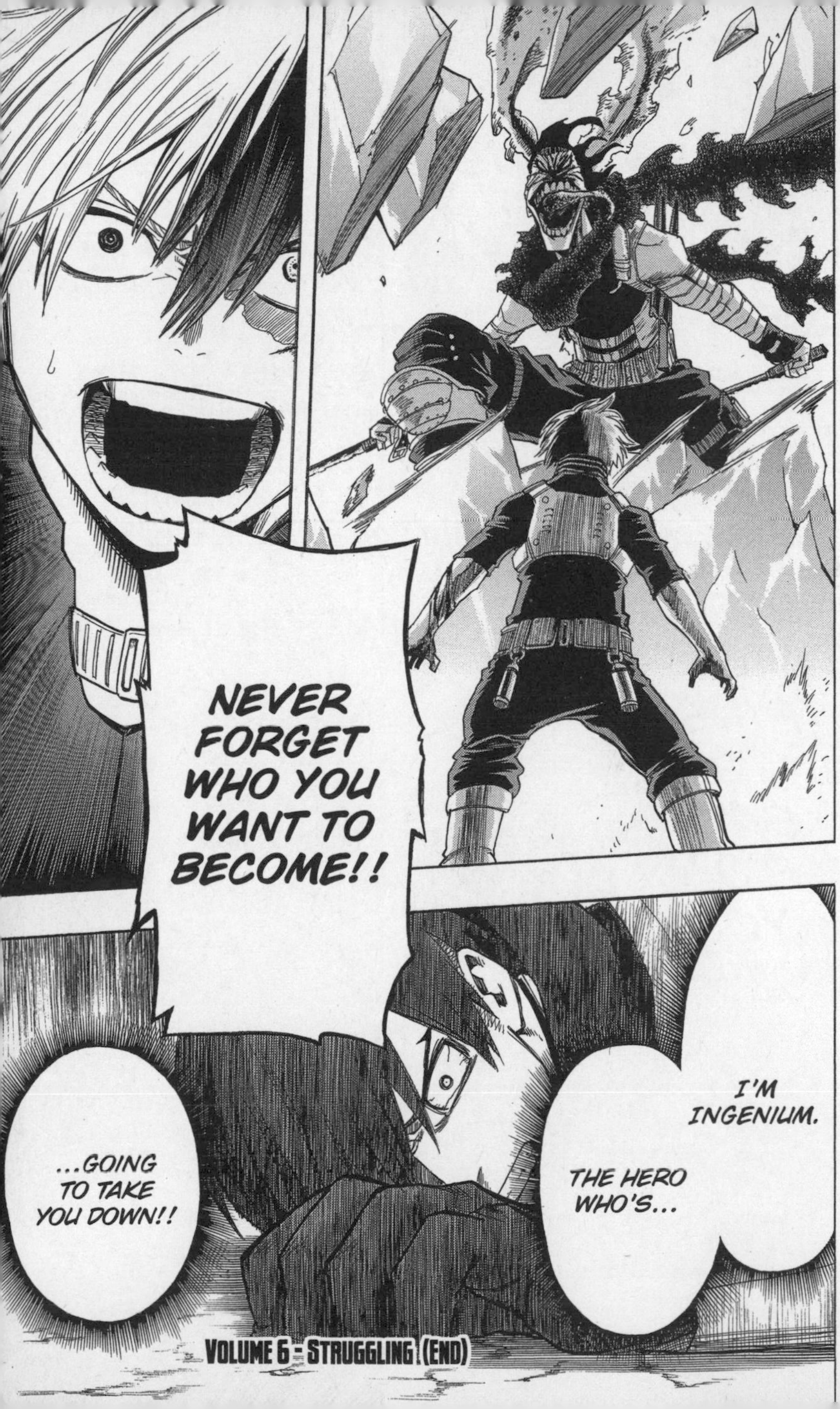
NEVER FORGET WHO YOU WANT TO BECOME!!
I'M INGENIUM.
THE HERO WHO'S...
...GOING TO TAKE YOU DOWN!!
VOLUME 6 - STRUGGLING (END)

ANIME VERSION!!

At last! The anime I've dreamed of!
It was only just announced, so I can't mention any details yet, but I'm super pumped for it!
Things might've changed since I was a kid, but I remember being glued to the TV watching my favorite shows, so I'm thrilled to think that boys and girls today will get to enjoy my work that way too. I'll keep working hard!

10/10/2015

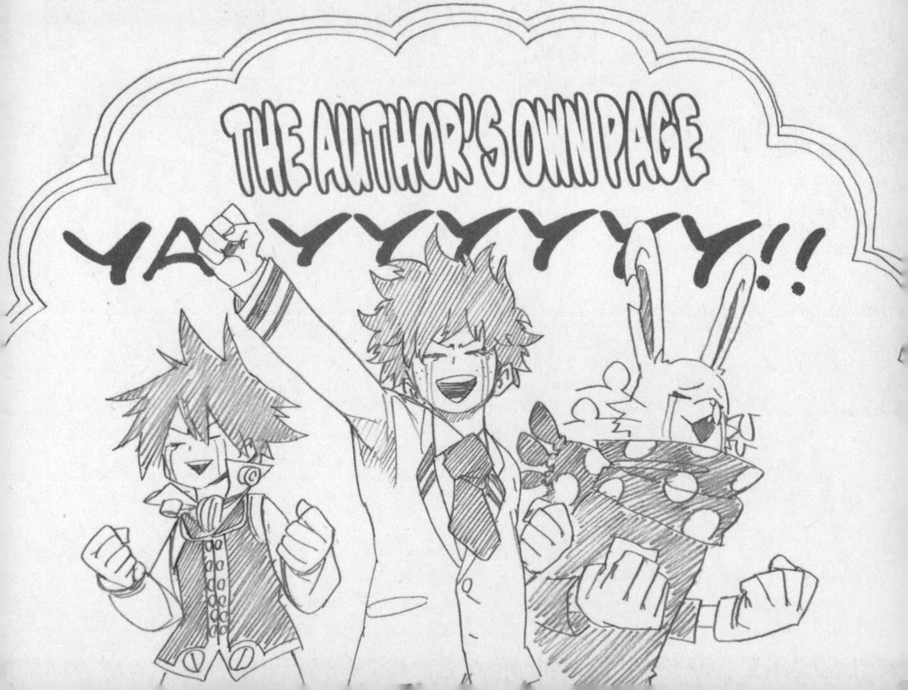
THE AUTHOR'S OWN PAGE
YAYYYYYY!!

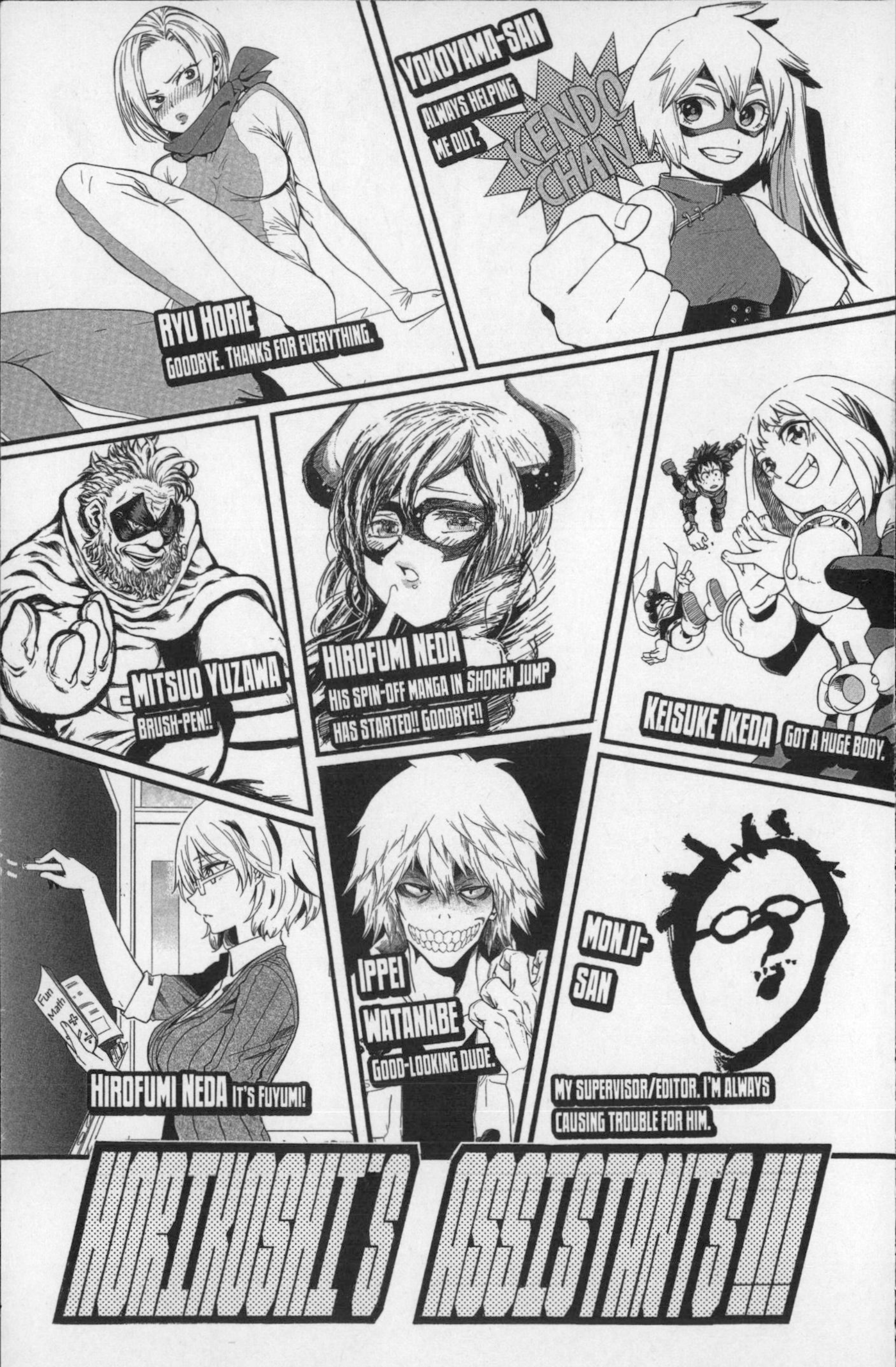

YOKOYAMA-SAN
ALWAYS HELPING ME OUT.
KENDO CHAN
RYU HORIE
GOODBYE. THANKS FOR EVERYTHING.
KEISUKE IKEDA
GOT A HUGE BODY.
HIROFUMI NEDA
HIS SPIN-OFF MANGA IN SHONEN JUMP HAS STARTED!! GOODBYE!!
MITSUO YUZAWA
BRUSH-PEN!!
MONJI-SAN
MY SUPERVISOR/EDITOR. I'M ALWAYS CAUSING TROUBLE FOR HIM.
IPPEI WATANABE
GOOD-LOOKING DUDE.
Fun Math
HIROFUMI NEDA
IT'S FUYUMI!
HORIKOSHI'S ASSISTANTS!!!

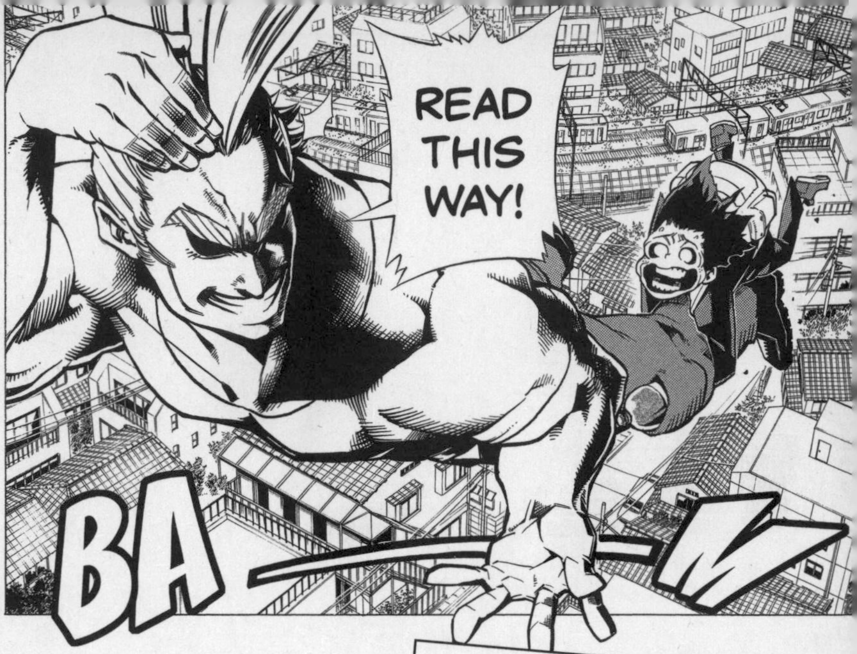
READ THIS WAY!
BA-M

MY HERO ACADEMIA

reads from right to left, starting in the upper-right corner. Japanese is read from right to left, meaning that action, sound effects and word-balloon order are completely reversed from English order.

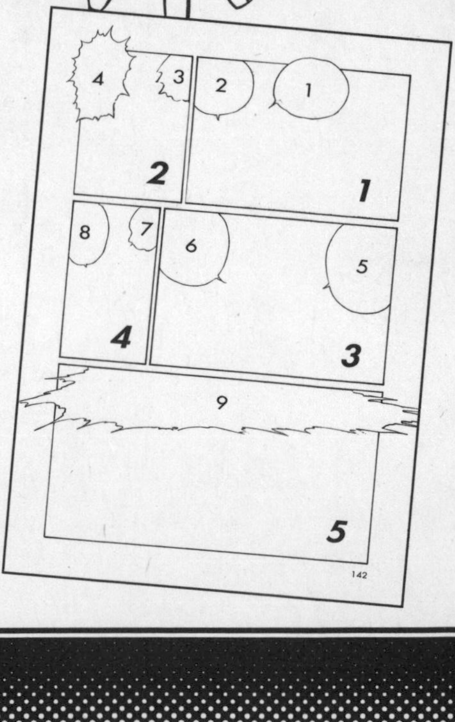
1
2
3
4
2
1
5
6
7
8
3
4
9
5
142